SIR CHRISTOPHER WREN

BRYAN LITTLE

SIR
CHRISTOPHER
WREN

A Historical Biography

ROBERT HALE · LONDON

ISBN 0 7091 5141 1

Robert Hale & Company
Clerkenwell House,
Clerkenwell Green,
London EC1R 0HT

Filmset by Specialised Offset Services Ltd, Liverpool
and printed and bound in Great Britain by
Redwood Burn Limited, Trowbridge & Esher

Contents

Illustrations

Preface

Of the many previous books on Sir Christopher Wren some have taken good account of the great architect's mathematical and scientific achievements as well as of his architectural work. Wren was also, however, closely and inevitably involved in the history and politics of his time. The career of an architect, more than those of most other artists, is conditioned by political factors and by economics and finance. For if his designs are to be rendered someone has to pay, and if the designs in question were those of a Court architect the sums needed were apt, in Wren's time, to be a considerable strain on the restricted finances of the Crown.

I have dealt, as any biographer of Wren must do, with Wren the architect, and in particular with his schemes, as revealed by drawings at Oxford and elsewhere, which could never be carried out. I have also expanded, more than in other works on Wren's life, on Sir Christopher and his kinsmen as figures in the history of their time, and on the impact upon Wren's career of political figures and historical events. I have dealt with Wren's personal and social life, and with activities which lay outside his architectural work – in the Royal Society, as a prominent member of the Hudson's Bay Company, in Parliament, as a businessman, and in his lesser (and whimsically varied) tasks as Surveyor General. My view of Wren is largely that of an architect whose building achievement was decisively conditioned by his place in Restoration society, and by the political events of an age full of the aftermath of a civil war, by dynastic crises and swiftly succeeding changes in sovereignty, and in Wren's later life by two major international wars.

B.D.G.L.
Bristol
July, 1975

Acknowledgements

Among many who have kindly helped me over archive research and other necessary enquiries I have, at Oxford, to thank Mr Clifford Davies, M.A., Keeper of the Archives, Wadham College, at All Souls' Mr J.S.G. Simmons, M.A. the Librarian, and members of the staff at the Codrington Library, Mr J.P. Cooper, M.A., Librarian, Trinity College, Dr J.F.A. Mason, Librarian of Christ Church and members of his staff, and Mr Howard Colvin, M.A., of St John's College.

At Cambridge I had valuable help from Dr P.A. Linehan and members of the library staff at St John's College, at Pembroke College from the Librarian, Dr I.R.J. Jack, from Mr A.J. Norton the archivist, and from Mr Denys Spittle, and at Trinity College from Dr R. Robson, from Dr J.P.W. Gaskell the Librarian, and members of the Library staff. Dr F.H. Stubbings (Librarian), members of the library staff, and Maj. Gen. E.F. Foxton, M.A., the domestic bursar, helped met at Emmanuel College.

At St Paul's Cathedral I had much kind help and attention from the Librarian, Mr A.R.B. Fuller, while Gen. Sir Charles Jones, G.C.B., C.B.E., M.C., the Governor of Chelsea Hospital, showed me the buildings there. Sir John Summerson, Miss Dorothy Stroud, and members of the staff were most helpful at the Soane Museum, while at the Royal Society I have to thank the Librarian, Mr N.H. Robinson, and members of the library staff. Again in London I was helped by Miss Margaret Swarbrick of the Archives Dept., Westminster Public Library, and by Miss E.G.W. Bill, Librarian Lambeth Palace Library.

In Wren's native county I am grateful to Mr Maurice Rathbone, A.L.A., Wiltshire County Archivist, and members of his staff at Trowbridge, and Miss Pamela Stewart, M.A., Assistant Diocesan Archivist at Salisbury. The Rev. R.H. Daubney, rector of Bletchingdon, Oxon. kindly showed me the church and its monuments, the rectory, and important Register entries on the Coghills and the burial of Dean Wren. Miss Cicely Baker, of the Buckinghamshire County Record Office at Aylesbury, put me in the way of valuable information on Winslow. At Portland Mr G. Reynolds, Masonry Works Manager, The Stone Firms Ltd. kindly took me over the old quarries and gave me other useful information.

Finally, I have had much help and courtesy from staff members of the library of the R.I.B.A., of the Public Record Office, of the Bodleian Library at Oxford and the University Library at Cambridge and, on specially frequent occasions, from those working in the City and University Libraries at Bristol.

Acknowledgments for help over single items are also to be found, as appropriate, in the notes.

B.D.G.L.

TO MY WIFE

*Lovingly, and with much
gratitude for her patience*

1
Laudian Beginnings

Few tracts of the western countryside are nowadays more delectable than the south-western corner of Wiltshire whose tangled scenery of wooded hills and lush valleys extends, between high and distant downlands, to the Dorset border and the beginnings of the dairy-studded Blackmore Vale on which Hardy's Tess, conferred literary immortality. The buildings include, or included, the fine church and spectacular mediaeval barn at Tilsbury, the ruined castle and the classical mansion of Wardour, the greatest of all 'follies' in the Gothick of Beckford's Fonthill, and the cool Grecianism of Pyt House not far from the highly picturesque village of East Knoyle. As in most counties the landscape which we now see, nicely diversified by parkland and cut through by the Salisbury to Exeter line of what was once the London and South Western Railway, is in large measure the creation of the last two centuries. But it must always have had its charms, and a pleasant rural setting must, in the 1630s, have surrounded the agricultural village of East, or Bishop's, Knoyle where the rector of the parish created no small stir by the changes, decorative as well as structural, which he made in the Norman chancel of his already ancient church. This was in 1639, the last full year of Charles I's personal rule and of Laud's forceful supremacy in the affairs of the Established Church. Seven years earlier, a house in the village had witnessed the birth of Christopher, the son and namesake of the rector, whose career as England's most famous architect was to be moulded and determined by the two turbulent decades which followed close on his father's replastering of his chancel.

An important mine of information on the activities of the Wren family, more helpful for personal than for architectural details, comes in *Parentalia*, compiled by the fourth Christopher Wren who was a son of the great architect, and brought out in 1750 by Stephen Wren the fourth Christopher's son. By no means all the architectural points made in *Parentalia* are correct, but for the Wren family and its background the book is widely valuable.

The Wrens were long settled in Co. Durham; like many others in the north-eastern counties they were also said to have been of Danish stock. Of the Wrens who were born, and who attained manhood, before the Reformation Geoffrey Wren was a priest, a canon of Windsor, and a confessor both to Henry VII and to Henry VIII in his early days as king.[1] By that time the family had moved south to find ampler fortune. Cuthbert Wren, Northumbrian in his christian name but by adoption a Midlander, had property at Monks' Kirby near Coventry. His only son Francis, born in 1552 at Monks' Kirby, settled in the City of London where he became a citizen and mercer; he lived, so it seems from the baptismal record of his elder son, in the parish of St Peter, Eastcheap whose mediaeval church was among those replanned by his eminent grandson.[2]

The architect's grandfather was well settled, by the later years of Elizabeth I's reign, among the traders and businessmen of the City. In such a setting a Puritan outlook, and anti-Stuart leanings, might reasonably have been expected. But Francis Wren's sons Matthew and Christopher, both of them sent to Merchant Taylors' School, followed a different bent. The family may, perhaps, have recalled the career, and the ecclesiastical dignity, of their forbear Geoffrey, a canon at Windsor and thus linked, in his clerical duties, to the Court and to the proudly royal ambience of the Order of the Garter. More palpably important, for both of them, was the High Anglican, and also royalist, influence of the great churchman Lancelot Andrewes, in the end Bishop of Winchester but in Elizabeth I's time a fellow, and for sixteen years from 1589 the Master, of Pembroke College at Cambridge; to him it may be due that Francis Wren's sons, like himself Londoners and alumni of Merchant Taylors', did not settle down in the City as Puritan merchants and eventual Parliament supporters, in the troubled times to come. Matthew and Christopher Wren followed no commercial career, but like Andrewes lived the lives of scholar-churchmen; the background, and the early career, of the third Christopher Wren can largely be explained in terms of England's two ancient universities and the High Anglican Establishment.

Matthew, the elder of Francis Wren's two sons was born in 1585 or 1586 and went up, in 1601, to Andrewes' College of Pembroke, Cambridge. He became a Fellow in 1605, remaining a protegé of Lancelot Andrewes and in 1615 becoming his chaplain while he was Bishop of Ely; he had, so *Parentalia* tells us, a "passionate affection" for his Church's ministry.[3] In 1621, by King James I's personal appointment, he became chaplain to Prince Charles who was now the heir to the throne, later going with him to Spain on that memorable journey when the Prince of Wales unsuccessfully (and to the joy of his Protestant countrymen) sought the hand of the Infanta. In 1625, the year when Charles became king, Matthew Wren became Master of Peterhouse at Cambridge; his building and furnishing of the chapel which still adorns that College was seen, then and later, as a controversially Laudian act. In 1628 he was the university's Vice

Chancellor; the same year saw him Dean of Windsor and also, in a plurality which had been automatic since the time of Edward IV, Dean of the Midland collegiate church of Wolverhampton. His younger brother Christopher was by now well forward in the clerical career which placed him in the very centre of the Stuart and Laudian Establishment.

The first Christopher Wren was born in 1589, the year after the Armada. He too, at Merchant Taylors' and elsewhere, came under the powerful influence of Lancelot Andrewes.[4] When he in his turn started his university career he was a little older than his brother had been as a freshman. He went to Oxford rather than Andrewes' Cambridge, to St John's which had been Laud's College. This was in 1608. He did well at Oxford, got his B.A. and M.A. degrees, took Anglican Orders and became a Bachelor of Divinity. He too profited from the Andrewes patronage, and it was the bishop who in 1620 presented him to the Wiltshire living of Bishop's Fonthill, following it in another three years with that of East (or Bishop's) Knoyle some four miles away. Both places had long formed part of the great Wessex estates of the bishops of Winchester, and though Wiltshire had long lain in the later diocese of Salisbury the ownership of the lands, and the gift of the two livings, had stayed with the Winchester prelates.[5] Here in southern Wiltshire the young cleric found his bride, marrying Mary, the only child and heiress of a local landlord, Robert Cox of Fonthill. It was at East Knoyle that, for some years, the elder Christopher Wren settled down, less eminent than his elder brother in his chosen profession but well set among the higher flights of the Laudian church.

The first of Chrisopher Wren's children were born at East Knoyle. Two of his daughters were Susan, important in her famous brother's life and (considerably younger) Anne, like her sister the wife of an Anglican clergyman, Dr Henry Brounsell who was a prebendary of Ely and the rector, out in the Fen country where his wife died young after a long series of illnesses, at Stretham between Cambridge and Ely;[6] by the time of her birth, so we note from the baptismal registers of East Knoyle, her father was Dean of Windsor as well as being the rector of his Wiltshire parish.[7] The elder Christopher Wren's appointment to his deanery came, as we shall see, in March of 1635,[8] But 26th December of 1634 is given as the date of his daughter Ann's baptism; from this point, and from other aspects of the way in which the registers were then kept at East Knoyle, we can see how confusion has arisen, in the minds of some who have studied the early life of Wren, over the actual year of the future architect's birth.

Though its entries start in 1538 the first volume of the East Knoyle registers, combining between the same covers the village's record of baptisms, marriages, and burials, is all, for nearly a hundred years, recorded in the same neat hand, perhaps that of a curate or of some conscientious parish clerk. Whoever wrote it must have copied the entries, from 1538 to his own time, in a new volume. But somewhere in the process he seems to have slipped a year, so that entries which should come into the year 1635–36 (old style) actually appear under 1634–35, the same error applying to earlier years which saw other events in the Wrens' family history. So on the page which covers February, 1630 (really 1631) there is the record of the baptism of "Elizabeth daughter of Doctor Wren". Against it, in different ink and in the rector's own handwriting which resembled that of his most famous child, there are the words "ffirst Elisab." Against 13th August 1633 there comes the record of the little girl's burial; one may reasonably add another year to the record. Her christian name, by a custom common in those times of heavy infant mortality, was soon revived for another daughter, the rector having already used the same device for two sons named Christopher.

Against 22nd November in the baptismal section for 1630–31 one finds the entry "Christopher sonne of Doctor Wren." The baby having failed to outlive the day of its birth the word "first" was later added in the rector's hand. Then, in the section for the year 1631–32 as recorded by whoever recopied the register, 10th November is given for the christening (three weeks after his birth on 20th October) of "Christopher sonne of Christopher Dtr in Divinitie e(t) rector". The word "2d" and the surname Wren were added by the boy's father and the whole entry, as befitted so renowned a son of East Knoyle, is underlined. The year, as we know from other sources, was 1632, not 1631, and the third Christopher was to live till George I had been eight years on his throne. Later, in the section containing baptisms in the Old Style year 1634–35 (given as 1633–34) December 5th appears as the christening day of a baby girl noted by her father, again at a later date, in different ink, and in his own hand, as the "second Elizabeth".

By the time of the future architect's infancy his father's clerical prospects were well beyond those of the ordinary run of country clergy. Since 1628 he had been a chaplain to the king, he was a Doctor of Divinity, and early in 1635 his brother Matthew became Bishop of Hereford.[9] Matthew Wren soon moved, full of Laudian reforming zeal which soon bore hard on the Nonconformists and Puritan-minded Anglicans of his new flock, to the more important bishopric of Norwich. He had now relinquished his pair of deaneries and in March of 1635 they went, within the Wren family, to his brother. Dean Christopher moved, for part of each year, from the rectory at East Knoyle, and in 1638 he added to his preferments the well endowed rectory of Hasely in Oxfordshire.[10] But he kept East Knoyle and it was there, in 1639, that he set about the redecoration of the chancel which at the time caused wonder and in later years, with the Puritans in full power, some sharp accusation.

Parentalia makes the point, important for the understanding of the varied influences which bore on the future designer of St Paul's and the City churches, that Dean Wren was highly skilled in all branches of mathematics, that he displayed a good knowledge of architecture, and that he used those talents in the invention of a "serpentine" to divert or disperse the current of a river.[11] The gifts of the son were clearly inherited from the father. More immediately Dean Wren made himself, and his parish church at East Knoyle conspicuous by the construction of a "very strong roof" over the chancel, and by the replastering of the chancel's ceiling and walls with decorations which soon aroused Puritan anger. I know of nothing, in the sense that the later roof of the Sheldonian at Oxford was of special interest for its construction, about the Dean's new roof timbers at East Knoyle. But the plaster decorations, put up when the Sheldonian's architect was an alert little boy aged seven, are certainly among the more curious and fascinating embellishments set up, in the Laudian years, in any English parish church. Jacob's Dream, the Sacrifice of Isaac, and the Ascension (but not the more 'Papist' Crucifixion) are shown, with an unsophisticated, vernacular artistry, in low relief; so too are a kneeling figure looking longingly at a dove, strapwork, some inscriptions, winged cherubs' heads, Biblical quotations, and a delicate frieze of rosettes and thin, curved mouldings intersecting to give a Gothic effect amid a somewhat naively Renaissance scene.[12] The plasterwork's imagery is, one would have thought, mild enough except for the most rabid of Puritan iconoclasts. Its artistry is more crude, and much less baroque than anything in the plaster ceilings put up by the craftsmen who in another half century worked under the rector's famous son.

But the royalist, Laudian world of Bishop Matthew Wren, and of his brother who was Dean of Windsor and rector of East Knoyle was soon to fall apart. The Long Parliament, assembling late in 1640, set in train the final events which led, inexorably in less than two years, to open civil war. Laud was soon arrested and kept in prison in the Tower. Matthew Wren, since 1638 the holder of the rich, important see of Ely, and with Cambridge in his diocese, was in 1641 arrested, impeached, and clapped in the Tower; luckier than Laud he survived his confinement and the years of Puritan power. Once war broke out Windsor, like nearby London, lay within the territory under effective Parliament control. Dean Wren, in the autumn of 1642, faced hostile soldiers whose commanding officer claimed a warrant from the king to search his deanery in the castle. He had hastily buried many of the treasures of the Order of the Garter which he, as its Registrar, had lovingly guarded. What he had concealed was safe for a while, though the hidden jewels were found later and sold. But the heavier goods still lay in the Treasury, and when its doors were forced they, along with the records of the Dean's beloved Order, were carried away; so too were many of his personal effects.[13]

Dean Wren, perforce, abandoned the castle and St George's chapel. His parsonage at Haseley was in somewhat debatable country. East Knoyle, till nearly the end of the fighting in a countryside controlled by the king, and with the Catholic pocket of Wardour and Tisbury a staunch royalist outpost not far away, was for some time the one of his preferments where he could still, without hindrance, continue his high Anglican ministry. He does not, however, seem to have spent much of the Civil-War period in Wiltshire, but to have taken refuge in Bristol, from 1643 to 1645 firmly held for the king, the economic if not the political capital of royally controlled England.

But in the short spell, less than two complete years, between the meeting of the Long Parliament and the martial raising, at Nottingham, of Charles I's standard, London was still a place where the tension between king and Parliament might still have been peaceably resolved. It was not yet, firmly and for nearly twenty years, a city embattled against its sovereign and unsafe for those with royalist sympathies. One could still reach it, without hindrance, from the royalist countryside and Puritan clothing towns of the West. So it was reasonable enough that, in January of 1641, when Dean Wren's precocious namesake son was only eight years old, his father sent him to continue the private tuition he had already had, to Westminster School. Later in that year, and certainly in 1642 when Charles I had left his capital and when war seemed certain, the Dean might have doubted his wisdom. But early in 1641 there were still good reasons for hoping that the fashionable school of Westminster, under the most termagant and royalist of headmasters, would be a safe, politically reliable seminary for a Laudian cleric's son.

The headmaster at Westminster, still in his thirties and by 1641 only a year in the post which he held till he died in office, aged almost ninety, in 1695, was Dr Richard Busby, an Oxford man and the most devoted of Laudian Royalists.[14] His powers as a teacher and as a (literally) strong-armed disciplinarian, his sturdy retention of his post through the Civil War and still more through the Commonwealth years, and his defiant gestures alike to Cromwellians and the restored Charles II, made him as legendary a pedagogue as the later Keate or Arnold. It is difficult to think of him, in later years, as having favourite pupils, though George Hooper, eventually a much loved bishop of Bath and Wells, is said to have been one. But the 1640s, despite many trials, were his earlier, more genial Westminster days, and the young prodigy from the ultra-royalist Windsor deanery seems to have found good favour with his teacher.

It is from just before the start of the boy Christopher Wren's first year at Westminster, and from a time when he was only nine, that we have his first letter to his father, a stilted, schoolboy Latin effort full of dutiful sentiments but a remarkable work for one of such tender years.

The Dean was proud to preserve it among the family papers.[15] For another five years the young Christopher continued his Westminster studies. With the Civil War still raging, and with a capital city controlled by the king's enemies, the wonder was that Dr Busby, the last-ditch Royalist, was still allowed to run Westminster School. His finances, precarious since the confiscation of the Abbey Dean and Chapter's endowments, he improved by the admission, as private pupils and for high fees, of the sons of many royalists. The school, despite its headmaster's unconcealed sympathies, continued all through the Civil War, so that Dean Wren's young son could still be there till 1646, remaining in London and then moving on, in the capital, to a sequence of private studies. The classics he had, as a matter of course, absorbed under Dr Busby; what now occupied his mind was his pronounced, and much less common scientific and mathematical bent.

Parentalia mentions, of the young Christopher, "the early appearance of an uncommon genius"; it merited some encouragement by more mathematical teaching. Astronomy was another, and kindred, subject in which the boy excelled. When only thirteen he invented what was described as a "panorganum astronomicum", a pneumatic engine, and some kind of an instrument for use in the making of sundials.[16] His mathematical tutor, an important figure in his family's history, was his brother-in-law, the husband of his older sister Susan; like most of the young Christopher's male relatives William Holder was a Church-of-England clergyman.

A son of a prebendary of the minster at Southwell Holder went up, in 1632, to Matthew Wren's College at Pembroke at Cambridge; the master at that time was Benjamin Lany, no less royalist than Matthew Wren.[17] For two years from 1640 Holder was a Fellow of Pembroke, giving up his fellowship when in another two years he married Susan Wren and became rector of Bletchington a few miles North of Oxford. Mathematical brilliance apart, Holder's talents ranged wide. He was a Doctor of Divinity, and his written works included treatises on harmony and a book called *Elements of Speech*; among his other achievements he taught a deaf mute to speak. His wife, as we shall see, also possessed, and extensively used, a gift of healing. Nor was Holder's mathematical tuition of the future architect his only service to his wife's kinsmen. For in the last, defeated years of Charles I's life, and in the Commonwealth period which followed. Holder's rectory in Oxfordshire was the refuge, and the last home of the widower Dean. When Bristol was no longer a royally held city, and when, in 1646, Christopher Wren was ejected from his Wiltshire living at East Knoyle, it was to Bletchington that he retired, sad and elderly but jealously guarding the recovered registers, and other papers, of his beloved Garter order. Aubrey points out that, as a result of his father's withdrawal, Bletchington was also, for some years, the real "home and retiring place" of the younger Christopher Wren. He employed his time on contemplation, study, and, as things turned out, on the first stages of romance. Aubrey adds that the future architect there made "several curious dials" which he set round and about his brother in law's rectory, and that these creations of "a youth of prodigious inventive wit" were still to be seen on the house. Holder's rectory no longer stands, as it was replaced in 1752, but in the church a Jacobean pulpit, and some fanciful bench ends of about the same date, are furnishings which the young Christopher Wren would have known. It was at Bletchington, in the early summer of 1658, that Dean Wren died, with his brother Bishop Matthew Wren still in the Tower and the Commonwealth still England's accepted, though disliked, régime. But Christopher, his son, was now well set on the career to which, in another two years, the Restoration soon brought opportunities and the promise of fame.

The years of Wren's teenage studies in London were also a time for some important, influential scientific and academic contacts. We hear, in particular, of the young prodigy's friendship with Dr Charles Scarborough, in London from 1648 onwards, after a spell at Oxford, a man prominent both in mathematics and as a physician; after the Restoration he was Charles II's doctor and received a knighthood.[19] Dr Scarborough had the young Wren as a patient and become his firm friend. Wren repaid Scarborough's kindness by helping him in some aspects of his work. Scarborough and Seth Ward, another clerical mathematician who became an important friend of Wren, made use in their studies of *Clavis Mathematica*, a work by William Oughtred and in those days a standard treatise on the subject. Wren is even said to have translated the book, for the benefit of Scarborough and Ward, from Oughtred's Latin. I imagine, however, that such learned men as Ward and Scarborough would have been well able to translate the Latin for themselves. Wren could, however, have helped them. One hears also, from this time of collaboration between the young prodigy and these men who were well established in their chosen field of science and mathematics, that Wren invented a weather clock which could, on a revolving cylinder, take records all through the night; he was also, so it appears, responsible for an instrument which could write in the dark. Another, more significant friendship of this time was that of Wren with a man of learning who was also a friend of his father, and who had visited the elder Christopher Wren in his Windsor deanery. He was John Wilkins, an Oxford man and a moderate supporter of the Parliament cause; from 1648 he held the post, in his own University, of Warden of the comparatively new College of Wadham.

2
Oxford Scientist

By the late 1640s, when the young Christopher Wren's further education had to be seriously considered, the Wren family had profound and intimate links with both of England's ancient universities. Matthew Wren, the future architect's episcopal uncle, was a devoted Cambridge man. The elder Christopher Wren was no less firmly in the Oxonian camp. Either university might, a few years earlier, have been suitable, and in both seats of learning the young man's relatives had many friends and helpful contacts. But Cambridge, for so royalist and Laudian a family, was wholly out of the running. Both universities, under Cromwellian sway and with dozens of royalist high Anglicans by now ejected from their fellowships and deposed from college headships, were drastically changed since the time of Charles I's personal rule. But Cambridge, of the two, was more completely under the Puritan shadow, with many Puritan 'hard liners' (particularly from the Puritan college of Emmanuel) in posts of importance. Oxford, though not without its difficulties, was, from the Wrens' point of view, a more sympathetic university, while Dean Wren himself, and William Holder his devoted son in law, lived close at hand in the rectory at Bletchington. Given Oxford as the chosen university, there remained the question of the most suitable, or least unsuitable college for a boy whose father was a deposed Dean of Windsor, and whose uncle the Bishop of Ely still lay in the durance of the Tower.

A dozen years earlier, Wadham would have been a most unlikely college for the young hopeful of so Laudian and royalist a family as the Wrens. Founded in James I's reign, with a strong preference for members from Somerset, Dorset, and Devon, and with its first admissions in 1613, the college soon took on the Puritan and Whig flavour which was long to distinguish it, making it one of the sparse Whig islands in mainly high Tory Oxonian sea.[1] Though Wadham men fought on both sides in the Civil War its most famous early member was Robert Blake, a Somerset man from Bridgwater, prominent as a Parliamentary commander on land and more famous still, during the Commonwealth, as England's great "General at Sea". But Wadham was less deeply Puritan than the new

Cambridge colleges of Emmanuel and Sidney Sussex. It soon became of fair importance and size and when, in the Civil War, Oxford was the headquarters of the Court it must readily enough have toed the royalist line. Like the Oxford colleges Wadham was swept, after Charles I's collapse, by the Puritan wave of ejection and change. John Pitt its Warden was ejected. But John Wilkins his successor was more congenial, to defeated royalist eyes, than most of those who now gained the headship of Oxford colleges. His presence in the Lodge at Wadham mainly decided it that his college, and not St John's which had, in times happier for the Stuart cause, housed Dean Christopher Wren in his undergraduate days, was chosen for the younger Christopher.

John Wilkins, for some years a friend of Dean Wren and well acquainted with his promising young son, was a vital figure in the early days of the man who, when he himself died in 1672 as Bishop of Chester, was planning the new St Paul's.[2] The son of a goldsmith in Oxford and born in 1614, he studied, successively, at New Inn Hall and Magdalen Hall, both known for their Puritanism; in the latter college he became a tutor. From his early days he showed an interest in science, including astronomy, but he duly settled, as a vicar in Northamptonshire, in the Anglican ministry. He was what one might call a 'moderate reformist', associated with the Parliamentarian Lord Saye and Sele and later a chaplain to Charles Louis, the Protestant Elector of the Palatinate in western Germany who was, till the shock of Charles I's execution, a princely supporter of the Cromwellians. Charles Louis, like Prince Rupert in later years, was an amateur scientist, visited Dean Wren at Windsor,[3] and got to know and encourage the budding scientific talents of the Dean's young son. Well before the Civil War broke out Wilkins and the Wrens were good friends; Wilkins' outlook of tolerant moderation, reinforced by Continental visits under the aegis of the Elector, made it reasonably certain that Wadham, under his wardenship, would be better than most colleges as a place of study for the youth whom he had already befriended, and with whose outstanding talents, well matured before the young Christopher Wren was seventeen, he must have been well aware. Wilkins' moderate Puritanism, far removed from what now prevailed in many Cambridge colleges, and in some at Oxford, made Wadham, somewhat surprisingly in view of its earlier history, a college in favour with royalist gentry who still, despite the changes that had come over Oxford and Cambridge, much wished to send their sons to a university. Bishop Sprat, Wren's friend and the historian of the Royal Society, makes the point that many country gentry, especially those known to the Commonwealth authorities as "cavaliers and malignants", sent sons to Wadham where they could be under Wilkins' care.

The precise day of the young Christopher Wren's arrival at

Wadham is unknown. But the record of the receipt, by the college's bursar, of his £5 caution money shows that it was some time, in the academic year 1649–50, before June 25th, 1650.[4] Already well known to the head of the college, Wren entered Wadham not as an ordinary undergraduate but as a Gentleman Commoner; in such a position of privilege his life, with meals taken at high table, would have been closer to that of a don than to the humbler existence of an ordinary student. He was, moreover, a little older, at the time of his entry, than most of the youths who then came up to the universities.

Wren entered Wadham at a good time in his college's history. Science, under Wilkins' guidance, was prominent among the subjects read in the college. The manciple at Wadham was well known as a mathematician and instrument maker, while another Wadham man in Wren's time, a half brother of the warden and originally at Trinity, Cambridge, was Seth Ward, a scholar of the college when Wren came up, a Fellow in 1651 when Wren became a B.A., and in his later years prominent in the Royal Society and one of Wren's episcopal patrons. But in these Commonwealth years Seth Ward, like many others among those in Anglican orders, suspended the active exercise of his ministry, turning over, to relax safely from dangerous political and religious topics, to the less controversial fields of science. Wadham, under Wilkins, continued as a college where Royalists and moderate Parliamentarians could happily and safely dwell together; the younger Matthew Wren, the Bishop of Ely's son and thus the young Christopher's cousin, refers to the "generous freedom" maintained in the college's regularly planned, Jacobean-Gothic-cum-Renaissance buildings. This was in 1657, after Wren's time at Wadham and a year after Wilkins, by his marriage to the widowed Robina French, had risen higher, as a brother-in-law to no less a figure than Cromwell himself, in the Commonwealth Establishment.[5] But all through the years of Wilkins' time as warden the same happy atmosphere had ruled in Wadham. These were also the years of Wren's steady progress, from Gentleman Commoner to B.A., to an M.A. degree in 1653, and later in that same year to a Fellowship at All Souls'; he was only twenty or twenty-one when he migrated to his new academic home.

Wren's time at Wadham had been one of close, equal association both with the warden and with others among the scientists who came, whatever their religious and political views, to this most tolerant of Oxford colleges. Wilkins, extending to his gifted Gentleman-Commoner pupil what amounted to the treatment of an equal, made his bachelor quarters in the warden's lodge available for the storage of various instruments and machines, some his own but others contrived by Wren. As was done in some other Oxford colleges Wilkins had a sundial set up in Wadham. Loggan's print of 1675 shows that out in the formal garden, itself in all probability laid out at this time, a curious artificial mound, with a stairway up one side, was capped by a figure of Atlas upholding a globe. The young Wren may have helped Wilkins in the design and setting up of the new device. Wren is also said to have had a hand, in the year 1653 which was that of his election to his All Souls' fellowship, in the design of the sundial "showing by rays and half rays the time to a minute" which was set up, for the sum of £32 11s. 6d. in his new college. At first it adorned the southward-facing side of the chapel. Then in 1659 William Byrd, a stonecutter and mason who was Wadham's college mason, and to whom Wren probably imparted the details of his technique for the staining of marble, carved the crudely Baroque frame which still, in a setting between two Hawksmoorian Gothic pinnacles of the library which houses many of Wren's drawings, encloses the dial. The dial itself may be the oldest, non-architectural but visible, piece of Wren's work.[6]

More important than a helping hand in the design of sundials were Wren's activities in the scientific circle now flourishing, with much help from the influential Wilkins, in the wider ambit of the university.

From soon after Wilkins' arrival at Wadham a club, or society of men devoted to experimental science, or natural philosophy as it was called at that time, started to meet at Oxford.[7] Their forgatherings were often in Wilkins' lodge or in the rooms of others in the group; a coffee house near All Souls' seems also to have been a later rendezvous. By 1652 some thirty members were meeting in this way. Many subjects were covered, architecture, structural problems, and maritime affairs being among them. On the sensitive topics of politics and religion wide tolerance, and even a touch of scepticism, prevailed among the members of the club, and one even gathers that the more zealous Puritans at Oxford did what they could to hinder these scientific studies. Thomas Sprat, the earliest historian of the Royal Society, made the point that these forerunners, and in many cases early members, of the Society had "minds . . . invincibly armed against all the inchantments of Enthusiasm". Wren was naturally among those who thus forgathered, while others who took part in the activities of what was, as things turned out, the forerunner of the Royal Society were important as his friends and patrons in his future architectural years. Ralph Bathurst, after the Restoration the President of Trinity, was among them, so too were Seth Ward and the devoted royalist surgeon Thomas Willis who attended the Anglican services still held, in private, by Dr John Fell whose sister Willis later married, and who later achieved disliked fame as the dominant figure in Restoration Oxford.

The young Christopher Wren, a Gentleman Commoner of his own college, and mixing more with men of proved academic eminence than with undergraduates, readily found his place among these scientific pioneers. Both as a Wadham man and as young Fellow of All Souls' he was very much one of them; for the next few years his activities flowed naturally from these Oxford associations. What we cannot tell for certain is how many of the schemes, theories, and inventions for which, by 1660, he is said, in *Parentalia*, to deserve the credit were evolved during Wren's junior membership at Wadham and the four years of his fellowship at All Souls'. The scheme, jointly contrived by Wren and Wilkins, for an eighty-foot telescope, to be powerful enough for the simultaneous viewing of the entire moon, seems certain to be a project of this time. Some anatomical studies and experiments also dated from the early 1650s. What is certain is that by the summer of 1654, when Wren was still only twenty-one, his reputation was such that a call on him, one imagines, in his rooms at All Souls', was an accepted item in a visit to Oxford.

So it was that when, in July of 1654, the ultra Royalist, high Anglican gentleman John Evelyn spent a few days in Oxford he called on the young prodigy whose promise and achievements were well known in the university, and whose obliging charm seems to have commended him to a wide circle of ultimately helpful friends. Their first encounter, probably at All Souls', was after dinner on July 11th. Evelyn says nothing of their conversation, but mentions the point, important to him as a Royalist and a devoted churchman, that this "miracle of a youth" was nephew to the venerated and imprisoned Bishop of Ely;[8] the point was significant for Wren's future opportunities, and for the part that Evelyn was to play, when times were happier for him and the Wrens, in forwarding Wren's interest. Two days later Evelyn and Wren met again, this time at Wadham enjoying the congenial, still bachelor hospitality of Wilkins, a good friend of Evelyn's and in 1656 much praised by him for the pains he had taken to save the universities from the unwelcome attentions of "the ignorant, sacrilegious commanders and soldiers" who yearned for an assault on all places and persons of learning. Evelyn saw the warden's strange group of "artificial, mathematical, and magical curiosities". A thermometer, a large magnet, and a conic section were among them. Most of them were of Wilkins' own contriving, but some had been worked up by "that prodigious young scholar" Christopher Wren.[9] Evelyn's present from Wren was prophetic of the young scientist's future interests in matters to do with stone – a piece of white marble which he had stained "with a lively red, very deep."

Wren's All Souls' Fellowship kept him in Oxford, in close touch with Wilkins and the others in the pioneering scientific club. Wilkins' strong influence in the university continued till, in 1659, he left Oxford for his short-lived mastership of Trinity at Cambridge. He had reinforced his position by his marriage to Cromwell's sister. Had the Commonwealth lasted he would have remained a leading Establishment figure. But the breadth and tolerance of his outlook were such that he happily survived the Restoration, living past it to a continued spell of position and preferment which coincided, in its last years, with Wren's rise to official eminence. By the time that Wilkins moved to Cambridge Wren held a post which caused him to divide his time between Oxford and London.

His appointment, made in 1657, was that of Professor of Astronomy at Gresham College in London. The college, a forerunner of the much later London University, was the Elizabethan foundation of Sir Thomas Gresham, the famous London merchant and the founder, on the model of Antwerp or Amsterdam, of London's Royal Exchange. Gresham's will provided for the eventual starting, in his own house off Bishopsgate, of a college whose professors were to give lectures in law, divinity, rhetoric, music, physic, geometry, and astronomy. By Wren's time the scientific subjects had come to predominate. The young Fellow of All Souls' was doubtful, at first, over the acceptance of a post whose lectures on his subject, given only once a week, would cause him, in those days when a seventy-minute journey from Oxford to Paddington was beyond reasonable prophecy, an absence from Oxford of at least half of each week. But Wilkins, Sprat, and others persuaded him to accept the post. Apart from a high-flown, long-winded inaugural address,[10] and apart from the actual instruction in astronomy which Wren gave in the arcaded courtyard of what had once been Gresham's splendid house, the appointment meant that he was again in frequent contact with the men of science who increasingly gathered in the capital.

He could also, as it happened, meet others besides Wilkins who had family ties with the chief holder of political power. Though Wren's own family connections, at this time of his father's death at Bletchington and of his uncle's continued imprisonment, were notably royalist his own interests, and the wide, unprejudiced scope of his own thought and study, made him an accepted friend of many in the Commonwealth camp. Among them was John Claypole, whose wife Elizabeth was the Lord Protector's favourite daughter.[11] He himself, the son of a gentleman in Northamptonshire, sat in Parliament and had been advanced to office in the days of his father-in-law's power. he held 'court' appointments and was a member of Cromwell's Committee of Trade. By the time that Wren knew him he had been made a member of the Protectorate's short-lived House of Lords. His was not, however, an extreme Puritanism. He had opposed the authority of Cromwell's much disliked Major Generals, and both he and his wife remained worshipping members of the Church of England. He was, moreover, a keen student of science and mathematics. It was as such that he became Wren's friend and frequent host in his London home; Wren's presence at dinner with the Claypoles gave rise to an incident well reported in *Parentalia*.[12]

During the meal Oliver Cromwell came in unannounced, recognised the young professor of astronomy as the nephew of Bishop

Matthew Wren, and told him that the long imprisoned bishop might "come out an he will". He added that Christopher Wren could take the message to his uncle as coming direct from the Protector's own mouth. But when Wren rushed to the Tower, and told his uncle what seemed to him to be such excellent news the bishop received the message coolly, adding that the offer was not the first of its kind, but that all earlier approaches had been conditional on his submitting to Cromwell's "detestable tyranny", and admitting that his release would be by the Protector's favours. The incident must have come early in 1658, the year in which both Lady Claypole and her father died; the aging bishop had two years to wait before the Restoration which gave him his chance, under very different circumstances both for himself and his nephew, to give Christopher Wren his first architectural commision.

Cromwell's death, in September of 1658, soon brought confusion, in the political field and to those who held the professorships at Gresham College. All but one had their lectures interrupted, and the college itself was rudely occupied by soldiers who turned it, in those days of borderline sanitation, into a polluted rookery. *Parentalia* tells us how Sprat informed Wren of the building's "noisome condition", and of "infernal smells" and other indignities, while the younger Matthew Wren told his cousin how his entry into the college had for a time been barred by a soldier with a musket. Christopher Wren himself had in the meantime retired to an expectant Oxford and the quiet quads of All Souls'. He was there, so it seems, till the late spring of 1660 and the restoration to his kingdom of a wary, travel-seasoned monarch.

The Restoration, with its renewed hope and prospects for those in the royalist camp, and with the chances of position and promotion vastly better, for such people, than they had been for nearly twenty years, was an event of vast future significance for the young Christopher Wren. Charles II's return had come too late to help the elder Christopher Wren in his exile from the Windsor deanery. But for Bishop Matthew, already released from the Tower, the Restoration meant a return to Ely, and seven more years of venerated influence. An important new post soon came the way of Gresham College's Professor of Astronomy. But in the meantime there had been an interesting display, in Oxford, at Wren's own college of Wadham. The occasion, so we find in *Parentalia*, was one of the early assemblies for the "advancement of Natural and Experimental Knowledge"[3]; one supposes that the occasion was after Wilkins had left for his short Cambridge mastership at Trinity.

Parentalia lists the "theories, inventions and experiments, and mechanic improvements" which the young Wren now put on display at the scene of his undergraduate studies. They must, one assumes, have been the fruit of some years deliberation; they certainly suggest not the specialist concentration of more modern times but the

Leonardian versatility of a Renaissance *uomo universale*. In England, as distinct from more fully matured Italy, the Renaissance itself, particularly in architectural matters, was still in a fairy early stage, and many of Wren's contemporary academics aimed, at least in theory, at a wider scope than seems possible in our more specialist age. Mathematical and astronomical items are predictably on this display list of 1660, while Wren's medical and astronomical interests come out in such items as an artificial eye and methods of plastering, dressing, or injection. Nautical and fishing matters, with such items as "ways of submarine navigation", and "easier ways of whale fishing", have their place; so too one finds the "fabric for a vessel of war". Agricultural improvements and a new technique for the embroidery of bed covers and hangings are less obviously in the main run of Wren's interests. "Probable ways of making fresh water at sea" would have introduced others beside sailors, while an idea for weaving "many ribbons at once with only turning a wheel" foreshadows the great inventions of the Industrial Revolution; one compares it with a scheme, mentioned by Aubrey, put up to the silk stocking weavers[14] "for a way of weaving seven to nine pairs at once"; when the weavers refused Wren's demand of £400 for the use of his invention he lost his temper and, in their presence, broke up the model.

More significant, from a young man whose father and friends were known to have included architecture and building among their more active interests, are various items directly bearing on what later became the main career of a man whose main talents still seemed to lie in mathematics and astronomy. Ideas for the much needed improvements of coaches, for pumping engines, and for rock drilling seemed, indeed, to belong more to the future science of mechanical engineering. But "new designs tending to strength, convenience, and beauty in building" bore directly on building technology, as also did Wren's ideas for some sort of composition material which would produce "a pavement harder, fairer, and cheaper than marble". Closer still to that blend of civil engineering and architecture which had engaged the talents of such masters as Michelangelo and Leonardo, and which in Wren's own time formed part of the work of such a 'court architect' as Carlo Fontana in Rome, were ideas for fortifications and projects (perhaps by the use of such Dutch devices as sluices and coffer dams) for clearing sands, fortifying harbours, and building forts, moles and other structures in, and on the edge of, the sea. It was, indeed, by way of coastal fortification, and the planning of the bastions and ravelins used by Baroque military engineers, that Wren was to be offered his first paid entry into the domain of building and architectural design. But his first new appointment, in those months of optimism for those whose families had fought and suffered for the Stuarts, was in his existing discipline of astronomy.

3

Emergent Architect

The restoration of Charles II, early in the summer of 1660, ushered in a time of happy congratulation for those of the Royalist party who had come back with their king from pinched years of Continental exile or who had stayed, in imprisonment or at best in clouded unhappiness, in Commonwealth England. Important posts, soon emptied of their Cromwellian holders, were abundantly available. Political revenge was an obvious demand. Yet it was modestly exacted. Charles II, a shrewd monarch and already no stranger to the subtler adjustments of kingcraft, was determined that he should never again "go on his travels". So the number of those actually put to death, all for their direct part in the execution of Charles I, was small by the standards of an age which held treason the most heinous of offences. Fervent royalist partisans, by the orders of the Convention Parliament, amused themselves more harmlessly, though with macabre repulsiveness, when on 30th January 1661, twelve years to the day since Charles I had died in Whitehall, they crudely exhumed from Westminster Abbey the bodies of Cromwell, Ireton, and Bradshaw, carted off the remains to Tyburn, there postumously hanging and burying the now execrated carcases; Mrs Pepys was among the great crowd that witnessed the scene.[1] Evelyn's happy ejaculation – "O the stupendous and inscrutable judgments of God!" echoed his gleefully pious invocation of divine providence when a few months earlier he encountered the men who bore from the gallows the hacked and reeking quarters of some of the regicides.[2]

Though much more had irrevocably changed since the sad 1640s than many jubilant Royalists imagined, the Restoration soon took effect in politics, at Court, and in matters of religion.

The Convention Parliament, which had summoned Charles back to his kingdom, and which had authorised the charade over the remains of three most hated Commonwealth figures, soon gave way to the Cavalier Parliament, recruited in the main from the royalist gentry whose sun had risen again. An extremist, vengefully oppressive régime might soon have gained the constitutional respectability of parliamentary approval. But in many respects this Parliament of cavalier squires proved moderate in tone, with a wary eye both on what were seen as the instruments of despotism and on the funds available to a monarch whose tastes might soon run to heady extravagance. The king himself might shine, in Whitehall, as the monarch and as the most conspicuous ornament of a reassembled court. But a few hundred guards apart he was allowed no standing army with which to dominate his kingdom. Nor was he generously supplied in the crucial matter of finance; Parliament saw to it that the Government's revenues, and the sums available for show and display, were spare and meagre. It was certain, from what Parliament decided soon after the Restoration, that Charles II would always be under tight financial restraint, and that however expensive his tastes might be no builder, be he Wren, Webb, or anyone else, employed by the restored Crown could provide his sovereign with the full architectural trappings of Baroque monarchy.

But the gay flamboyance, the theatricals, and the licence of the Court soon showed that Baroque monarchy, Continental in its cultural flavour and remote both from sober Puritan restraints and the rumbustious crudities of many country squires, was what Charles II wished to see flourishing in the jumbled, mainly mediaeval purlieus of Whitehall, at Windsor where his father lay buried, and in the rambling variety of his other residences. Abroad, in the despotism of Louis XIV, he had seen such a monarchy in full action. Himself half French, a linguist in Spanish and Italian as well as in his half-native English, Charles neither looked nor thought like the general run of the subjects among whom he had not lived for ten years. His preferences were for the political circumstances, and the way of life, of a king who was both absolute in power and unrestrained in his outlay. Yet his 'travels', and the poverty of much of his exile, had taught him much. He soon knew, better than many of those around him, how little the Court of Whitehall, and the public buildings of his capital, could resemble those sponsored by his royal cousin in France.

So in some respects the Restoration fell short of the hopes of Royalists who imagined that the restored kingship could, in the 1660s, go blithely back to the palmy days of Carolean absolutism which the Long Parliament of 1640 had restrained and, in the end, overthrown. But in some gay superficialities the picture at Court was of a burgeoning luxuriance. Full bottomed wigs and low cut silken dresses replaced close-cropped heads and the high-collared severity of Puritan women's attire. Court ceremonies returned, and the restored King promenaded, with "abundance of gallantry" as John Evelyn put it, in Hyde Park. Henrietta Maria the Queen Mother came back from France, and the theatre recommenced after a bleak spell of interdiction. It was too soon, in those first few months after the King's return, for the Restoration to gain its architectural expression. But the political seedbed for new building work was there, given peace and financial provisions more lavish than seemed likely, or were ever in fact achieved.

But in one respect, specially relevant to the fortunes of the Wrens, Restoration promise soon blossomed into reality. The Anglican Church soon regained its position. Those who had secretly, and like the Catholics with their masses in their own houses, held Prayer-Book services, could do so openly, while many who had lost livings and preferments could look forward to their return. Though the full enforcement of religious unity was not attempted for another two years the first, most obvious steps were soon taken. From 8th July 1660, as Evelyn happily noted in his diary, the Prayer Book Liturgy was publicly read in the churches whence it had long been banished, while a few months later, in the King's presence, the service was performed, as formerly and by contrast to the unmusical devotions of the Puritans, "with music, voices, etc." No less evident, in these first joyous months, was the flood of latter-day Laudian divines to fill leading clerical posts which death or deprivation had temporarily emptied. The important dignities of bishoprics and deaneries were sought with special zeal. The year of the Restoration saw most of England's bishoprics vacant; those of their elderly holders who had survived the Civil War and the years of the Commonwealth were in prison or in unmolested but inarticulate retirement. The episcopal general post which got under way in 1660 soon brought new preferments, and new chances of patronage, to clerics who figure large in Wren's life. Bishop Juxon of London, nearly eighty years old and a prelate who had, for devoted royalists, gained veneration from his attendance on the fateful scaffold in Whitehall, was fittingly promoted to a three years' tenure of the see of Canterbury. But age and frailty, which curtailed the part he played in the Coronation ceremony, soon heavily hampered him. Dr Gilbert Sheldon, a strongly anti-Puritan Oxford man who had, for a year by now, resumed his wardenship of All Souls', became Dean of the Chapel Royal and Juxon's successor in London. As a man on the spot in the main centre of power he, and not the aged archbishop, officiated at the Anglican ceremony when, in 1662, the king married Catherine of Braganza. Next year Juxon died and Sheldon, significantly for Wren the budding architect, became, in name as he already was for many practical purposes, the primate of the Anglican Church.

More important, perhaps, for the young astronomer-mathematician whose reputation stood high, but who had yet to choose a career outside his learned subjects, was the venerated, influential position of his uncle. For Bishop Matthew Wren, restored to the fulness of his Ely bishopric, soon resumed his Laudian ways. His palace and cathedral apart, he had his London residence, near Holborn, at Ely House. There, in February of 1661, Evelyn saw him at a service in the splendid mediaeval chapel;[3] after all was done the bishop, a true lover of ceremony and the decencies of worship, gave the blessing "very pontifically". The old bishop lived, for another six years, to be one of the last survivors in high clerical office of those who had held sees in the days of Laud and Charles I. He had, in the meantime, been mindful of his old college of Pembroke at Cambridge, starting there, in his old age, a chapel, as he had long before done, when he was the Master of Peterhouse who started a new chapel. It was there at Pembroke, not in his vast cathedral, that in 1663 he carried out, in a spirit of reinstated thanksgiving, the vow he had made as a prisoner in the Tower. His prestige, like that of Juxon, stood high, and it was no accident that his family flourished under Charles II. Earliest of them in the field of high preferment was his eldest son Matthew, aged thirty-one in 1660 and first cousin to the future architect. For he soon became secretary to the statesman-historian Lord Hyde, the powerful Vice-Chancellor and in another year the Earl of Clarendon. Seven years later, on Clarendon's fall, Matthew Wren came closer still to the centre of power when he moved on to become secretary to the King's brother (and Clarendon's son-in-law) James, Duke of York. By then, however, his cousin Christopher, though not yet Surveyor general or official Court architect, had been favoured, by accident as well as his own talents and the influence he could command, with opportunities putting him past the need of recommendations by his relatives.

Yet the positions of others among Christopher Wren's kinsmen confirmed him in the official and clerical Establishment. Bishop Matthew, while he still lived, was the family's most prominent member, while his eldest son's contacts with the great ones of the land were of the closest. The younger Matthew Wren was a Member of Parliament as well as the holder, in succession, of two highly placed secretaryships. His premature death, in 1672 in the naval battle of Solebay against the Dutch, probably kept him from yet higher posts; he was buried, in Pembroke College at Cambridge, in the fine new chapel which his cousin had designed for the reinstated Bishop of Ely.[4] The younger Matthew's brothers also fared reasonably enough. Dr Thomas Wren, the bishop's second son, was a doctor of physic who combined his medical knowledge with a love of music and a clerical career. The Commonwealth interlude found him, like Dean Wren and William Holder, living close to Oxford; he was there, so we find from *Parentalia*, to be near the Bodleian. But the Restoration renewed his clerical chances; though he fell short of a deanery and a mitre he settled down, at Wilburton in the fen country, as Archdeacon of Ely. In later years his younger brother Charles became Member for the borough of Cambridge, while William, the bishop's youngest son, ended up with a knighthood.

Members of Dean Christopher Wren's family also had their share of place and prominence; the younger Christopher's sisters were, in this connection, of more note than the Dean's other sons. Anne, short of stature like her famous brother, became the wife of Dr Henry Brounsell, no humble and ordinary clergyman but a Canon of Ely and rector of Stretham, a parish next to that of his wife's cousin Dr Thomas Wren. Anne Brounsell was long an invalid and died worn out with various maladies, in 1668. More important, and alive all through Charles II's reign, was Susan Holder, the architect's other sister of note. As her husband, after leaving Bletchington, combined other preferments with a prebend, in the end residentiary, at St Paul's she often found herself in London. Other qualities apart, she appears, so we find from her monumental inscription in the crypt, of her brother's cathedral, to have skills, in an amateur capacity, in what are described as "medicinal remedies"; she cultivated her gift "in compassion to the poor". So expert did Mrs Holder become that, in the words of the inscription which her surviving husband may have composed "thousands were happily healed by her, no one ever miscarried". One would gladly know more of what seem, when compared to the efforts of most physicians of those times, to have been remarkable achievements. Her funerary tribute adds the point that Charles II himself, Queen Catherine, and many courtiers also "had experience of her successful hand". Aubrey too mentions Mrs Holder's "strange sagacity" in curing wounds by considering their causes, circumstances, and effects. He mentions an episode when a poultice of hers, applied in an emergency to one of the king's hands which the royal surgeons had made worse, gave Charles II immediate relief and later, "to the great grief of all the surgeons", effected a full cure.[5] Such a standing in high quarters, till her death in 1688 after forty-five years of happy marriage, could have improved her architect brother's good standing. Susan Holder's husband, and the young Christopher's good friend in his youthful days, died, aged over eighty, in 1698, the year after the first service had been held in the new cathedral choir wherein he held a prebend's stall.

Such was the historic setting, all-important for a man who aspired to high position as a designer of buildings for Court and Church, in which Christopher Wren rose to architectural eminence. Had his background and political loyalties been those of, say, John Milton who could compose *Paradise Lost* in circumstances like those of many royalist clergy and gentry in the Commonwealth years, no important buildings by Wren could ever have arisen. He might never have got as far as the committal to paper of architectural designs, preferring or being constrained to the quiet obscurity of a mathematician-astronomer with little in the way of salaried work. Wren the architect was the creation of Restoration politics. But his first appointment, and his prominence from the start in the new scientific organisation whose work tuned in with the enquiring spirit at work in an age in which the episcopal survivors of Laudianism could, as Pepys noticed,[6] be scorned as strange relics of a past and forgotten era, lay close to his recognised studies. But before, in the early months of 1661, Wren took up his new post he played a major part in the founding of a famous organisation which formally continued the enquiring studies, at Oxford and elsewhere, of the loosely knit groups in which Wilkins, Seth Ward, and Wren himself had been prominent.

The idea of some such body as the Royal Society was not new in 1660. Cromwell's government, which had also considered the notion of a northern university at Durham, had given thought to the matter. Richard Cromwell, one gathers, had been specially interested, but nothing was done in his short Protectorate. But as the right people, of varying political beliefs, were readily available a move was made very soon after the Restoration. In November of 1660, after one of Wren's astronomical lectures at Gresham College, some men of science, Lord Brouncker, Robert Boyle, and Wilkins being among them, gathered and agreed to form a Philosophical Society whose meetings, of an enquiring and scientific bent, would occur every week. Wren himself was active in forming the new body which, in the following March, with the King's approval and interest, became the Royal Society, whose activities, more than in later times, reconciled science and religion.

By that time Wren had taken up his new post. This was the Savilian professorship of astronomy at Oxford; its previous holder had been Wren's old Wadham colleague and lasting friend Seth Ward, now appointed to the deanery of Exeter, soon its bishop and later Bishop of Salisbury. Wren now gave up his All Souls' fellowship, living elsewhere in Oxford when his presence was needed there. For an observatory he used the topmost storey of the Jacobean Gothic tower of the Old Schools' Quad; it was there, in October, 1664, that John Evelyn found him, with a telescope, attempting an observation of the sun.[7] But Wren's London activities still claimed much of his time; it was not long before they came, for new reasons, to dominate his life.

A recent writer on Wren has suggested that John Evelyn was the man who first brought the future architect of St Paul's to the direct notice of Charles II. He was certainly well in the King's confidence, and architectural matters were among the many topics which the King and his faithful courtier discussed. On October 1st, 1661, Charles and Evelyn out with him in one of his yachts, and there amid the sea breezes discussed the (presumably classical) "improvement of gardens and buildings"; he told Evelyn that such matters had not gone far in England compared with what he had seen on the Continent.[9] But there were other ways, more aligned to Wren's activities as a scientist and astronomer, in which Evelyn, and other members of the new Royal

Society, could bring the Savilian Professor to the King's direct notice. Not long after the Society's inauguration Wren, a most talented draughtsman, sent the King some drawings of insects as seen through a microscope. He followed the gift by a large, and in the knowledge of those times, realistic model of the moon.[10] Charles II may well, in the small-scale high society of his reign, have been aware of the gifts of the young man of science whose background was so impeccably royalist, and whose family had suffered much in the Stuart cause. But this achievement of 1661 gave Wren a personal interview with the sovereign with whom he was to have many future consultations.

But however Evelyn may have helped Wren to high patronage it was from his cousin Matthew, Lord Chancellor Clarendon's secretary, that Wren had his first firm invitation to concern himself in building; the occasion for the offer was in essence political. For in 1661 negotiations were completed for the marriage of Charles II to the Portuguese princess Catherine of Braganza. The actual marriage occurred next year but an earlier, though financially incomplete start was made with the handing over of Catherine's dowry. The territorial items were Bombay, Portugal's northern trading position on India's western coast, and Tangier, long held by Portugal on the Moroccan side of the straits of Gibraltar, a convenient springboard for a country which wanted, as England had done since Cromwell's time, to become a Mediterranean power. Tangier, being the closer of the new acquisitions, was the earlier of the two to be taken over; preparations for occupation were in hand in the autumn of 1661. It was probably then that Wren got the offer of a well paid commission to survey, and generally to supervise the work needed if Tangier was to become, as Gibraltar did later, an effective base. The items mentioned were the new mole, the harbour works, and the fortifications of the newly gained town. *Parentalia* states that Wren's expert knowledge of geometry was the main reason for an offer as notable for its incidentals as it was in itself.[11] But it must also have been known, particularly to Wren's cousin, that building and architecture were among the family interests, and that the "inventions, experiments, and mechanic improvements" already shown by Wren included "offensive and defensive engines" and the building, in the sea or on its brink, of such items, very relevant at Tangier, as forts and moles. In an age when definitions had yet to be drawn between various professions it was reasonable that a man best known as a mathematician and a scientist should also, in a spirit of Renaissance universalism, concern himself with civil engineering and architecture.

The incidentals of the Tangier offer were, if anything, more important than the actual post. A good salary might reasonably have been expected, though Wren might, under the Restoration monarchy, have found its actual payment somewhat chancy. Oxford University was to be cavalierly treated, with a temporary royal dispensation for its Savilian Professor of Astronomy to be away from the duties of his post. But the main point in the scheme was the accompanying offer of the reversion, on the death of its existing holder, of the post of Surveyor General of the Royal Works. The current Surveyor General was Sir John Denham, better as a poet than as a builder, and a 'gentleman architect' to whom the post had gone for devoted service to the exiled King.[12] His death, which actually occurred in 1669, did not then seem a speedy likelihood. But the fact that Wren, famous as a geometer and not without potentialities as a military engineer or an architect, was offered such a post suggested that his future might lie with buildings rather than stars.

Giving his health as a pretext Wren politely declined the Tangier offer, asking the King to "command his duty" in England; he may, on consultation with his cousin and others, have realised that his own country might soon give scope for his architectural interests.[13] He never went to Tangier, but the fortress on the fringe of Barbary later claimed some of his attention. For in 1669, when many of Pepys' papers dealt much with building work at Tangier, and when Sir Hugh Cholmeley was on the spot in charge of the mole and the defences a "modell", or scheme, for further work was sent in by Cholmeley; four hundred of the six hundred yards intended for the mole had by then been built.[14] Wren, now Surveyor General, had a wide supervision to exercise in such matters. So without giving the Tangier scheme any detailed work he "perused this modell" and reported the latest scheme to be sufficient for its purpose.[15] The episode reminds us that paper work, as well as actual building operations, pertained to the high post which Wren eventually held.

A time followed, in 1662 and 1663, when scientific and architectural activities alike occupied Wren's attention. As Savilian professor at Oxford he lectured on spheres, on Pascal, and on navigation as this was aided by astronomy. In the summer of 1663 the French traveller Balthasar Monconys came to Oxford, there visiting Wren at All Souls'. He commented, as did others who knew the Savilian professor, on Wren's small stature. He found him one of the most polite and frank of the scientists he had met in England; their discussions turned largely on Wren's weather clock.

It was probably about this time that Wren carried out a scientific task which was, by a curious chance, to leave us the earliest of his surviving drawings. Thomas Willis, well known by now as a physician, and since the Restoration Sedleian Professor of Natural Philosophy at Oxford, was also a staunch royalist, and a devoted Anglican in whose Oxford house Prayer Book services had been held all through the Commonwealth.[16] He was now writing the book, on the anatomy of the brain, for which he became best known; the work came out, with a dedication to Archbishop Sheldon, in 1664. In his preface Willis pays tribute, among other helpers, to Wren. For not only had the Professor of Astronomy watched many of Willis' dissections and discussed their results but he had also found time, amid many other preoccupations to make, *eruditissimis suis manibus* as Willis puts it, several of the drawings which appeared as the fine illustrations of an epoch-making book. As the work was ready for the printers early in 1664 Wren's kind help to an old associate in the Scientific Club at Oxford cannot have been given later than the previous year.

Wren's refusal of the Tangier offer might, under some monarchs, have blighted his future chances of building work. But his friends at Court were influential, and Wren's hope that his services might be sought in England seems soon to have been fulfilled; a different offer, with unexpectedly great implications, came jointly from the sovereign and the Church, so that Wren's professional discourses at Oxford suffered from a cause much closer than the Barbary Coast to the University.

The conditions of St Paul's cathedral, impaired by the fire of 1561 which destroyed its tall spire, was deplorable in the centenary year of that disaster. Though Inigo Jones had recased the outside of the nave, and had added a great Corinthian western portico, the Civil War had delayed any repairs on the shaken piers of the central crossing. The years of Puritan power, with some interior damage and desecration, had not made things better. The refurnishing and repair of the cathedral, a conspicuous reminder, in England's largest city, of the power and prestige of a reinstated Church, came both as a political and a religious gesture. Gilbert Sheldon, the new, energetic Bishop of London, and those at Court who aimed to restore the pride of the Church of England, were at hand to press for an overdue process of repair. Some early consultations, in advance of a special commission and more detailed schemes, occurred in 1661. It seems certain that Wren was involved, marking the first stages of what proved a lifelong connection with London's cathedral.[17] *Parentalia* quoted a letter, racily written to Wren by Thomas Sprat, another Wadham man, at the College, under Wilkins, when Wren was there, and an early member of the Oxford scientists' club. Sprat achieved some note as a witty man of letters, and was praised by Evelyn for his direct and ready turn of expression. An early member of the Royal Society, in 1667 he became its first historian, while his clerical career led him to the joint tenure of the Westminster deanery and the see of Rochester. His crisp note does not belie Evelyn's praise; its reference to Dr Richard Bailey, the reinstated though aging President of St John's, as Vice Chancellor at Oxford dates the letter to 1661.

Sprat confessed that he had "some little peek" against Wren,

having the occasion to tell him some bad news about Dr Bailey's
displeasure with his university's Professor of Astronomy. For the Vice
Chancellor, worried at Wren's absence so long after the beginning of
term, had asked Sprat for news of Wren's whereabouts and the reason
for his absence. Sprat had done what he could to stand up for his old
friend, reminding the Vice Chancellor that Charles II had been
declared absolute monarch, and that it was the king who had kept
Wren in London. He argued the point that activities in Sir Henry
Saville's school were of less concern than the fortification of Tangier or
the rebuilding of St Paul's – these being the works on which the
"extraordinary Genius" of the Savilian professor was then thought
necessary. After some discussion the President of St John's told Sprat
that Wren could not, at this juncture, think of him merely as his friend
Dr Bailey, but, more augustly, as the university's Vice Chancellor; as
such he "most terribly" told Sprat that he took it very ill that Wren
had given him no explanation of his absence from his post at Oxford.
For our understanding of Wren's career the importance of Sprat's
letter lies in its proof of his concern, only a year after the Restoration,
in the knotty problem of the restoration of a damaged and neglected
mediaeval cathedral.

It was now nearly time for Wren's first purely architectural
commissions. With Tangier sidestepped he soon found patrons not
merely for restoration jobs but for wholly new buildings. One of these,
from a man who must have known him for various reasons, but in a
special degree from the idea that old St Paul's should be put in good
order, was Gilbert Sheldon, on Juxon's death, in the summer of 1663,
at once moved from London to Canterbury. The other was Wren's
venerable uncle of Ely.

4

The Growth of Ambition

The idea of the Sheldonian Theatre at Oxford was not that of the prelate who paid for its building and gave it his name. Soon after the Restoration, with the air full of ideas for the restored position and dignity of Crown and Church, the university itself bought the site, on the southern side of Broad Street, for the worthy performance of the degree congregations, and other university ceremonies, which had long been held in the university church. Though religious in origin, those ceremonies had become secular in their general character, and not without elements of buffoonery which made them, in the eyes of restored and zealous Laudians who now again held sway in Laud's old university, quite unsuitable for performance in the sacred setting of a church. The problem was to find money for a building fit for its ceremonial purpose. Gilbert Sheldon, still Bishop of London but virtually certain of the Canterbury succession once the aged and ailing Juxon died,* took the matter in hand in the early months of 1663. He held no competition, but went straight to Wren, the mathematician, geometer, and from his standpoint well connected Oxford man, as his designer for a building whose roofing required much theoretical and technical skill. Late in April Wren showed a first model of his project to his colleagues in the Royal Society.[1]

As the new building was to hold large gatherings, and as those present needed both to see well and to hear what was said, the design of a classical theatre was a suitable precedent; England's climate, however, made it needful for the new auditorium to be roofed. The Theatre of Marcellus at Rome, rising clear on all sides and with none of its semi-circular seating abutting on a hillside, seemed to Sheldon and the university authorities a good pattern to follow. Wren could, moreover, have known, from works by Vitruvius and Serlio which he could consult in England, of the general appearance, and stylistic treatment, of the 'built up' theatres by Roman architects. He may therefore have based his first Sheldonian design on what he knew of Roman theatres. But it seems, from what Evelyn says of his meeting

*He actually died in June of 1663; Pepys remarked, the very next day, that Sheldon was "to have his seat".

with Wren in the autumn of 1664, and of his visit to the building site, that the actual design of the building was not yet final. Evelyn, who unlike Wren had seen the Theatre of Marcellus and many other buildings in Rome, adds the point that Wren, still an architectural novice, did not disdain his advice on a few points.[2] It seems that the Sheldonian, like St Paul's much later in Wren's career, saw stylistic changes, if not alterations in its basic design, as work went along.

An auditory space, with clear sightlines towards the Chancellor's chair and the picturesquely projecting rostra whence orations were delivered, needed a broad ceiling with no obstruction from supporting pillars. A dome, at that moment of Wren's architectural experience, was out of the question. So Wren, displaying mathematical and structural ingenuity, contrived a single-span ceiling whose roof was a constructional tour de force, and whose decoration somewhat quaintly recalled the *velaria*, or awnings, which in the heat of an Italian summer were spread across the open-air auditoria and amphitheatres of ancient Rome.

By the time that he needed to make his final designs for this roof he may have come back from the visit to France which he made in the summer and autumn of 1665. He may well, during those months in Paris, have seen and studied the Salle des Machines, or opera theatre, which had been built, between 1659 and 1662, in the Tuileries Palace.[3] Cardinal Mazarin had sponsored the scheme. The architect, recommended him by his niece who was Duchess of Mantua, was the Mantuan architect-engineer Gasparo Vigarini who had worked on other theatres in Italy, and who sent for Italian carpenters to perfect the flat ceiling over his auditorium in Paris.

The main element of Wren's roof structure, replaced in 1802 by the Sheldonian's present roof, was a series of transverse timber trusses. As the carpenters could get no beams as long as the seventy-foot span of the theatre Wren composed each truss of a series of timbers, strongly and ingeniously jointed together and firm enough to uphold the vertical beams which rose above to the lowpitched roof and to the simple cupola which originally capped the theatre, and which Blore attractively replaced in 1838. A balustrade, comparable to that which Wren in later years disliked at St Paul's, capped the sides and the polygonal northern end, while an assertively picturesque feature, as it was finished in 1669, was a set of oval dormer lights or lucarnes, a central one being topped by Charles II's crowned monogram, the others by mitres to honour the Archbishop who gave the money – over £14,000 – laid out on the building.[4] Dormers of this upright oval type, prominent on the roof storeys of some recently built country mansions in France, could have been noted by Wren on his one journey abroad. Robert Streeter, Sergeant Painter to the King, worked in London on the canvasses for the painted ceiling, an elaborate Baroque work with putti rolling back an awning, just as slaves rolled back the Roman velaria, thus revealing the allegorical scene of Truth descending on the arts and sciences. Imitation cords, standing out in relief and gaily gilt, recalled those of the Roman velaria and interrupt the sweep of Streeter's paintings which Wren (but not Pepys) seems to have rated higher than those by Rubens in Inigo Jones' Banqueting House in Whitehall.

Wren's Sheldonian exteriors held a wide variety of Vitruvian and Renaissance references. Books and engravings had to be his main sources for a building whose sides, and whose polygonal northern end, had to be much simpler than the more triumphal facade which greeted graduands as they processed (through a new Gothic doorway perhaps designed by Wren) to get their degrees in the new ceremonial hall. Such modern critics as Sir John Summerson, Dr Margaret Whinney, and Dr Kerry Downes have traced influences from Bramante, Serlio, and Palladio in the theatre's elevations,[5] while Alberti's church facade at Rimini, as well as Palladio's work in his two Venetian churches, could have been a background factor in the double pediment of the southern frontage with its array of Composite and Corinthian pilasters and half columns. A main interior feature, akin on a smaller scale to what one finds in the more ordinary run of theatres, is the shallow gallery on its curved sequence of Corinthian pillarets.

The new chapel at Pembroke College, Cambridge came from a straightforward act of patronage within the Wren family. It was built simultaneously with the Sheldonian, but as it was started first, and was finished four years before the auditorium at Oxford, it fairly ranks as Wren's earliest building.

The college already had its chapel, a somewhat humble building of the fourteenth century. But Bishop Matthew Wren, a devoted Pembroke man, had vowed, when he was Cromwell's prisoner in the Tower, that if Crown and Church were restored, and if he himself lived to reoccupy his see at Ely, he would give his old college a new and more imposing place of worship.[6] The chapel at Pembroke fulfilled the bishop's vow; it also counted as a memorial to Bishop Andrewes to whom Matthew Wren and his brother Christopher had owed much during their earlier years. Historically speaking, the new chapel was a parallel to the one which Matthew Wren himself had started, across the street, at Peterhouse. But Pembroke's new chapel had none of the reminiscent Gothicism of the building at Peterhouse. Its spirit was that of the fully Renaissance classicism for which its designer, and his fellow scientists, stood in the Restoration age when Gothic was outmoded, and when the Italianate idiom pioneered in England by Inigo Jones was fully accepted by the 'architects', in 1663 more established as such than was Christopher Wren, who enjoyed the highest patronage.[7]

As the new chapel's foundation stone was laid in May 1663, Wren must have worked on the designs early that year. Unlike the Sheldonian the chapel is simple and rectangular; it caused no special problems of construction. A drawing in the college shows a five-bay northern elevation, not one of four bays as actually built.[8] Rusticated pilasters appear between the side windows, and above the parapet there is a row of pineapples. There is no western cupola, and some other details differ from what one actually sees. The somewhat battered model, likewise with no western cupola, has four bays and is much more like the actual building; it is important as the oldest survivor of a technique of demonstration much favoured by Wren.

The chapel's side walls are faced with brick, but stone was used for the window frames and for other dressings. The interior, with its joinery by the prolific Cambridge woodworker Cornelius Austin, was simpler at first than it is today.[9] For the sanctuary, with its plain eastern window on the 'Venetian' pattern, was not then parted from the body of the chapel by the dignified pillars and arch put up by the younger George Gilbert Scott when, in the 1880s, he lengthened the building. But the altarpiece, with its triangular broken pediment, and the fine Baroque plasterwork of the ceiling, foreshadowed much of what was done, under Wren's supervision if not to his detailed designs, in conditions of church replacement unforeseen in 1663 or 1665. More important, and a revelation to Cambridge as the most fully classical building work so far seen in the university, was the western facade, successfully capped by a well proportioned bell turret. Its four plain Corinthian pilasters, with simple niches in the narrower intervals and a window in the broader central space, display Roman and Renaissance references which showed, as did the Sheldonian, how fully its designer had turned from mediaeval or Laudian Gothic. The chapel's associations with the Wrens did not end when Bishop Matthew consecrated it on 21st of September 1665 – his patron-apostle's festival. In another two years the bishop's splendid funeral was held there, and not in his cathedral. In five more years his son Matthew was buried in Pembroke College after his gallant death in action. Later still, the chapel was the place of worship of Sir Christopher's namesake son, sent not to Oxford to his father or grandfather's colleges but here to the college of his uncle whose high position had forwarded his family's fortunes.

The year when Pembroke chapel at Cambridge was finished saw Wren at work on an Oxford building whose style was, for that university, no less of a revelation. The college was Trinity, Wren's patron being his old friend and fellow scientist Ralph Bathurst, a leading influence in his college before 1664 when he started his forty years' spell as its President. He soon thought of new buildings for his college, and he naturally turned to Wren, whose Sheldonian Theatre was arising across the Broad. As Bathurst's biographer pointed out, "the venerable beauties of Gothic magnificence" had prevailed in Oxford before Bathurst, with Wren as his designer, first gave his university a taste of the "just and genuine proportions of Grecian architecture";[10] the new chapel at Brasenose, started in the 1650s and still incomplete, was a strange Gothico-Renaissance hybrid. As it happened, Wren's building was none too impressive and had some backward-looking features; it was, however, the occasion for some lively, biographically revealing correspondence.

Ralph Bathurst had got quickly to work on the raising of money for new buildings in a college which his régime was to make prosperous and fashionable.[11] Archbishop Sheldon (a Trinity man) contributed generously and work could soon start. Wren's ideas on what should be built differed widely from those of the College's benefactors. He wished to build a single block, or 'pile', out in the Grove to the East of Trinity's ancient Durham quad and separate from the college's other buildings. But a new quad, or at least its evident beginning, seemed more likely to coax money out of the college's well wishers. So Wren, in a letter of 22nd June 1665, told Bathurst that he, like Machiavelli and others, was sure that the world was "governed by wordes". As the idea of a quadrangle would carry more weight with the benefactors, and as a quad was what loyal Oxford men would readily finance, a quad they had better have "though a lame one somewhat like a three-legged table.[12] What Wren built for Trinity was in fact a single block, but so placed as to be the nothern side of an eventual new quad, three-sided in a manner more that of Cambridge than of Oxford, looking out across the Grove towards his own old college of Wadham. His two lower storeys survive (the attic storey, with its mansard roof, having been rebuilt in 1802). The work one sees, and the building as Loggan showed it in 1675, differ in a few respects from the corresponding drawing in the Wren collection at All Souls'. In the central section, at first capped by a small pediment and with its main windows sub-divided by the mullions and transoms still in vogue, a niche lies between the two windows of the ground-floor storey. The building, which only contains two staircases, is of no great distinction, while the niches, in the end wall and in the middle of the building's southern wall, are shell-headed in an almost Jacobean manner.

The rest of Garden Quad was finished later, closely following Wren's pattern but with differences in the joinery of the stairways to reveal its varying dates. Had Wren been free to go ahead with a single block he might have produced a finer building than his one side of Trinity's Garden Quad. He had certainly felt that he could, with the appropriate sketches, have convinced the prospective donors of the merits of his idea. When, in his letter of 22nd June 1665, he wrote thus to Bathurst, he added the point that if such a demonstration failed he could "within a fortnight", appeal to "M. Mansard or Sr. Bernini".

By the spring of 1665, with three building commissions under way, and already, perhaps, consulted by the Commission which had, for two years now, considered the future of Old St Paul's Wren could see, more than ever before, that his future lay mainly in architecture. He had come into a sphere of activity where professionalism, as modern architects know it, had hardly started, but where the fully classical Renaissance style, pioneered in England by Inigo Jones, had gained acceptance in great mansions and for such court buildings as the monarchy could afford. Only in the more vernacular architecture of the remoter provinces, and in some of the buildings put up by the Established Church, did Gothic idioms still fight a rearguard action.

Very few of England's most prominent designers of new buildings had what we should now call an architect's training – Hugh May, with useful observations in the Netherlands leading him to the designing of mansions in the Dutch manner, and Sir Roger Pratt whose buildings ran closer to the Palladianism of Inigo Jones, were 'gentlemen architects' of the type that now became important in England's building history. A far more experienced and competent designer was John Webb, the nephew, pupil and working associate of Inigo Jones. John Webb was, when Charles II returned to his kingdom, the best qualified man available for the post of Surveyor General. The job should really have gone to him and not to the courtier Denham, and as things stood in the early years of Charles II's reign the reversion to the post should have been given, as indeed it was unavailingly promised against Denham's opposition, to Webb and not, as it was given in 1661, to the architecturally inexperienced Wren. Webb was, however, allowed some compensation in the limited post of Surveyor General for the Palace at Greenwich, where Charles II intended that a new riverside grouping should replace the rambling mediaeval buildings. So the dignified 'Charles II' block, pedimented in the middle and with pavilion ends above giant Corinthian pilasters, was started in 1664; its alignment was to affect Wren's later planning on the same site. Webb was secure, as was May at Windsor Castle, in this particular domain. But elsewhere such court architecture as could be afforded lay within the province of Denham and, in due course, concerned the rising architect who was to be his successor.

Dr Kerry Downes has suggested that Wren may, with the King's knowledge, have got out some designs, for the palace at Whitehall, as early as 1664. These would, so it seems, have meant the duplicating of Inigo Jones' Banqueting House and the filling of the space between the two Palladian blocks with a somewhat ill-composed building whose main feature was to be a two-tiered, pedimented portico, flanked by sculptured panels and statues in niches.[13] The year was one when such schemes would normally have fallen to Sir John Denham. But he may not always have been fit for such work, so that

Wren may already have expected, reasonably soon, to become the official architect of the English crown.

Samuel Pepys, in a diary entry of 15th August 1664,[14] records a conversation with his friend Sir John Minnes in which Minnes, who seems to have had chemical knowledge, told Pepys of various cures he had achieved when abroad with the King. A particular success had been the cure, miraculous by the standards of that time, of Sir John Denham who had smallpox so badly that the disease amounted to "an ulcer all over his face". Though the episode seems to have occurred some years before 1664 the after effects of so severe an attack, in such a position, could have been considerable, not least on the mental state of a man who later showed strong symptoms of insanity. In 1666, the year when Denham, a widower, just turned fifty, married an attractive teenage wife who promptly became a mistress of the Duke of York, his health was poor and he looked old. He may, by now, have shown signs of the physical and mental collapse which soon afflicted him. If so, Wren could have felt, about the beginning of 1665, that Denham's sickness, retirement or even death might soon confront him with the opportunities of the Surveyorship. It was certainly with Denham's knowledge, and perhaps with his active encouragement, that Wren had, by early April of 1665, laid careful plans for an architectural pilgrimage to Paris.

5

Paris and St Paul's

For a man who probably hoped to become Surveyor General, or official architect, at the court of the restored Charles II the supremely suitable city for study and adaptation was the Paris of Louis XIV and his highly efficient minister Jean Baptiste Colbert. Of all Europe's despotic and ceremonial monarchies that of Louis XIV was now, after a spell of turmoil and civil strife, the richest and the best organised. If the building achievements and ceremonial régime of any monarch were to serve Charles II as a pattern in the smaller-scale circumstances of England they were those of his richer and more absolute cousin in France. Rome, with its papal and theocratic flavour, was less suitable as a precedent for a king of Protestant England, while the planning and building achievements of the Baroque popes had now, in any case, nearly run themselves out. No lesser despots in Italy or Germany had yet followed the building precedents of Paris, or those even more dramatically set, in later years, at Versailles. For important current work, and an atmosphere of excitement and architectural achievement, any aspiring builder had, in this precise year of 1665, to turn to the French capital. Other countries apart, Wren's good friend John Evelyn could, as he had said in his letter of April 4th, give Wren the addresses of friends in Paris,[1] helping him both with introductions and with ideas for buildings he should see during what was obviously a visit carefully planned, not to avoid the Great Plague which had not started when Wren decided to go to France, but well in advance, with all the needed correspondence, for a purpose directly bearing on Wren's intended architectural career.

Wren's reasons for going, just when he did, to the French capital are best understood from a short sketch of what was happening in Paris in the second half of 1665; as always in Wren's life the exact realities of history bore largely on what he did and saw. He must, when planning his journey, have known much of the architectural situation in the city which had yet to be replaced, as the normal headquarters of the French King, by the still modest residence of Versailles.

By 1665, with Louis XIV still in his twenties and coming to the

Sir Christopher Wren, from a portrait by Kneller, 1711, and Wren's signature from his letter to Faith Coghill, 1669

CHRISTOPHER WREN, D.D. DEAN OF WINDSOR.

VIRTUTI FORTUNA COMES

Christopher Wren, Dean of Windsor; below the heraldic blazon of the Wren arms: "argent a chevron sable between three lions' heads erased azure with three wrens argent on the chevron and on a chief gules three crosslets or." (*V.C.H.* War. *Vol. III, p. 217*)

East Knoyle, Wiltshire: Dean Wren's plasterwork, 1639

John Wilkins, Warden of
Wadham and Bishop of
Chester

Wadham College, Oxford,
c. 1675, from Loggan's
Oxonia Illustrata

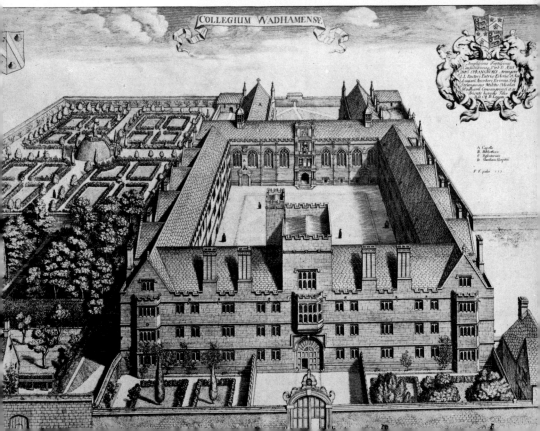

William Holder

(*left*) All Souls' College,
Oxford: Wren's dial (*right*)
the human brain: Wren's
drawing in *Cerebri Anatome*,
1664

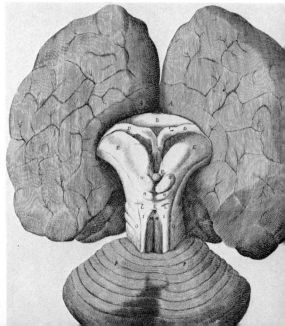

John Evelyn

FRIENDS AND PATRONS

(*left*) Archbishop Sheldon
and (*right*) Archbishop
Sancroft

Pembroke College, Cambridge:
the chapel, West end

FIRST COMMISSIONS

Sheldonian Theatre, Oxford

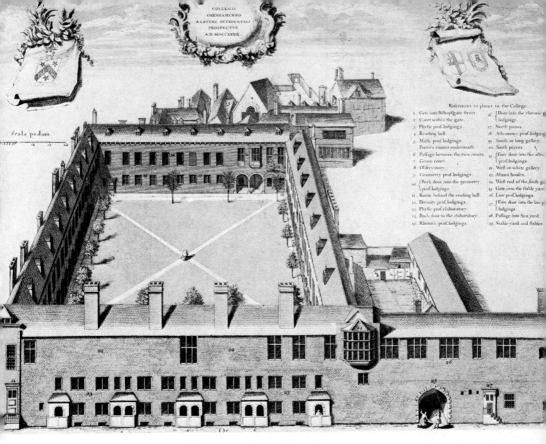

Gresham College, London

City of London: Wren's proposed layout, 1666

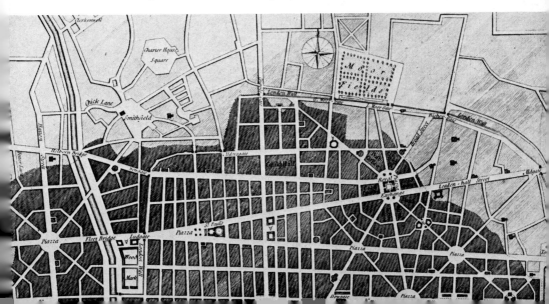

Paris, the Sorbonne: the dome of the church

FRANCE

Colbert: bust by Coysevox

maturity of his lavish tastes, France had recovered from the bloody bickerings and economic upheaval of the Fronde. Mazarin had died four years earlier, and the energetic organiser Jean Baptiste Colbert was all powerful, particularly in financial matters, as the chief minister in a state whose resources were more ample, and better available for engineering and building schemes, than they had been when Louis was still a minor. Since the first day of 1664 Colbert had added to his other posts that of Surintendant des Bâtiments du Roi. His policy was to make Paris the home of the king and his court, and the main focus of government in a centralised state. Despite Louis' growing liking for Versailles, as late as the summer of 1665 Colbert's policy still prevailed. A vital part of that policy was that the Louvre in Paris, and no out of town hunting lodge, should be improved and enlarged as the king's principal residence. In the city the improvement and better lighting of ancient streets, the opening out of new thoroughfares, and the further restraint and embankment of the river, were all planned to create a more worthy setting for the splendours of a despotic monarchy. New churches, though several were built, were less spectacular than the display of royal urbanism. The Paris of Colbert, as distinct from the later elaboration of Versailles, had much to teach an English designer who might soon be asked to rebuild, or recreate, riverside residences for his own less wealthy, yet politically triumphant monarch.

Apart from his introductions from Evelyn and other friends Wren's best contact in Paris, and the source of many valuable meetings and introductions, was the English ambassador at the court of Louis XIV. For some unnamed friend, who may have known of his bright architectural prospects in England,[2] had recommended him to Henry Jermyn, since 1660 the Earl of St Alban's and many years later Wren's patron for a well known building scheme in London. A devoted Royalist and well known as a courtier, diplomat, and gambler, Jermyn had a long experience of France; he must, from what we know of his career and of his long service to Queen Henrietta Maria, have had excellent contacts in France and possessed, so one imagines, a good knowledge of French and the French cultural and political scene. We gather, from one of the two valuable letters on Wren's stay in France, that Jermyn used the aspiring Surveyor "with all kindness and indulgence imaginable".[3] With such a friend to help him Wren's sojourn in Louis XIV's capital was not that of a stranger without contacts or connections. What Jermyn could do for him must have been a large element in his plans for the trip.

Something of what Wren expected in Paris, in this opportune year of 1665, is clear from his letter, of June 22nd, to his friend Ralph Bathurst at Oxford.[4] Some of it (see page 45) dealt with the position, as a single block or as an element in a new quad, of the new building which

Wren was then designing in Trinity. We have seen how Wren later made the point that he would soon be able to appeal, over any doubtful point of architectural judgment, to "M. Mansard or Sr. Bernini". His contacts were such that he could be confident of introductions to two of the leading men then present on the Parisian building scene.

François Mansart, by now in his late sixties and in semi-retirement, had once been the leading architect in Richelieu's France; his difficult attitude to clients had lost him work he might still have had under Louis XIV. He had, however, designed several important buildings; he ranked, as did Wren himself in another forty years, as the Grand Old Man of French classical architecture. Bernini, Neopolitan by birth but long established as the leading architect, in Papal Rome, was a more transient Parisian phenomenon. Wren's assumption that he would meet Bernini proves how closely he was, by correspondence, in touch with the current French scene. His hopes of a full interview were actually to be much disappointed. But before he set out he could reasonably suppose that he could have ample consultations with the architectural maestro of his age. The cause of Bernini's much heralded presence in Paris lay in Colbert's schemes for completing the Louvre by putting up an imposing eastern side to the existing court. Le Vau's plans were laid aside by Colbert when he became superintendent of the King's buildings. There was trouble, not unusually, with François Mansart, and Colbert was little pleased with the schemes sent in by various other French designers. So he turned to the Baroque fountain-head of Rome, the choice being eventually narrowed down to Carlo Rainaldi and Bernini. Rainaldi's project found no acceptance. Bernini, back at home, got out two sets of designs, one of them of a pronouncedly Baroque, curvaceous character. For a third project, which he must have hoped to be final, he made his quasi-royal progress to the French capital. He arrived, a little before Wren, in June of 1665; his stay, a fiasco as it proved, was shorter than that of Wren who may now have been kept in France both by the deterrent effect of the London plague and by the exhaustive keeness of his studies.

Of Wren's two companions on this trip to Paris one was Edward Browne, at Trinity, Cambridge during Wilkins' short mastership and a son of the famous physician-author Sir Thomas Browne; a letter from him is one of the two giving details of the stay.[5] His other friend, of a staunch and aristocratic royalist family which fought and suffered in the Civil War, was Henry Compton, sixth son of the Earl of Northampton who had fallen in battle for the king.[6] Born in the same year as Wren, Compton had just started on a clerical career which in the end, for most of a long London episcopate, made him Wren's employer as the architect of the new St Paul's.

Wren must have reached Paris in July of 1665. I do not know where he lodged, and no sequence of visits and interviews can be worked out from the somewhat scanty details available. At some time he and his friends travelled north of the capital. The short meeting with Bernini, something of a fiasco as was Bernini's whole visit to Paris, must have occurred before the end of October, while Wren was back in England about Christmas time. At some time, so we find in *Parentalia*, Wren was troubled with pain in his kidneys; we are told that as a result of a medical tip conveyed in a dream, he eased the problem by the consumption of some dates.[7] It is clear, from his own letter quoted in the same family record, that he busily filled his time by visiting, drawing, and sketching a wide range of buildings, both in Paris and in the adjacent countryside. He was, of course, exaggerating when he told his correspondent that he would bring "almost all" France on paper.[8] Unlike Evelyn in 1650 he never toured the French provinces. But he seems to have made a thorough study of the relevant (i.e. Renaissance) buildings of Paris and the Ile de France. Direct introductions apart, his old friend Evelyn would have told him, from his own experience of Paris, of what Wren, with the ambitions which held his mind in that particular year, ought to see amid the architectural bustle of the Paris of Colbert and Louis XIV.

The buildings in and near Paris most obviously of interest to Wren were royal palaces, the hôtels, or grandiose town houses, of the nobility, out of town royal residences such as Fontainebleau or Versailles, and the great country mansions, in various Renaissance idioms, which high officials and great nobles had built for themselves near the capital. Churches, for an aspiring architect who had no great expectation of ecclesiastical commissions, were probably of less interest to Wren than the buildings being put up by the monarchy and the court. But the domes lately completed, by Lemercier on the monastic church of Val de Grâce commenced by François Mansart, and by the same architect of his chapel at the Sorbonne, may have helped to edge Wren towards the unconventional solution he was soon to put forward for the weakened crossing of Old St Paul's. Less obviously relevant to any Anglican needs was François Mansart's domed, and at the same time centrally planned convent chapel of Nôtre Dame de la Visitation whose main and central space was a domed circle.[9] But if Wren was able to get access to the chapel of so strictly enclosed and contemplative a convent the intellectual appeal of such a building to a scholar with so mathematical a mind may have made some slight contribution, when the need had arisen for a wholly new St Paul's, to the working out of the design which its architect most favoured.[10] As a Protestant Wren may also, like Evelyn, have gone to the French Protestants' Temple out at Charenton, plainly rectangular with a barrel ceiling and with simple Roman Doric pillars upholding a double tier of galleries whose occupants could see the liturgical focus made by the lofty pulpit.[11] There was a basic likeness between this 'auditory' interior and some of

those which Wren built for the Anglican worshippers of the City of
London and on the Earl of St Albans' West-End estate. If he saw it in
1665 he would not have forgotten the Charenton Temple. But no fire of
London could then be foreseen; the building, so unlike the mediaeval or
tentatively Baroque Catholic churches of Paris, would have been no
more than marginally relevant to a man whose expectation looked more
to the splendours of royal residences.

The quotation in *Parentalia* does not say that Wren met François
Mansart. But from what he told Ralph Bathurst such an encounter
seems to have been likely, while Mansart, who had designed several
buildings which Wren saw, and who died next year, then had little
work in hand and may have had time to spare for the enquiries of an
English visitor who came with good contacts and introductions. He
had been among the French architects who, at Colbert's behest,
produced designs for the eastern wing of the Louvre. He was also the
designer for an ambitious scheme, never carried out but astonishing
both for its impressive scale and stylistic incongruity, for a vast
church, centrally planned and domed, to be added directly on to the
eastern apse of the early Gothic abbey church of St Denis, and to be
used as a mauseoleum for the Bourbon royal family.[12] If Wren met
Mansart, and saw his drawings for this pompous royal burying place,
he would have found its Greek cross plan mathematically appealing.
He could also have revived the essential idea when, in the middle
years of the next decade, he designed the domed mauseoleum of
Charles I which was, with little artistic respect for the existing Gothic
church, and actually involving the demolition of its eastward
extension, to have been built immediately East of St George's chapel
in Windsor Castle.

Lord St Alban's, with his high position as ambassador, must have
been Wren's most valuable source of introductions in Paris.[13] Wren
mentions a few others, three of them priests. The Abbé Bourdelot, a
kindred   spirit   who   was   a   physician   and   an   'experimental
philosopher', had an 'Academy' in his house every Monday afternoon.
The Abbé Bruno showed Wren the literary treasures, and the medals
and intaglios, of the Duke of Orleans' library, while it was through
the Abbé Charles that Wren got his short interview with Bernini.

Though   buildings,   especially   palaces   and   chateaux   in   the
Renaissance style, were the main purpose of Wren's visit it was not
surprising that he soon paid admiring attention to leading works of
civil engineering. So it was natural that a man who had earlier
exhibited schemes for building in deep water and for moles to be
thrust into the sea, and who had been offered the task of erecting such
structures at Tangier, should   especially   admire   the   *quais*,   or
embankments, by which the turbulent, shifting currents of the Seine
were then being confined. Some of them had been made under Henri

IV and Louis XIII. Colbert, as ever energetic in the improvement of
the city for which he still planned the principal role in France, gave
orders that the length of the *quais* should be much increased.[14] Wren
must have been able to see, with absorbed interest, work in progress
as well as work complete. So much did he admire the progress of
Colbert's engineers that he told Browne, after a few weeks in Paris,
that these river embankments were, in his opinion, "the greatest
work about Paris, and that in their cost, and in the volume of materials
used, they surpassed the two greatest pyramids.[15]

The most numerous group of buildings seen by Wren was that of
the greatest Renaissance chateaux not far from Paris; it was on his
return journey, out to the north of the city, from Chantilly, Liancourt,
Verneuil, Raincy, and the town of Senlis that he and his friends saw
Louis XIV, driving fast back to Paris in the company of his reigning
mistress Louise de la Vallière.[16] Some of the country houses which he
saw are listed in his own letter. They, and others unnamed, comprised
a substantial gatherum of varied achievement; as things happened in
Wren's later career they must have been less useful than he hoped as
quarries of inspiration for his English commissions.

Three of the chateaux which Wren saw belonged to the French
Crown. Fontainebleau, whose scenery Wren mentions rather than
actual building, and St Germain (an "antique mass") were little to his
architectural purpose. Nor, at this moment, was Versailles of much
moment to a student of palaces. Wren saw the chateau twice, and
called it a "cabinet" rather than a full palace. As also at Courances,
its mixture of brick and stone could have strengthened a liking for this
blend of materials; the additional presence, at Versailles, of blue tiles
and gilding made Wren think of the exterior as a "rich livery". He
complained (attributing it to femine influence) of the fussy, over-
decorated interior, crammed with what he called "little Curiosities of
Ornament"; he felt, in his dislike of "works of Filgrand and little
knacks", that building work should "have the attribute of eternal".[17]
Versailles was, perhaps, among his less happy French experiences. In
1665 it was, however, no more than the somewhat glorified hunting
lodge designed by Lemercier and Le Vau.

Private chateaux showed Wren a wide range of styles and tricks of
design. The most important were François Mansart's Maisons, and
Vaux le Vicomte which Le Vau had built for Fouquet in his palmy
days of financial power.[18] Wren called them "incomparable villas";
the connotation of "villa" was not, of course, that of Victorian
suburbia but of the Renaissance or Baroque grandeur of Frascati,
Tivoli, or Caprarola. At Maisons he could have noted a grouping of
rectangular masses, with Doric columns or pilasters, and what
Professor Blunt calls a "severe richness" in the decoration of the
vestibule. Vaux le Vicomte, Le Vau's greatest country house and

quickly built between 1656 and 1661, had two different, impressive façades, a variety of high-pitched rooflines, and a great oval saloon as the central element of a dominant residential block.

Of the other chateaux seen by Wren and his friends[19] St Maur les Fosses and Chantilly, being early works of the French Renaissance, and with Chantilly not yet altered by the younger Mansart, were somewhat outdated by 1665. At Verneuil, as also at Maisons, Wren saw the various classical orders placed one above the other; the building was, however, a work of the previous century and not in the taste of Wren's French contemporaries. Liancourt, seen in September, was by Lemercier, with two wings, and part of a third, round its main courtyard; it seems, however, to have been of more note for its ornate gardens than for the actual house. Raincy, another September target, was a recent work by Le Vau, important for the giant order of its pavilions, for high-pitched roofs of a type which Wren came to dislike, and for its central saloon, a straight-sided oval, which corresponded to the great oval room at Vaux. At Rueuil, which Lemercier had designed for Richelieu, and which Evelyn saw in 1643, gardens, fountains, cisterns, and the orangery were more notable than the actual building; cisterns and other 'waterworks' also featured at Essonne which Evelyn may also have recommended to Wren. At Meudon Wren must have seen Le Vau's alterations for the owner who jointly superintended the royal finances; a pedimented central storey had a lofty, tapering, somewhat graceless central roof. Issy, with its grotto now a century old, was in the main a great house of the sixteenth century. Taken as a whole, Wren must have found these chateaux of great splendour and interest, but of more use as a repository of details than as basic designs of mansions likely to suit English clients.

But if Wren was eventually to become Surveyor General in England the Parisian buildings of most interest to him were palaces. At the Tuileries the Salle des Machines may well have been the most helpful, at once for the final stages of the Sheldonian and perhaps, in another nine years, for Drury Lane. The Palais Mazarin seems to have impressed him more for its furniture than for its fabric. Mazarin's great testamentary benefaction, the Collège des Quatre Nations, by Le Vau on its riverside site across the Seine from the Louvre, could have given Wren an exemplar for what he planned for Whitehall and achieved at Greenwich.[20] He admitted that Le Vau's three-sided court was much admired. But Wren, with his remark that the architect had deliberately sited it "ill-favouredly" to display his skill in coping with an awkward site, spoke a little scornfully of what was, in 1665, among the unquestionable glories of Paris.

The Louvre, and the work Wren knew to be in progress on its eastern wings, may have been the main goal of his visit to Paris. In the existing palace he frequently saw the Queen Mother's quarters, admiring the furnishings and other works of art, lately moved from Mazarin's residence, which filled her "glorious apartment". More to his purpose, lately started and to Bernini's final design which was more severely classical, and had less emphasis on swelling curves, than the second scheme which the Pope's architect had prepared in Rome, was the eastern wing. Bernini himself, concerned both with building work in Paris and with his vigorous bust of Louis XIV, was still in Paris and had, among other activities, been shown the plans for urban extension got out by le Nôtre, an artist better associated, as Wren later found at Hampton Court, with gardens than with the planning of towns. So it came about, through the good offices of the Abbé Charles, that the future architect of St Paul's in London had a few minutes with the great artist who had, in Rome, laid out the doubly curved, monumental approach to St Peter's. Wren leaves no record of any conversation or discussion he may have had with Bernini, but his reference to "the old reserv'd Italian" suggests that little small talk passed between the maestro of sixty-six and the young English mathematician-astronomer, less than half Bernini's age and, architecturally speaking, the merest tiro.[21] Bernini seems, on this brief occasion, to have lived up the phase *aspro di natura* coined by his own son who was his biographer. He did, however, give Wren a few minutes' glance at the "five little designs on paper" for which Colbert had paid him highly. They were, one assumes, some sketches of his third Louvre design, and Wren only had time to copy them "in fancy and memory", later making a crayon sketch which has not survived. Bernini's final design for the Louvre's eastern side had, however, some kinship, in the straight, uncurved line of its façade, with schemes which Wren eventually evolved for Whitehall.

More to his purpose was what Wren saw of the building operations at the Louvre, soon given over to designs by others than Bernini. For a time he went on site every day. What much impressed him was the large number of men simultaneously at work.[22] A thousand were constantly on the varied tasks of foundation laying, hauling up large items of stonework "by great and useful engines", on masonry, and on a wide range of fitting and furnishing. Altogether they made up what Wren rightly, and perhaps enviously, called a "School" of architecture; it was probably, in 1665, the best in Europe. Teamwork on such a scale was what Wren himself aimed at, and largely achieved, when he himself supervised the building of St Paul's. No less impressive than this simultaneous work of many craftsmen was their regular payment, every Sunday. Colbert himself came to the Louvre every Wednesday, and on Thursdays if he could; Wren, with his good introductions, could well have met him on some of these visits of superintendence. Another architect whom he may have encountered, and who is mentioned in *Parentalia*, was Thomas Gobert, a man whose main career still lay before him but who, by 1665, styled himself *architecte des Bâtiments du Roi*;[23] in such a post he would often have been on site at the Louvre.

By the spring of 1666 Wren was back in England. He was still Savilian Professor of Astronomy at Oxford, so that his old university (with the Sheldonian and the work at Trinity still unfinished) may well have claimed his time as well as concerns in London. At Cambridge, Pembroke College chapel, the first of his buildings to be completed, had been opened while he was abroad.

Not long after his return from France Wren became more closely involved with the problem of what should be done about old St Paul's. Though not among the Commissioners of 1663 he had been consulted, two years before that date,[24] on measures to combat the gathering catastrophe of the cathedral's central crossing. Now in the early months of 1666 he was back in England, full of architectural knowledge of a type possessed by few, if any, of his compatriots. Denham's increasing ill health, and Wren's enlarged experience, made it more likely than before that he might duly become Surveyor General. Along with his old friend Evelyn he became a full member of the Commission, with him were the 'gentleman architects' Roger Pratt and Hugh May, John Webb with his experience gained from Inigo Jones, Thomas Chicheley one of the Masters of the Ordnance, and some others with technical experience. The clerical members were, expectedly, Humphrey Henchman the elderly Bishop of London, a staunch royalist whose earlier days as a Wiltshire clergyman had made him a friend and colleague of Wren's father, and the new, energetic Dean of St Paul's in whom we meet another of Wren's good friends and important patrons.

William Sancroft may not, in his early years and as a senior member of Emmanuel College at Cambridge, have had much contact with Wren. But from 1662, when he became the reforming Master of the college which had been so notable a Puritan stronghold he came fully into the circles wherein Bishop Matthew Wren was prominent and in which the bishop's nephew moved. Early in his short mastership he planned to do as Bishop Wren was doing elsewhere in Cambridge, and to build for Emmanuel a chapel more fitting than its predecessor for a college now orthodox in its Anglicanism. He may, in fact, have had Christopher Wren brought to his personal notice, in this particular connection, before he moved to the deanery of St Paul's, succeeding Dr John Barwick, who had died prematurely, at the end of 1664.[25] He now became actively aware of the schemes for the repair of London's vast mediaeval cathedral. He may not, however, have had much time to consult Wren before his future architect left for France. On Wren's return it was, however, a very different matter.

During the spring and summer of 1666 the Commissioners worked on their ideas for the strengthening, or total rebuilding, of the central area of the cathedral. Wren must have worked with great speed and concentration, for he had, at the beginning of May, handed in a report which was critical of the existing structure and revolutionary in what he proposed for the central space.[26] On 27th August the Commissioners forgathered at the cathedral for an important meeting. A good account of what happened comes from Evelyn, prominent on the Commission and a strong backer of his old friend Wren.[27] Apart from some disagreement, between Pratt and Chicheley on one side, and Wren on the other, as to whether the cathedral's arches had been forced out of the perpendicular by the steeple's added weight, Evelyn supported Wren on deeper matters of policy and style. The main problem was that caused by the condition of the central crossing. Pratt and Chicheley wished to prop up, and where necessary to augment by extra masonry, the piers which still held up the central tower. But Evelyn and Wren, in the end with the acquiescence of Sancroft and the others, proposed a wholly different, more spatial solution; with one reference to a unique English mediaeval masterpiece Wren's general proposals for old St Paul's continued what Inigo Jones had done while also drawing on his Parisian experience.

Inigo Jones having given St Paul's its great Corinthian western portico, along with a Renaissance outer casing for the nave and transepts, what Wren proposed in 1666 followed logically from this earlier work. In the nave the arcades and the triforium stage were still to have round arches, though they were to be given a Renaissance flavour. But between them giant Corinthian pilasters, running up to a sequence of vaults and saucer domes, were to give a new classical character to a Romanesque interior; a plan shows that a large circular chapel was to be contrived in the southern aisle. The Corinthian order was to be used for the giant pilasters of an utterly changed central space.

Wren proposed to demolish the crossing piers and the tower, and in the manner of his uncle's cathedral at Ely to create in Old St Paul's a great central octagon; beyond it, bar one bay destroyed to widen out the crossing, the Gothic eastern limb was to stay intact.* Above the octagon, with Evelyn's full argumentative support, Wren planned "a form of church-building not as yet known in England" which must have seemed revolutionary to their fellow Commissioners.[28] For what Wren proposed, and what he must have had in mind for some time, was "a noble cupola", not without splendour but as incongruous over St Paul's as were the Renaissance Façades clapped onto a few Gothic churches in Paris. The design of his dome, with its tall, continuously

---

*Other bays were similarly to be pulled down in the nave and in the two transepts.

pillared drum and its soaring silhouette, owed much to Bramante's project for St Peter's which Wren could have known from engravings. But its double design, with an outer dome masking what one was to see from below, and with much constructional interest in the timber work which was to support the lantern and the outer skin, showed what Wren had learnt from Lemercier's dome at the Sorbonne. Above an internal lantern a free-standing spiral staircase, constructionally daring and sweeping more widely than the shut-in 'vices' of mediaeval stairway turrets, led up to the wierdly elongated, unhorticultural pineapple which was the one artistic disaster of the scheme.

If Wren had not already, by the time of his report in May, made the drawings which still survive for his projected refashioning of Old St Paul's he must, after the gathering on 27th August, have worked fast to produce them. For on the night of September 2nd there came the opening of the fiery tragedy which made most of these ideas irrelevant beyond recall.

6

A City to Rebuild

The historic fire of September, 1666 laid most of the City of London waste; it roared west of the little River Fleet so that it only just stopped short of the lawyers' precinct of the Temple. The blaze had started, not far from London Bridge, in the city's eastern sector. Had the wind been in the more normal south-western quarter most of the urban area, including St Paul's, could readily have been saved. But a wind from the east had allowed the flames to spread into the main part of the crowded town; only the Tower, and the north-eastern section of the densely built city, remained untouched.

This fiery calamity, and the burden of the Dutch war from early in 1665 to the late summer of 1667, meant that nothing could now be done to fulfil any royal ideas for new palaces. Whitehall must wait, in all its jumbled confusion, till things down river were in a better state. Wren, and any other designers and builders called in to help, could concentrate on the vast problem posed by the needful rebuilding of England's chief single source of commerce and wealth.

On the basic policy that the city, between Temple Bar and the Tower, should soon be rebuilt there was never any doubt. For one thing, the destruction of the historic commercial area had not been complete. A fair section of the city had been spared by the flames, and the Guildhall had not been wholly destroyed. The towers of some gutted churches had sturdily survived, while some observers held that at least a part of St Paul's could be fitted up for continued use. No one doubted that the City of London should keep its place as a great centre of commerce and exchange. Nor had such factors as the larger ships of the nineteenth century outdated the ancient river port just below London Bridge; still less had modern container ships banished much of the port's traffic far down the river to Tilbury. Some sort of a city was bound to arise again in the devastated zone. But the wholesale destruction of the narrow streets, and the timber-framed houses of the mediaeval London of Falstaff and Shakespeare had created the opportunity for a more open, geometrical plan of straighter streets and more spacious points of intersection than those which had long prevailed. Those who drew their notions of planning and style from what they knew of Renaissance and Baroque planning abroad, and from Inigo Jones' piazza at Covent Garden, must long have envisaged some such urban planning on a London site; they could, however, have entertained few hopes of its actual creation. But Wren, and others with an interest in such matters, now got to work with a swiftness so astonishing that it suggested long previous thinking on what had now, by a grim accident, become a pressing task.

A few days after the fire had died down Charles II, being "infinitely zealous" (as Evelyn put it)[1] for the rebuilding of the devastated city set up a Crown Commission to supervise the daunting task. It was also made clear, in a proclamation dated as early as 13th September, that new buildings were not to be timber-framed, but that their main structures were to be of the more fire-resisting materials of stone or brick.[2] Though he was still the Surveyor General the ailing Sir John Denham was not on this Commission. Sir Roger Pratt and Hugh May had considerable knowledge of architecture, while Wren, still fresh in his experience of Paris, with his involvement in St Paul's, and with his reversion of the Surveyorship soon likely to mature, was an obvious choice; friend as he was of the courtier John Evelyn he now had little need of the influence such an associate could give him. The City Corporation named three members to balance those appointed by the Court. One of them, Robert Hooke, already knew Wren and long remained his friend and collaborator; he was genuinely important in the process whereby more than three-quarters of the city arose from the ashes of 1666. Three years Wren's junior, and like him a clergyman's son, he had, like Wren been at Westminster School under Dr Busby. When at Oxford he was a protégé of Wilkins and a member of the experimental scientists' club. He was the most active of the City members of the rebuilding commission, not only in two-dimensional planning but as the probable architect of various buildings.

Wren and his fellow Commissioners soon produced plans for an almost wholly realigned city, with many buildings on sites other than those occupied by their predecessors. Wren's project went in as early as September 11th. John Evelyn, not a Commissioner but important in the whole process, worked out another scheme, presenting it to Charles II on September 13th, the day of the proclamation which banned the future use of timber structures.[3] Six days later Hooke exhibited his scheme to the Royal Society, and two other designers tried their hand. All were quick off the mark; Wren, in particular, must have worked as hard as he must have done, a fortnight before, on his scheme for Old St Paul's. Neither he, nor the others who sent in plans, could have had time for thorough consultation with the distracted members of the City Corporation, or with the merchants and clergy whose future was to be determined by anything done in the City during the next few years. So drastic were the proposals of Wren (as also of the Renaissance-minded Evelyn) that they would, if put forward under our modern conditions of planning decision, have led to the long, tedious processes of a public local enquiry. As it was, the gulf between City thinking and that of Wren and his like-minded friends was what led to the setting aside of what Wren now somewhat high-handedly proposed.

Both Wren and Evelyn based their plans for a new City of London on what they knew of Renaissance town planning in some important Continental cities. Neither of them put forward such totally new schemes as those of the sixteenth century for such inland, virginally sited, and rigidly geometrical towns as Palma Nova; the Thames, as London's immutable southern boundary, would alone have prevented so geometrical a solution. But the Thames, like the Seine whose *quais* Wren had so much admired in Paris, gave a scenic opportunity which Wren and Evelyn were both anxious to exploit, with a splendid, continuous embankment, and public buildings of various kinds along the length of that promenade, to give a river frontage far finer, if less commercially useful, than what was actually created. Long, straight streets, some radiating from scenic points and several of them converging on piazzas or open spaces, recalled the *sistemazione*, by Renaissance and Baroque Popes, of Rome which Evelyn knew in person and which Wren could have apprehended from available engravings and from his friend Evelyn's accounts. Not only was the new London's street plan, as swiftly sketched by Wren while the ashes of the old city were still hot, to be more geometrically aligned, with a radial or grid pattern of straighter streets than the mediaeval town, but many of its leading buildings, St Paul's and the gutted Guildhall excepted, were to be ruthlessly pruned or resited. Private houses and shops were, of course, to arise again in large numbers, but few owners, away from the city's north-eastern quarter, could expect that their new properties would stand on the old sites, or that they need be particularly near their old haunts of social or business forgathering. A start was to be made, as was actually done, on the replacement of gutted churches. The new places of worship were not necessarily to be on the ancient sites, and their "conspicuous and insular" positions were planned with an eye to their effect on a new townscape.[4] From what we know of Wren's later views on places of burial we can assume that none of them were to have adjacent churchyards, and that Wren would lastingly have avoided the foetid, Dickensian horrors of bulging City burial grounds. The prevention of such scandals was on a par with similar proposals whereby the more obnoxious trades and industrial processes were to be kept out of the City. A new Royal Exchange was to dominate a fine piazza, with straight sides and an *esedra* at each end, in the eastern zone of the City,* while the twelve

*Evelyn's Royal Exchange would have been on a riverside site.

leading City companies were to be moved from their old headquarters, and were to have their new halls grouped in a single square enveloping Guildhall. The streets were to be of the standard widths of ninety, sixty, and thirty feet, the "narrow dark alleys" of the ancient city being carefully avoided.

The splendour, intellectual daring, and reforming ruthlessness of Wren's scheme for a renewed City were beyond question. Had his plan been for a totally new city, with no forerunner on the site and no survivals from an older town, it might have been accepted as a business proposition and for the creation of a fine new urban scene. But it was better suited, and could more easily have been realised, as the ceremonial and governmental capital of a Baroque despot than it could ever have been, in an age which knew little of commuting, as the living and working place of a business community whose habits and customs, and whose workplaces, had grown piecemeal, and as practical needs determined, over many centuries. Only the quays along the widened Fleet, and the part of the City west of the Fleet, with its fine radial plan cut through its middle by Fleet Street, might have been practical politics as a fine link zone between the City and the nation's capital at Westminster.

But most of Wren's scheme had poor chances of happy acceptance either with the City clergy or with their commercial parishioners. Many parishes were, however, duly merged with others, so that over thirty destroyed churches were never rebuilt. Yet parish boundaries, whether of unaltered or merged parishes, remained as they had been, and the churches rebuilt, or in part repaired, by Wren arose on ancient, and in many cases challengingly inconvenient sites. The clergy, with the Restoration a recent and happy memory, and with their firm royalist loyalties, were perhaps more amenable to enforced change; more churches were, however, replaced than the thirty-nine allowed for in the London Rebuilding Act passed in the following year. But the merchants, many of whom had been prominent, in the Civil War, among Parliament's supporters, were often less ready to collaborate with a government of which they were, not unreasonably, suspicious. The vistas, the new open spaces, and the grandiose, mathematical planning of Wren's scheme for the City seemed a poor compensation for the loss of cherished sites and accustomed streets. Nor need one assume that obstinate self-interest was the only driving force behind the merchants' dogged opposition to the changes implicit in Wren's plan. The City's effectiveness as a place of business had come to depend, as it continued to do for long after Wren's time, on the concentration, in various close-knit areas, of particular trades, and on the nearness to each other, within easy strolling distance, of business houses of the same type. The scattering, and enforced resiting of such businesses could lead, so it seemed, not only to the

weakening of hallowed customs and links but to an actual fall in the
efficient conduct of trades in which ready man-to-man contacts were a
real element in success.

So the objections to Wren's plan, some of them selfish and narrow
but deeply rooted in shrewd commercial experience and in a very
reasonable dislike of government procedures, are easy to understand.
As *Parentalia* somewhat unfairly puts it, what frustrated Wren's
schemes, and what could equally have blocked what Evelyn proposed,
was the "obstinate averseness" of many citizens to the alteration of
property boundaries and the setting back of building lines for the
creation of new and wider streets.[5] More to the point, in the political
circumstances of 1666, and a factor still relevant in our own time, was
the merchants' unwillingness to make over their property, under
nominal promises of return, to Public Trustees or official
Commissioners. No promises of the eventual return of surrendered
sites, or of compensation should land be kept back for such purposes
as the realignment of streets, could overcome the deep-seated,
perennial suspicion of business people against central or local
authority. So the Halls, with continuing inconvenience but with a
swift return to commercial prosperity, mainly arose on the traditional,
commercially convenient sites. Though their fitting and furnishing was
achieved by craftsmen of the school which also worked on the City
churches, Wren himself cannot certainly be connected with any of their
architectural designs. With the churches, in later years, the story was
quite otherwise.

Wren's plan of the City, as it was soon after the fire, shows the
surviving streets and walls, and also contained the ruined St Paul's on
its full mediaeval plan.[6] But his manuscript plan of a rebuilt City[7]
shows an intersting first version of a cathedral to replace the great
building, over six hundred feet long and the longest cathedral in
England, which the Romanesque and high Gothic builders had
completed.

As Wren presented his scheme for the City a mere five days after the
fire had ended it would not have been easy, or even safe, for him to make
a detailed survey, on the actual site, of the ruined and surviving
buildings. At St Paul's, as we know from descriptions and drawings,[8]
the choir limb was far more thoroughly ruined than the nave. Much of
the Norman western limb was still standing, while Inigo Jones'
portico, though damaged and calcined, may not have seemed wholly
past repair. Wren himself may genuinely have thought, in these early
days, that the western half of the name could be used again; such was
the instinctive feeling, and perhaps the desire, of Sancroft and the
cathedral clergy.

What Wren inserted into his plan of September, 1666, was a
cathedral with a western portico which was, perhaps, meant to be less

ambitious than that of Inigo Jones, a rectangular nave of modest size, and to the east of that nave a square block whose upper part was to be a circular dome. The whole building would only have been about a third as long as the mediaeval cathedral, so that the future Bishops of London, like their brethren of Bristol, Oxford, and Carlisle, would have had to be content with ceremonial headquarters far smaller than the original sizes of the churches concerned. But St Paul's would still have had a sanctuary, or auditory space, of considerable dignity, enhanced, as were the Parisian churches which Wren knew, by the enfolding curvature and soaring height of its eastern dome. The nave could have been new, but it could also, as things seemed in those first few days of smoking embers and of Londoners camping out in the fields, have been contrived by the repair and reroofing of some of the Norman nave with its outer casing by Inigo Jones. But as the months passed, and as Wren could survey the ruined cathedral and better realised its true condition, he saw that the surviving pillars and walls of the Norman nave were beyond permanent reconditioning. Sancroft, so it seems, was privately aware, though at first without full conviction, of the newer thoughts of the architect whom he now employed on a pleasant commission away from London.

The year 1667, with the second Dutch war going badly, and with hostile fleets causing havoc in the Medway and in the James River of tidewater Virginia, was an unpromising time for major building work on churches or a cathedral in London. The rebuilding Commission continued in being, and the early prohibition of the future use, in London's new houses, of timber framing was carried over in to the London Rebuilding Act which was passed that year, and which provided for the "speedy Restauration", and for "the better regulation, uniformity and gracefulness"[9] of the many houses and shops which were soon to arise to give new life to England's chief commercial centre. Four types of houses, much standardised and with their proportions, and the scantlings of their timberwork, strictly laid down in the Act's clauses, were to line the streets.[10] Those streets were here and there to be widened, and a few new streets were to be laid out, but they were, for the most part, to be on the pre-fire lines. "Noisome" trades, and those with a strong fire risk, were to be forbidden in the main streets, while conduits, which had picturesquely blocked some ancient highways, were to be moved from their old sites. So keen were the citizens to get back to their business life that those who were replacing their houses were supposed to do so within three years[11];* strict powers were taken, with the certainty of a building boom, to regulate wages in the building trades and the prices

*The target was not exactly achieved.

to be charged for bricks, tiles, and lime.[12] Furthermore, by its imposition of a duty on the seaborne coal that came into the port of London, the Act opened the way, at a time when English insurance was still in its infancy, to the financing of a stupendous task of reconstruction.[13] Wren was, however, little concerned in this great surge of domestic building. For his activity we can, for a moment, turn to politics and academic architecture, both of them linked to the University of Cambridge.

Wren was not, in his own education, a Cambridge man. But he had received a doctorate there, and while his uncle was still alive as Bishop of Ely his contacts and influence were strong in the university. So when, in the summer of 1666, Sir Richard Fanshawe, the university's Member of Parliament, died in Spain, Wren's name was put forward as Fanshawe's successor. The contest took place in March of the following year.[14] By a margin of a mere six votes (118–112) Wren lost to Sir Charles Wheler, once a Fellow of Trinity and lately distinguished for the help he had given to Londoners distressed by the calamity of the Great Fire. But Wren remained well placed for prominence both in Court and academic circles. Though his uncle, the Bishop of Ely, died in May of that year in September his son, the younger Matthew Wren who was the architect's first cousin, became secretary to James, Duke of York, the king's brother and still a powerful, respected figure at Court and in the country. For Wren's architectural activity we can, for the moment, turn to Cambridge for another of his buildings.

In 1662 William Sancroft had taken over the mastership of Emmanuel, the most Puritan of Cambridge colleges. He set about its doctrinal and physical re-orientation. Not least among his concerns was the replacement of the Elizabethan chapel, not only by a building more stylish than the severely plain structure in which Emmanuel men had so far worshipped, but by one whose east to west alignment would, as he put it when he mentioned his scheme in a letter of June, 1663, rid Emmanuel of the "great mark of singularity" which, to his royalist and Laudian mind, unhappily distinguished it in Cambridge.[15] His short mastership ended in May, 1665, by which time he had settled into his deanery in London. By then, however, he could well have decided on the site, and on the basic plan, of the chapel, flanking loggias, and gallery which are now the main architectural glory of Emmanuel. The scheme of the buildings with which he enclosed the eastern side of his college's main court was clearly inspired by what had been done, not long before the Civil War, elsewhere in Cambridge at Peterhouse. The man who had initiated that scheme, still alive as the restored Bishop of Ely, and still actively interested in his old university, was Matthew Wren. His brilliant nephew, by the summer of 1663 the designer of the new chapel at Pembroke which was started in May of that year, was the obvious man for the bishop to recommend as the designer of Sancroft's new chapel at Emmanuel. Wren and Sancroft could, as early as 1663 or 1664, have worked together on the essential design of Emmanuel's new buildings; they seem certain to have done so, at a time when the Dean knew Wren as his architect at St Paul's, late in 1666.[16]

As far back as September, 1664, a stone-mason had been at the college to bargain over work on any chapel that might eventually get started. He pointed out that he could not estimate materials or prices till a model and a "platform" (ground plan) were available.[17] It was therefore decided, as at Pembroke, that a model of Emmanuel's new chapel should be made. Nothing was done for over two years, but Dr John Breton, Sancroft's successor as Master, referred, very early in 1667, to the policy of having such a model.[18] It was made in London, and work went on, under Wren's supervision, during 1667. Breton's letters to Sancroft make it clear that the Dean of the now ruined St Paul's took a generous interest in the building project in his old college.

The letters from the college to London were not sent direct to Wren but to Sancroft; the dons relied on him not only for money and other encouragement but for contacts with their architect. By the beginning of 1667 Wren had probably worked out the essentials of the scheme, but the dons still hoped for some advice on the spot. They had, in March of 1667, sent Sancroft some information to pass to their designers.[19] In July Breton, having heard that the model was progressing, wrote that "Dr Wren deserves to be remembered among our best benefactors"; no thanks were sufficient to be given for his or Sancroft's "grateful kindness".[20] The model, which cost £13 5s.0d. with 7s.8d. for its carriage from London to Cambridge, arrived in September and the Emmanuel dons were delighted. Their one extra wish was that more height should be allowed, and that in the absence of an east window those on each side should be of a generous size.

As the time drew near for the starting of actual work the dons still hoped for a personal visit from their architect; two somewhat plaintive letters, written by Dr Breton early in 1668, revealed their worries.[21] On 28th January the Master told Sancroft that they were preparing for the chapel's foundations, but much desired Wren's advice "upon the place"; he forwarded a letter for the Dean to pass to the architect. A little later, on February 5th, in a letter in which he revealed that the devastation of the City of London had ruined many of the college's hopes of financial aid, Breton reported progress but admitted that the Emmanuel dons still greatly needed the advice of an architect; he heartily wished to have that of Wren, but did not know how to proceed, in such a matter, but by Sancroft's help. Then on 19th February, in a letter reporting that he had been to the Ketton quarry to deal there with masons who gave better terms than those of

London, he told Sancroft that Wren had sent him "a very civil answer" to his queries of three weeks back. Wren had told him (presumably from Oxford) that he might soon be in London and then, perhaps, in Cambridge, but warned the Master (rightly as it proved) not to delay a single day in any expectation of his coming.[22] Wren seems, from now onwards, to have confined himself, apart from his Oxford duties which continued for a few more years, more and more to the London area; there was, in those days of slow travel, little of the personal supervision of a job now expected of the partners in an architectural practice. But in July of 1669 Dr Breton went to London "about chapel affairs" and other matters.[23] He may well, on such an occasion, have consulted Wren on the work at Emmanuel.

The design of Wren's range at Emmanuel is in essence that of the building which his uncle started at Peterhouse. The main point of difference from the earlier pattern is that the simply panelled long gallery, a very late example of this mainly Elizabethan or early Stuart feature, runs all the way across the eastern side of the court, so that the chapel is set more to the east than its equivalent in the older college. The central façade, with its broken pediment, clock, and a cupola poised above the middle section of the long gallery, is set tight between the open loggias which contain the gallery's outer reaches; above the clock, in a small eyebrow space, the figures 1673 make this Wren's one structurally dated building; the year was that when the main fabric was complete. Almost all the decorative emphasis is on the western frontage with its Corinthian pilasters and half-columns, its frieze of garlands, festoons, and a cartouche, and with urns, little oval windows, and more floral decoration leading to a slightly heavy, but charmingly composed cupola which is more of a *tempietto* than its equivalent at Pembroke. The side walls, plainly faced with stone, have simple foliate carving in their window spandrels, while the eastern wall, stone-faced and deliberately devoid of a window, is pedimented above its plain expanse.[24] Wren's drawing in All Souls' suggests that the western façade was meant, at a time when Emmanuel's buildings were less completely of stone than they were by about 1780, to be in a mixture of stone and brick. But in the end the charming monumental front, in a few other details different from those shown in the drawing at Oxford, was cased all over with the creamy pink mixture of facing stone from Ketton.

The building process, from early in 1668, is well documented from Breton's letters to Sancroft and from the college records. The details, with their references to Squire, the college carpenter, and the other Cambridge craftsmen who worked on the chapel, and to such activities as brickmaking in a kiln near Trumpington, the carriage and laying of clunch for the foundations, the freightage along the Fenland waterways of timber, iron, lead, and stone and the carriage of the waterborne goods, for the last mile of their journey, through the town are more a part of the building story of Cambridge than of the architect's life.[25] The one thing lacking was a visit from Wren himself.

The early months of 1668 soon involved Wren in the temporary reparation, and the final catastrophe, of Old St Paul's. He seems soon to have abandoned his early ideas for a short nave with a domed auditory space to the east. Once the embers had died down he went to the ruins, with Pratt and May of the existing Cathedral Commission, and with Hooke and two other Commissioners for the rebuilding of the City as a whole. He soon got to work on a report more tempered by experience than his hastier scheme of September. His report, written during the winter months, admitted the shattered cathedral's "deplorable condition".[26] But whatever his misgivings he proposed, as a temporary measure, that a short choir and an auditory nave should be fitted up, with a flat ceiling below the older clerestory level, in the western half of the Norman nave.[27] Time could then be allowed for the planning of some "more durable and noble fabric" on the eastern part of the ruined site.[28] The Commissioners as a whole were of much the same mind, so that in the middle of January, 1668 they ordered that such a cathedral should be provided. But Wren seems to have had gathering doubts, expressed in private to Dean Sancroft before he left for Oxford for a spell of professorial residence.[29]

Trouble soon overtook the cathedral authorities as they cleared rubble and started to botch up their temporary place of worship. Though they had done some casing, in the southern nave arcade, on the third pillar from the western end, the whole pillar soon crashed down; collapse seemed imminent along the whole of what had survived on this side. Sancroft himself seems not to have been surprised; as he pithily put it in an urgent letter to Wren, "what you whispered in my ear at your last coming is now come to pass".[30] It is now generally clear that nothing more could be done to make a place of worship, however temporary, in the western sector of the long Norman nave. Positive action was, however, harder to determine. As Sancroft wrote to his friend, Wren was now "absolutely and indispensably necessary"; without him the Commissioners and the clergy could "do nothing, resolve on nothing".[31] From now onwards, for over forty years Wren's was, in the matter of London's cathedral, the decisive voice. He soon came to London. Whatever pleas may still have been made for restoration Wren's view, in those midsummer months of 1668, prevailed. Late in July a Royal Warrant gave the go ahead for the demolition of what was left of the nave, and for the saving and storage of any re-usable stone. Wren, in the meantime, turned to other matters of interest.

Before the fire the Royal Society met in Wren's old haunt of Gresham College; the courtyard, with something of an academic aspect, had been Sir Thomas Gresham's mansion. Lying off Bishopsgate it escaped the fire; it was soon pressed into service both as a Guildhall and as a Royal Exchange. Wren and his colleagues in the Royal Society had to find some other venue. The Earl of Arundel kindly allowed the society to meet in his mansion in the Strand. It was for this site between the City and the haunts of the Court that Wren and Hooke made designs for what could have been seemly, well planned headquarters for their society. Behind a pedimented frontage, with Corinthian pilasters and a dignified stairway,[32] provision was to be made for a large meeting room, offices, rooms for experiments, and a small observatory dome. The design must have been made in that summer of 1668. But in the next year the Society's firm acquisition of other buildings outdated the scheme for this more central site.

Chelsea College had been founded, on 'Oxbridge' lines, by James I; its purpose was to create a training place whose clerical alumni should combat the theological forces of Counter-Reformation Catholicism. Ambitious collegiate buildings were to make a spacious setting for this Anglican counterpart to the Tridentine seminaries. But only part of this college was built, and few Fellows ever took up residence. Under the Commonwealth the one completed block housed Dutch naval prisoners and although, in 1664, it was arranged for Charles II to give the building to the Royal Society the second Dutch war saw its renewed use as a prison. In 1667 the incomplete, damaged building was granted to the society, being a possible site for its lasting home.[33] There were still some legal difficulties, and the Patent which finally confirmed the grant came in 1669. Wren, admiring neither Jacobean Gothic nor dilapidated buildings can hardly have been happy at the society's acquisition, and by the middle of 1668 no work had been done to convert the block. All that actually happened, in the first years of the society's ownership, was the carrying out of some basic repairs. As late as the summer of 1668, Hooke's design being preferred to that of Wren, a new building off the Strand was still actively proposed.

As it happened, the Jacobean structure of Chelsea College was never of any use to the Royal Society. From November of 1669, the Council, including Wren as an active member, often pondered on what it should do with the property, and in 1670 Wren proposed, without result, that some "rich citizen" should be found to lease what was clearly, and for some years to come, an increasing embarassment.[34] Two years later Evelyn proposed that the building should yet again house Dutch prisoners of war.[35]

The summer of 1668 saw Wren on a short, but doubtless pleasant visit to the cathedral city of his native county; he was there again, so we find from the Chapter Records, in the summer of 1669.[36] Seth Ward, his old friend and Wadham contemporary, and his successor (still in office) as astronomy professor at Gresham College, was his host; for a year now he had been bishop of Salisbury. Ward had summoned Wren to advise on the structural state of the great cathedral whose choir he had not yet had time to refurnish. The Close and its dwellings were still as George Herbert had known them, more mediaeval than they are now in their outward appearance, with no Mompesson House of William III's reign and none of the warm red brickwork, Queen Anne or Georgian, which now fronts many of the houses round the lawns, and the placid residential precinct, which gave Trollope his first notions of Barchester. The separate bell tower still stood north of the cathedral, and James Wyatt had yet to trim off the late Perpendicular chapels, one each side of the Lady Chapel, which were the only additions to the first ground plan of England's pattern-book cathedral.

His visits must, for Wren, have been congenial times of ripe companionship, and of thorough application, as he expeditiously surveyed another, but intact, mediaeval church of the front rank. Pepys, in June of 1668, had found Salisbury cathedral "most admirable".[37] Wren, aesthetically disposed to favour classical disciplines over the Gothic styles, was none the less fair in his judgment on Wiltshire's great cathedral. He agreed, in a report which Aubrey called "a curious discourse", that "the whole pile is large and magnificent, and may be justly accounted one of the best patterns of architecture in that age wherein it was built".[38] He commended the stark, chastely proportioned beauty of an early Gothic building whose predominant lancets he preferred to the traceried windows of later churches which were, as *Parentalia* puts its, "more elaborated with nice and small works". He rightly criticised the cathedral's "low and marshy" site. He disliked what he reckoned to be its poor foundations, and the fact that Bishop Poore's original designers had not raised its floor above the level of the Avon's frequent floods. His mathematical mind perceived that the substructure was too weak for the weight of the upper tower and spire; he does not seem to have realised that the steeple was a century later than the main fabric. His survey, in which he used a plummet from the ceiling of the tower to its second floor, showed that the spire, whose masonry was only seven inches thick, leant several inches to the south-west; the masonry of the tower below it was only a "slender hollow work of pillars and arches", and its walls were liberally braced with corroding bands of iron. Wren hoped that the spire would incline no more. But he feared, if more settlement overtook the foundations, that the only cure would be an unsightly octet of additional flying buttresses running up from the walls of the nave; any more binding with iron would, as he vividly put it, "be but as pack-thread". Finding that the spire was a little bent towards the top he suggested that it be secured by a "curbe of iron", to be constructed at some seaport where anchor smiths were experienced in heavy ironwork. The band could be in eight sections, jointed to each other and tied back to vertical bars of iron inside the spire. Wren's other suggestions included repairs to the timbers inside the tower and spire; the whole problem of the fourteenth-century steeple was clearly among the "most clamorous decayes".

Despite the urgent terms of Wren's report it does not seem that enough was done, in the next few years, to carry out what he suggested. The Dean and Chapter did, indeed, follow Wren's advice, and started work in the summer of 1669, using what financial reserves they had and paying in a portion of the residentiary prebends' stipends.[39] But in the autumn of that same year they were forced to appeal to the non-residentiary canons. A letter went out, and one finds that Isaac Barrow, later on, as Master of Trinity at Cambridge, an important patron of Wren and already his friend, was among the contributors. But the fabric bills for 1669, and the years immediately following, with their entries for such items as plumbing, nails, and the ironwork of windows, suggest that no really exceptional sums were laid out on the cathedral at this time. The payment, in 1671, of £56 for timber does, indeed, indicate that something was done to carry out Wren's ideas for roof repairs.[40] The iron braces which secure the flying buttresses running down from the corners of the central tower may also have been put up at Wren's suggestion, but the band, or "curbe" of iron which Wren advised to give extra strength to the spire seems not to have been installed. For when in 1691 Thomas Naish, the cathedral's Clerk of Works, surveyed the fabric[41] he referred to the *long-existing* irons (many of them small mediaeval clamps) which bound together the stones of the spire. His suggestions for "work proper to be done" included three iron bands, to go round the spire and with bars on the inside anchored through its stonework. This was, in essence, the same device that Wren had suggested; its estimated cost much exceeded any single structural item carried out since Wren had reported. So it may be that the iron band actually cast round the base of Salisbury's spire was put in place later than the time of Naish's report. What can be proved is Wren's share in the later refurnishing which his friend Bishop Ward carried out in his cathedral's choir.

Another job, with which Wren was, about this time, at least partly concerned was the design and building of a new Customs House in London; the swift replacement of the building lost in the fire showed how keen were the authorities to see London's commerce swiftly regain its place. On a water-side site, with a spacious forecourt flanked by wings on open colonnades, and with Ionic pilasters to adorn its principal storey, it was a less stylish, more provincial building than the riverside Collège Mazarin which Wren could, from his Parisian experience, have used as an exemplar. The new Custom

House, being a Crown building, also showed him more closely involved with the activities of the Royal Office of Works.

The year 1669 was highly important for Wren's life story. The year started with an increasing likelihood that he would soon, by Sir John Denham's disablement or death, succeed to the respected, well paid position of Surveyor General. For Denham was now far gone in physical and mental decay; he must long have done little in a post for which his talents had never suited him. Early in March he was persuaded "on account of his weakness" to ask the King to make Wren his official deputy.[42] John Webb, more experienced than Wren in actual building, and already employed on such jobs as fortifications and the Court Theatre at Whitehall, was naturally disgruntled, and had already said as much. He declined to work under Wren whom he felt to be "by far his inferior"; he condescendingly suggested that he would, if jointly appointed with Wren, instruct him "in the course of the Office of Works", in which official business Wren admitted his ignorance.[43] By the end of March Denham was dead, and Christopher Wren came into the fulness of his reversion; it was a formality that the financial officials were not told, till December, of the new appointment.[44] Wren soon showed his hand, with a touch of knowledgable vigour beyond the imbecile capacity of Denham. For early in May a Royal Warrant went out to the authorities of the King's manor in the Isle of Portland. Wren saw how great would be the need for durable stone in the City of London. Even if houses were to be mainly of brick, public buildings, parish churches, and a wholly new cathedral would need a more silvery material. So the shipping of its splendid stone from the great central feature of the Dorset coast was forbidden without the new Surveyor General's leave.[45] Demolition had already started on the ruins of Old St Paul's. Here, in addition to what he could re-use from materials of the old cathedral, was Wren's guarantee of a superb medium for the classical idioms and sculptured details of numerous ecclesiastical buildings.

In July of 1669 the Sheldonian at Oxford was opened, with ceremonies of unusual elaboration graced neither by the donor nor by the architect of their university's new auditorium.[46] But Wren, that summer, was preoccupied with a more personal matter. His position and income assured, he was about to marry.

The lady of Wren's choice was an old friend, from back in the days when, in his father's last years and in the tenure of its rectory by William Holder his brother in law, he was often at Bletchington. She was Faith Coghill, aged thirty-three and like Wren of City-of-London stock. But her father, Thomas Coghill, had in the 1620s moved out of London, buying the main estate of Bletchington.[47] He settled down as a country gentleman and in 1632, the year before his knighthood, he became High Sheriff of Oxfordshire. A royalist gentleman like many

others in his time Sir Thomas Coghill, like Dean Wren, just failed to
outlive the Commonwealth.

For Faith Coghill it was, for those days, a late marriage,
affectionate no doubt but not, perhaps, marked by high flights of
romance. Wren's one surviving letter to her, dated in June and
perhaps of 1669, is somewhat contrived though obviously sincere,
couched in studied language very typical of the seventeenth century.[48]
Miss Coghill had dropped her watch into salt water, and Wren had
seen to its repair, envying the timepièce which would, when pinned to
the lady's dress, "be so near your side, and so often enjoy your eye".
He had, he added, put such a spell on the instrument that every beat
of its balance would tell his beloved that "'tis the pulse of my heart
which labours as much to serve you, and more trewly than the
watch". But whatever the warmth of Wren's summer sentiments he
and Faith Coghill were married in the Temple Church (for which he
later designed an altarpiece) in December, 1669. As he settled, by the
end of that momentous year, into his official house in Scotland Yard
the newly married Surveyor General, with a flow of work on routine
matters as well as his concern for more monumental schemes, could
well, at the age of thirty-seven, feel that the world was at his feet.

7
Knight and Widower
1670—1675

The first years of the 1670s were decisive for Wren's dedication to architecture and for his standing in the Restoration scene. By the end of 1675 Dr Wren, no longer a Professor of Astronomy though still interested in the subject and an active member of the Royal Society, was a knight, deeply involved in the planning of a new St Paul's and by now the designer of the first new churches in the City. His main sadness lay in the recent death of his first wife. But within eighteen months he was to marry, as his second wife, a lady of higher rank than the squire of Bletchington's daughter.

The City apart, he had also to cope with the varied duties of the Surveyor General of the Royal Works. It is possible, though not certain in view of the lack of a date on the relevant drawing, that about now he got out designs for a fine new palace at Whitehall; the heraldry of the central pediment, as it appears in the drawing, proves that the design was for Charles II or his brother James II.[1] The years just after 1670 were not, moreover, an unlikely time for such a project. England was, for a few years, at peace with the Dutch, while the Treaty of Dover, secretly made in 1670, eased Charles II's financial position with its subsidy from the Sun King, now fully committed to the splendid expansion of Versailles and more than ever a magnet for such other monarchs as his cousin of England. Whenever they were made the designs for a new Whitehall Palace were for buildings of modest size but of great dignity. Inigo Jones' Banqueting Hall was to be repeated, flanking wings were to be added at each end of the whole composition, and between the two Palladian blocks a central element was to have statues above its pediment and an arrangement of giant pilasters, 2·1·1·2, which foreshadowed a main element at Blenheim.

Much of Wren's time was now filled by the varied, often trivial duties of his Surveyorship. The actual building of such structures as royal palaces did not yet figure large. Much of what he did was on jobs which would now fall to the office, and within it to junior members, of a municipal planning department. The short, wiry, birdlike figure of the active, still comparatively young Surveyor General must have been seen, busy on the minutiae of his official work, in many places in or near Whitehall and round the confines of the ravaged City.

Some of Wren's work was what a Surveyor General, or court architect, might expect to encounter, and at that time to tackle with no large staff to help him. The lesser minions of Colbert must, in Paris and now to an increasing degree at Versailles, have coped with similar tasks of minor routine.

Wren was in part concerned with the fabrics and precincts of royal residences. In April of 1671, when the King had it in mind to go to Windsor for that year's Garter ceremonies, Wren was ordered to inspect the royal quarters in the castle, and to see what state they were in for the reception of Charles and his retinue.[2] Early in 1673 he was concerned with the work done, for over three years by that time, on the building of a new house for the King to occupy on his frequent visits to Newmarket. The designer, so we hear from Evelyn who thought poorly of a building which he considered "mean enough and hardly fit for a hunting house",[3] was William Samuel who supervised the subcontractors and paid them for what they had done. Early in 1672 two of these men, Edward Ronan a bricklayer and a carpenter named John Scudamore, complained that Samuel had denied them payment, insisting on what they called "unreasonable abatements".[4] The papers went, for checking and a report, to Wren; within a month he had probed the matter. Ronan and Scudamore went back on their claim; Wren's report, and their "recantations" were sent in for the King's satisfaction;[5] we shall see how similar tasks of checking came to Wren from the cathedral at Salisbury. In the spring of 1675, so Hooke tells us,[6] Wren was himself at Newmarket, one assumes on royal business, on one of his comparatively few trips out of town.

The situation of Newmarket, and its popularity with Charles II and his brother James, strongly bore on Wren's concern, for over thirty years, with another royal residence whose temporary fame as such has been largely forgotten. The house, nicely placed in the hilly terrain of north-western Essex, was the great mansion of Audley End. It had been built, near a headwater of the Cam and on the site of the Benedictine Abbey of Walden in Saffron Walden parish, by Thomas Howard who held the Suffolk earldom. It was the third Earl, well placed at Court and in the confidence of Charles II, who arranged for the king to buy the house and its immediate surroundings. With Windsor in great disrepair the king often felt the need of some residence out of town. Audley End could meet his requirement, the more so as it could be a highly convenient staging post on the royal journeys to and from Newmarket; the king was more than once there before the deal was formally concluded.[7]

The sale was arranged in 1669, three-fifths of the £50,000 purchase price being paid at once and the rest left on mortgage on the security of the Irish hearth tax. The mansion, soon known as 'The New Palace', was a great Jacobean complex with two main courtyards, a long gallery, and a stately hall. It was not, of course, a building of the type which Wren and other architects of the time could equate with their fully developed Renaissance taste. John Evelyn called it "a cheerful piece of Gothic building, or rather *antico moderno*",[8] while Wren, a quarter of a century later, held that the fabric had, when the king bought it, been weak, and badly built "after an ill manner rather gay than substantial".[9] Such a cross between two architectural traditions was clearly a building that Wren would have preferred to replace. But for a house so occasionaly used no such policy was likely. Repairs, which in 1669 Wren reckoned would cost £10,000, were the second best expedient, and though no such lump sum was forthcoming £500 a year was allowed and with this, so Wren said later (*see* page 188), a good deal was achieved. Work on this new royal residence was an obvious chore for the Surveyor General and his staff. From 1670, in which year the future King William III was at Audley End on a journey from Cambridge to London official visits, by Wren himself or perhaps at times by deputies, were a constant item in the business of the Works Office. The records of Wren's "riding charges" (at 4s. 10d a day) frequently mention Audley End;[10] like the kings he served Wren must often have combined Audley End and the royal racing haunt in his journeys away from the capital.

The close neighbourhood of Whitehall Palace also came under Wren's inspection. Late in the summer of 1673 he certified that the building activities, in Old Spring Gardens, of a widow lady named Hester Hoare were not, despite some encroachment on the foundation line of the palace's boundary wall, prejudicial to the King's privacy.[11] In another three months the Surveyor General was again concerned with Windsor. For Sir Christopher (as he was by now) and other officers in the Works Department had to inspect the "extraordinary rails" used by one Simon Smith for impaling paddocks and gardens in the Great Park, and to determine their proper price.*[12] Next spring Wren was back on the lesser problems of Whitehall, with a royal request that he should view, and have lowered, some earth which had been banked against the wall of the King's garden in St James's Park; it was piled so high that it spoiled some fruit trees.[13] Later that year Wren authorised Peter Brent, the King's plumber, to search houses whose owners were suspected of tapping water from the pipes which supplied Whitehall Palace and the royal mews.[14]

*In the summers of 1674 and 1675 Wren was personally at Windsor; *see* Hooke pp. 112 and 173.

Wren, as Surveyor General, was also consulted over the holding of official posts in the various building trades. Early in 1674 John Grove, the master plasterer of the royal works, petitioned about the arrears in his payments. The matter was turned over to Wren, who certified that Grove, for new work and repairs, was owed the large sum of £1031 13s.10d; some of the repairs had been on Sir John Denham's house, and as Denham had died early in 1669 the money, not untypically at that time, must have been well over five years overdue.[15] In April of 1675 Wren did Grove another good turn, recommending that his son, John Grove the younger, should have the reversion of his father's post.[16] Royal commissions, and work on many public buildings had, he said, been done by the younger man who was "sober, diligent, and as skilful in his art as any of that profession". In the same year Charles Atherton, the brother in law and apprentice of Peter Brent the master plumber, petitioned for the succession to that post. Wren reported, in Atherton's favour, that he was "an able and honest artisan", and fit for the job.[17]

The most important of Wren's subsidiary concerns arose from the Government's efforts to control excessive building round the City of London, and to regulate such matters as drainage and water supply. The burning of most of the City, and the need for accommodation not far away, had caused a strong demand for new houses. This meant that areas, so far open ground or used as gardens, were taken up for building, with the diversion to this out-of-town housing of materials also needed in the devastated City. So in April of 1671 the King issued a proclamation whose intent it was to forbid, or at all events to restrain, the building of new houses in these peripheral districts. It fell to the Surveyor General, acting very much as a Planning Officer would act nowadays, to control these operations; other decisions which Wren made concerned various work in the City itself.

Not long after the royal proclamation, Wren ruled that various building permits, already granted in Knightsbridge and in St Giles's parish, were not against its intentions; his one stipulation was that the new houses should, as in the City, be of brick or stone.[18] Next year Wren had to consider a warrant, from as far back as 1664, under which Sir William Pulteney and Sir John Denham were allowed to build some new houses in Piccadilly, a low-density, quality development with no more than ten or twelve residences, each one to cost at least £1,000. He visited the site, and saw the plans of John Chipps their designer. As the proclamation did not forbid such buildings Wren let them go ahead, of brick with adequate walling and timbers, and without brewhouses, or buildings for "offensive trades" whose odours would upset the smart promenaders in St James's Park.[19] Those same years also saw Wren concerned with points relevant to the planning and rebuilding of the City.

As a new riverside embankment was to run from the Temple to London Bridge some of the muddy foreshore had to be taken from the unconfined channel of the tidal Thames. But for some years at least the projecting Paul's Wharf was needed for the unloading of materials (timber and Portland stone among them) required for what must now be a wholly new cathedral. So in 1671 some of the embankment's site was cut out, at Wren's insistence, from the new feature's unimpeded length; cranes and other apparatus were to be set up to handle the incoming supplies.[20] Another point concerned a site not far away. John Bill desired to build a printing house on a site near Blackfriars. Its structure had to be such that Wren, as a Commissioner for the City's rebuilding, could approve it. He inspected the site, and early in November he issued his report, agreeing to the scheme and to the scantlings proposed. There was, however, to be an open area, not less than fifty feet across, on the new building's southern side.[21]

More important, as an exercise in planning control, was Wren's supervision of various building projects outside the confines of the City; the eastern reaches were under pressure as well as the more fashionable western outskirts. Early in 1673 Wren was asked to report, with that result I do not know, on a petition by Lady Wentworth who wished to build on her land at Mile End.[22] By now, moreover, Wren was involved on a long controversy over building activities, just outside the City, in what was then the eligible district of Spitalfields. In August, 1672 the Wheeler Trustees had asked permission to build in the area.[23] Wren and the Lord Mayor of London considered the scheme, recommending consent for what they reckoned to be "no great addition" to what had already gone up in the district; the new property would still, moreover, ensure that the fields, in the manner of a modern green belt, would remain "square and open". But they did not consider that the building should spread over more easterly areas, or to obscure places less subjected to good Government. The Lord Mayor, one assumes, felt strongly on the enforcement, by the City's magistrates and constables, of law and order. For a time Wren was troubled no more with what might happen in Spitalfields; the subject was, however, to crop up again.

In Charles II's time the public supply of water was still haphazard and patchy. But it was not by any means wholly neglected. Springs and wells played their obvious part. So too, more riskily, did supplies from the none too pure water of such rivers as the Thames. In the autumn of 1674 Wren had to report on a scheme to raise water, by means of some kind of pump, from the river to St James's Park, Piccadilly, and Charing Cross.[24] Wren inspected the "engine", and saw the promoters' designs. As the works moved easily and without noise he did not think that the project would, as an incidental to its main purpose, cause annoyance or nuisance to the select purlieus of the Court. In the autumn of the next year he had to deal with a similar project for a less fashionable district. Thomas Neale had built a "water house" at Shadwell which distributed water in Stepney, along Ratcliff Highway, and elsewhere in the East End. Here again Wren personally viewed the water house, and the streets, alleys, and lanes which it was to flush with river water. He reckoned, not only that the scheme would be no annoyance, but that it would help districts otherwise poorly supplied; it was, moreover, to be encouraged as a check on the still topical peril of conflagration. He, or some member of his staff, added the practical point that the streets through which Neale's pipes were to run must at once be repaired and made good by "well ramming" the earth disturbed by trenching.[25]

Early in the 1670s Wren was concerned in a building project at Oxford, small but involving some leading personalties. Joseph Williamson, not yet knighted or advanced to the Secretaryship of State, but already rich from various official posts and a devoted member of the Queen's College where he held a fellowship, was anxious to start a scheme whereby his college's somewhat rambling mediaeval buildings should, like those of St Catharine's at Cambridge in a few more years, be replaced by more symmetrically planned, more stylish Renaissance work. He started with the building which still, enlarged and much altered, runs along Queen's Lane to the north of the main buildings which are also indebted to Wren's refashioning of English architecture. Williamson, readily able to consult the Surveyor General who was also his old Westminster school-fellow, must first have approached Wren in 1670. For early in January of 1671 a letter went to him, not from Thomas Barlow the Provost of Queen's but from Dr John Fell, now Dean of Christ Church and already unlikeably dominant in Restoration Oxford.[26] Fell had heard that Wren, before designing the new block, required "a more exact measure on the ground". The measurements would duly be sent, but Fell did not reckon that Wren need make a model for so modest a work. Later in the same month he told Williamson that if a drawing were dispatched foundations could be started,[27] while in another two months the Dean told the college's benefactor that "Mr Surveyor" would help him draft a contract, also advising him on the dimensions, style, ornament, and construction of the new block.[28] Wren must therefore have been the designer, though perhaps with some on-site changes by Anthony Deane of Uffington who was the contractor, of the block still known by its donor's name. Loggan's print of Queen's shows it newly completed,[29] of two main storeys with dormers to light its attics, with mullioned and transomed windows, and with a curiously cramped central grouping whose pediment rises above windows which, on the two main floors, flank central niches, an agreeable building but vernacular by Wren's later, more sophisticated standards.

In the City of London Wren's work was now more on its parish churches than on its new cathedral. St Paul's, at the moment and for a few more years, was a demolition job. Work started on the more completely wrecked eastern limb, on the piers of the crossing, and on the nearer part of the nave, this being the site of the comparatively modest cathedral for which Wren was asked to make designs; the nave's western end, and Inigo Jones' great Corinthian portico, still stood for some years to come. The initial clearance, with pickaxes, was reasonably straightforward though it was both dangerous and tedious.[30] The crossing piers, and the remains of the central tower, were a tougher proposition. Wren started with gunpowder, using a charge of only 18 lb to bring down the massive weight of the north-western pier and two bays of the Norman nave. Another explosion, set off when Wren was out of town, was a failure, and caused alarm when a flying stone crashed through a window in a nearby house. Demolition with explosives was then forbidden, so Wren turned to a device with which he clearly enjoyed himself. It was Wren the engineer who contrived a battering ram, hanging a larger iron-tipped beam from a triangular frame, and rejoicing, as the ruins yielded, that "he had recovered this notable Engine" which the besiegers of the ancient world had used to assault fortified towns.

With no insurance money to hand, and with no coal tax as yet diverted to finance a new cathedral, Wren's first commission for St Paul's was for a cathedral whose size and cost would perforce be moderate; his design was probably made late in 1669 or early in the following year. What he proposed, on part only of the mediaeval site, was a building, far from cathedralesque by England's accepted standards, which would none the less combine a large rectangular choir space with a noble vestibule crowned by a dome.[31] The choir, with its communion table at one end, was, in the mediaeval manner of old St Paul's, to be long and narrow. Galleries, lit by large roundheaded windows, and very much in the manner of those which Wren set up in some rectangular parish churches, were to flank this auditorium. But the 'aisle' spaces were not to look inwards or connect with the choir, but were to lie open, to the churchyard outside, as arcaded loggias or promenading spaces. A model, preserved in St Paul's, shows Wren's ideas for the curiously planned 'choir limb' of this proposed cathedral. We are less certain on the details of the domed vestibule, for that part of the model has gone. But the entire building, about 250 feet long and a grander version (though with its dome at the western end) of what Wren had sketched in his quickly drawn scheme for a rebuilt City, would have been impressive yet manageable, a larger version of what Wren himself later achieved in several parish churches, of Archer's St Philip's at Birmingham with its domed western tower, or of the two noble blocks with which Wren, in the full maturity of his architectural achievement, later flanked the upper court of his palatial hospital at Greenwich.

Wren's earliest version of a new St Paul's was soon superseded by more ambitious ideas. In the meantime he got to grips with the great task of replacing about half of the City's burnt churches; Hooke, as several entries in his diary prove, was also, as a leader among the City Surveyors, considerably concerned both with the clearance of ruins and the supervision of new work. Wren's own idea for totally new places of worship, free-standing and in positions of dominance in a new townscape, and with little if any relationship to the ancient sites, had been dropped. Where churches, in most cases with the amalgamation of small parishes, were to be replaced they were to arise on old, and often irregular sites. Churchyards, despite Wren's hygienic preference for out-of-town cemeteries, were still, with the grim results which Dickens later depicted, to accompany the new buildings. Wren had also to apply his clear, scientific thinking to the liturgical needs of new churches whose worship would differ much from that once seen in the Londoners' recently burnt worshipping places. The whole process of building some fifty new churches was inevitably long, most notably so in the completion of some of their steeples. But important principles were laid down, and some notable churches were started, in the first five years from a starting date of 1670. Though Wren must often have had close personal dealings, friendly, contentious, and often convivial, with the clergy and the churchwardens of the parishes concerned the main principles, rather than the details, of what lay behind his great work of replacement are the more important for the understanding of his outlook and career.

A few of the burnt City churches were not damaged beyond repair, while in some others the bases of the towers, being relatively sturdy, could in part be retained to support new upper stages. Two churches in which Wren's work amounted to heavy repairs rather than total replacement were both on the fringe of the main area of devastation. At St Dunstan's in the East, from a starting date as far back as 1668, repairs were needed rather than complete rebuilding, though Tuscan pillars and arches replaced the mediaeval arcades.[32] The steeple, of great interest and with a possible reference to the main source of the coal taxation of which was so vital for London's new cathedral and parochial churches, came thirty years later in Wren's career. St Sepulchre's, Holborn, was a church whose western tower, and whose outer walls and south porch of the fifteenth century, substantially survived the fire, so that the Roman Doric arcades of Wren's interior reconstruction contrast with the late Gothic of the outer shell. St Mary at Hill, though classical inside, may also have kept some mediaeval outer walling.[33] But for the most part Wren was free, within the sometimes awkward confines of existing sites, to design churches whose plans, and whose style, could differ greatly from those of the mediaeval buildings which had lasted, with new liturgical use for over a hundred years before their destruction, from the turbulent Reformation decades till the year of the Great Fire.

Most of Wren's City churches were therefore wholly new buildings. Though not aisled, basilican interiors must often have partly repeated what had been there before chancels and sanctuaries were less emphasised than in the lately destroyed pre-Reformation buildings. In a few of them, mostly started later than 1675, Wren found that he could exploit ideas of spatial planning so far unknown to Anglican worshippers. His clear, realistic mathematician's thinking was applied, successfully and with a lasting influence, to the creation of new buildings for rites in which the vernacular had replaced Latin, in which those who attended wished both to follow the Prayer-Book wording and to hear sermons (often of great, though post-Puritan length) which were still more important than they had been before the Reformation. The new churches must also be buildings in which Matins and Evensong had replaced the Mass as the main rite; the Communion service, though important and devoutly celebrated, was said far less often, and with less ceremony, than the masses of pre-Anglican days. Short unemphatic sanctuaries were, for this new liturgical purpose, more useful than deep, screened-off mediaeval chancels. Interiors were thus needed where Communion tables stood, unobtrusively but before some elaborate altarpieces, at one end, or one side of auditoria whose main furnishings were their pulpits, high and ornate beneath their opulent sounding boards and well placed to command those seated down in the pews and, where congregations were large enough, in sloping galleries. These 'auditory' churches were suffused with copious, unmysterious light pouring through windows of clear glass, reflected by the creamy whiteness of plaster and glinting off the gold of such details as modillions and winged cherubs' heads. French Protestant 'temples', such as Wren had seen at Charenton, and Dutch Renaissance churches, like the Nieuwe Kerk at Haarlem, and the Lutheran Church at Amsterdam, whose massively pulpitted interiors he could have known from prints and engravings, may well have influenced his planning and the ordering of his interiors for a cool, post-Laudian Anglican liturgy.[34] Though most of Wren's earlier interiors were rectangular (like that at Charenton) his 'auditory' planning was sometimes rendered with a new spatial effect where domes, so far unknown to English congregations, rose sweepingly above central spaces, with slim pillars and side ceilings so arranged, within broad rectangular or nearly square spaces, as to give cruciform or transeptal impressions. St Mary-at-Hill and St Stephen's, Walbrook, both started early in the 1670s, showed their designer as a bold essayist in spatial and illusionist planning, while at St Benet Fink an oval dome rose above a nave shaped as an elongated decagon.[35] But most of Wren's departures from the basilican rectangle came later in his career.

The sites of the City churches, often shut in and only seen from one or two sides, severely limited the exterior effects which Wren could give his new buildings. Even at St Clement Danes, where an island site presented a clearer opportunity, the sides and eastern end of Wren's new church were unimpressive, with elaboration mainly reserved for the interior, and for the steeple whose actual completion, though achieved in Wren's lifetime, was by Gibbs.[36] But some east and west ends, and a few good side elevations (as one still sees at St Martin's, Ludgate) showed Wren as an inventive, resourceful designer, drawing ideas from several facets of Continental Renaissance or Baroque.

More dramatic, and widely influential in the coming century, were the steeples with which Wren adorned many of his City churches. There had, of course, been towers or spires over most, if not all, of the churches lost in the fire. Some replacements – plain or pinnacled towers and simple spires like that of St Margaret Pattens – followed the basic designs of earlier examples, while even the more fanciful spires, such as the brilliantly adorned steeple of St Antholin's, differed little, in their silhouettes, from mediaeval predecessors.[37] Where Wren was more inventive was in the churches, such as St Mary Abchurch and St Martin Ludgate, where needle-thin spires were poised on lead-sheathed cupolas or other carefully composed designs, or where steeples, capped by little cupolas or spirelets, were elaborate architectural compositions of small Baroque stages, diminishing in size as they rose towards their finials. Here were steeples expressed in the decorative terms of the French or Italian Renaissance. But although such steeples, over churches different from those planned by Wren, were not unknown in Italy the basic conception of these most inspiring London towers may have come to Wren from Renaissance towers, over churches or various public buildings, in the cities of the Netherlands. Wren had never been to Holland, but Evelyn and some others among his friends knew the country. All could readily have consulted the engravings in various Dutch architectural books which were available in England. *Architectura Moderna*, brought out in 1631 by Cornelis Danckert and featuring church steeples, and secular towers, put up in Amsterdam by Hendrik de Keyser, was an important volume, while Wren, like Hooke when in 1674 he consulted Storey the master mason just back from a visit to the Netherlands,[38] could have discussed things with those who had seen Dutch buildings for themselves. Among these towers are built-up steeples, like some of Wren's with stages of gradually lessening sizes and various Netherlands Renaissance detail, which adorn their own towns as Wren's more spectacular designs glorified the skyline of a rebuilt City of London.

Internal fittings, mostly of wood but including the ornate plasterwork of ceilings, were also vital for the beauty of the City

churches, whose steady rebuilding got under way in the 1670s.
Altarpieces and altar rails, panelling, galleries, pulpits, fonts, and
organ cases all combined, in varied ways, to create interiors of a sober
splendour. But here, as in the refurnished choir at Salisbury, Wren's
part in the achievement was more by way of general supervision, and
the approval of craftsmen's schemes, than the getting out of detailed
designs. For some churches he may, as with Alexander Fort and his
work at Salisbury, have got out drawings for the general guidance of
the joiners and carvers. But the fittings of the churches were, as a rule,
less directly Wren's responsibility than their main fabrics of stone or
brick.

I have said that Robert Hooke, Wren's most important colleague on
the Commission for rebuilding the City, was certainly involved in
work on the parish churches. But the extent of his participation is
uncertain, and the greatest responsibility lay on Wren. Dr Kerry
Downes thinks it likely that the two designers worked together[39] on
the striking urban ornament which soon arose, and was complete by
1676, to commemorate the event of the Great Fire. It was soon
decided that a monument, eventually planned to take the form of a
tall, suitably embellished classical column, should arise on or near the
site of the baker's shop and oven where the fire had started. As with
other similar schemes, more than one design was put forward. The All
Souls' collection contains one drawing,[40] no particular credit to Wren,
for a tall, Roman Doric pillar, unfluted and with metal flames
spurting out, at intervals, in an inept parody of the none-too-attractive
Roman idea of the rostral column. The final, more dignified design
was for the column, fluted and with no interruption of the vertical line
above its sculptured plinth, which actually adorns Billingsgate. As
with Wren's later idea for a giant order of columns for the western
front of St Paul's trouble arose over the size of the Portland stone
blocks required for the work. But the job went ahead as planned,
though a phoenix, a statue of Charles II, and a symbolic figure of
London, were all rejected as a final feature, and a ball spurting
multiple flames, whose price, per pound of metal, was negotiated by
Hooke, [41] capped the topmost composition above the abacus of the
Monument's capital.

The early 1670s were also the years when the new Temple Bar was
built as a stylish entrance to the City from the West. It was
supposedly to designs by Wren, though Eduard Sekler has pointed
out[42] that there is no documentary proof of his authorship. A
charming composition, more Baroque in character than many of
Wren's definite buildings, the bar was akin to many ceremonial
gateways, permanent or temporarily set up for special occasions, built
in several countries about this time. It could also have been by Hooke,
or by one of the teams now being gathered alike in the Office of Works
and for rebuilding the rest of the City.

Whatever was, or was not done about the main fabric at Salisbury Cathedral the years 1671 and 1672 saw Wren concerned with his old friend Seth Ward's refitting of the choir. In October of 1671 Bishop Ward, without mentioning Wren, issued a decree on the ornamentation, above the surviving late mediaeval choir seats, and behind the still standing mediaeval screen, of that crucial part of his cathedral;[43] the document referred to the re-laying of the pavement and the repair and decoration of the stalls. Next month an agreement between Dean Ralph Brideoak and Alexander Fort, a Wiltshire man but described, in the official papers, as a citizen and joiner of London, laid it down that Fort should do all carpenter's work, joinery, and carving on the repair, "new modelling", and adornment of the choir; the prebends' stalls and a "very decent and handsome" seat for the Dean were to be the main new items. Fort's joinery and carving were to be "according to the modell [drawing?] already drawn by the Rt Worshipful Dr Wren".[44] Early in the following year a somewhat similar agreement provided that Fort should erect a new throne for the bishop. Here again the work was to be according to a "form and modell" by Wren, which Fort was to consult over the work's proper performance;[45] its cost was to be £58. Wren himself was a witness to the agreement and the design, which one would gladly have now since the work itself has disappeared, was to be left with Fort and produced as needed. Here and elsewhere the details in the papers make it clear that the bishop's choir furnishings were to be richly classical, a Renaissance contrast both to the early Gothic structure and what Wyatt later inserted.*

The work must have been done in 1672 and early in 1673. For in May of the latter year Wren had to comment and arbitrate on disputes which arose over payments to some of the craftsmen and over what was said, by the Dean and the prebends, to have been done over and above the agreement with Fort.[46] Matthew Foulson, a carver who claimed £60 for what he had done, got £40, with the balance submitted to Wren for his ruling. More important was the dispute, also referred to the Surveyor General, over such items as brick walls laid beneath the stalls, and whether classical vases and other details in the stallwork, and cantilever supports for the organ should be paid for under the agreement with Fort made late in 1671. Wren reported on the first day of June. The brick walls (not, in view of the conditions of a low-lying site, an unreasonable idea of Fort's) had not been mentioned in an agreement only covering woodwork. Only the Dean's stall had been meant to have rich ornament; the vases and other Baroque details elsewhere were beyond Fort's contract. It was also

*Some portions of the simple panelling put up behind the prebends' stalls survive in a house in The Close; I have not been able to see them. *See* N. Pevsner, "Wiltshire", p. 385.

reasonable that Fort should make deductions for various items not carried out on the organ. At about the same time it was stated that any doubts that might arise from agreement, for painting and gilding in the choir, with John Walford, citizen and painter of London, were to be referred, as with the woodwork which Walford was to paint, to Wren's judgment.[47]

Wren's designing connection with Salisbury seems not to have gone beyond these items in the cathedral. For when in 1682–83 Bishop Ward arranged the foundation and building of the beautiful, H-shaped, brick and stone College of Matrons his extremely detailed contract with the builder, one Thomas Glover of Harnham in Salisbury, did not mention Wren.[48] Sir Christopher could, of course, have given his old friend some ideas for what turned out to be a building more vernacular in its manner than those he was certainly designing at that time. But the supervision of the building, in matters of materials and quality of workmanship, was entrusted to Thomas Marsh, the cathedral's Clerk of Works; its design was such that many provincial masons and builders of Wren's time could well have evolved it.

While refurnishing was going on in the cathedral of his native county Wren was also concerned with the problem of a new St Paul's. Ideas for a totally new cathedral must, in these preliminary years, have been revolving in his mind. But for the moment the awkward realities of demotion and site clearance were more relevant than new building work. But from about the middle of 1670, with the assurance of considerable funds from the tax on London's seaborne coal, Wren could confidently plan for a large new church. He also had borings made through the subsoil on which the new foundations must be laid, piercing sand, "pot earth", and water before his drills reached London's natural bed of hard clay. He struck trouble, near the north-eastern corner of his site, where cavities and subsidence resulted from ancient diggings for pottery clay. An inverted arch, not unlike those he was to build in the soft riverside Cambridge soil beneath the library at Trinity, was his remedy for this "softness and disturbance".[49] He now decided that the main axis of the new St Paul's was to lie slightly slantwise across the older alignment. Site values, and the alignment of new streets and houses already put up since 1666, ended his chances of a roomier, more piazza-like site than he actually obtained for his new cathedral.[50]

With the knowledge that "the generality were for grandeur"[51] Wren was from this time onwards actively concerned with his ideas and designs for a large new St Paul's. There seems, however, to have been little dialogue or discussion between the architect and the main body of the future cathedral's clerical users. The first two designs which Wren displayed were splendid, and could be reckoned as the mathematician's dreams of a Renaissance intellectual. More doubtful was their fitness for the liturgical task which any new Anglican cathedral in London must needs discharge.

Wren's first design was for a mathematically satisfying church, domed and on a Greek cross plan, perfectly symmetrical and with gracefully curved walls to connect the limbs of the cross. A pedimented Corinthian portico was to terminate each limb; the whole composition was beautifully even. But a problem lay in its liturgical dispositions, and in particular in its provision of a choir. A space, from the easternmost pair of dome piers and the church's eastern wall, was, indeed reserved for this purpose, with curved sets of stalls planned to face each other across the screened-off space.[52] Such a position, behind the high altar and confined within the curvature of an eastern apse, was not uncommon in the Renaissance or Baroque churches of some friaries in Catholic Europe. But in those churches the main worshipping activities were the sermons and masses in the frequently used main spaces of capacious naves. In what Wren now proposed for St Paul's the liturgical activity of an Anglican cathedral would have been relegated to a relatively obscure space, with processional ways round the dome, and the great circle beneath the dome itself no more than an auditorium for occasional preaching.

The same defect appeared in the second design, from late in 1673, for which we still have the splendid Great Model,[53] raised on its plinth and eighteen feet long, so that one can walk inside and gain an impression of how its unfurnished interior would have appeared. The mathematical perfection of the Greek cross design was little changed, though a shallow apse gave eastern emphasis to the choir space, and at the ends of the transepts porticos were replaced by open pediments, Corinthian pilasters, and columns in *antis*. The dome, with its projecting ribs above brackets at its base, and its row of small windows high up in its structure, paid a tribute to that of St Peter's in Rome. The main difference between this design and the Greek cross scheme lay in the lengthening out, as in an embryonic nave, of the western limb. The vestibule now projected between the dome and the cathedral's main facade could, in its own right, have been a fine polygonal church, domed and with circular windows in its dome and with a convincing cupola. The idea of such a vestibule, allied to the conception of some Romanesque or Gothic naves but akin to the notion of a *westwerk*, appear in Wren's actual cathedral. The 'Model' design's final element, after a portion which was to contain a library without raising high enough for a pair of western towers, was a colossal eight-columned portico of fluted Corinthian columns, simply pedimented and to that extent an enlargement of what Inigo Jones had earlier achieved. What defeated this idea, as it had nearly frustrated the scheme for the Monument, was the impossibility of getting blocks of Portland stones large enough to form the component drums of so vast a set of columns.

The 'Model' design, with its giant Corinthian pilasters, at intervals, round its central space and with upper windows to light that space, was Wren's favourite scheme for a new St Paul's.[54] His preference was a little surprising, as the Greek cross scheme, with no western addition to mar its symmetry, was more mathematical, in an almost Platonic harmony, than the design three-dimensionally revealed, early in 1674, by means of the model.

The 'Model' design, whose model had been commissioned late in October of 1673, was approved by the King on 12th November.[55] Commissioners were appointed to carry out the scheme; it must have seemed that the design, on any count a splendid Renaissance concept, would duly adorn a restored City. But objections, not unreasonable in terms of liturgy though timid of novelties in design, caused the rejection of what was now displayed. For the cathedral clergy were accustomed, as were their pre-Reformation forbears, to the chanting or recitation of the choir offices in the long, rectangular setting of an antiphonal choir. Beyond it, less elaborate and more seldom used than the mediaeval high altar, the Communion Table was decently set and duly respected. None of this, they felt, could be achieved in the small, circular choir space allowed for in Wren's Greek cross and 'Model' designs. Any new cathedral, though by pre-Reformation standards sparsely used and with no mediaeval profusion of side chapels, shrines, and chantries, must none the less, in the 1670s, be built to an essentially mediaeval plan. The nave, as in mediaeval cathedrals by the time of the Reformation, would only serve occasional uses. So the 'Model' design was rejected some time in 1674, to Wren's bitter chagrin and, so we are told, tearful disappointment.[56] He went back to work on a more conventionally cathedralesque ground plan, retaining his cherished concept of a domed central space but meeting the canons' longing for a collegiate choir.

But among "persons of distinction, skilled in Antiquity and Architecture"[57] Wren's standing was high and his third design, once displayed and before prebendal criticism assailed it, found approval at Court. It can have been no accident that Charles II's approval of a design, whose chances of being realised at first seemed good, soon brought the Surveyor General a signal honour. For almost at once the forty-one year old architect was knighted. The actual date, as both Hooke and the Oxford antiquary Anthony Wood reported, was 14th November 1673,[58] and, so Wren's son Christopher said in 1742, it was about now that the younger Edward Pearce made his brilliant Baroque bust of the architect, presumably from sittings in London. The bust could fitly have commemorated its subject's knighthood, and for this reason would have become a much prized family possession. On many counts Wren deserved the honour, but the King's formal approval of what later got known as the "unexecuted" design was an obvious occasion for accolade.

Hooke added, to his brief note of Wren's Knighthood, that Sir Christopher had "gone to Oxford". The occasion for his journey was neither academic nor architectural but political. For he now made his second attempt to become a member of the House of Commons.

A few days before Wren's knighthood Sir Heneage Finch, who was one of the university's representatives in Parliament, was made Lord Keeper of the Great Seal. Wren saw himself, and was supported, as Finch's successor. His eminence as an Oxford man, his prestige as the recently knighted Surveyor General, the memory of his recent professorship which he had given up in the spring of 1673,[59] and his recent completion of the Sheldonian all seemed to unite in his favour. From mid November onwards he was in Oxford to work up his supporters; the election itself was held in January of 1674.

The main contest was between Wren and Thomas Thynne, a cousin of the notorious Thomas Thynne of Longleat, who later emerged, till his spectacular murder in London, as a leading supporter of the Duke of Monmouth. Anthony Wood, who supported Wren and disliked the more flamboyant Thynne as a "hot head" and "a person now much against the King's interest in Parliament" racily records the election.[60] Despite Wren's obvious claims on Oxonian sympathy Thynne's high pressure campaign among "the pot men" was devastatingly effective. As adept as his cousin in Wiltshire at "hospitable treats" he poured out money, for a week or ten days, in keeping an open table for the Masters of Arts, frequenting the coffee houses, and the common chambers, "to court stinking breaths".[61] Sir Christopher, as we can imagine and as Wood ruefully recorded, "was not so expert this way". His defeat, by 125 to Thynne's 203, was worse than what he had suffered at Cambridge. He was, however, Vice President of the Royal Society, and in the same year he, Bishop Ward, and Hooke (who often mentions the matter in his diary) were on a commission to study the vital navigational problem of correctly finding longitude at sea.

The making of the Great Model took Wren and his colleagues well into 1674; Hooke "walked through it" on February 21st. There were also the discussions which led to the discarding of Wren's favourite design. The same year had seen him concerned, amid many preoccupations, with designing works foreshadowing what soon came to him in Cambridge, for the authorities of another great cathedral. For in June of that year, one assumes after earlier design work done in London, a contract was made between William Evison, a Lincoln builder, and the Dean of Lincoln.[62] It provided for the building, along the northern side of the cloisters and above a new, round-arched loggia, in a somewhat backward-looking style not unlike that of the ranges already flanking Nevile's Court at Trinity College, Cambridge, of a library whose style no more respected the Gothic of the cloister arcades than Wren's stalls and throne had deferred to the Early English at Salisbury. The donor, a Cambridge man and a friend of Sancroft, was Dean Michael Honywood of Lincoln who held the post from the Restoration year till he died in 1681. There was no likelihood of Wren's on-the-spot supervision, but details in the contract, over which he may have advised, lay it down that no softwood timber was to be used but for the floor, stairs, and the boarding just under the lead roof; the remaining structural woodwork was to be of good, well seasoned oak. With its square-headed, transomed windows, cartouches with Honywood's arms over two of those windows, and a Corinthian interior doorway with the same arms in a segmental pediment of Baroque character, the library is wholly in a Renaissance idiom. The bookcases, which may be from drawings by Wren, were at first meant to project, at intervals between the windows, from the southern wall.[63] But in fact those of Wren and Honywood's time run lengthwise along the other side.

Another building which was finished in 1674, and with which Wren's name is linked, was the new theatre in Drury Lane; if he was, indeed, commissioned to design it his work on the Sheldonian, and what he had seen at the Tuileries in Paris would have furnished him with precedents. The earlier playhouse, built by Thomas Killigrew to house the performances by what came to be known as the King's Company of players, had been finished in 1663; it was, however, burnt out in another nine years. Money was raised for another playhouse on the same site. By the end of 1673 the building was far advanced, and in 1674 it stood complete.[64] If Wren was indeed its designer he must have worked on his drawings not later than the early part of 1673. But his authorship, though not inconceivable, cannot completely be proved, nor can we be absolutely sure that the drawing at Oxford,[65] with its view-impeding series of giant pilasters along the sides and round the semicircular end of the auditorium, is of this second theatre in Drury Lane. The new theatre, put up for private individuals and not, for some years to come, styled the Theatre *Royal*, did not fall naturally within the scope of a busy Surveyor General. But the presence of the drawing, if in fact it is of this theatre, within the Oxford collection of Wren's drawings suggests that Wren was at any rate consulted by the proprietors. The likelihood of his share in the work is reinforced by Colley Cibber's later opinion that "it were but justice to lay the original figure" which Wren had given it. The theatre of 1674, with alterations probably made by 1696, was the one which served, in 1764, as a model for the still existing Theatre Royal at Bristol.

These years of the 1670s saw Wren busier than ever before on architectural work, acknowledged not only as Surveyor General but as the prime designer of new places of worship in the City. Now was the time of his knightly honour; it is also a period when we may look, without the material for a really detailed study, at some sides of his personal and private life. He was widely esteemed and, as his character deserved, much liked, though he lacked a profusion of small talk or the more unbent forms of mirth in which Pepys delighted. He moved among a wide range of friends, increasing his circle as he and his two successive wives had dinners, or other gratifications, from those in authority in some of the City parishes. Wren's short, spare, figure was familiar in the small-scale, restricted London Society of his time. The coffee houses, like the City vestries, knew him well; he seems, moreover, like his present biographer, to have been much fond of the comparatively new "Arabian cordial". He was also, so Hooke tells us, a smoker, though one cannot envisage his excessive indulgence in "the weed". Of his other diversions we know little, but once in the summer of 1674 he and Hooke went to the theatre and saw *The Tempest*.[66]

The diary of his close colleague Robert Hooke is an important source, for these years and later, for Wren's personal and informal activity. They often met, sometimes three or four times a week, for the most part on business arising from their respective surveyorships, and often for the purpose of checking the accounts of various builders and craftsmen. But they were often together in a more social way. They frequently dined together, more often in Wren's house in Scotland Yard than in Hooke's bachelor quarters, and even more numerous were their forgatherings, often with other friends present, in London coffee houses. They sometimes walked together, conveniently near Wren's official residence, in the formal pleasance of St James' Park, with the frequent chance there of friendly meetings with Charles II for whom the Park was a favoured promenade. Hooke, as one readily finds, is a more exhaustive source than Pepys or Evelyn for Wren's none too fully evidenced doings.

Wren's health, concerning him far less than the minutely and revoltingly recorded disorders and purges of the fussy, hypochondriac Hooke, seems not, by the standards of the age and in a man of so slight a frame, to have been a major worry. Hooke does, however, mention that in March of 1675 Wren was "sick of stone".[67] Though the architect seems not to have been a person of much unconstrained mirth or boisterous humour he seems, for a man whose professional activities must often have tried his patience, to have been equable enough. Only once, when he suggests that Wren was jealous of him, does Hooke (who was, in any case, a warped and over sensitive man) give the impression of any unreasonable failing.[68] This was, however, a time when the two were anyhow in dispute over the working accommodation that Hooke should have in or near Whitehall Palace. Hooke, whose surveyorship concerned the City rather than the Court, first complained that Wren did not want him to have a room in the Palace Gallery, and that he wished to see him "thrust into the Park". But the kindly Surveyor General soon promised his colleague a chamber "by the Park stairs" which must, in the jumbled warren of the old Whitehall Palace, have seemed a reasonable compromise.[69]

Many of Hooke and Wren's meetings and discussions concerned such scientific points as lighthouses, Hooke's invention of the spring watch, and the problem of longitude with which both were officially involved. But other points in Hooke's record reveal more of Wren's personal circumstances and family affairs. In 1672, for instance, Hooke speaks of the Surveyor General's "neatly furnished rooms" in his official house at Scotland Yard.[70] He mentions how on one occasion some china was bought, by John Fitch a leading master bricklayer much employed by Hooke and Wren, as a present for the first Lady Wren.[71] Sir Christopher himself, in July of 1675, ordered a clock, when on a visit to his workshop, from the famous Thomas Tompion.[72]

Wren had married in 1669, and in October of 1672 his first child was born. The boy was christened Gilbert, a name new to the family, and he may have been named after Archbishop Sheldon; I have, however, been unable to find, from the baptismal entry in the registers of St Martin-in-the-Fields,[73] or from other sources, whether the Primate was his godfather. But little Gilbert failed, like all too many children at that time, to survive infancy. In September, 1673 he had convulsive fits,[74] and in March of the next year he died, being buried in the chancel of old St Martin's.[75] But in February of 1675 the next Christopher Wren, who was long to outlive his father, was born; his tragedy, very common in those days, was that he soon lost his mother. For late in August Hooke noted that Faith Wren had been "five days sick of small pox".[76] On 3rd September she died and was buried, with her infant son, in St Martin's chancel.[77] It seems that her mother was with her at the end, for a few days later Hooke dined with Sir Christopher, and Lady Coghill his mother-in-law.[78]

In this same year, 1675, one of Wren's smaller designing jobs had about it the flavour of family piety. For between 1675 and 1677 the chapel of St John's College at Oxford was extensively refitted,[79] the new furnishings including a screen. For this feature Wren provided a Baroque design, with fluted Corinthian columns and the arms of the College over a swan's neck pediment.[80] He took no payment, and the free provision of the design would have been a happily fitting gift to his father's old college. The last months of 1675 thus saw Wren a widower and burdened, as was common in those days of heavy mortality, with the care of a motherless infant. Compensations lay in his ever more absorbing work, and in the prospect of another marriage. From June of the same year he had been involved with a building, modest in bulk but of great interest to him both as a leading architect and as an astronomer. More important for the building process of his greatest current project he now had official permission for work to start on the latest, though not, in terms of the third dimension, the final version of his new St Paul's. The foundation stone, had indeed, been laid, in June, exactly at the time when the first moves were being made on the scheme for Greenwich.

8
London Concerns
1675–1680

One

Storms, shoals, and rocks were by no means the only hazards which faced the sailing ship mariners of the seventeenth century. A more baffling terror could be their inability to be sure of their precise position east or west of any point of departure or intended port of arrival. Latitude they could plot with reasonable accuracy, but longitude remained a daunting problem. It was, in fact, well in the eighteenth century before accurate chronometers provided a solution; by that time many ships had been cast away and Anson, in the 1740s, had lost hundreds of men in the Pacific as he groped for Juan Fernandez and as scurvy devastated his crew. But in Charles II's time, with a Board of Longitude at work, and with Wren among its members, it was still reckoned that more accurate stellar observations could provide a major help. For such observations, and "for the finding out of the longitude of places for perfecting navigation and astronomy",[1] the available telescopes must be suitably housed. The idea of such an observatory led Wren to the erection of his first building in the place which later saw the rise of what is arguably the greatest of his architectural compositions.

A leading spirit in the scheme for an official observatory in England was Wren's friend and fellow mathematician Sir Jonas Moore, Surveyor General of the Ordnance and hence accommodated in the Tower. John Flamsteed, the first Astronomer Royal, was appointed to make the observations; he started work on the top of Moore's official dwelling.[2] Once the project had the King's personal approval a search could be made for a site which was both free of smoke and commanded an unimpeded view. The first proposals were for Hyde Park, and for Chelsea College, a site soon otherwise adorned by Wren. But the Surveyor General himself preferred the more easterly, more elevated site of Greenwich Hill, already crowned by a ruined mediaeval tower.[3] There was no idea that this tower should be reconditioned. Wren preferred a wholly new observatory, modest in size and inexpensive, but suitable both for observations and for "lodging rooms for our astronomical observator".[4] Predictably enough Charles II's Royal Observatory was to be less monumental than its opposite number in Paris, put up, under Colbert's instructions, to Claude Perrault's designs and finished four years before work started at Greenwich. Wren may have known of this building, square and massive with its two polygonal corner turrets, its northern projection, its round-headed windows, and a large square room, of a ceremonial character, along most of its southern side.[5] He could not hope to rival the size or the dignity of the Parisian Observatoire; he could, however, have adapted its conception of a semi-practical grand saloon.

On 22nd June 1675, a Royal Warrant for the building of the new observatory went out to Moore's immediate superior, Sir Thomas Chicheley the Master General of the Ordnance who had been a colleague of Wren's on the pre-fire Commission for Old St Paul's. He was to build and fence it, with all convenient speed, to a "plot and design" by Wren. Materials were to be brought up river from Tilbury, where the Elizabethan fort was then being rebuilt and improved, and money was to come from the sale of "old and decayed powder"; the entire monetary outlay was not, however, to exceed £500.[6] Hooke refers, on the day when this warrant was issued, to a visit to Sir Christopher "to direct the Observatory in Greenwich Park for Sir Jonas Moore". The foundation stone was laid in August, and progress was swift, for by Christmas the new building was roofed; the provision of instruments, some of them lent by the Royal Society, was a longer business. Flamsteed's main astronomical work was done in the comparatively humble buildings, almost wholly rebuilt less than a century later, which lie south-east of the main block which rises on the crest of Greenwich Hill. It was in this main block, with its two dominant turrets, its terrace, and its charming pair of flanking summer houses, that Wren designed "the observator's inhabitation", and adorned it, in the Parisian manner, "a little for pompe".[7] Flamsteed's rooms, with a curious prevalence of fireplaces in their corners, comprised a modest suite on the ground floor. The upper rooms of this building in brick and stone, marked on an old plan as *Camera Stellata*, is the one which best displays Wren's designing skill and decorative accompaniments. Octagonal in plan, it does not, on its northern side, correspond to the outer shape of the building. It has pedimented doorways and wainscoted walls, a shallow dome, and a charming plaster frieze whose foliate decoration is punctuated by the crowned initials C.R., crossed sceptres with the crown above them, and the royal cipher of Charles II; the same cipher surmounts the

Baroque plaque, over the main doorway, whose inscription records the supervision of the Observator's building by Sir Jonas Moore.

A greater concern of Wren in this year 1675 was his further designing work on the new St Paul's. Liturgical criticism, not wholly unreasonably, had caused the rejection of the 'Model' design. For the rest of 1674, and in the first months of 1675, Wren must, among other activities, have been busy on the replanning of the new cathedral; it seems certain that, in this process, he re-used many ideas going back to the early months of 1666. His next plans, accepting the points made by the clergy and allowing for a choir limb of mediaeval length, must have been ready in the spring. For on 4th May 1675, a Royal Warrant went out for the execution of the design. Those who issued it could hardly have foreseen how much the elevations of the finished cathedral would vary from what they approved.

As with the 'Model' design, there are some drawings and sketches which suggest that some details of the "Warrant' design followed a process of drawing board trial and experiment;[8] there is also the interesting idea, which I shall later discuss, that Wren was at work, simultaneously with his preparation of the 'Warrant' design, on drawings a good deal closer than the 'Warrant' sketches to what was actually built. But the 'Warrant' design, and some practical factors which led to its official adoption, are worth considering. For in its ground plan the 'Warrant' design, insipid or bizarre in its elevations, came close to the cathedral which was actually built.

What the 'Warrant' design allowed for was a choir limb, of three long bays, a shorter section, and a semicircular east end; it was to be of considerable length and fully comparable to the eastern limbs of some mediaeval cathedrals. Not only would such a plan satisfy prebendal demands for what was reckoned to be a cathedralesque choir, but the eastern limb, with a good sum of money now to hand but not yet enough to finish a complete cathedral, could be "put in great forwardness" before the rest of the cathedral was complete. A domed central space, and two deep transepts, were to lead to a nave of five bays and a short vestibule bay lying between two modestly capped but attractive western turrets. A western portico, with ten columns along its frontage as against the eight put up by Inigo Jones, was none the less to do deference to the old cathedral's much admired western adornment. Only the two chapels which flank the western portion of the actual nave made a real departure from the basic plan which the King and his advisers accepted.

Inigo Jones' work on old St Paul's must have influenced what Wren now suggested for the exterior of his 'Warrant' design. For the elevations of his conventionally aisled and clerestoried nave and choir were to have been similar, with plain pilasters between their round-headed windows, to those which Jones had evolved from his

ROYAL PATRONS

(*above left*) Charles II (*right*) James II (*below left*) William III (*right*) Mary II

(*above left*) Emmanuel College: the chapel
and gallery, dated 1675
(*below left*) Trinity College: the Library
from Neville's Court

CAMBRIDGE

(*above*) Wren's proposed Senate House and
Library (*right*) Trinity College, the Library:
foundations and superstructure

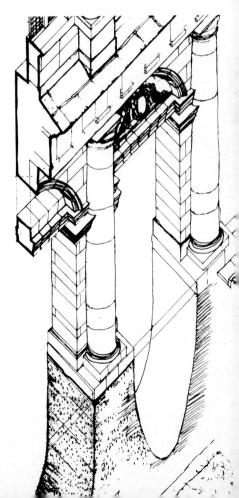

Lincoln Cathedral: the Library, 1674

London, St Lawrence Jewry: East end

London, Temple Bar

Greenwich: Royal Observatory, 1675, the *Camera Stellata*

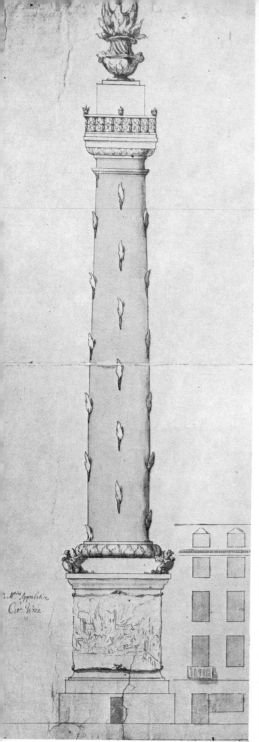

MONUMENT

A rejected design   The actual pillar, 1676

(*top*) Hampton Court: drawing
for a *tempietto* and colonnade
(*above*) designs for capitals
(*right*) drawing for an ornamental
urn

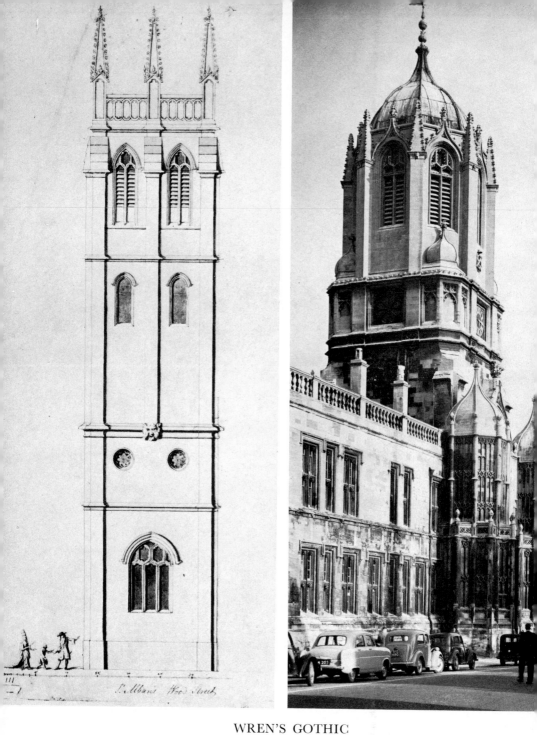

WREN'S GOTHIC

(*left*) London, St Alban's, Wood Street (*right*) Christ Church, Oxford : Tom
Tower, 1681–2

Renaissance recasing of the Norman nave. Only the row of round windows, one above each aisle window, were left out of Wren's composition, while Wren's aisles, a little surprisingly in view of his protests a few decades later, were to be crowned by a balustrade. Some features in the 'Warrant' design's transepts, most notably the Baroque brackets linking the aisles and the clerestory stage, also carried over some points from what Jones had done in the 1630s; the whole scheme is more akin to Wren's thinking of the 1660s than to his more mature phase of 1675; Sir John Summerson has even suggested that large elements of the 'Warrant' design may come from a time closer to 1666 than to 1675,[9] when Wren could have sketched various schemes for a new cathedral in London.

Up to its roof level the 'Warrant' cathedral would have been a competent, well detailed, but somewhat unexciting building; tall Corinthian pilasters, unfluted like those which Wren had intended for a transformed pre-fire nave, would have risen high between the rounded arches of the nave and choir arcades; the triforium stage which was, before September, 1666, to have been kept from the Norman nave would have disappeared in this new, basically kindred version of what Wren had proposed for a repaired mediaeval cathedral.

The central space of the 'Warrant' cathedral, under the first stage of a shallow dome whose curvature would have recalled that of the Pantheon in Rome, would have been roomy and of some dignity; above it, the drum of a comparatively small upper dome would have acted as a lantern. The double structure of that dome, and the timber supports which would, as at the Sorbonne, have held up its outer skin, came through from what Wren had put forward before the fire;[10] so too did the free-standing spiral staircase, twisting up to the cathedral's highest point. It was the outward appearance of the great central feature that displayed outright ugliness and an inept confusion between the nature of a dome and the qualities of a steeple.

Wren's combination, in one design, of a shallow dome and a smaller one of the more normal Renaissance kind would have deprived the 'Warrant' cathedral of the full merits of either type; the upper dome would, moreover, have been too small for the dignity of the building as a whole. Above the upper dome, and rising higher than the cross which tops the lantern of the actual St Paul's, a tall steeple of six stages would have much resembled the beautiful steeple to be built above the tower of Wren's new church of St Bride. The topmost composition now suggested was less grotesque than the slim pineapple of the design worked out in 1666; in neither case does Wren, as yet untried in the actual design and building of monumental domes, seem to have realised that the upward termination of a dome should never overtop the height of the dome itself. If the lantern of

St Peter's in Rome is somewhat small for its dome, with Wren's actual lantern at St Paul's about right in size, his proposals of 1666 and 1675 were far too tall.

Though the 'Warrant' design in many ways revived Wren's project, only nine years before, for a refurbished Old St Paul's he must soon have decided to abandon some important aspects of its three-dimensional rendering. The warrant itself, with its reference to "liberty in the prosecution of his work, to make variations rather ornamental than essential" gave Wren fair latitude provided he adhered to the liturgically important ground plan. Very soon, perhaps with the connivance of the King, of Archbishop Sheldon, and of Dean Sancroft, he made variations of importance both for the structure and appearance of the new building. Before the end of the year he could also have had consultations, relevant to the new cathedral he was about to build in the City, with his old friend and Paris travelling companion Henry Compton, moved in December from the bishopric of Oxford to that of London.

Even before his plans (perhaps in essence a few years old) for the 'Warrant' cathedral were formally presented, accepted by the clergy, and royally approved Wren may also have made at least one set of sketches for a cathedral closer than the 'Warrant' building to what was in the end perfected. In the drawings preserved at Oxford, for what has been called the 'Penultimate' design,[11] points of variance from what was sanctioned late in the spring of 1675 concern the dome and the lighting of the space below it; another scheme bears on the walling arrangements for the nave and choir. The first two Oxford drawings, survivors from what may have been the fruit of much activity in Wren's brain and at his drawing board, are for a dome, comparatively low but more nicely rounded than the main one of the 'Warrant' design. The base of this dome would have been lit by a row of oval lucarnes,[12] and although its topmost termination is not shown one presumes that it would have had no surmounting steeple as inept as that of the 'Warrant' design. More important for the structure of this dome would have been its piers arranged, not at equal intervals as for the 'Warrant' dome, but, as in the actual St Paul's, with arches narrow for the aisles and wider for the transepts, nave and choir. Windows, as in the great Gothic octagon at Ely, would have pierced the walls above the four narrower arches.

This 'Penultimate' design was never carried out. But another drawing at Oxford, perhaps of about 1675, shows the southern elevation of a domed cathedral very similar, bar its unrusticated walls and the design of its top hamper, to the actual St Paul's.[13] The transepts have their curved porches, and the nave has chapels flanking its western sector. More important, as a visual and structural variation on the 'Warrant' elevation, are the upper walls which rise above the aisles. They are as high as the cornice of the clerestory behind them and, from any viewing point on the ground or a fairway above it, mask its very existence. They give the illusion, repeated in the cathedral as built, of a 'greater' church whose aisles, like those of the choir limb of the cathedral in Bristol, are as high as the central compartment. Walls of this type had, moreover, a structural purpose, as abutments for the thrust of a central dome and as a concealment for the unclassical device of flying buttresses behind them; this came as an addition to the new effect which they would give to what was still to be a conventionally (or mediaevally) designed cathedral. The aisle windows were still to be of the same type as those shown in the 'Warrant' version, but the pilasters between those windows were now to be in pairs. But in the screen, or sham, walls no windows need appear. The clerestory windows could now, in their screened obscurity, be the plainest of openings, while in the equivalent spaces of the upper screen walls attractive Corinthian aedicules, with simple triangular pediments, could (and do) make a delightful contrast to the aisle windows below them.

Whatever the detailed processes behind Wren's new designs to replace details made public when the warrant was granted work actually started, in that midsummer month of 1675, on a cathedral considerably different from the building foreshadowed a month earlier. As Dr Margaret Whinney has pointed out, the walls of the actual aisles, having to support the weight of the screen walls, had to be evidently thicker than those shown in the 'Warrant' ground plan.[14] The masons, especially Joshua Marshall, the Master Mason to the Crown and hence an official associate of Wren's, who built the southern side of the choir, must at once have known how great were the 'variations' to be carried out. On 14th June 1675, the first contracts were signed with Marshall, and with another London mason, Thomas Strong;[15] both were already at work, under Wren and Hooke's direction, on City churches. Another document, of 17th August, specifies rustication, not the plain ashlar of the Oxford elevation drawing, for the outer walls.[16]

Clearance on site, apart from what had already been done to remove the wreckage of the mediaeval choir limb, must already have started. It is from this early stage, when points on the ground were being marked for staking, that *Parentalia* gives us the pleasant little story of what must, for Wren, have been a happy and auspicious moment in a busy life. For when, to mark one spot, he was handed a scrap stone, he turned over what must have been part of a tombstone in the southern part of St Paul's churchyard. He found the word RESURGAM (I will arise) engraved on its surface.[17] This happy chance must have led to the fitting word's repetition, along with a sculptured pheonix rising from the flames, in the pediment of the south transept which projects close to the scene of the find.

The new cathedral's foundation stone, more genuinely the

beginning of the main work than such stones are apt to be nowadays, was laid, apparently without special ceremony, on 21st June. Work then proceeded apace, clearance being done at the same time as laying of foundations and the putting up of new walls. Carts, to remove unwanted rubbish, came to the site while others brought sand, lime, and other materials for mortar.[18] Not all the rubble of the burnt cathedral was wasted, and fair quantities of the old St Paul's humbly served for the foundations and mortar of its successor.[19] Watchmen were paid to keep an eye on the site after normal working hours, and Wren could securely feel, as 1675 drew to its close and as Henry Compton succeeded Humphrey Henchman as Bishop of London, that the greatest of his commissions was well under way.

Two

The early months of 1676 saw Wren hard at work both on St Paul's and on an increasing number of City churches. He was still a widower, and we know nothing of his arrangements, through nurses and housekeepers, for the maintenance of his house and the upbringing of the infant Christopher. Hooke's journal is still, with a tantalizing slightness of detail, valuable both for the architect's doings and for their collaboration over the City churches, and over the Monument (including details of the inscription to be placed on it). More than most men Hooke seems to have had some admission, and not only on the frequent occasions when he came to dinner, to Wren's small family circle. In September of 1676 he mentions the ordering, at a cheap rate (which turned out to be 14s.) of a "cradle horse for little Wren".[20] On 21st October the hobby horse was dispatched to the little boy. It was the day after his father's forty-fourth birthday. The evening before Hooke had been with Wren, and other friends, for a relaxed evening of celebration at the Palgrave's Head, a well known tavern by Temple Bar. There had been "good discourse", and the festive architect had "paid all".[21] A little later, Hooke mentions the death of "Sir Christopher Wren's Frenchman" – presumably a valet or some other personal servant.[22] He himself, so frequent a visitor and often given lifts in the Surveyor's coach, took pains to keep in with Wren's staff, giving generous tips, early in 1680, both to the coachman and footman.[23]

Six months earlier the widower architect had let his house, not, one assumes, his official one in Scotland Yard but a dwelling of his own.[24] He may not, in that spring of 1676, have expected that within a year he would again be a married man. But on 24th February 1677, at the Chapel Royal, Whitehall, Sir Christopher married a lady whose name was unknown to Hooke, or had slipped his memory, when he laconically recorded the event.[25]

The lady concerned was Jane, a daughter of William, the second Baron Fitzwilliam of Lifford in Ireland. The family were gentry in Northamptonshire, and the second Lady Wren's brother, being an Irish peer, was Member of Parliament for Peterborough.[26] The Fitzwilliams had not long been ennobled, and Jane Wren's mother, from whom she took her christian name, was the heiress of a London alderman. She was probably in her thirties when she married. How she and her husband met is unknown, but Wren could have been friendly with the family either at Court or through his increasing connections, at vestry dinners or in discussions about new churches, with prominent City men. Jane Wren is an even more shadowy figure than Faith, the architect's first wife. Hooke must often have met her particularly when he stayed to dine on such dainties as pudding (of a type unspecified) and, on 4th July of 1678, on bacon and beans, and he mentions her occasionally. Late in 1678 he promised to produce her "Mahomet's book", perhaps the *Koran*; the episode suggests that Jane Wren had some curiosity over philosophic and religious matters.[27]

It is, however, on Wren's more public and social life that Hooke favours us with more numerous glimpses. His home life remains obscure and may well have been uneventful; had the architect of St Paul's left a diary it would, I imagine, have been a record less vivid, and much less salacious, than that of Samuel Pepys. As with some prominent men in classical Athens he may have found his brighter encounters, and his best conversation, away from home. His equivalents to the *agora* and the *stoai* of Socrates and his friends would have been the London taverns and coffee houses which flourished as the forerunners of the West-End clubs at which, had he lived a century later, Wren would surely have been a popular member. Walks in St James's Park added to their many encounters. Occasionally, as in earlier years, Wren visited Hooke in his own quarters. He was there, for instance, with two other friends, on an August evening in 1676; Hooke notes, apart from "claret, one bottle", that they stayed till the modest, but darkening, hour of nine.[28] It was St Bartholomew's Day, at a time when London was still annually enlivened by the long revelry of Bartholomew Fair. Two years later Lady Wren spoke of the occasion when Hooke called and next year he and Sir Christopher amused themselves, in a leisured hour, at the booths and sideshows, seeing an elephant wave flags and perform the trick of firing a gun.[29] Hooke also met others among Wren's kinsmen. He often speaks of encounters with William Holder, while early in December of 1676, on a day when they went on to see Holder, their dining companion was a cousin of the architect, Thomas Wren, the son of Bishop Matthew, who had risen in the Church to become Archdeacon of Ely.[30]

Nearly all these encounters seem to have been friendly and good humoured, with business talk as well as a wide range of social conversation. On Hallowe'en of 1677, falling sickness, cats, and a "curious gardiner of Amsterdam" was discussed;[31] on other occasions, over wine or coffee, they would talk on such things as maps and the Atlas in whose production Wren was concerned. Man's, Jonathan's, and Garaway's were coffee houses which Wren particularly favoured, but he was frequently seen at many others.

Though Wren was normally a man of charm and restrained, conversational geniality he had his more petulant moments. Admittedly he had much to try him, but he may at times have been bad at the glad suffering of fools. So in January of 1679, when Wren and Hooke were in financial dispute with the widow of the mason Joshua Marshall, Hooke found, when the three of them met to discuss the matter, that Mrs Marshall was irate, and that the Surveyor General was "not kind".[32] There were other times when Wren seems to have made no secret of a testy, displeasure at schemes, like one of Hooke's for some buildings for the Earl of Oxford, whose details were shown to him.[33]

Almost all Wren's architectural activity now concerned buildings in or near London, and the range of his journeys remained narrow. Trips to Woolwich and Windsor must have been on jobs, or on the discussion of jobs, falling to him as Surveyor General,[34] while a short journey to Fulham, in August of 1677, may have been made to consult the Bishop of London on his new cathedral. Wren never journeyed abroad, and seldom elsewhere for pleasure, recreation, or cultural curiosity. But in October of 1676 he, and Dr Holder his brother-in-law who now, along with other preferments, held canonries both at St Paul's and Ely, left London for Cambridge,[35] work now being in hand on the most important of Wren's three buildings in that university.

The man behind the plan to build a spacious new library in Trinity College, Cambridge, was an old friend and fellow spirit of Wren and his associate, at Gresham College and elsewhere, in mathematical studies. Isaac Barrow, two years Wren's senior, had first been at Peterhouse, but in the 1660s found his lasting academic home at Trinity. Though he briefly held the Greek professorship and was famous as a liberal-minded, enlightened divine, and as the exponent of a religious outlook much akin to that of Wren it was as a mathematician that he most notably shone.* It was on a recommendation from Wilkins, Wren's old friend and teacher, that in 1662 he obtained the geometrical professorship at Gresham College,[36]

---

*Evelyn, in a laudatory reference, also calls him a "most humble person".

and like Wren he was an early Fellow of the Royal Society; the whole nexus of their association bore a less Laudian stamp than those which had caused Wren's earlier advancement. Barrow was soon, as Professor of Mathematics, more lastingly in Cambridge, making way, in 1669 and of his own free will, for his brilliant pupil the young Isaac Newton. In 1672 he commenced his unforseeably short mastership of Trinity, and in 1675 he became the university's Vice-Chancellor. His tenure of that post probably led him to ask his friend Wren for what turned out to be an important set of unachieved designs.

Many Cambridge dons were worried, as Sheldon and others had been at Oxford, over the holding in the university church of the increasingly secular, often rowdy degree ceremonies. They considered it a "profanation and a scandal" that the requisite scaffolding should cumber the interior, and that "rude crouds and outcries" should defile its peace.[37] Spurred on by the example of Wren's Sheldonian Theatre Barrow and some supporters pressed for the erection of a building which, unlike its Oxonian counterpart, should include in one composition both a Senate House and a University Library less cramped than what was provided in the unfinished court of Cambridge's Old Schools. So Wren, almost certainly at Barrow's insistence, produced designs for two parallel blocks, of two main storeys in the Venetian Renaissance or Palladian manner, and a more sophisticated version of the library he had lately designed for the cathedral at Lincoln.[38] But the building was to have a two-tiered attic storey which would have given a feeling of excessive bulk and height; of the two ranges the library would have been longer and higher than the hall of assembly. Barrow argued hard in favour of the scheme; he is said to have made the shrewd point that if a "magnificent and stately" building seemed sure to surpass the Sheldonian ample contributions would come in from loyal Cambridge men.[39] But for financial and other reasons, and in some ways to the architectural advantage of Cambridge, the project was dropped. What happened, half a century later, when a mere third of Gibbs' three-sided Library-cum-Senate House court was actually built suggests that Wren was spared the galling frustration of a project less than half achieved. But he found his compensation, without asking for a fee, in a Cambridge building over whose commencement his friend Barrow had a more complete control.

The story goes that Barrow, enraged at the rejection of the Senate House-cum-Library scheme, went straight home to Trinity and there, that very afternoon, staked out the site for a college library which would be finer and more costly than the library element of the scheme which he had failed to get accepted. The anecdote smacks more of Bentley than of the milder Barrow. It seems, moreover, that Trinity College had for some time intended to replace the congested upstairs

library, with its straining floor, in the northern range of its Great
Court.

Shortage of library space, a problem not unknown to learned
societies, already pressed Trinity when in 1671 the death of its
devoted alumnus Bishop Hacket of Lichfield brought the matter to a
head. The bishop's benefactions, already manifest in the building of
the Bishop's Hostel, meant that the college would get large annual
additions to its stock of books. A separate library building was
essential, and Barrow may well, in the first year or two of his
mastership, have consulted Wren. Some months at least before his
Senate House designs were rejected Wren could have worked on his
plans for a circular library. He seems certain to have done so a
considerable time before January of 1676[40] when an appeal went out,
to Trinity men and other friends of Cambridge, for money to build a
new library, almost certainly the rectangular one of Wren's second,
and completed, designs; its fabric, adjoining the two lengthened wings
of Neville's Court, would turn it into a "fair quadrangle".

Wren's first version of a library at Trinity may go back to some year
before 1675.[41] It too was for the site at the riverward, or western end of
Neville's Court. Its square main bulk was to be linked to the
unlengthened ranges of the court by modest curved *esedrae* whose low
walls were to be capped by railings. Above the square, a dome was to
crown and light a fine circular interior space; had it been speedily
finished this would have been Wren's earliest completed dome. A
likeness to Palladio's original, high-domed design for the Villa
Rotonda near Vicenza was to be reinforced, on the library's eastern
side, by a pedimented Ionic portico. This attractive scheme,
anticipating what Oxonians later saw projected by Hawksmoor, and
built by Gibbs, was early abandoned. What Trinity actually got, with
its kinship to Sansovino's library at Venice, could be reckoned as a
finer version of the two lower stages of what Wren had designed for
the university's books. Its scheme, of a balustraded library block
seemingly raised on an arched loggia, was akin both to the cathedral
library at Lincoln and to what Wren had planned, at Cambridge, for
the site of the Old Schools.

The Trinity dons decided, on 22nd February of 1676, to build the
library; work started the next day.[42] The task was constructionally
daunting as well as being of great practical and aesthetic note.

The riverside site, though level, was soft and alluvial. It had,
moreover, been cut through by one of the many ditches and slow
watercourses which in Cambridge run on each side of the river. Wren
was faced, in this part of Trinity, with a considerable problem of
foundations which he solved with great skill. Above a lowermost bed
of riverine gravel he laid sleeper walls, along the length of his proposed
building, of local clunch. Above each of these sleeper walls a course of

brick supported a series of brick arches, inverted and running down to pointed bases.[43] These arches gave firm support to the piers which uphold the book-laden floor and the roof structure above them. The whole scheme of these complex supports is as much a work of high talent as are the Renaissance design and structural contrivance of the building above pavement level; there is, in fact, a complete and essential integration between the two.

The main structural interest in the actual library is that what seem, as one enters Neville's Court from the hall screens, to be rounded arches in its loggia are a sham, their blind tympana being filled with sculptured detail. including a fine central plaque of Ptolemy Philadelphus in the Library at Alexandria. The vertical piers, resting on the supports which come up, below ground level, between the inverted arches, are the building's main support. On the side of Neville's Court, looking in towards the rest of the college, they have attached to them a lower row of Roman Doric three-quarter columns, with similar Ionic features between the large round-headed windows with their mullioned and transomed subdivision. The library floor, upheld above the loggia's ceiling by angled timber supports of an ingenuity typical of Wren, lies not above the rounded tops of the blind arches seen in Neville's Court but just above the top level of the square headed openings from the court to the loggia. This side of the library, with its statues by Cibber, its sculpture, and its pronounced Palladian idiom, was at first the library's more important and more often-seen side. The river elevation, more familiar now when thousands throng the Backs in a way unforeseen in 1676, is much more severe, with a classical order (Roman Doric) confined to the three entrance ways, with their fine Baroque ironwork by the London smith William Partridge;[44] Wren made the point that such an elevation gave "grace enough for the views that way".[45] Between the windows there is no architectural ornament and a feeling of solidity is conveyed, at ground floor level, where a wall is pierced by square-headed, unglazed window spaces. It is on this more austere side that one best appreciates the creamy pink of the Ketton stone which here, as in the chapel of Emmanuel, was Wren's favoured exterior material in Cambridge.

Wren sent his drawings to Trinity with a full letter of explanation and instructions. The copy which survives is unsigned and, more inconveniently, undated, but late 1675 seems the most likely time for its writing.[46] Though the letter is long, the copy attached to the drawings in All Souls' is all in Wren's handwriting; however much of a building team he was now assembling, and whatever clerical staff he had as Surveyor General, he seems still, for his private commissions, to have lacked an amanuensis or a secretary. He had, moreover, now learnt many of the tricks and ways of the building trade. For he asked for the return of his drawings, well knowing that "in the handles of workmen they will soon be defaced". So the surviving drawings are clean and intact, and Grumbold and his assistants must have made working copies. The letter contains some pithy explanations. Wren starts with the point that "a building of that consideration you goe about deserves good care in the design and able workmen to performe it"; he adds that the open loggia, with its central pillars, was based on precedents in antiquity. He claims a French parallel for "the appearance of arches . . . fair and lofty" as the supports for the library floor. Rejecting a pedimented central section facing Neville's Court he explains, when confining his demand to four statues above the balustrade, that any other central emphasis would be "impertinent". But if the Trinity dons wished to save money they could confine three-quarter columns, with their bold projection, to four which would flank the three middle "arches". The effect would, however, be "best as designed", and as Trinity was a wealthy college, three-quarter columns in fact project all along both storeys of the library's eastern facade. Having designed the furniture, including the projecting book presses which were to have had plaster statues above their ends Wren told his clients that "there are Flemish artists that do them cheap".

As the ground had been broken for the library in February of 1676 the important foundations could have been well advanced, and perhaps complete, by the early autumn. So Wren's visit early in October could have been to inspect progress before much work started above ground level. The Trinity records make no mention of Wren's presence in the college; he would probably have stayed, as Barrow's private guest, in the master's lodge. He could also, while in Cambridge, have seen his completed chapel at Pembroke, and at Emmanuel he could have visited the chapel which, though structurally finished, still awaited its furnishings and was not consecrated till the following year.[47] But Wren could have personally discussed the fittings with the Cambridge joiner Cornelius Austin, in due course the maker of the library furnishings which Wren had designed for Trinity. Wren's visit to Cambridge could not have taken him long, for Hooke saw him, on 20th October, on the festive occasion of the architect's birthday. But Wren's journey to the university, whose colleges looked much as they did when Loggan's prints came out in another twelve years, would have come as a pleasant autumn interlude in his busy London life.

Wren never seems to have gone again to Cambridge, but London visits by Grumbold kept him in touch with progress at Trinity. The Cambridge mason, later an architect in his own right, was in London in 1676 and again, a few days after Barrow's unhappily premature death, in May of 1677; he could then have reported that the library's walls had reached three quarters of their ultimate height. Building progress was little interrupted and by 1680, in which year Grumbold went twice to London to see Sir Christopher, it was time to buy lead to cover the roof.[50]

Three

From the spring of 1677 Wren settled back into the domesticities of married life. We still know little of Lady Wren, and there are no Pepysian glimpses of their life together. Two more children swelled the number of Wren's family. Their daughter Jane was born in November of 1677 and baptised on the 13th.[51] She took her name from her mother and Sir Christopher, whose favourite child she was, may later have seen in the girl some continuance, sweet-natured and talented, of the second wife whom he was soon to lose. The second child was a long source of sadness to his father. William Wren was born on 16th June 1679 and christened, so John Evelyn tells us, on 17th June.*[52] Evelyn himself, an old friend of the father, was one of the godfathers, the other being Sir William Fermor of Easton Neston in Northamptonshire; the name which the boy got from him was also, conveniently, the one normal in Lady Wren's family of the Fitzwilliams. The godmother was the Viscountess Newport; her husband long held high Court office as Treasurer of the Household. We shall, however, see how "poor Billy's" life of sixty years belied an auspicious start.

At the end of 1677 Archbishop Sheldon died. His successor, unexpectedly as he had held no previous bishopric, was William Sancroft, Wren's old friend and patron at St Paul's; the occasion brought forth a letter of congratulation, warm in its terms though somewhat stilted in its language, from the Surveyor General.[53] He had, for a few days, been out of town, and had only just heard the news when, on the last day but one of the year, he wrote to the archbishop elect. He could not "defer to congratulate Our Church in general", and in particularly St Paul's that the King had made "soe wise and exact a choice for the service both of Them and Himself". He needed "expression for my zeale", heraldry for his superscription, and time to kiss his Grace's hands, but he presumed on his friend's clemency that he would accept his "most humble and most obliged servant's" sincere profession of duty. Next day, when Hooke called on him, Wren told him of the appointment, and that Stillingfleet was to succeed Sancroft in the St Paul's deanery. But Hooke, as he tartly records in his diary, did not favour the dean's elevation to the high post which he was to vacate in turbulence.[54]

*The baptismal registers of St Martin's in the Fields give the date as 18th.

Late in 1677, or very soon after the start of the new year, Wren must have been at work on drawings for one of the finest of his unexecuted works; its main defect would have been incongruity with mediaeval surroundings.

Wren's plans were for a magnificent domed rotunda, to be built in Windsor Castle as a mausoleum for the remains of Charles I. Its site was to be that of the large chapel which Henry VIII started, east of the main fabric of St George's, as a place of burial for Henry VI and for himself. But the scheme for such a chapel was dropped in favour of Westminster Abbey. The Perpendicular Gothic eastern chapel (now known as the Albert Memorial Chapel) was never finished, and in the seventeenth century it lay unused and forlorn. Charles I had thought of turning it into the royal burying place which it has, more recently, become. Charles II, with no feeling for the derelict building in the unfashionable Gothic style, now proposed to replace it by a new building which would nobly commemorate his father. On 30th January 1678, the anniversary of the fateful beheading in Whitehall, the Cavalier Parliament voted £70,000 for the "solemn and ceremonial" funeral which Juxon had been unable, in the circumstances of 1649, to conduct at Windsor, and to pay for a monument whose splendour would worthily honour the royal martyr.[55] Three days later Hooke and Wren discussed the matter, and a week later Wren showed Hooke his designs.[56] Wren's estimate for the building, with a monument within it, came to £43,663 2s.0d.; of this sum £8,200 was to be for the late king's actual memorial.[57]

Had it been built Wren's mausoleum at Windsor would have derived from the peak period of the Italian Renaissance. On a vaster scale, and with rusticated masonry to link the Corinthian order of its lower stage, it would have recalled Bramante's famous *tempietto* design.[58] Its dome, in a simpler version, would have recalled that of St Peter's. Inside, four shallow curved recesses would have led out of a square space, with light descending from the windows and lunettes of the dome. To make way for this mausoleum the early Tudor chapel would have disappeared, and though the new rotunda would have been girt by a shallow moat it would almost have touched the eastern end of the main chapel of St George. Such an incongruity between Gothic structure and Renaissance addition is not unknown; one has it, on a modest scale, in the polygonal Baroque chapel which the Maes family had only lately finished as an eastern feature of the great church of Ste Gudule in Brussels. But this chapel, though contrasting with the Gothic of an apsidal choir, is modest in size and does not dominate its setting. The Windsor mausoleum, more than a hundred feet high, would have been an overpowering accompaniment to the late-Gothic St George's. Its main inspiration seems clear – the great domed chapel for the Bourbon tombs which Mansart designed as an eastern addition to the Gothic abbey of St Denis, and whose drawings Wren may have seen in Paris.[59] The noble Corinthian interior of his Windsor tomb chapel would have enshrined a Baroque monument to Charles I. Grinling Gibbons made two draughts of "statuary design"; the surviving sketches give two versions, one for brass, the other for marble, for this most strikingly conceived of England's royal tombs. Allegorical figures, and the motif of apotheosis, are prominent in both versions of the memorial.

But history, perhaps fortunately for architectural good manners, decreed that this splendid building was never started; it was left, successively, to Hawksmoor and Gibbs to plan a monumental rotunda for Dr Ratcliffe's library at Oxford. The turbulent, panic-stricken months of the 'Popish Plot', the Covenanters' Rising in Scotland, and the tense crisis years of the Exclusion controversy meant that the Cavalier Parliament's £70,000 remained unspent. The sad comment on one of Wren's drawings expresses a royalist view. For though the scheme had been evolved (*excogitalum*) in 1678; it had not yet (*eheu conditionem temporum*) been put in hand.[60] Those bracketed Latin words, well loaded with political meaning, could explain the fate of some others among Wren's finest projects.

The affairs of the Royal Society, and discussions elsewhere on science and discovery, were still among Wren's main pre-occupations. Discoveries in the remoter parts of the world were also among his interests. When, in September of 1676, he heard that a new ambassador was soon to leave for Russia he suggested to Charles II that the envoy's attention should be drawn to the exploration of the north-eastern, or Siberian parts of the Tsar's domains.[61] In July 1679, the Hudson's Bay Company, with its interests elsewhere in the far north, was a topic talked over coffee by Wren and Hooke.[62] In taverns and coffee houses, and often during their walks in St James Park, their discussions ranged wide. Square ships, chariots, astronomy and theories about the moon, a new type of shorthand and Wilkins' old hobby horse of a universal language received their attention; so too did flying machines, pumps and cylinders, water condensing, and marble tools. They also discussed such inventions of Hooke's as a weather clock and his spring motion for watches.

Late in 1679 Hudson's Bay, on which Wren had earlier conversed with Hooke, became important in the architect's life. That year he started to buy stock in the Hudson's Bay Company,[63] and in November he was elected to the committee, remaining an active member for four years. He had no mean interest in the company's success, for by early 1683 he held £1,200 worth of its stock[64] and more than once, when cash was tight, he lent money (at good interest) to help pay the tradesmen's bills. The Governors, while Wren was on the committee, were Prince Rupert and, after his death, James, Duke of

York. Most of the rest, like Sir James Hayes who had been Prince Rupert's secretary and was normally Deputy Governor, were City business men. Wren joined them as an eminent figure with a wider experience of society, with many influential contacts, and with skill as a negotiator; one notes that when Hayes was away in the country it was Wren who normally chaired the committee meetings and who was, twice in 1680, named Acting Deputy Governor[65] of an organisation whose main concern was in hazardous northern navigation and the fur trade, chiefly in the beaver skins much in demand for fashionable beaver hats, in the wooded and watery fastnesses of the Canadian Far North.

On the last day of 1679, and in February of 1680 Wren and a colleague were asked to see Sir Robert Clayton,[66] a leading financier and then Lord Mayor, to seek a further loan to the company and to discuss the repayment of money he had already lent. For the rest of 1680, as chairman or otherwise, Wren was at many committee meetings, often at the "Golden Anchor" in Cornhill, later in a room rented in the house of one of the merchant members. These business journeys to the City could, of course, have been combined with the on-site supervision of new parish churches and St Paul's, while the 6s. 8d. which a committee-man got for each attendance would have met much of what Wren spent, on the relevant days, in taverns and coffee houses.* Negotiations with Clayton apart, discussions were what one might expect of such a committee; some of it must also have interested a man of such wide knowledge and curiosity as the Surveyor General who was also prominent in the Royal Society. We find, for instance, that in Wren's first Committee year, and at meetings which he attended, they dealt with such subjects as the sorting of elk hides and beaver pelts, the choice of hatchets and muskets for use in the sub-arctic wilds,[67] the hiring or building of the tiny ships thought large enough for the shallow estuaries of Hudson's Bay, and the use of moose skins for making snow shoes. One day in May, Hayes, Wren, and some others went down to Deptford to go on board the little *Prudent Mary* which was soon to sail for the Bay,[68] and which they insured (wisely, as she was soon lost) for £6,000; between them they gave the crew £2 in tips. On a more solemn note Sir Christopher, probably the best educated of the committeemen, was asked to "overlook and correct" the form of the oath of fidelity to be taken by the company's employees.[69]

Shortly before the end of 1675 Wren spoke to Hooke about what he called "the grand design".[70] On New Year's Eve, which Hooke spent with Wren and Holder, there was the beginning of a new 'club' for "natural philosophers" (i.e. scientists) and "mechanics". The next

---

*Wren attended 49 committees in 1679–80, and 31 in 1680–81.

day, at Wren's house, the New Philosophical Clubb was formally started.[71] Those present decided not to talk of anything revealed *sub sigillo* at the meetings of what seems to have been a more specialist group within the diffused, and in some cases amateur, membership of the Royal Society. Though its members must also have been Fellows of the Royal Society the 'club' was clearly for serious, skilled experimentalists. They first discussed light; on 5th February, with many other gatherings to follow, they covered the more mundane topic of cures for toothache.[72]

So prominent had Wren been, from its commencement in 1660 and from back in the days of Gresham College, and the Oxford gatherings, in the Royal Society's affairs that his rise to high office could readily be presumed. Late in 1677 he had his first chance of its Presidency.[73] Many Fellows then felt that the time was ripe for a successor to Lord Brouncker who had, from its inauguration, been the society's President. Discussion, lobbying, and perhaps some in-fighting and intrigue followed. Some fellows, Hooke among them, were for Wren as Brouncker's successor. On 10th October Hooke discussed the matter with Sir Christopher; next day he noted that "all things seemed to go well" for Wren to take over. But as November drew on towards the anniversary election on St Andrew's day opinion swung towards the less charismatic, but politically more influential Sir Joseph Williamson; as Secretary of State he may have seemed a valuable friend at Court. So on 14th November some fellows met at Williamson's house.[74] Wren and Holder his brother-in-law were there; so too were Hooke, John Aubrey, Evelyn, and others. They were "nobly treated" and "very kindly welcome". By the time they left all present favoured the Presidency of the Secretary of State. The top post disposed of, Hooke had his own ambitions and hoped for the Secretaryship left empty by the recent death of Henry Oldenburg. Next day he mentioned the matter to Wren and Holder,[75] hoping that they would put in a favourable word with Williamson. But Wren, not wholly surprisingly when one recalls the somewhat warped personality of a man he knew really well, objected against him. In the upshot, the Secretaryship was shared between Hooke and Dr Nehemiah Grew. Predictably enough, Wren stayed on the society's council; a few days later Williamson nominated him a Vice-President.[76]

As a very active Vice-President Wren soon made up for his failure to get the society's highest post. Thomas Birch's detailed history of the Royal Society's early years records Wren's attendance at council meetings, his chairmanship of those meetings from 1677 to 1680, and something of what he said in the wide range of the Fellows' discussions. He was at many council meetings; occasionally, with Wren himself in the chair, these occurred in the cosy privacy of his house.[78] The Secretary of State being a busy man Wren chaired several successive autumn meetings in 1679; at one it was agreed that he should "perfect" his draft of what was probably a tart letter of reminder to members behindhand in their subscriptions.[79] Some points he made harked back to his days of anatomical experiment. Late in 1677 he told how, nearly twenty years back, he had found eels to be viviparous, while a little later he explained to his colleagues how he had once taken a perfectly shaped lobster from its parent's egg.[80] In 1678 he recounted his dissection of an otter's heart. Dissection, particularly of "exotic animals", being of interest to the society's medical members Wren and Thomas Henshaw undertook, in 1680, to use their interest with the keeper of the menagerie in St James's Park to procure the bodies of any such creatures as died under his care.[81] A few days later a meeting which Wren chaired heard of the birth, at Isle Brewers deep in the Somerset countryside, of the Siamese twins (named Agnilla and Priscilla) whose birth was seen, by Andrew Paschall the staunchly royalist rector of Chedzoy, as a portent of political trouble from Monmouth and his supporters.[82] Early in 1681 they heard, from Paschall himself, of an earthquake at Chedzoy and elsewhere in the county; the news gave rise to a discourse by Wren on the causes of earthquakes.[83] Other subjects coming up when Wren was in the chair, or discussed by Wren himself, included the causes of springs, the gravity of air, the composition of Chinese ink, and cures for wasp stings. Earlier, at the end of 1677, Wren had suggested Bermuda, with its temperate climate and isolation from other land, as a good place for barometric tests. But Sir Jonas Moore pointed out that similar observations (by the young Edmund Halley) were already in hand at St Helena.[84]

The last years of the 1670s also found the society, and Wren in particular, much concerned with an old topic which ended in their literally clearing the ground for one of Wren's most important new buildings. Chelsea College had never been fitted up as a headquarters for the society. Nor had it been let to any tenant. The society's meetings continued, more centrally for many of those concerned, at Gresham College in the City. At Chelsea, decay and dereliction reigned; by the spring of 1678 the real problem was that of an alternative use for a largely agricultural site. On 4th May a council, at which Wren presided, agreed that the property should be surveyed, and that Hooke should negotiate with a possible tenant.[85] A few days later Hooke recorded a scheme which Dr Holder liked, but of which Wren his brother-in-law disapproved.[86] On 30th another council chaired by Wren set up a sub-committee on the college's disposal;[87] in another fortnight we hear of the building's demolition being taken in hand. In the next two years the council mulled over various projects for the building development of the site, or for its agricultural lease.

Hooke tells, in the autumn of 1679, of himself and Wren seeing a "module" or ground plan of the site.[88] By late in 1680 it was still on the society's hands. But a scheme, of whose nature, and of whose preliminary discussion, Wren may already have been aware, was soon to come up which decided both the fate of the college site and Wren's concern with the new buildings which duly filled it.

In 1678 the Royal Society, and Wren as one of its most prominent members, became concerned with a project of geographical note. In the spring of that year Moses Pitt, a London bookseller and publisher,[89] explained to the Society a scheme whereby England could vie with Dutch progress in the publication of maps and atlases. He planned to bring out a splendid atlas, with some 900 printed pages, and 600 maps or engravings, and covering the whole known world as no English atlas had done before. He asked the Royal Society for its help; Wren, Hooke, Sir John Lowther and a few others were made a committee to consider the matter and report back.[90] A few weeks later the State Papers, coming from the office of Williamson who was both President of the Royal Society and Principal Secretary of State and who, like the King, Prince Rupert, and the Duke of York, allowed Pitt to use some of his maps, refer to the scheme.[91] Pitt's object, with the help and advice of Wren and his colleagues, was to publish his atlas in eleven volumes, each to cost £2 to those who were asked to subscribe; in the middle of November Hooke showed Wren what seemed to be suitable paper for the printing of Pitt's monumental work.[92] In another two months, when he, Wren, Pitt himself, and some other friends were supping with Williamson, the Atlas, along with the 'Popish plot' and Popery in general, were among the topics of their talk.[93] It was not till January of 1680 that the Royal Society again discussed the matter. Pitt was asked to meet members of the Council, presumably including Wren, to take account of the scheme's progress.[94] It was, in fact, in 1680 that Pitt issued the first of the five fine volumes which actually came out.[95] He dedicated it to Charles II, also printing a promise, made in May of 1678 by Wren, Hooke, Isaac Vossius, and three others that they "not doubting that this work will be of great use and for the honour of the Nation" would "from time to time, at spare hours" advise Pitt, reporting his progress to Williamson or whoever might at any given moment, be the Royal Society's President. Wren himself was to hold that office for some of the relevant time; what is less certain is how many "spare hours" he could actually devote to a scheme which alike embraced his astronomical interests and his wider scientific concern. Along with Hooke (who mentions various meetings with Pitt) and Evelyn he naturally featured in the long list of subscribers to a work which none the less failed to profit its initiator.

In November of 1680 the members of the Royal Society held their annual elections; a main item of business was the choice of a new President to replace Williamson.[96] They chose Robert Boyle, "that excellent person and great philosopher" as Evelyn, who thought that Boyle should have been the post's first holder, enthusiastically called him.[97] But a few days later Boyle wrote declining the honour. Early in 1680, on 12th January, Wren was elected in Boyle's stead, and so started his two years' spell of office.

The year 1680, in which Wren stowed the first of Pitt's Atlas volumes in his well stacked shelves, also saw another crisis in his life at home. We still have few glimpses of his family circle, or how Lady Wren coped, as many mother had to do in those days, with a young stepchild as well as two children of her own. In September, 1680, as Hooke relates, she recovered from some illness.[98] But her respite was pitifully short, for on 4th October (a Monday) she died, being buried in another two days at St Martin's in the Fields.[99] Wren passed again, and lastingly, into the sorrow of marital bereavement. We know nothing on what he arranged for nurses or others to tend his young family. His more public concerns must claim our attention. Among them, for the past five years and for the rest of Charles II's reign in a peak period of building and furnishing activity, was that of increasing work on the renewal of the City churches.

9

The Ending of a Reign

One

Wren's concern with new churches in the City reached its climax in the ten years between 1675 and the year of Charles II's death. After 1685 there were few new commencements, while only on the uppermost, most ornate stages of some steeples did much have to be done in the last decades of Wren's own life. What remains to some extent uncertain is the full degree of Wren's personal credit for the main fabrics and the varied furnishings of the buildings whose steeples, along with the dome and bell towers of St Paul's, were long, unchallenged, to glorify the City's skyline.

The last ten years of Charles II's life found Wren immersed in the varied duties of his surveyorship. He was increasingly committed to the building of a new St Paul's, while other commissions, Chelsea Hospital and work at Oxford and Cambridge being among them, claimed his concern if not, in all cases, his personal presence. He was an active member of the Royal Society, and for two busy years its conscientious president. It would have been an astonishing, though not perhaps an impossible feat for Wren to have given his personal care to every detail of the main design of each London church for whose authorship he is credited. But the way in which rebuilding was done could have enabled others, especially Robert Hooke, to have a hand in the design, the building control, and the financial supervision of the new City churches. When, moreover, in 1679 Dr Busby planned to build a new church on his country estate at Willen in northern Buckinghamshire it was to Hooke, like Wren his old pupil at Westminster School, that he turned for designs which are, when one allows for a rural, free-standing site, very much in the manner one associates with Wren.[1]

Hooke's diary amply proves his deep involvement, along with Wren, in this matter of the City churches. Numerous entries made from 1670 to 1675 make the point clear; for the next five years the record is no less eloquent.

Early in 1676 Hooke was at St Mary Aldermary over the demolition of the fire-shattered mediaeval church, while on 29th February of that leap year he was with Wren on the important site of St Mary le Bow. On 11th April he met Wren, who must again have been visiting Bow church, in Cheapside; they strolled together, close by Guidhall, to St Lawrence Jewry; Hooke noted that in his church he himself designed the new seats.

Other meetings between Hooke and Wren involved discussions with craftsmen and contractors. Late in April Hooke dined with Wren, another guest being Joshua Marshall, the mason not only for some work on St Paul's but also for the new tower of St Bride's and for activity on other churches.[2] In a few days Hooke, with Wren, John Scarborough who was a senior clerk in the office set up to deal with the City churches, and John Fitch another London mason made agreements over the new fabric of St Michael Bassishaw;[3] James Floory was another mason employed on the same building. To judge by Hooke's numerous references to site visits this seems to have been a relatively troublesome job, but early in 1677 Fitch was commissioned to build SS. Anne and Agnes, Gracechurch Street. September 19th was a busy church day for Wren and Hooke, for they looked in on St Nicholas Cole Abbey, St Magnus' near London Bridge, and St Benet Fink whose elongated decagon, with an oval dome upheld by six pillars, was another of Wren's finer ventures in auditory planning; *Parentalia* speaks of "a fine piece of architecture" and of "a very commodious form for the auditory".[4]

The passing of the bills sent in by the masons, joiners, and other craftsmen was another of Wren and Hooke's joint tasks. In December 1676, they met at Wren's house, and approved some bills for St Magnus'.[5] In August of the same year they had passed Marshall's bill for St Stephen's, Coleman Street.

Other days, as 1677 wore on, were well filled with site visits. On 26th June, after a start at St Paul's, Hooke and Wren went on to Coleman Street, to St James's Garlickhythe, and not far away to St Michael Queenhythe, while on 5th May they had busily visited Bow church, St Olave's Old Jewry, St Benet's Gracechurch Street, All Hallows Bread Street, and Garlickhythe. As Hooke adds "etc., etc." to the list, those five churches seem not to have completed a busy round. These supervisions, and the paper work that went with them, had their social side. For on 26th July, 1677, having, on the previous day, seen the church wardens and vestrymen of St Stephen's, Walbrook on the subject of a new porch, Wren, Hooke, and others dined at the Swan in Fish Street with the officials of that wealthy parish.

The year 1678 was no less busy, for the passing of workmen's bills, for the discussion of such vexed topics as St Michael's Bassishaw, and visits to sites. In the spring of 1680, having gone by water to Wren's house, Hooke advised on problems to do with the new church of St Clement Danes,[6] not in this case a matter of making good a loss in the fire, but the replacement by Wren (who charged no fees) of a decayed mediaeval church. From 1681 onwards Hooke's journal is sparse and sketchy; were it still as full as the record of 1672-80 it would probably be illuminating on a complex subject which both he and Wren must have found a major preoccupation.

Designs apart, the years 1675–85 were a time when rectangular or simply domed parish church plans went simultaneously with some others less conventional in their spatial effects. At St Mary Abchurch and Christ Church, Newgate Street, one had churches built smaller than the sites originally allowed. One also has the impact of these numerous churches on the busy lives of Hooke and Wren, and evidence on the way in which the task of rebuilding was carried out.

The first step in the replacement of the City churches due for rebuilding had been the clearance of rubble and the putting aside for re-use, where its condition allowed, of stonework from the gutted buildings. Some mediaeval walling could be worked into a few of the new fabrics, and though many ruined towers had wholly to be dismantled there were others whose lower stages could bear newer work. This was specially true at St Michael's, Cornhill, while St Christopher le Stocks and St Peter's, Cornhill were other churches whose destruction had been less than total. St Mary Woolnoth was a repair job rather a complete rebuild; its total replacement, though started in Wren's lifetime, was achieved by the colleague and pupil who came to be at least as great an architect as Wren. There were also St Andrew's Holborn and St Clement's, undamaged by the fire but replaced by Wren during his great burst of churchbuilding. Both of them, more notably St Andrew's with late mediaeval windows which can still be seen, kept much of the structure of their ancient towers.

Though Portland stone, and occasionally brick, were Wren's favoured materials for his church exteriors Kentish rag and Reigate stone were also used, in St Peter's Cornhill for instance, for repair work on the inner cores of walls.[7] Rubble from Old St Paul's also came in useful, presumably for foundations or the cores of walls; many payments were made, for loads of it to be used in St Olave's Old Jewry and other churches, to John Tillison the cathedral's clerk of works.[8] An initial measure had been the building of temporary 'tabernacles' so that worship could continue. New houses, and rehoused inhabitants had, one recalls, come earlier than the bigger task of the replacement of some fifty churches. Wren had a responsibility for these buildings, plain and simply furnished, as well as for the permanent churches, and he passed money to the Commissioners to pay the modest sums involved. At St Martin's Vintry, for example, the bricklayer, carpenter, glazier, and other workmen got £183 14s.2d.[9]* while £210 19s.5d. was laid out on the

---

*This particular burnt church was never, in fact, replaced.

tabernacle which preceded the permanent All Hallows' Bread Street.[10]

Most of the money spent on the City churches came from the coal tax. But Wren and his colleagues found that useful sums were given by private subscribers. Some of the cost of St Mary le Bow came that way, and at St Mary Aldermary, before ever the coal tax yielded any funds, a private benefactor left money for a new church, and for the repair of the lower stages of a damaged mediaeval tower; he insisted that the church should, like St Alban's, Wood Street, reappear as a mainly Gothic fabric.

A special office had to be set up to administer the great work of rebuilding the City churches. Papers throw light both on the more regular, humdrum aspects of that office's working, and on a few more personal transactions in which one can sense the preferences and personality of Wren.

The office needed its equipment of stationery, also an occasional book for professional reference. Samuel Wells, a City stationer, had payments, from time to time, for drawing paper, parchment, pencils, pens, albums, an iron chest and other fixtures; similar payments also went to Andrew Phillips. On one occasion Phillips also sold Wren's office a book on Vitruvius, also a Statute Book;[11] it was also through Phillips that Wren and his colleagues arranged such things as coach hire, "waterage", and the supply of office furniture.[12] Modern "Securicor" methods were anticipated when, at some unknown date, 7s. 6d. was spent on a bag and a hired coach to bring back from Guildhall some money in specie.[13] Thomas Lane got money for copying drawings and designs, while Thomas Heisenbuttel, a carver presumably of German origin, got £5 15s.0d. for his model of a "spire or tower" for Christ Church, Newgate Street.[14] John Scarborough, the chief clerk, got allowances for office expenses, including letters by penny post. Nicholas Hawksmoor, in the office from 1679 as a clerk and in time, despite his modesty, its chief personality after Wren, got £9, for a twelvemonth ending in September, 1687, for finding paper, ink, copying books and other items, while he later got £10 "in part" for transcribing and engrossing the book, needed so that the Exchequer could get a consolidated account, which contained the parishes' bills and work records.[15] Later still, for a period ending in the middle of 1693, Hawksmoor got £35 for "extraordinary pains" in extracting and engrossing yet more accounts.[16] This date did not, of course, wholly end the story of the City churches' steady replacement. For not all of the steeples had by then been finished; the top stages of some of Wren's towers awaited a completion considerably later than that of their main fabrics.

The replacement of the City churches also presented some personal problems. As the buildings had not, as Wren had hoped, been started on island sites dangers came from the nearness of other buildings pressing closely upon them; these could arise not only from new work but from the demolition of wrecked mediaeval churches. Some tiles on a roof were smashed by the fall of stones coming down from the old tower of St Martin's, Ludgate, while the demolition of the same tower caused damage to an adjacent shed which involved £2 compensation to John Fisher.[17] Building work on the close-girt St Mildred's, Bread Street, more than once damaged a house which literally touched the church; on one of these occasions £2 5s.7d. was spent on necessary repairs.[18] Injuries to workmen were another item of compassionate expense. Thomas Hudson, a labourer, got £1 for some hurt received, on 4th May 1672, at St Mary le Bow. In September,1674, when working on the same church, he broke a leg; "he being a poor man" Wren personally ordered the payment of another £1 for what seems to have been a result of Hudson's carelessness and not a contractor's liability.[19] The seamier, all too familiar side of building came when lead was stolen from the works on St Swithin's, Cannon Street. Somewhat surprisingly the lead was recovered, and the parish beadle got £1 10s.0d. "for apprehending the felons".[20] Wren himself, for his work as Chief Surveyor of the City churches, got the modest annual salary of £100. But he deservedly reclaimed his carefully recorded expenses. About 1693 the sum of £67 13s.7¼d. went to him and his assistants. It covered the entire period up to that time, and was for coach hire, "waterage", and other sums "by them disbursed and craved" for that long period.[21]

The planning problems of the City churches, and the detailed aesthetics of their design, have been much studied and discussed; full appreciation is somewhat confused now that it is realised that the designing of these churches was not the work of the single man Wren, but that others were also involved. A few more churches departed from the rectangular basilican plans which had presumably been those of their mediaeval precursors. False transepts in the ceiling plans at St James's, Garlickhythe and, initially, at St Magnus's gave cruciform illusions, though less daringly so than in Wren's great achievement at Walbrook. Elliptical plans, like the one pioneered at St Benet Fink, remained exceptional, though St Antholin's, whose spire was specially delicate and brilliant, had an elongated octagon contrived inside mainly rectangular walls. The finely domed, unimpeded interiors of St Mary Abchurch and St Mildred's Bread Street were of the late 1670s or the following decade, while a single aisle, perhaps following what had stood before 1666, was all that the site allowed for the specially charming church, of brick and stone in a Dutch vein, of St Benet, Paul's Wharf.

But the two-aisled basilican plan remains, presumably at the insistence of many City parishioners, a favoured design; what Wren and his colleagues did, with galleried naves, minimal sanctuaries, and high, canopied pulpits was to rationalize the plan for the worshipping (and mainly preaching) needs of Restoration Anglicanism. So some of Wren's leading City churches, among them St Bride's, St Andrew's Holborn, St Andrew-by-the-Wardrobe, and Christ Church were on this plan, while in two churches where no post-Fire rebuilding was involved the aisled and galleried plan appeared on important island sites. Wren used it, from 1680, at St Clement Danes; the precedent was followed, late in Wren's lifetime and not, perhaps, without his knowledge and encouragement, at St Martin's in the Fields. At St Clement's the new chancel was apsidal and interestingly linked to the galleried nave by two curved walls. Curvature, with a nice touch of design unknown in the City churches, was also planned in an attractively domed southern porch. Further West the wholly new church of St James was built, on land he had developed as a smart suburb, by Wren's old friend from Paris days, Henry Jermyn, Earl of St Albans. Though the church is now considered to be in Piccadilly its original main entrance was through an elaborate Ionic doorway, in the middle of the nave's southern wall and looking, across the street to which the landlord gave his name, down York Street to St James's Square. Unlike Wren's City churches the new building became a feature in an achievement of planned urbanism. Basilican, barrel-vaulted, and galleried, with a shallow recess for its Communion table and some fine plasterwork in its ceiling panels, the building was akin to such City churches as St Andrew-by-the-Wardrobe whose commencement was a little later than St James's building date of 1682–84. Wren seems to have thought highly of a church whose location at once made it fashionable; despite domed or polygonal spatial experiments he himself considered this lofty, spacious interior his best solution for contemporary problems of Anglican worship.[22] Evelyn reckoned that the church, which he visited late in 1684, was "elegantly indeed built", and much admired the altar and Grinling Gibbons' carving near it.[23]

The book on Vitruvius bought for use in the City churches office suggests that Roman and Palladian precedents were often in the minds of Wren and his colleague, while for interior decoration they sometimes drew on Flemish Baroque. Design touches of a Baroque character are best found in the fanciful terminal of some of Wren's steeples; one notes, not without significance for the later phases of Wren's career, that a few of them were put up considerably later than the main fabrics of their churches.

Wren's ecclesiastical projects outside the City did not end with St Clement's and the new church off Jermyn Street. In 1679 there was a project, some decades ahead of its realisation by Hawksmoor, for an Ionic church in the Bloomsbury area whose development was about to get under way.

A decorative achievement, carried out in 1682–83, must have had its sentimental appeal for the twice widowed architect. The Temple Church had, in 1669, been the scene of his first marriage. Now in the 1680s the benchers asked him to survey their historic building.[24] Wren reported that it was "ruinous"; the adjective may have applied less to its fabric than to the state of its furnishings. Wren reckoned that £1,300 would be needed for repaving the church, and for the installation of new pews and panelling, a screen, a pulpit, and an altarpiece. All these were duly provided, Wren passed the bills, and all was done by early February in 1683. The handsome altarpiece, with its segmental pediment, and a fluted Corinthian supporting order, is now back in the Temple after its sojourn in a North-country museum.

To achieve so great a feat of church building, carried out when many other structures, including public buildings and the halls of livery Companies, were going up in the City, Wren and his colleagues had to draw heavily on the varied craftsmen available in London, and having secured their services to weld them into a working team; their co-operation was something for which Wren himself could claim much credit.

The main structures of the churches, in stone or brick, were spread among several contractors.[25] Some, like the mason George Turley who did some of the work at St Dionis's, and the well known Jasper Latham who mainly built St Mildred Poultry, were only lightly employed. Edward Strong (the son of Thomas Strong who worked on St Paul's), Joshua Marshall before his death, Samuel Fulkes, and John Thompson were all important contractors on City churches; so too were Christopher Kempster and Thomas Wise who were also much concerned with St Paul's. External carving, as well as basic structure, also came within their scope.

The carpentry of roofs, floors and other woodwork was also widely spread. John Longland, wholly or in part responsible for the heavy woodwork of Christ Church, St Bride's, St Lawrence Jewry, St Stephen Walbrook, and nine other churches, was the chief contractor. Robert Day and Israel Knowles who worked on St Augustine's hard by the East end of St Paul's, on St Andrew-by-the-Wardrobe and five other churches, were also important; so too were Thomas Woodstock and Matthew Banks. Henry Blowes did carpentry in St Benet Fink, St Martin Ludgate, and two other buildings. Some other carpenters only worked on one or two churches, or shared with a colleague the woodwork of a single church. Jonathan Willcox was on his own on St Vedast's not far north of St Paul's.

For joinery the distribution of contracts was wholly different. Though several craftsmen were involved, a few of them on one church only and with Roger Davis responsible for the important St Stephen's, Walbrook, William Cleer was overwhelmingly predominant. In whole or in part he provided the joinery for thirty churches, while for the two commissions of All Hallows Lombard Street and St Andrew-by-the-Wardrobe payments went to his widow who must have continued to run a substantial concern.

The plasterwork of walls and ceilings, and ornamental plaster in the classical taste or with Baroque touches, was another sphere in which one concern was easily the leading contractor. Though John or Thomas Sherwood worked, alone or with other craftsmen, on some half a dozen churches, and though Thomas Mead had the important contract for St Lawrence Jewry, the vast bulk of the work went to the partners Henry Doogood and John Grove. They often worked in collaboration, but on some churches, as when Doogood had the contract for St Antholin's or when Grove by himself was the plasterer for St Benet Fink and St Bride's, one or the other of the partners is named alone. John Grove's son, named after his father, also worked on some of the partnership's numerous London jobs. Painting work was another aspect of the churches' embellishment in which two men enjoyed a massive predominance. Edward Bird, with others or purely on his own account, was employed on many of the buildings, while Robert Streeter, the King's Sergeant Painter who had painted the ceiling of the Sheldonian, did much of the work before he died in 1680.

Two

I have shown how Wren became President of the Royal Society early in 1681. His term of office was a busy period not only for the society's routine concerns but for the frustrating management, and eventual sale of Chelsea College. The active tenure of such a post, filling much of the time left over from his architectural work, could, for the Surveyor General as he neared and passed his fiftieth birthday, have been some solace in his second, and lasting spell of a widower's life. He had, however, his personal friendships, some of them closely bound up with his activity as a leading member of the society. John Evelyn was still among his closest confidants; of special interest is Evelyn's note of the time, on 5th May 1681, when Wren, and Sir William Fermor who had stood godfather to the young William Wren, came to dine with him. The conversation, on what must have been a relaxed, agreeable occasion, sparked off his remark that "a wonderful genius had this incomparable person".[26]

Wren's presidency of the Royal Society was anything but a sinecure. He chaired twentyseven of the twentynine Council meetings held during his spell of office. He was also present, as chairman, at many of the meetings held on council days or on separate occasions; only occasionally was he absent (as on one occasion when Evelyn deputised for him), while from one gathering he was called away on urgent business. The subjects covered were richly varied, occasionally coming close to Wren's particular interests, though never including architecture. Early in 1681 Wren mentioned a scheme, got out by a Middle Temple barrister named John Adams, for a new survey of the whole of England. Wren, Hooke, and Flamsteed the Astronomer Royal, had already advised him, and Isaac Newton had promised help.[27] In May Adams presented detailed proposals which led him to four years' journeying up and down the country and to the later publication of a revised map, six feet square, of the entire country.[28] A little later in the same year Wren, still actively interested in astronomy, took part in two discussions on comets. On 27th April Wren told his colleagues how he often noticed the luminosity of fresh prawns,[29] while late in June, when the assembled savants viewed the prodigiously spread horns of what must have been an Irish elk Wren thought that they came from a "moose deer" and went on, with his good knowledge of the activities of the Hudson's Bay Company, to tell his friends of the feeding habits of moose.[30] He took part in a discussion on beavers, speaking of their "strange sagacity" in felling trees and building dams, and he gave a good account of the Eskimos met in Hudson's Bay. Wren went on, in what must have been an entertaining evening, to observe "that all wholesome food should have oils". On 7th June 1682, the discussion was on the well worn, baffling topic of pendulum clocks and longitude, while in October Hooke read a paper on comets.

The meetings of the council dealt with all aspects of the society's business. In March of 1681 those present had to consider the society's printing arrangements, Robert Chiswell being chosen, in the following month, as the society's printer; this was at one of the few council meetings not chaired by Wren. Early in May the society's finances were discussed, while on 16th November, at a meeting at which the council decided to spend £10 a year on books, Wren himself promised to give £5 for works on geometry.[31] But the two most frequently recurring topics of Wren's spell of office were those of members in arrears with their subscriptions, and of the disposal of the property, now a burden rather than a boon to the society, of Chelsea College.

From early in the Royal Society's history its membership, easy to obtain at that time, had been divided between those with a deep, and often professional interest in the subjects within the society's scope, and members, many of them men of rank or high position, whose interest was more nearly that of keen amateurs of a subject holding an increasing, fashionable appeal. So it was always likely that there would be variations both in steady enthusiasm and in the regular payment of subscriptions.

At a council meeting held in January, 1682, the Treasurer read a list, perhaps of some length, of members who were in arrears or did not pay at all.[32] The council decided that he, the two secretaries, Sir John Hoskyns the Vice President, and Wren should meet, every Monday evening at Wren's house, to consider the arrears and devise means for their recovery. Gatherings on this delicate topic were duly held, and in March of the same year the President reported that some defaulters would pay up, without continuing their membership; other cases remained under discussion.[33] On 10th May, when it transpired that some of the backsliders who were, or had been, on the society's council were "more intimately concerned" in its work the council decided that these members should be asked to give a good example by paying what was due.[34] In the end, a new rule was made about council members in financial arrears, while twentythree obstinate defaulters, one hopes a small proportion of those considered in the privacy of Wren's house, were expelled from the society.[35]

Despite many calls on his time Wren now served both as President of the Royal Society and as an active member of the Hudson's Bay Committee. In the latter connection he was still assiduous, with thirtyfive attendances in the year 1681–82. Some matters came up, in 1681 and 1682, important for the company's well-being and in a minor way relevant to Wren's architectural and building interests.

Twice in 1681, while Sir James Hayes was out of London, Wren again acted as Deputy Governor.[36] He was at many sessions of the committee; at one, which he chaired, there was a report on a special warehouse hired, for storing beaver skins impaired by sea water, so that the smell of the sodden pelts should not lessen the saleable value of those which were sound.[37] Then, as at other times, some of the Company's more important out letters – commissions and instructions for ships' captains and the governors of trading stations – were jointly signed by Wren along with others. Late in 1681 they had to prepare, with copious supplies of sack and claret for the fur dealers, for the sale of furs come in from the Bay,[38] while the buying of such items as Stroudwater red cloth (for bartering with the Eskimos) and snow-goggles came up at meetings when Wren was present. His knowledge of buildings came in useful when, early in 1682, Hayes, Wren, and two others inspected, and reported favourably on, the Scriveners' Hall which was soon rented as the Company's normal place of business.[39] In September of the same year, when a warehouse for over 18,000 beaver skins had to be inspected, such shutters, bolts, and locks as Wren should "judge fitt", were to be made to secure these valuable goods.[40] Earlier in the year instructions had gone out, over the names of Wren and others, to John Bridgar who had been chosen as the Governor of a new trading post which the Company was to set up at Port Nelson on the western side of the Bay. Other matters apart, Bridgar was to choose a good site for a fort and for a combined dwelling house and warehouse. He was, so the letter told him, to do it according to a "model" (presumably a ground plan with sketches) already sent him; one can imagine that Wren may have cast an expert eye on the plans for these log buildings with their glazed windows.[41] He was soon, moreover, involved, as a committeeman and as acting chairman, in a serious turn in the company's affairs. For in June of 1682 news came that a one-time member of the committee, who had earlier been expelled, intended to sail to Hudson's Bay as an intruder into the company's preserves. Despite the time of year they at once decided to send a ketch into the Bay to compete with their adversary. But on 12th July, at a meeting which Wren chaired, the hasty project got "long and serious debate".[42] The members present, perhaps with their knowledge of the voyage aided by Wren's scientific and meteorological learning, reckoned that a suitable time was "allready relapsed". They insisted on a short delay; Wren himself was to convey their resolution to the Deputy Governor. But the buying and equipment of the *James* was eventually allowed to go ahead; the little ship was, however, tragically lost on her way out to the Bay.

The affair of Chelsea College was a still greater preoccupation; for Wren it led, by contrast, to one of his happier commissions.

For most of 1681 the society's discussions on Chelsea still assumed its continued ownership of the property. The councillors considered whether they could pull down any of the surviving structure, and in April they discussed, and referred to a committee of Wren and others, a proposal by one Thomas Hutton, to rent the property and build paper works on a part of the site.[43] Nothing came of that project, but they still had discussions on a dispute with Lord Cheyne the neighbouring landlord, and on whether they should buy all or part of the land between the college and the river. But other, more decisive ideas soon circulated. For on 5th October Wren disclosed some crucial discussions he had had, over the property's future, with Sir Stephen Fox.[44]

Like Wren a Wiltshireman by birth, and of humbler origin than Sir Christopher, Stephen Fox kept his deep ties with his native county, and his family have remained prominent in the west of England. Farley near Salisbury was his native place, and it was there, in 1681–82, that he built the almshouse row, with the Wardenry as its central house, whose design is less plausibly by Wren than that of the church across the road. Fox himself, devotedly royalist and an exile in the Stuart cause, was of special service, in the crucial matter of money, to the Court in exile. After holding various official posts he was promoted to the important, inevitably lucrative position of Paymaster General to the Forces. His official post brought him naturally into the Court and official circles in which Wren moved; he was, in any case, the kind of man one naturally found among Wren's patrons and confidants.

As a high official in the Army's administration Fox, like others,

would have known of the distress caused, even when the standing
Army was small, by maimed, disabled, and broken down soldiers. On
a much larger scale the same problem existed in France, where in
1670 Louis XIV had founded the Hôtel Royal des Invalides. The
Duke of Monmouth, more competent as a soldier and military
administrator than he was as a political figure, twice visited Les
Invalides, and told his father what he had seen. As an institution, Les
Invalides was as important an influence on the foundation of Chelsea
Hospital as its dome was, for Wren, in the eventual design of the
dominant feature of St Paul's. It was, however, in Dublin, at
Kilmainham Hospital, started in 1680 for disabled Irish soldiers, that
the idea of some such retreat as Les Invalides first took root. But it was
late in the summer of 1681, well before Sir William Robinson's
buildings at Kilmainham were complete, that Charles II, in close
collaboration with Fox, took steps that led to the building of the Royal
Hospital at Chelsea.

   The first active discussions occurred early in September of 1681
when Charles II asked Fox to arrange for the building of an English
veterans' hostel on the lines of Kilmainham.[45] On 11th September Fox
asked Evelyn for his help over the purchase, not far from his own
home, of the Royal Society's Chelsea property.[46] Evelyn soon told his
friend Wren of what was afoot, and the three of them must soon have
met to discuss a possible sale. For on 5th October, as we have seen,
Wren took the council of the Royal Society into his confidence.[47] He
told them of the "treaty" on Chelsea which he had lately had with Sir
Stephen. He and Evelyn were empowered to negotiate with Fox on the
sale, not only of the semi-ruinous college buildings but of the "whole
concerns" of the society's Chelsea property. The price was to be
£1,500, or at all events not less than £1,400; the council was to be told
if Wren and Evelyn could not get Fox's agreement to the lesser sum.
Hard bargaining seems to have followed, with ready money a strong
inducement to Wren and Evelyn not to stick out for too high a price.
For on 11th January 1682 Wren told his colleagues that he had sold
the college and its land to Sir Stephen Fox "for His Majesty's use"—[48]
The price, in money down (from Fox's own purse) was £1,300; despite
their earlier insistence the members present agreed that the President
"had done a service to the Society". Approving the sale, they thanked
Wren for what he had done. In less than a month the deed of sale was
sealed, the purchase money being invested in the East India
Company.[40] Fox had already told Evelyn more on the King's
resolution to build the Royal Hospital; the two men discussed staffing
arrangements, with Evelyn urging the inclusion of a library for the
literates among the old soldiers.[50] By now, moreover, the Surveyor
General, as obvious a choice for such a designing commission as
Robinson his Irish opposite number had been at Kilmainham, was at

work on the designs of a building whose foundation stone the King laid as soon as 16th February.[51]

Wren may well have seen Robinson's plans for Kilmainham, and the Irish soldiers' hospital may have had some influence on the more grandiose buildings at Chelsea. In each building the main range has its hall and chapel *en suite* with a vestibule between them. The scheme anticipates what was later done, by Hawksmoor and others, in the further rebuilding of Queen's College, Oxford, and Chelsea, like Kilmainham, has more about it of a college than of an almshouse, or of the far more palatial setting which Wren later perfected at Greenwich for naval veterans. At Chelsea the main buildings round Figure Court, without their flanking additions, were those which were far advanced in Charles II lifetime. They were carefully thought out for their charitable purpose, while one feature, completed after 1685, looked forward to one of the architect's major constructional feats.

Though Charles II had, in February of 1682, been hasty in his laying of the foundation stone, some details had still, at that time, to be settled. Back in January Evelyn and Fox had planned to discuss the scheme with the Primate as well as with the King, and on 25th May Fox, Wren, and Evelyn went over to Lambeth, taking with them the "plot and description" of the proposed hospital, and intending to get Sancroft's "approbation" for the project. They achieved their end, settling down thereafter to dinner with the Archbishop.[52] Before work started, and well aware of the shakiness of the finance behind all too many Government building schemes, Wren got Fox to promise that the contractors' bills would be promptly paid.[53] The promise was honoured, but much of the money had to be Fox's own. Initially, Wren himself accepted no fee, but eventually, to ensure an official record that he, and not the Earl of Ranelagh who yearned for the credit, had been the controlling genius, he was paid £1,000.[54]

Many of those who worked on Chelsea Hospital were also employed on City churches or on others among Wren's official jobs, while Roger Davis got £50 for a model of the buildings. Wren's favoured mason Thomas Wise worked, in Portland stone, on the Roman Doric porticos. The younger John Grove was on the plasterwork, while John Scarborough, of the office which controlled work on the City churches, surveyed the property and made two maps of the site.[55]

Work on the buildings, attractive in their homely blend of stone and brick of differing yet mellow colours, went reasonably fast as finances allowed. Though much had to be done under James II and William III great progress had been made by the early weeks of 1685. The hall and chapel block, and the two accommodation blocks, each of three main storeys and an attic stage, were roofed in by early February. It must have been to see this stage of the work that Charles II, at the beginning of that month and thus immediately before the seizure which soon proved fatal, came over to Chelsea to inspect the buildings. The fitting and furnishing of the buildings, and their eastern and westward extensions, came later in the story of Wren's achievement. He must, however, in these early days have decided on the main architectural elements of his design, in particular on the pedimented Roman Doric centrepiece of the northern front, and on the similarly designed, severely simple Roman Doric portico which overlooks Figure Court. He would also have planned the more humble colonnade, with its paired columns, beneath whose shelter the veterans could look towards the Thames down a vista of formal gardening completed in later years.

In the last months of 1681, and early in 1682, Wren undertook a task which must have brought back family and boyhood memories, and whose performance must have given him no small pleasure. The Dean and Chapter of St George's at Windsor asked him to survey the chapel, and to report any defects that might need attention. Sir Christopher, so the Chapter records put it, took "great pains and care" in examining the noble Gothic chapel of which his father had been the devoted custodian.[56] He brought down some workmen, perhaps from the staff of the Royal Works. The men were duly "gratified" by the Chapter, while Wren got his out of pocket expenses. But he seems to have taken no fee for what must, in such a place, have been a work of filial piety. So in May of 1682 the Chapter gave him a piece of plate worth £20; two of the canons took the gift to Sir Christopher, along with the thanks of the clergy of St George's.[57] Copies of the report had by now been made so that all the canons could consider its terms.[58]

Wren's work at Windsor recalled the survey he had made, over ten years earlier, on Salisbury Cathedral. A leading problem arose from the low pitch of the late Perpendicular vault which was, as Wren explained, "designed with boldness enough low and flat to ostentation." To check it Wren pointed out how he had, for his own satisfaction, "Taken with care the section of the church". He noticed defects, above the daring main vaults, in the timbers and leadwork of the chapel's outer roofs; of the roofs themselves he made the point that as "the architect lived too near the forest" they contained too much timber for structural necessity. As a result of his climbing and scrambling Wren also picked out several faults in the chapel's late Gothic stonework. The daring vaults showed several cracks and were only just supported by their flying buttresses. The pinnacles needed pointing, and many of the "king's beasts" which had once surmounted all of them were broken or had fallen into the gutters. Wren suggested that all of those surviving on the nave pinnacles should be taken down, and that stone pineapples should, in the current taste, replace them as a coping for the pinnacles. Wren's main concern lay, however, with the outer roof. He could not recommend a new one, but put up several suggestions for the repair both of its timbers and of its lead covering. The repairs to the stonework would include many points of detail, but the "vulgar eyes" of those who would not see the more vital work done on the roof would get the impression that little else had been done to the chapel. Nor did Wren confine his recommendations, with their total cost of £1,012, to the immediate necessity of repair. With wise foresight he also suggested, as a lasting insurance, that some "workmen and servants of the church" should spend a day each quarter inspecting the chapel's roofs, cleaning its gutters, preventing the growth of weeds and noting drips before the water could do harm. They could then, as "a shilling seasonably expended prevents greater charges, and sometimes intolerable damages in such fabrics as this" report any trouble to the treasurer of the Chapter.

The Dean and Chapter of Windsor, being well placed for money, at once put the work in hand, and the beasts were duly dismantled to await recent reinstatement. Wren's directions were to be followed, and he was, as in other commissions, to approve or allow the bills before they were paid. The papers from Windsor would, of course, have come to Wren separately from those pertaining to his royal surveyorship or to his ecclesiastical work in the City of London.

When Evelyn recorded his visit, with Fox and Wren, to the archbishop at Lambeth he noted that Chelsea Hospital's quadrangle was to be "after the dimensions" of the first quad of Christ Church at Oxford. The measurements of the two quads are not, in fact, the same, and the two buildings have no stylistic kinship. But the spring of 1682 was a time when Tom Quad figured large in Wren's mind, for it was in this year that the best known feature of Christ Church was finished to his design.

The leading figure in the story's Oxonian aspect was that unliked Dean-cum-Bishop John Fell. The Dean, who in 1676 had started his ten years' tenure of the see of Oxford, had already completed the domestic buildings which surrounded his college's noble entrance quad; under his dispensation the western front was of a more Renaissance symmetry than that allowed for in Wolsey's late mediaeval plan. When Fell proposed to complete the great entrance feature of Wolsey's Cardinal College he turned to Wren for what had, both in the existing situation and by Wren's choice, to be a Gothic design.

Transactions started late in the spring of 1681,* and as Fell was in a

*Earlier in the same year Wren or his assistants had been otherwise concerned, at Oxford, over the preparations, in the Schools where the Lords and Commons were to meet, and in Christ Church where the king and queen were to lodge, for the dramatic Oxford Parliament of 1681.

hurry things moved faster than Wren, with his architectural judgment now matured, could really approve. On 26th May Wren told Fell[59] that he had sent his designs to Oxford; though he felt, for reasons of basic sympathy with Wolsey's initial work, that the tower should be Gothic he had drawn his detail "less busy" than in what the Cardinal's master mason had left.[60] Constructionally speaking, the main feature of Wren's upward continuation of the gateway was his reduction, without laying new foundations, of an oblong structure (running east and west) to a square which was, in its turn, to end in a handsome octagon. Diagonal arches, at each corner of the early Tudor foundations, were to underlie piers which would underpin the stage of transition, reducing the space of the gateway to a square which could then contain what Wren wrongly calls the "tracery" of a fine though belated fan vault. He asked Fell for the prices and transport costs of Burford and Headington stone; when he got them he could, with his close knowledge of wages and other building costs, send an estimate for building work which he could finish by Christmas of 1682.

More perplexing was the choice of a master mason. Remembering, perhaps, his earlier Oxford experiences Wren told Dr Fell that he could not "boast of Oxford artists, though they have a good opinion of themselves"; the great days of the two William Townsends still lay in the future. So Wren recommended Fell to employ Christopher Kempster, the quarry owner and mason of Burford in the Cotswold foothills.[61] Kempster had just built the Town Hall at Abingdon, whose design Wren may have approved and even modified, while Wren had already employed him on "good works" in London and found him "modest, honest, and treatable". He had lately seen him as he was about to return to the fine quarries near his lovely home town, and he had persuaded him to travel via Oxford and there to call on Dr Fell. Whether or not the interview was pleasant we cannot tell, but Kempster was the mason who got the prestige of this commission. Worse problems arose, however, over Fell's eagerness to make a speedy start.

Wren heard, by 11th June when he next wrote to the mitred Dean,[62] that the foundations for the new work had been started; one assumes that this was without considering the points he had made. Unless there was a new start he was "out of hope that this design will succeed". He expected "unexcusable flaws and cracks, explained the technique whereby secure foundations could lie on a base of well rammed earth, and was "jealous that your workmen, beginning so giddily, will proceed accordingly." His plea may well have been heeded; the next controversy concerned the way in which the plan, and the detail, of the new tower was to marry up with Wolsey's unfinished work. Points which one could now resolve by telephone, or better still by a day trip from London to Oxford, had then to be covered, at all events initially, by correspondence. But Wren soon asked Kempster to see the situation for himself, and to report with his own ground plan; he pointedly remarked that "from two witnesses we shall find out the truth".[63] From his wealth of experience he pithily added that "a thing well settled at first prevents more trouble", and that "to piece well is a more careful business than to erect a new thing where there is no constraint".

These difficulties of detail seem to have been ironed out; there remained the problem of what Kempster and the Oxford masons might respectively consider a proper working pace. Wren's letter on this topic also pleasingly illuminates the summertime régime of the architect himself. For late in the summer of 1681 Wren excused himself to Fell for some delay in their correspondence. For he had been "using his horses and enjoying the summer a little".[64] He does not say where he had ridden or driven through the countryside whose scenery, less planted and enclosed than it would be in another hundred years, was very different from what one can now discover in the country. But this rare glimpse of Christopher Wren in a holiday mood suggests moments, in an increasingly busy career, when he could relax away from London and the Court. His main point concerned possible disputes between Fell's masons and Kempster who would be "apt to mend their pace". But Wren, who had heard, as one might have expected, that the masons were using Burford stone and were well ahead with their work, was confident that Fell would "find satisfaction" in Kempster. But before the end of 1681 a really serious crisis arose; had it been settled as Fell wished the famous silhouette of Tom Tower would not have been as it is.

Late in 1681 Fell conceived a scheme whose carrying out would have been architecturally disastrous and scientifically out of date. What he suggested to Wren was the alteration of the new tower's top stage so that it could, like the tower at the Bodleian, become an observatory. When Wren heard of the Dean's notion he laid other work aside to consider this radical change in the whole design. On 3rd December he wrote to Fell; while he tactfully held back from the outright rejection of his prickly client's scheme he clearly found it hard, as a onetime astronomer and an architect of genius, to be polite about a project which he obviously found preposterous.[65] He explained that if the tower were to carry an observatory it must have a flat top, without the Baroque ogee cap which gives Tom Tower its unique character. A balustrade, rather than the pinnacles which normally cap Oxford's flat-roofed Gothic towers, would have to surmount the whole, while the windows, if they were to suit the projecting telescopes of the astronomers, would have to be without mullions and tracery. Having started the tower in the "Gothick manner" they would have to finish it, as Wren explained in a rare mood of sympathy with mediaeval idioms, with "such proportions as will not be well reconcilable to the Gothick manner"; all in all he feared that the gate tower-cum-observatory would end in "an unhandsome medley".[66]

Worse still, and here Wren spoke as a one-time astronomer who had kept abreast with changes in "the Trade . . . I was once well acquainted with" an observation room of the type that Fell proposed was "not necessary for observations as now they are managed".[67] He explained that at Greenwich Observatory the real work was done not in the tower block but by using instruments housed in lower buildings down in the courtyard. He could, if the necessary apparatus were provided at Christ Church, accommodate it "for less charge than a pigeon house". His arguments must have prevailed with Fell, and Tom Tower, though a little crude in some of its Gothic detail, and especially in its two little rose windows, was spared the harsh adaptation which would have ruined a silhouette much loved in Oxford. Fell's scheme was not, however, the end of the idea that an observatory could be perched on a Gothic tower. Early in the coming century an observatory, for the new created Professor of Astronomy at Cambridge, was built on top of the early Tudor Great Gate at Trinity. The aging Wren seems not to have been consulted, nor need one suppose that had he expressed his thought his ideas of 1681 would have swayed a college head far more of a termagant than John Fell. But an architectural cum astronomical dispute between Wren and Bentley could surely have provided some memorable passages of arms.

Tom Tower's main structure was finished in November of 1682. But the college's disbursements book shows that work went on through 1683 and 1684,[68] and the bell Great Tom was not hung, in Wren's fine timber frame of sturdy baulks, till the second of those two years. The exterior of the tower, with its ogee-headed corner turrets and outer squinches, its octagonal lantern stage, and its leaded ogee cap, is very well known. No less remarkable are some structural devices only seen inside the tower. In the square-planned stage which houses the ringing platform the central panels of Wren's large, late-Gothic windows, adorned outside with their figures of Wolsey and Queen Anne, are in reality sturdy piers giving extra support to the upper tower. In the octagonal upper stage the corner squinch-arches are plain and sharply pointed, while all of Kempster's masonry is finely jointed Burford stone. One approaches the topmost stage not by the cramped and enclosed stone "vice" which Wolsey's builders would have erected but by a fine free-standing spiral stairway, in timber and with banister rails in the manner of the 1680s. The device recalled what Wren had intended, back in 1665, for the stairway below the wierdly elongated pineapple he had sketched as the finial for his pre-Fire dome at Old St Paul's.

At the new St Paul's work went steadily during these last years of a monarch who was not, by a long margin, destined to see the new cathedral complete. Wren himself, in the manner of Colbert's regular, twice weekly visits to the Louvre, was at the cathedral every Saturday;[69] here at all events was a building job whose personal supervision gave him no trouble or tedious journeying. He shrewdly insisted that the new cathedral should not, as was first intended, be built "by parts".[70] So work was simultaneously in hand on the choir limb, on the transepts, and at least on the beginning of the nave. Outer walls, pillars and arches, and some of the great cornice above those arches, were all in progress by the beginning of 1685. But the cathedral could, as yet, make less impression on the skyline of the City than the first completions among the steeples of the parish churches.

Trinity Library at Cambridge also continued to claim some of Wren's attention though not, so far as one can tell, any personal visit. Some time in 1680 Robert Grumbold the master mason called on Wren in London,[71] while early in the summer of that year, so it appears from the handsome gratuity of £10 15s.0d. which the college paid to "Wren's man",[72] Sir Christopher must have sent some trusted emissary (who could have been Hawksmoor) to report progress. The upper floor above the library's ceiling was laid in 1683, and in 1684 the scaffolding was taken down. In the latter year, with the main structure complete and awaiting the attentions of plasterers and furnishers, Grumbold went three times to London to see the architect.

Wren was still concerned with some lesser minutiae of his Surveyorship. In March of 1681 the king consulted him on the problem posed by those who had, without official leave, erected doors in the wall of St James's Park, thus giving unauthorized entry, and easy escape, to "lewd and disorderly persons"; others had even presumed to demolish some of the wall and build over its site.[73] Wren was told to ensure the stopping of these illicit gaps and to prosecute the trespassers. Yet 1681, with severe pressure on the royal finances and acute political tension arising from the Exclusion crisis, was also a time when Charles II was less at Whitehall than had been his custom. As Wren told Fell on 25th June, he had just been to Windsor.[74] With Hugh May still, till his death in 1684, the Controller of Works at the castle the visit was unlikely to have been about building work at Windsor by Wren himself; consultation with the King on various matters would more readily have explained this spell of absence from Scotland Yard. The visit could, however, have led to his commission to survey the state of St George's Chapel.

The year 1682–83 was Wren's last as a member of the Hudson's Bay Committee. He attended thirtynine times, with a total of 154 attendances by the time that he left. Routine matters, like the choice of furriers for sorting beaver skins, and the buying of goods for use or barter, still came up when he was present. He was also involved in matters of deeper concern. When Prince Rupert died, and when the Duke of York was chosen to follow him as Governor, Hayes, Wren, and two others called formally to tell the Duke of his appointment.[75] Later in 1683 the problem of interlopers, whether English or French from Quebec with the backing of Colbert, came up again. The committee heard that Benjamin Gillam, who had sailed from Boston in New England, had been in the Bay, so legal steps were taken to arrest him, and others in the same position, on their return to port.[76] For this, royal orders were needed. So in August of 1683 Wren, with his good official contacts, was asked to approach William Blaythwayt, the Colonial Secretary of State, and (with later repayment) to pay him and his clerks "what he judges fit" for his trouble in the matter, as also for the letter which, on 12th August, went out to Governor Bradstreet of Massachusetts; the King's orders were that the Governor was to sieze any interlopers found to have traded within the boundaries granted, by its charter of 1670, to the Hudson's Bay Company.[77] Then in the autumn a busy time followed for the committee when two of the company's ships arrived back in the Downs, while on 20th November, the last committee meeting which Wren attended, an item approved was a fine gift of furs to Sir James Hayes' wife.[78]

The year 1683 was to see Wren immersed in one of the most important of his official commissions. But minor tasks still arose from his Surveyorship; among them, in 1683 were various works and reports in London. In April Peter Moulong, an armourer employed near Wren's house in Scotland Yard, asked for a "work house" so that he could make firearms as well as service and repair them. Wren was asked to put up a suitable building "at some convenient place" within the official precinct.[79] Then in August Capt. Thomas Cheek, an official in the Tower, asked Secretary Jenkins to have Wren install, in the prisoners' lodgings, a suitable set of strong doors and iron bars; there were, so he said, "not so ill houses in any prison in the World as in the Tower".[80] Back in June Wren had been told, by the King's personal direction, to install writing tables for the Treasury clerks in what had been the King's bathing room at Whitehall,[81] while in July the Surveyor had to report on a scheme whereby one Patrick Lamb and his son William, who in the jumbled purlieus of the palace kept a wooden shed which they used as a tavern and tobacco shop for the palace servants, wanted to enlarge and improve their facilities.[82] Such tasks would have been small matters for Wren and his colleagues. By now, however, the Surveyor was deeply busy on a really important royal building whose design and supervision automatically arose from his official post. The building itself, and its abandonment when unfinished, again proved how much the achievements of Wren's career turned on the ups and downs of Stuart politics.

The summer of 1682, with Shaftesbury still in England, with Monmouth still his threatening cat's paw, and with danger to the King and his brother James from Whig plots and political designs, was still, from the Court party, an uncertain, dangerous time. The London area, including Windsor with its nearness to the capital and riskily distant from the south coast, was anything but a secure district for lasting royal residence. A safer, and pleasant place seemed to be the ancient city of Winchester. Linked to monarchy for some thousand years, it stood in a friendly countryside well dominated by royalist gentry. Its chief buildings were the great cathedral, the college, and the homes of its bishop and of its inevitably royalist clergy. Among the townspeople a large Catholic element reinforced the Church and King sympathies of most Winchester folk. The nearby countryside, whether it was the heaths and glades of the New Forest or chalky downlands closer at hand, was splendidly suited to the outdoor sports in which Charles II delighted. More significant was Winchester's location as a vantage point less readily observed than London for routine political contacts with the French Court. It was also conveniently close, should the situation make it advisable for the King again to "go on his travels", to Southampton or, better still, to the ramparts and naval anchorage of Portsmouth whence a loyal warship would easily take the King to exile, or to a temporary retreat, in his cousin Louis' realm.

Charles II was at Winchester late in August of 1682;[83] he seems then to have actively considered Alfred's ancient Wessex capital as a site for what he might, perhaps, use as his main residence. Before the end of the year the castle was examined as a likely location. The flight, and speedy death in the Netherlands of the Earl of Shaftesbury who was Dryden's "Achitophel" made no difference to the project. For in January of 1683 the Secretary of State sent the King's appreciation of the "frankness" wherewith the Winchester justices (who must actually have had little choice) had shown themselves ready, for Charles' "better conveniency in building" to part with their county hall; Sir Leoline Jenkins assured them that "the county will be made very happy by his residence among them".[84] The fine thirteenth-century hall of the castle was happily spared. But most of the old fortified site, along with other ground adjacent to it, was soon available for the buildings on whose layout and design the Surveyor General must already have been at work.

By the beginning of 1683 Wren had been Surveyor General for fourteen years, and the building of royal palaces was, from the time of his visit to Paris, among his chief ambitions. But the Winchester commission was his first chance of supervising the actual erection of such a building. Predictably enough, what he proposed for the hillside above Winchester showed much French inspiration, and the palace was to be but the main element in a ceremonial layout akin to what Wren must, by 1683, have known to exist at Versailles. As with some of his other projects he got out some designs which differed from the one on which work actually started.[85] One of them allowed for a main façade whose middle element would have been a single-storeyed portico above a base of rusticated arches. But Cosimo III, the Grand Duke of Tuscany who had, in 1669 and before his accession, visited England and befriended Charles II, made a gift to Charles of six massive columns of white marble, probably from the quarries at Carrara. The final design had thus to include these columns as the supports of a much larger portico. The rest of the exterior was to be of red brick, with dressings of Wren's much favoured Portland stone. Behind and above the portico a flat topped dome of the 'Mansard' type was the dominating feature. Its top would have commanded a superb view, though one may doubt that warships lying, over twenty miles away, at Spithead would normally have been seen in the southward prospect.

As was shown in its Mansard dome, the general character of the proposed Palace was very largely French of the late seventeenth century. On its hillside site its three-sided court recalled the riverside Collège des Quatre Nations in Paris. The main buildings, with 'stepped' recessing for their two flanking wings, and with groupings of composite three-quarter columns adorning two of the corners so created, would have been French in feeling. Two small 'areas', or enclosed courts, would have anticipated features later put in by Wren at Hampton Court. Two chapels, one Anglican and a Catholic one for the Queen, were to be in the wings, while the central block, approached by the main portico, would have contained the main ceremonial rooms. The Louis-Quatorze feeling of pomp and splendour would have been reinforced, past a spacious forecourt, by a ceremonial avenue cutting down, through ground cleared by demolishing many houses in the city, direct to the west front of the cathedral. Somewhere in the gardens a stream let in from the western downs would have ended in the foaming Baroque splendour of a thirty-foot cascade.[86]

The palace at Winchester was Wren's most important building well away from the London area; had it reached completion we could reckon it among his leading works. For two years it was one of his main preoccupations, and it was of financial note for him in that he was, in addition to his annual retainer of £45 12s.6d. as Surveyor General, paid £500 a year "for his care and pains in and about the building of the said Palace".[87] Apart from his cognisance of such things as the felling of five hundred loads of New-Forest timber, the shipping of stone from Portland pier, and the making, by London brickmakers of bricks from locally dug earth, the job was one which demanded some personal visits.[88] Wren was at Winchester, over land negotiations, quite early in 1683;[89] he was there again, late in the summer of that year, "to view and contract for" land for the large hunting park which the King, in a gesture not unworthy of William the Conqueror, planned west of the city.[90] Nor were these trips the end of Wren's professional acquaintance of Winchester in these last two years of Charles II's reign. For when, some time in 1683 or 1684, the officials in the City-churches office wished to consult Wren on some financial problem, they had to consult him at Winchester, spending £2 10s.0d. on coach hire for the journey there and back.[91] April, 1684, was another month when Wren was certainly down at Winchester.[92]

Some of the contractors for the new palace were men from the team which Wren had built up at the office of Works and for the City churches. Christopher Kempster and Edward Strong were engaged to lay the foundations; Wren's insistence on "well rammed" rubbish, and on the use of "heavy paviours' rammers" recalled what he had told Fell about foundations for Tom Tower.[93] Thomas Wise was to be among those who procured Portland stone, while James Grove and Matthew Banks were to work on carpentry. John Grove and Henry Doogood were hopefully commissioned for internal plasterwork but, as the Wren Society has plausibly pointed out, progress may never have been such as to require the "at least ten trowels, or more if required" they were to keep at work.[94]

If the palace at Winchester was a major opportunity for Wren its completion was no less desirable for his royal master; the building also inspired other architectural feats elsewhere in the city. Politics apart, Charles II must soon, as Evelyn noted and as Defoe later realised, have found Winchester "infinitely preferable to Newmarket for prospects, air, pleasure, and "provisions"; it was thus a place highly suitable for his "autumnal field diversions".[95] The palace's foundation stone was laid on 23rd March 1683; on the day before, unknown to those working at Winchester, an accident had much strengthened the Wessex city's claims. For a serious fire at Newmarket destroyed much of the town and damaged its royal residence. The King was there at the time; his premature return to London decisively upset the timetable of the Rye House plot. From now onwards the Winchester scheme surpassed Newmarket in Charles' thinking; as Defoe put it the palace in Hampshire would certainly, if completed, "have diverted the king from his cursory journeys to Newmarket". It would also, perhaps, have been rather more than a summer hunting seat. In August, 1683, and for some of the next month, the Court was down at Winchester.[96] With spells of royal presence and Wren's supervision work went fast and money, in those comparatively easy last years of Charles' reign, was made readily available. Early in 1683 the Paymaster of the Royal Works was allowed to spend up to £36,000 on the palace,[97] and the Treasury books show that regular sums, enough for most of the liabilities incurred, were paid monthly. By the end of 1684 most of the outer walls (but not the Grand Duke of Tuscany's columns) had been put up and the palace had, as Evelyn put it, been "brought almost to the covering".[98] Late in the previous August the King and his retinue, trundling down in coaches and with Yeoman of the Guard in attendance, had been at Winchester.[99] But exactly a year later Charles was in his grave, and in the great hall of Winchester's castle Judge Jeffreys was at work trying Dame Alice Lisle for her entertainment of two leading followers of Monmouth. The new King had shown no desire to finish the Hampshire palace. As Wren reported, less than a month after Charles II had died, £35,110 had been received against work done to the value of £37,664 15s.1½d. About £5,000 was due for work done and not yet measured, while his estimate for the completion of the shell came to £5,250. Many materials, among them the Carrara columns, were ready should the job be pushed forward; all Wren could do for the moment was to secure the completed work and have the books made up to the month of the late King's decease.[100]

The year 1684 saw Wren on several tasks which came to him from his official posts. Early in February, after two reminders, he surveyed, and reported on, the new Navy office building in the City of London.[101] Its predecessor, to Pepys's surprised satisfaction, had just escaped the great blaze of 1666. But seven years later it was burnt, and this building, put up by one Ward, was its somewhat belated successor. Wren had already, in August, 1682, been asked to advise on the project;[102] then and at this time when he inspected the completed building he may well have had an official encounter with Samuel Pepys.

In March, after Hugh May's death, Wren followed him as Controller of Works both in the actual castle at Windsor and in various buildings in Windsor Forest; he thus added to his guaranteed income the modest retainer of 6d. a day.[103] Work soon came to him from his new post, for in June he had to consider a petition from the Keeper of the Home Park on repairs to posts, gates, palings, and bridges, on the cleaning of ponds, and even on so humble a subject as the levelling of mole hills and the cutting of thistles and nettles.[104] The matter must have given Wren the excuse for a pleasant country jaunt to Windsor's green retreats, for next month he reported that the palings were "in ill condition", that the ponds needed scouring, and an annual sum of over £50 would for some years be needed, on the receipt of his proper certificates, for the carrying out of various works.[105]

The month of June brought Wren two different commissions. One was when the petition of a certain Henry Bradbury was referred to him; what Bradbury wanted was permission to build, within Whitehall Palace, a cockpit and its accompanying pens "for his Majesty's entertainment and diversion".[106] His second task, at the Secretary of State's direction, was to consider plans made, for the increasing Huguenot congregation which used the Savoy Chapel, for that chapel's enlargement; in another two months these refugee French Protestants got formal leave to enlarge their worshipping place "according to a draft made by the Surveyor General"; it would seem that Wren's final part in the project was more than merely advisory.[107]

Later that year, and at the start of 1685, Wren had cognisance of a scheme of Francis Gwyn, a groom of the Bedchamber, to rebuild his lodging in Scotland Yard, and to augment it, for the benefit of the King's wind musicians, by some building more convenient than the mere shed in which they had long hung their instruments. Wren reported, in the middle of December, 1684, on this site near his own home which contained various lodgings. He agreed that the current users were happy with their quarters, but tartly added, as he had "continually found by experience", that their present content might not extend to their successors. He added that Gwyn's scheme for a house much taller than those adjoining it would much impair the use of those lower houses whose chimneys would be below the level of its eaves. There would, moreover, be heavy expense to the State if all the other houses in the area had in the end to be rebuilt to match that of Gwyn. Yet Wren could not deny that what Gwyn, and Lady Pye who had a similar project, desired would "much better become the Court" than the "contemptible sheds" which at the moment cluttered the ground.[108] The problem, like one discussed, earlier in the year, about the haphazard erection, within the chaotic purlieus of Whitehall Palace, of other lodgings and buildings, was relevant to the difficulty bound to occur should the King seriously plan to do what Wren must have hoped he would do, and "reform, beautify, or new build" any part (or better still the whole) of his hopelessly haphazard dwelling place between the Strand and Westminster.

Wren had, in the meantime done some work, near Whitehall but of an ecclesiastical character, which involved him with another of his more interesting clerical patrons.

Dr Thomas Tenison who was, under William and Mary, made Bishop of Lincoln and then Archbishop of Canterbury, had for some years been the rector of St Martin-in-the-Fields; the church in which he officiated was, of course, the late mediaeval fabric, much altered but still to be replaced by Gibbs's famous building. Though a staunch Anglican, who had lain low under the Commonwealth, Tenison was of a "broader", more liberal churchmanship than the high Laudians, such as Matthew Wren, among whom Sir Christopher had been brought up. His wife, moreover, was a daughter of the one head of a Cambridge College (which was Tenison's own) who came through the Commonwealth undeprived and yet, at the Restoration, got advancement to a rich deanery. In these last years of Charles II's reign he came closer than those earlier churchmen to Wren's enquiring, unbigoted churchmanship; only when Tenison came to his strong advocacy of the Hanoverian succession which in the end cost Wren his Surveyorship could there have been a divergence of views between the two elderly men. But in the 1680s the rector of St Martin's and his parishioner the Surveyor General must have been close in each other's confidence.

Wren had already been concerned with some work about the church in which he must often have worshipped, and where his infant son and his two wives lay buried.[109] Late in 1681 the parish vestrymen resolved that the Senior Churchwarden should consult Wren about the ordering and alteration of the churchyard. William Deane, the official in question, duly waited on the Surveyor, taking a mason's estimate for the stonework needed for the alterations. This was on 26th January 1682; Sir Christopher approved the scheme, and held its cost "very reasonable". In another two years Tenison called on Wren for a more considerable work.[110]

Being close to Whitehall, and to the houses of many magnates and high Court officials, St Martin's had among its parishioners many young clergymen who were chaplains or tutors in noble households. When Tenison complained that these young clerics spent too much of their time at such haunts as coffee houses or taverns they told him that if they had ready access to books they could use some of their spare time on reading or serious study. So the rector, in those days when no public libraries existed, decided, so he told Evelyn early in 1684, to build, within his parish and at his own expense, a public library. He asked Evelyn and Wren to help him over "the placing and structure thereof".[111] During the rest of the year Wren must have spent a little of his time on what was, in the whole context of his achievement, a minor if pleasant work. In March of 1685 he was asked to erect what amounted to a dual-purpose building, with a school downstairs, a segmental headed doorway at each end, and the library and schoolmaster's room upstairs. A large central window, like those below it, and at each end of the first storey, with a segmental head, was to light the main storey; it was flanked on each side by two round windows set high, one assumes, to allow space for bookcases below them.[112] In September, 1685, perhaps in connection with this school cum library, Wren was made a vestryman of St Martin's.[113] I do not know when the building was finished, but Evelyn records how he went to see "Dr Tenison's library" on 15th July[114] 1685, the day of which the Whig rector of St Martin's spent a part attending Monmouth on the scaffold.

The death of Charles II, on a cold day early in February of 1685, had no effect on Wren's tenure of his Surveyorship. It did, however, put an end to the Winchester project. Wren was still a busy man during James II's short reign. But his works for the Court, though of interest, were, by comparison to the unfinished palace in Wessex, in a minor key.

10
James II:
Quiet Interlude

The new reign started smoothly and with no disturbance; few could, for the moment, or even after Monmouth's failure in the summer, foresee the shortness of its duration or the turbulence at its end. Though James's personal morals were little better than those of his brother, his backslidings were more discreetly concealed than those of Charles had been and, as Evelyn soon noted, court life was to be less flamboyant, with less gambling and flaunting of vice, than under the Merry Monarch's genial régime. As the diarist put it, the king himself affected "neither profaneness nor buffoonery", while "a more solemn and moral behaviour", with the pious queen Mary of Modena a more prominent figure at court than Queen Catherine had been, was now to prevail. More relevant, from the approving standpoint of such steady public servants as Pepys and Wren, the new king was a sounder, more meticulous administrator than his adroit, charming, but lazy brother. Had his political sense equalled his administrative ability he might well have kept his throne far past the fatal year of 1688. It could then have been for James II, not for his daughter and her Dutch husband and widower, that Wren could have got out the designs and supervised the buildings of his time of mature architectural perfection.

Wren's position as Surveyor General, both for Windsor and for other normal royal residences, was soon put in order; the transition bears the marks of efficient administration. His grant of the Surveyor General's post had been made late in March of 1669; Charles II's death had ended, or was supposed to have ended the appointment. But on 21st April 1685, a royal warrant renewed Wren's grant of the Surveyorship of the Works, within the Tower of London and of all the royal residences normally in use. The retaining pay, 2s. a day for himself and 6d. for his clerk, was to be what he had received under Charles II; he also had 4s. a day to cover the "diet, boat hire, and ridings" of himself and his deputies.[1] Wren also got the renewal of the post, worth 6d. a day and held since the previous year, of Controller of

Works in Windsor Castle and Forest.[2] On the same day Matthew Banks, Wren's tried colleague who had, for almost two years, been the Chief Carpenter of all the King's Works, likewise got his tenure renewed.[3] Wren's continuation in his two offices had all along been assumed, for back in March he had been asked to certify what was due, for work started while May was still in charge at Windsor, to Antonio Verrio, the Italian mural painter who had, for Charles II and now for his brother's enjoyment, painted the Baroque ceilings which still adorn some of the castle's ceremonial rooms.[4] Wren was, moreover, already involved in a task which had not come to him under Charles II. He had to make the preparations, in Westminster Abbey and elsewhere, for the new king's coronation; sums of money, in advances of £400 each time, were regularly provided till Wren's estimate had been met.[5]

The late spring of 1685 was also the time when Wren first entered Parliament, soon finding himself immersed in six weeks of active House of Commons business. The Parliament, summoned early in James II's reign, was carefully packed, to the exclusion of Whigs and possible Monmouth supporters, with reliable Stuart adherents. The Secretary of State, in a letter sent to trusty political managers in various counties, clearly pointed out how important it was that "good Members" should be chosen; he urged them, at the king's insistence, that "persons of approved loyalty and affection to the government" should be elected. Not only did such a description fit tried provincial Tories, but it seemed in no way incongruous that important State officials, such as Pepys and Wren, should join eminent landowners and country squires in a reliable assembly. Nor need a functionary like the Surveyor General find it an uncongenial task to sit in a Parliament whose main functions included the voting of a steady Crown revenue, free of the secret factor of French subsidy which had, under Charles II, made up much of the money available to the king. Should such revenues equal those available in the previous reign, and should tranquillity, of the type expected in those early months of the new regime, prevail in the political scene there were good reasons for supposing that royal building activity, of a type constantly impeded under Charles II, should at last be commissioned from the office over which Wren presided.

The constituency for which Wren sat, without personally visiting it, was the small south Devon town of Plympton St Maurice, long a Parliamentary borough, too small for its honour and with a village population. It had, for some years, been partly controlled by the local family of the Trebys. In the previous Parliament one of its Members had been Sir George Treby,[6] a prominent Whig lawyer, the manager, at the time of the Popish Plot, of the impeachment of the Catholic peers and in 1681 a member of the Committee which had, before the famous dissolution at Oxford, drafted the Bill which was, so he and friends expected, to exclude the future James II from the succession to his brother's throne. There could be no question, in any Parliament called by the new King, of so strong a Whig partisan resuming his seat; for a renewed representation of his native town, and also for high office as Attorney General, he had to wait for the reign of William and Mary. Some other Members of this Parliament must soon have been determined; as early as March of 1685 it must have been evident that Wren was to be one of them. For on 11th March a warrant went out, as many others did at this time when many boroughs had been obliged to surrender their charters, for the renewal of the charter which regulated the affairs of Plympton. The first 'modern' mayor and the nine 'modern' magistrates were named, so too were the 'modern' burgesses from whom the future magistrates were to be chosen. Most of them were local men, one assumes of assured Tory loyalty to the new sovereign. But there were also some important extraneous figures, among them the Lords Lieutenant of Devon and Cornwall, William Strode of the prominent local family which was to provide Wren's colleague in the representation of Plympton, Sir Nicholas Slanning a prominent Cornish royalist, and Wren himself.[7]

The new Parliament met on 19th May, Members were speedily sworn, and the King addressed the two Houses on 22nd May. From then onwards, and not, perhaps, foreseeing the speedy interruption of business by warlike incidents in the West country, Wren and his fellow Members got actively to work. The Commons Journals have no record of their speeches, but they make it clear that, as a committee man, the Surveyor General in Parliament was much busier than many of his colleagues.

Three days after the King's speech leave was given, no doubt to Wren's pleasure, to bring in a Bill for the rebuilding and finishing of St Paul's, while on the next day Wren found himself on the Committee to enquire into laws which had expired or were soon due to expire; next day he was put on another committee whose task it was, with petitions from shoemakers and leather merchants to be taken into account, to consider the revival of an Act for transporting leather. A few days later the House received a petition from Sir George Treby on the recent election at Plympton. It was referred to the Committee of Privileges, but there was no chance of countermanding action on a contest which need not have involved Wren and Richard Strode his colleague in any financial corruption, but which was certainly a ruthless device of political management.[8]

For the whole of this Parliament's brief session Wren was extremely active in its committee work. Some of the committees on which he sat were concerned with topics relevant to his architectural profession; others were more remote from Sir Christopher's more obvious

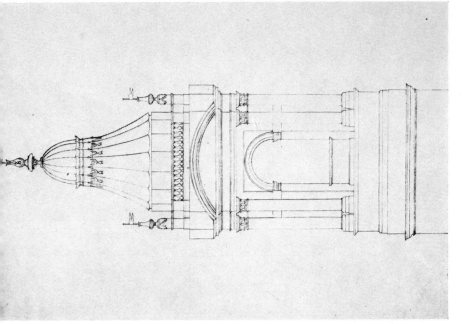

CITY CHURCHES

(*left*) St Antholin's (demolished 1875) : interior (*right*) St Bride's: projected
tower and cupola

London, St Stephen, Walbrook: domed interior

CITY STEEPLES

(*left*) St Mary le Bow, finished 1680 (*right*) St Bride's, 1701–1703

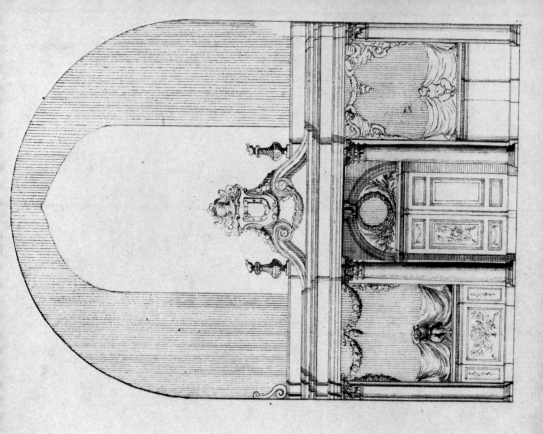

(*left*) Drawing for a gallery with organ (*right*) St John's College, Oxford: screen design, 1675

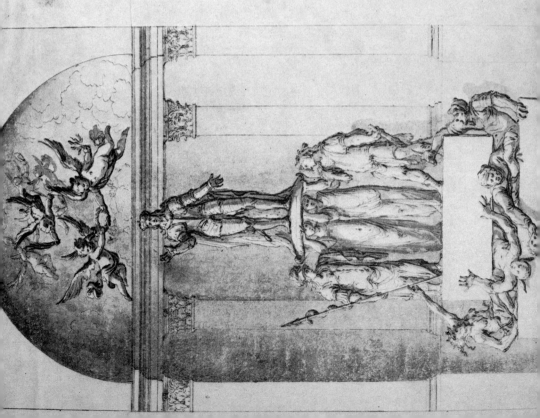

(*left*) Windsor Mausoleum : a drawing for the monument of Charles I (*right*) Hampton Court : a drawing for the Britannia Fountain

Bust of Sir Christopher Wren by Edward Pearce the younger, 1673

Drawings for a polygonal vestry

SCHEMES FOR ST PAUL'S

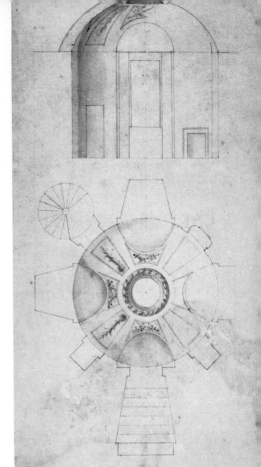

The 'Penultimate' Design,
before 1675

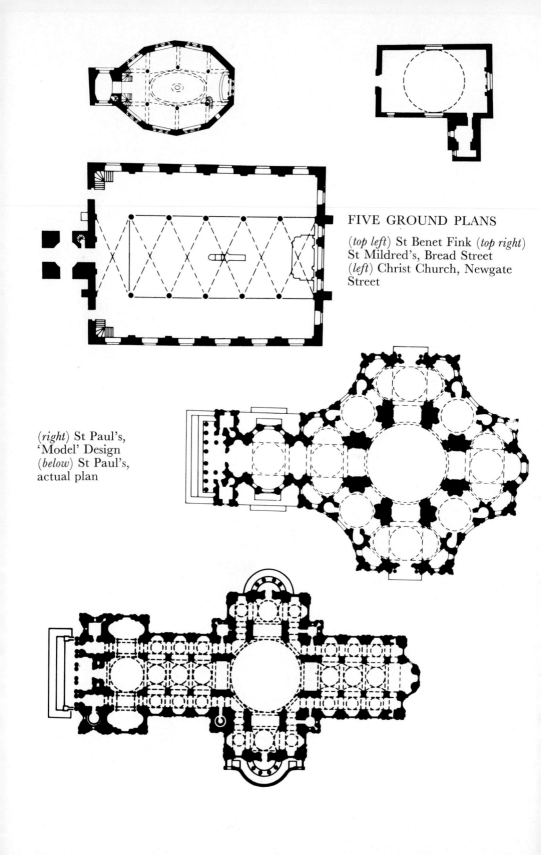

FIVE GROUND PLANS

(*top left*) St Benet Fink (*top right*)
St Mildred's, Bread Street
(*left*) Christ Church, Newgate
Street

(*right*) St Paul's,
'Model' Design
(*below*) St Paul's,
actual plan

concerns. Those less clearly relevant to a man who was both a scientist and an architect were the committees set up to consider and report on Bills for the recovery of small tithes, on keeping up the prices of wool and corn, on the revival of an Act to provide land or water transport for the Navy and Ordnance, against the import of tallow candles, on the general registry of estates, titles, and encumbrances, and on the relief of widows and orphans in the City of London;[9] the last subject would, of course, have been familiar to a man who was so much in touch with the officials and clergy of the City parishes.

Wren's other Parliamentary committees were all appropriate for the presence of the Surveyor General. Naturally enough he was on the Committee, which reported on 20th June, which was to examine the Bill setting up the new parish, whose church he had designed, of St James's, Piccadilly.[10] Early in June he and Pepys, who as Secretary of the Navy Board had an interest in such a matter, were on the committee whose task it was to consider a Bill for the repair and improvement of the harbour at Great Yarmouth. As on other committees, Wren and his colleagues got quickly to work, for on 13th June, the day on which Parliament heard of Monmouth's landing in Dorset, they reported to the House, having agreed some amendments and added a clause.[11] In another two days the Commons gave the Bill a third reading, while in their main business that day Wren's must have been one of the votes which, *nemine contradicente* on a Bill of Attainder, destined Monmouth, without trial, to the block on Tower Hill.[12]

The campaign in the West soon brought the proceedings of this Parliament to a premature end. On 18th June the King sent a message expressing his desire for a Recess, but also asking for special funds to suppress the rebellion. On the same day a committee was set up to estimate the yield of a proposed tax on new buildings. This, of course, was a natural for Sir Christopher; the *Commons Journals* here mention him, not by name but as "Mr Surveyor". His cousin William Wren was another member. The matter being urgent they made an interim progress report in as little as two days.[13]

Despite what had now become the main political preoccupation some Parliamentary work went on as before. On 22nd June a committee was asked to consider the rebuilding of St Paul's, being empowered, in addition, to put in a clause for finishing four City churches. Wren was an obvious member, so too was Lord Ranelagh with whom he was, over Chelsea Hospital, to have relations none of the happiest. The committee worked quickly, and one may reckon that Wren's presence aided its deliberations; in another three days the Bill got its third reading.[14] At the end of the month the Surveyor General found himself on yet another Parliamentary committee – one to consider a Bill for regulating Hackney coaches, and preventing nuisances, in the streets of the City,[15] Southwark and Westminster; it was no fault of his that the measure failed to reach the Statute Book. For on 2nd July, a day when Monmouth was toiling back to Bridgwater and the scene of his swift disaster, Parliament adjourned for a month; its business was then, in the assumed absence of most country members, to be carried out "by such members (Wren included) as shall be about the Town".[16] But as things turned out, that Parliament of James II met only briefly after a single day's business on 4th August. It was adjourned till November; its debates in that month found it divided and, from the King's point of view, awkwardly restive over money for a standing army and over the advancement of Catholic officers. On 20th November it was prorogued, and all through 1686 it was frequently prorogued again.[17] The same thing happened twice in 1687, and on 2nd July of that year, with its dissolution, Wren ceased to be a Member. But those hectic weeks in 1685 had shown how active as a Parliamentarian a man of his wide talent and official position could be.

We still know very little, for these years of his mid-fifties, of Wren's personal or private life. Hooke was still, for the replacement of the City churches, his close colleague, but his journal is no longer available to throw light on their doings. They must, however, have continued to confer as often as they found it necessary, and we can assume that Wren was still a familiar, gladly greeted figure in London coffee houses and taverns. He was, moreover, involved about now in a new business venture. In 1685 he and his old friend Sir Stephen Fox got letters patent allowing them to take over the licence of Hungerford Market, just off the Strand and on the site of Charing Cross Station. The market had been built, a few years earlier and on the site of his town mansion, by Sir Edward Hungerford. Wren and Fox now bought it and took over the licence allowing the sale of grain and other goods, and they were also to receive the market tolls.[18] They also hoped for a share in the vegetable trade, but Covent Garden's competition was already strong, and their ownership of the market seems never to have brought much profit to Fox and Wren.[19] They kept it, however, till Fox died in 1716; it was sold in the following year.

We can tell nothing for certain on how Wren the widower ran his home or arranged for the care, and early tuition, of his three young children. The third Christopher, who did not go to Eton till 1691 when he was sixteen, was ten in these early months of the new reign; he may already have shown signs of the genuine though minor talent which he inherited from a brilliant father. Jane was eight by the end of 1685; she may, by now, have displayed her budding musical talent, also the sweetness of disposition which was, in coming years, to be her elderly father's greatest consolation. Less happy, one assumes, was the problem of William, the architect's youngest son whose sixth birthday fell as the Court was in turmoil over Monmouth's advances in the west. For "poor Billy" may already have shown sad signs of the lasting, incurable mental debility which made him a permanent burden to those who had the care of him.

Within three weeks of his coming to the throne James II asked Wren to give him an estimate of what it would cost to secure the unfinished buildings at Winchester against vandalism and other damage.[20] But although the King was there in the coming September, lodging in the deanery and availing himself of the "autumn diversions" which his brother had much enjoyed James seems to have been less keen than Charles on the delights and political convenience of the historic Hampshire city. As Evelyn put it, he "did not seem to encourage the finishing it",[21] and Wren's active commitment ceased with what could have been among his leading buildings. He was still, however, kept busy with various jobs which came to him, and to his increasingly experienced colleagues, from his Whitehall and Windsor surveyorships.

In the jumbled purlieus of Whitehall Palace Francis Gwyn's building request came over from the previous reign. Gwyn now asked that his lease should also cover the site of some "old ruined buildings" belonging to Sir Paul Neale. Wren's report allowed, in June, 1685, for the overruling of Sir Paul's objections.[22] The day before Wren had been asked, as a result of Queen Mary's commands, to alter and recondition the lodgings, within the palace, of Lady Waldegrave, while later in the same month he was asked to comment on workmen's bills, to the tune of £1,304, for work lately done on St James's Palace.[23] Later that summer Wren advised on a scheme, put up for Windsor, by Sir Samuel Morland, a hydraulic expert and wide-ranging inventor of whom Evelyn thought highly, and on whom Pepys had written much less favourable comments. What Morland proposed was the building of a wharf to protect the mill, and the other "waterworks" which conveyed water, uphill, to a point within the castle. The King, who was at Windsor that autumn when Jeffreys came back from his historic western assize, was personally anxious that Wren, as surveyor for Windsor Castle, should deal with a matter for which the money required was to be made available.[24]

In the winter of 1685–86 some jobs, and what was, perhaps, an amusing controversy, arose in Whitehall and St James's Palaces. A petition by one Patrick Lambe was referred to Wren on 9th November. Relying on Charles II's verbal promise of a base, Lambe had built a house on a site next to the Office of the Pastry; he now asked for his lease to be put in order. Wren promptly reported that the house, five rooms and two closets and built for £600, had actually improved the royal pastrycooks' quarters. But it was not till April,

1686, that Lambe's *fait accompli* was regularised.[25] Early in December the Earl of Mulgrave, who was Lord Chamberlain, said that his office was so badly decayed that it had actually to be propped up. He asked for its complete rebuilding, and Wren seems, in a report of 18th January, to have agreed with the Earl. But the King ruled, in the following July, that repairs, presumably to be done under Wren's supervision, must suffice.[26] At the very end of 1685 Wren had to report on a request of one Joseph Radcliffe, who had, since the Restoration in 1660, supplied goods to the Works Office, for the official post of Purveyor to the Works; he revealingly added that over £41 had, since 1665, been owed to him for fitting up the "Masking House".[27]

On 11th February 1686, Henry Guy, the Secretary of the Treasury, sent Wren papers which bore on a flare up between the Italian Court painter and a highly born lady. Antonio Verrio, born in Lecce down in the heel of Italy, was well established in the royal service and had worked at Windsor and on other commissions for Charles II. A gardener as well as a painter he was a friend of Evelyn who visited the Italian's garden at Windsor and said, of the royal garden at St James's Palace, that Verrio had made of it "a very delicious Paradise". The painter-cum-gardener from Apulia had lodgings at St James's which he now proposed to enlarge; the site he had in mind for his extensions was that of a greenhouse, put up in the late king's time, against the garden wall of Lady Susanna Williams' house. The lady claimed "annoyance" from the painter's scheme to build a house, of two or three storeys, which would, so she said, block her view and impede her light. So Wren, whose diplomatic gifts were held to be considerable, was asked by Guy to "accommodate" between the two parties; one can imagine a tense interview, partly perhaps in French which Verrio knew, between the Court lady, the middle-aged architect, and a hot-tempered Italian painter.[28] Nor was this episode the end of Wren's concern with Antonio Verrio. At the end of 1686 he had to comment on a memorandum sent in by the decorative painter. The paper must have dealt with the sums due to him for what he had done, particularly at Windsor, for in another six months Wren was told to pay £100 to the Italian for his work on the early Tudor chapel east of St George's, still standing now that nothing had been done to build Charles I's mausoleum for which, in 1678, Wren had made so splendid a circular design.[29]

At Windsor and nearer to Whitehall Wren's two surveyorships brought him varied commitments. The erection of iron railings, before the Treasury Chambers and Lord Sunderland's office, was a matter of minor routine;[30] so too was the request to report on an estimate for new chests to be used by the Exchequer officials.[31] More significant, in November, 1686, was the Lord Treasurer's reference to Wren, for his assurance that the workmen's charges were reasonable, of bills for such permanent structures as a bakehouse, granaries, barns, and a hospital put up in the politically controversial military camp on Hounslow Heath;[32]* the camp, and the whole matter of James II's raising of the larger standing army which Monmouth's rising had shown to be needed, were factors not only in the King's political decline but in his inability to afford the proper palace which he and his queen would probably have liked.

Late in 1686, and at other times during the rest of James II's reign Wren was considerably concerned with repairs, and new projects, in the royal stables and mews; the duties of his surveyorship were apt, from time to time, to impinge on those of stablemasters or of the keeper of a menagerie. The All Souls' drawings suggest that he had got out plans for splendid stables for the new palace at Winchester;[33] he had now, nearer home, to deal with James II's equestrian requirements.

In September of 1686 Wren was asked, by Lord Dunmore, the Master of the Horse, to advise over a scheme for repairs, and new buildings, in the stables at St James' Palace. Matthew Banks, the Chief Carpenter to the Royal Works, had got out designs for both categories of work. When he came to the basic design the Surveyor General, reckoning the officials in the royal stables to be the best judges in such matters and supposing the scheme to be suitable for its purpose, made no variations. He did, however, have something to say on Banks's costing. Some items he had found to be "miscast" below what he reckoned to be the right figures; as a result the estimate went up to £2095 17s.0d. There were, however, some optional details, while some of Banks's prices could be cut. Thorough as ever, Wren sent Dunmore new drawings, a new estimate, and a convenient abstract of the buildings' entire cost.[34] In another report, of 22nd October 1686, Wren referred both to the current use of the St James's stables, comparing them, with their housing for eighty-two horses, with the much larger Royal Mews nearer to Whitehall. He also referred to the King's idea that that stables should be contrived, in or very near the palace of St James, for 160 "horse upon the Guard". Wren pointed out, no doubt from close personal knowledge, that the Royal Mews had thirty coach houses, stabling for 300 horses, staff lodgings, and ample room for such mundane items as water, hay, provender, and manure, with infirmary space for sick horses; for none of these, he told Dunmore, was there room at St James's. But should the King need guard horse stabling at St James's the Surveyor General reckoned that such a building "decent enough and sufficient for use", could be put up, for £1,000, in the Green Mews. In such a position,

*The barns, which Wren valued at £500, but not the hospital and the bakehouse, were pulled down in 1692. *See* Calendar of Treasury Books, Vol. IX, p.1779.

shielded from public gaze, there need be less "care for outward beauty", while no special screening walls need be put round water tanks, drains, or manure heaps.[35]

In the meantime, on 18th October 1686, various repair and rebuilding items, all in the royal stables, were referred to Wren for his estimate of their cost. The Surveyor General, as was his wont, got his staff quickly to work and reported in less than a month. One item was the proposed building, over a coach house, of lodgings for one of the King's coachmen who was otherwise unhoused. No single item was of any great value, but most of them, so it seems, were considered "of absolute necessity". They included such picturesque details as "a press for the Queen's rich harness", a "ladder for ye servants to goe up to bed", paving, rack staves, arrangements for watering horses, and a new lock and keys for the horse pond. Wren's main estimate came to £677 16s.0d. But allowing for extra items, and for arrears due on earlier work, he gave a total of £954 12s.0d. He explained that some of the jobs could be cut out, but all of them were put in hand under his direction.[36]

About the same time, in November, 1686, the Secretary of the Treasury sent Wren a long list of estimates for repairs proposed in the royal parks at St James's, Greenwich, and Hampton Court.[37] Wren's report well shows how his professional concern could lie with other and humbler things than the cornices, pediments, and architraves of palaces or churches. At St James's he had to cover such items as a lodge for the planter of trees and shrubs, with the repair of walls, with seed, malt, oatmeal and duck baskets for the ornamental birds, and with hen houses, pens for the "feeding and fatning of fowls", and cages for the vultures which were a notable feature of the royal aviary. At Greenwich the plantations presented problems, while at Hampton Court Wren had to see both to plantations and, as at St James's, to the maintenance of chicken runs and a "volary". He was also asked to report on the condition of the "new river" which had been cut, from springs at Longford over nine miles away in what was then rural Middlesex, to supply Charles II's canal and other sheets of ornamental water in the palace garden. The sum of £300 was suggested for the clearing out of this artificial watercourse.

On 13th December Wren, who must have made some prompt winter journeys to the more outlying sites, sent in his report.[38] He had, so he put it, "with ye best care examined every particular" of what Henry Guy had sent him. On some items he offered little comment. A planter's lodge, with two small rooms and a chimney, could be put up in St James's Park for £20, while £80 could be allowed, as in the Treasury estimate, for a large new birdcage. But there was no need for a new decoy, while when Wren came to the vultures' cage he pointed out that the King could save himself £20 by repairs for £10 rather than the £30 proposed for a new structure. At Greenwich the Surveyor General at once saw that the reconditioning of the plantations would run to far more than the figure put to him; he would not, for the moment, survey the job unless the Lord Treasury specially asked him. At Hampton Court, "not knowing what fowles are kept there", he could not judge the yearly cost of pens and the feeding of the birds, but he sensibly added that if the trees in the park were to be newly boxed in the work should, because in the last months of the year the trees were "more lyable to be barked by ye deer", be done before the coming winter. On the new river, where repairs were obviously "summer work" Wren agreed that it should certainly be cleaned out, and that various new bridges should be built to span it. But he believed, allowing for the taking of proper measurements, that the cost of the job would much exceed the suggested £300. It would, however, be much cheaper if, instead of scouring the whole channel, the "tumbling bay" at Longford were so restored as to give a lastingly stronger head of water.

Routine tasks of Works administration, and problems connected with the deferred payment of craftsmen, also concerned Wren at this time. Early in 1687 he and others had to help check the accounts of Philip Packer, the Paymaster of Works who had lately died, and to advise what financial security should be asked of Thomas Lloyd his successor.[39] Petitions for payment came from artificers who had worked, under Charles II, on the late king's lodgings at Whitehall, and from others who had been on the "waterworks" at Windsor. Wren also had to deal with financial claims by some artists of note. In April of 1687 he got a petition from the sculptor John Bushnell who pointed out that he had, at Charles II's command, made statues of St Peter and St Paul for Queen Catherine's Catholic chapel at Somerset House; he claimed that £100 was still owing.[40] In July of the same year Grinling Gibbons claimed that Charlers II had allowed him £100 a year for cleaning and repairing carved work at Windsor Castle; he had had nothing, on this account, since James had succeeded his brother.[41]

At Whitehall Palace rebuildings and extensions, rather than a complete new Palace, were still the order of the day. In July, 1687, a single storey was to be added to some lodgings above the buttery.[42] More important, and evidenced by drawings at Oxford[43] and from other sources, were new buildings for social and business purposes, and for the public devotions of the King, the Queen, and their Catholic courtiers. There could, in the military and financial circumstances of James II's increasingly difficult reign, be no question of a wholly new palace. But additions, for administration, receptions, lodging, and devotion could be made to existing residences.

It was clear, to James II's orderly mind, that arrangements for

Council meetings and other activities of State, were inadequate in the jumble of Whitehall Palace as his brother had known it. So Wren was asked to design an important new building which would tidy up a part of the palace which needed it, and which would help to remedy the defect. Drawings at Oxford,[44] and townscape views, show the building, of brick with dressings and ornamental features of stone, which was put up, in 1687-87 , for over £30,000. A Council Chamber, a Privy Gallery, social apartments for the Queen, various other rooms, and an important Catholic chapel were leading elements in this "New Building".

For the block containing the Council Chamber, a drawing in the collection at Oxford shows a rusticated arcade at ground level; above it, pairs of Ionic pilasters appear as the main adornment of this particular building's frontage. The Queen's drawing room, facing the river, was a charming Baroque building of six elements, with the two central ones projecting beneath a pediment. Triangular and segmental pediments crowned the front windows, while at the back a central window composition had a pediment above two windows which, in their turn, had a niche between them.[45] Panelling and staircases apart, rooms such as these were suitable scenes for Verrio's display. He had certainly worked, by the end of 1686 when Wren considered his accounts, on the Queen's bedchamber, on her closet, and on a small chapel.[46] More important was what he painted in the large, ornate chapel whose building was supervised by the Surveyor General.

The Whitehall Chapel, whose furnishing and Catholic services made so great an impression on Anglican observers, was of no special architectural note. Much of it was incorporated in the main fabric of Wren's "New Building", and as it was of no great size its sanctuary end did not project far from the southern side of that new wing. Its note, and in Protestant eyes its notoriety, lay in what one saw inside. On the walls and ceilings Verrio, who asked £1,250 for his work, and for whom Wren certified £800 for what he had done by the last weeks of 1686,[47] painted what Evelyn called "a world of figures", the Assumption being the central feature of a typically Baroque ceiling decoration. No less striking, destined for a chequered future, and still in part surviving in the Somerset church of Burnham-on-Sea, was the architectural and sculptural decoration behind the High Altar. Here Wren was involved in a composition far more lavish, and pictorially more exciting, than any of his City altarpieces. From a pencil outline[48] it would seem that Wren had a hand in the design of the marble altarpiece, in two main tiers and over thirty feet high, while Gibbons and the Flemish immigrant Arnold Quellinus carved the free-standing figures' and the reliefs (by Quellin) which completed the ornate composition. The chapel, so Evelyn tells us, was opened at the end of

1686, with all the fullness of ceremonial long hardly known among England's Catholics as they endured the restraints of penal times. The Baroque ensemble included appropriate music, with a famous castrato singer brought from the queen's native Italy.[49]

St James's Palace was also chosen for some special apartments for Mary of Modena. In March of 1686 Wren signed an estimate for the alteration of some rooms so that space could be made for a new Council Chamber.[50] It was to measure twenty-two feet by seventeen feet ten inches, its wainscoting was to cost over £70, and it was, in these years before their more general popularity under William and Mary, to include four new "shass" (sash) windows to be glazed with Normandy glass. The total estimate came to £238 13s.0d.; the Queen's treasurer was duly asked to pay any sum, not over £240, that might be needed for the work.

The building of the City churches, and Wren's general supervision of their construction and furnishing, continued during James II's short reign. The process, now well over half complete, was little affected by the new factor of enlarged tolerance for Catholics and Protestant Nonconformists. Few of the new churches were now commenced, but some which were started late in Charles II's time were completed. Much internal decoration and furnishing, under Wren's surveillance if not in all cases to his detailed designs, was done between early 1685 and the end of 1688. Of these whose building was now somewhat belatedly started St Andrew's-by-the-Wardrobe was, in essence, another rendering of the galleried basilican plan only recently completed in St James's in Jermyn Street, while at St Margaret Lothbury a simple, one-aisled building got an interesting variety – round-headed, rectangular, and circular – of window designs in its nave and clerestory. A rainwaterhead of 1687, presumably from near the completion of its main fabric, makes it a rarity among Wren's City churches in being dated to a particular year. Another church of this late period was St Mary Somerset; its surviving tower strangely blends pinnacled Gothic survivalism with a generality of Renaissance design. The back of the great task of replacement was now, to the swift advantage of the cathedral, broken now that twenty years and more had passed since the Great Fire. But some of Wren's towers, significantly at a time when his style was moving to a more Italianate Baroque phase, had still to be given their ornamental tops.

At St Paul's work went steadily and soon, with more money available, at an increased pace. Early in the new reign Wren's commission as the new cathedral's architect was renewed, while on 11th May 1686, Wren was asked to report on the Dean and Chapter's authorisation, under the Privy Seal, to quarry stone for the cathedral at Portland.[51] The clerics had asked for a renewal of their authority; one assumes that, with Wren's consent, they had their wish. The main fabric of the choir limb, of the transepts, and of the supports for the eventual, but still unfinished dome was now far advanced. The nave was, however, in a more interesting stage. We can discount the idea that the two large chapels off its western end were an idea of a Catholic king hopefully expecting that they would one day be used for the rites of his Church. The chapels had been shown in a drawing (*see* page 98) which may have been made not long after the 'Warrant' design of 1675, which Sir John Summerson has held to be from some earlier date, and which in any case seems certain to have been made well before James II's accession. The actual cathedral would, moreover, have had ample space, even without those nave chapels, for the side altars and shrines of the type that lavishly grace the High Renaissance and Baroque churches of Counter-Reformation Catholicism. What did happen, before the end of 1686, was the laying of the lower courses of the west front, on whose main structure an augmented team of masons was working by the end of 1688.[52] Wren thus ensured, so far as he could do short of some major crisis or disaster, that the new cathedral's length, though much less than that of Old St Paul's would be all that he had planned. As it happened, the available finances were soon more favourable to the achievement of his full scheme.

As most of the new City churches had now been finished more money could now be made available, for St Paul's, from the continued levy of the tax on seaborne coal. Much extra money could thus reinforce what had come in from gifts, and from such ecclesiastical expedients as the monetary commutation of penances which had, under Charles II, been made over to the financing of the new cathedral.[53] In 1687–88, for instance, the cathedral authorities got nearly three times as much coal money as they had received the year before, while in the eight years from Michaelmas in 1687 they received £150,500 as against a mere £31,000 paid to Wren for the parish churches.[54] Wren could thus be sure that work on the nave, including its two lateral chapels, could proceed steadily and without disruption, throughout the time when James II was on the throne. What was not yet apparent was the final artistry of the most conspicuous features of the finished cathedral. But for the structure of its dome a hint existed in what Wren was doing elsewhere in London.

The Royal Hospital at Chelsea was a job on which progress was steady under James II. Though the main buildings in Figure Court had mostly been finished before Charles II died some important features had still to be completed. Much had to be done, within the four-storeyed main blocks, on such ornamental items as the panelling and fine plasterwork of the Council Chamber where John Grove was the plasterer and where William Cleere, Wren's Master Joiner at the Works, made the bolectioned panelling. In the blocks where most of the veterans were to live partitioned cubicles had to be fitted up. A thoughtful touch, very typical of Wren, appeared in the main stairways. For the stairs themselves were wide, with each tread conveniently low for slow climbing by elderly warriors; this same feature of gently rising stairs appears in the stairway whereby one reaches the library and gallery in St Paul's. A more notable forerunner of what Wren achieved in his great cathedral came at Chelsea in the way in which he supported the stone lantern rising high above the octagonal vestibule which parts the chapel and the hall. The lantern, like that which eventually crowned the dome of St Paul's, being large and heavy could rest neither on the roof timbers nor direct on the crown of the domed ceiling below it. So Wren inserted a hollow brick dome, above the ceiling of the octagon and unseen from the floor of that splendid space, so as to support the lantern which surmounts the great dome of London's new cathedral. Work was being done in 1686 on this structural device at Chelsea.

As the inscription along its colonnade tells us, James II augmented Chelsea Hospital, adding considerably to the number of old or disabled soldiers borne on the strength. To house these extra numbers the site was surveyed, and in 1686 Wren designed the two flanking courts whose buildings, of comparatively low elevation but even so with a pedimented feature in the middle of each block, make an admirable foil to the more massive ranges of the original court.[55] Work started in the last year of James II's reign, and his fall had no effect on their building or on the completion of the whole hospital. Nor, while James II was still king, were there undue financial complications. In July of 1687 the Earl of Ranelagh, the Paymaster of the Forces who was, in many ways, to prove a bad neighbour to the hospital, got a Treasury warrant to pay various craftsmen, for work done at Chelsea in the previous year, the sum of £6,363 2s.10½d.[56] The western wing of Figure Court, the hall, the great Roman Doric portico, and the cloister with its paired columns were covered by these accounts. The executors of Thomas Wise, Thomas Hill another important mason, Matthew Banks the carpenter who was owed more than £1,000, and Charles Hopson, a joiner to whom the sum of £1176 12s.3½d. was due, were among those named. Wren's faithful henchman John Scarborough was to get £7 5s.0d for his survey of the ground, while £20 was the fee for Leonard Gammon the Clerk of Works. Wren had already investigated the accounts, for his certificate, dated 18th April, assured the Treasury officials that he had "diligently examined" the account, comparing prices with contracts and, where he thought it necessary, correcting and cutting the demanded sums. But on the whole he judged that "the total charge may be reasonably allowed as it is cast up". Early in April of 1688 the Treasury told Ranelagh to make payments, amounting in all to £12,150 7s.9d., for work done in 1687; the items excluded the lantern over the octagon porch.[57]

Another of Wren's jobs, within his cognisance but still without his personal visitation went steadily on during these four eventful years. The library at Trinity, Cambridge, now drew near to its structural completion. Robert Grumbold the master mason saw Wren twice in 1685, while in 1686–87 the internal walls and the ceiling were plastered.[58] Wren's trusty associates Matthew Banks and John Grove worked on the timbering and plaster, the latter being done, within the rectangular confines of a richly modillioned cornice, with an absolutely plain surface. The panelled ceiling which Wren had designed was omitted, perhaps for reasons of expense, and was only set up during William Whewell's Victorian mastership. The whole task was one in which Wren could rely, in his absence from the scene, on men whose capacity he well knew.

There remained the tasks which still came to Wren as Surveyor General of the Royal Works. Within the chaotic purlieus of Whitehall Palace there were alterations and additions to the lodgings of various Court officials. Directions on such matters could still be given when the King and his entourage were out of town. For when, in the late summer of 1687 James II and Mary of Modena were at Bath, hoping that the warm waters would aid the Queen's fecundity and help to secure the dynastic fortunes of a Catholic monarchy, Henry Guy consulted the Treasury Lords, who were present at the spa, on various matters which Wren had raised.[59] Later in the same year Sir Christopher dealt, one assumes with sympathy, with a petition from his old Wiltshire friend Alexander Fort, who claimed that he had, on the death of its existing holder, the reversion to the post of Master Joiner of the Works. But he had, at a critical moment, been busy on the Baroque pile of Monmouth House in Soho. As a result, for reasons which became clearer in a few more years, he was "misrepresented", and at the King's insistence missed the promised position.[60] Another matter within Wren's scope concerned the most remote from London of any building whose future he had ever to consider. For in August of 1687 he was asked to report on an estimate sent in for repairs to the royal residence at Berwick on Tweed; the idea was to make a suitable dwelling for the border town's Governor. At such a distance, this was not a job which Wren could supervise in person. So John Etty of York, well known in his own city as an architect, carver, and designer of monuments, and the master to whom the young Grinling Gibbons had been apprenticed, was asked to deputise. But by early December the King had changed his mind, deciding to build a chapel rather than reconstruct the house in the fortress. So the Surveyor General was asked to value the materials available, and to say how they would serve the King's more pious intentions.[61] In the following April Wren wrote to Etty on the repairs done at Berwick. Etty had been there, and Wren expressed himself obliged to him for his journey, travell [travail?] and skill.[62]

The year 1688 was also one in which Wren, legitimately and with no prejudice to his official post, struck out on a property venture of his own. He and one Roger Jackson laid out the considerable sum of £4,400 on some land, for housing development on the northern fringe of the rebuilt City of London, in the area of the Barbican which has now become the scene of massive modern reconstruction.[63] I do not know how large a proportion of the outlay fell to Wren's share, or how much he made from the joint venture. But the results of his purchase would respectably have added to his income; the actual building work, in conformity with the London Rebuilding Act of 1667, need not have diverted him from the designing and building work which came his way as Surveyor General.

In the summer of 1688 Wren had a personal sorrow which presaged a degree of family isolation in his old age. For on 30th June his sister Susan, the wife of Dr William Holder the canon of the still uncomplete St Paul's, died at the age of sixty-one; she had been the closest to Sir Christopher of his brothers and sisters.

In November of 1688, five days after William of Orange had landed in Torbay, Wren got, from the Treasury, what must, with its recalling of astronomical times, have been an agreeable enquiry. One William Mar, back in Charles II's reign, had received a lump sum for "new delineating the dial in the Privy Garden"; he now petitioned for another grant, claiming that what he had done, by that late time in the now crumbling reign of James II, had equalled his previous work. It was for Wren, with what results I do not know, to look into the matter.[64] A few days later, with William of Orange already in Exeter, Wren was asked to deal with a matter bearing on the building activities of his old friend Sir Stephen Fox. Sir Stephen, so it appeared, had, as a leading financial official, spent £1,000 on the lodgings allocated him; he had, so he said, made a large house of the building. Wren speedily certified the improvements which Fox had made. So on 17th November a royal warrant went out, guaranteeing to Fox his occupation of the house till he had been paid his £1,000.[65] It would, however, be for the next king to honour the bargain. For Wren soon found himself at the beginning of the reign, short but from his standpoint most significant, which was to see him evolve his most memorably Baroque designs and, in his sixties, to reach the mature perfection of his style.

11
William and Mary
I   1689–1691

The coming to power of William III and Mary II, and the Glorious Revolution which accompanied and followed that abrupt change in the sovereignty of Britain, could have brought widespread disaster to public servants who had held high positions under James II. But the new queen, like her father, was wholly a Stuart while William, as a grandson of Charles I, was of so pronounced a Stuart descent that he could, on his own, advance a claim to the English throne. So there could be, and was, a measure of continuity between the two regimes. Sir Christopher Wren, a devoted and conscientious servant both of Charles II and his brother, was no fanatical supporter, in the manner of his Laudian father and uncle, of the more extreme aspects of Stuart kingship. He was open-minded enough, in the spirit of the century's enquiring last decades, to work for monarchs who were in the Stuart succession and whose rule need not harm him in politics or religion. Unlike Pepys, whose loyalty to James II, his old official superior, was such that he could not well continue as Secretary of the Navy, Wren found that he could stay on in his official post. As it happened, the new reign, though short, brought him discerning royal patrons, and also fine opportunities for architectural achievement at a time when his designing genius may be said to have reached its peak.

There was thus no obstacle to Wren's reappointment as Surveyor General. On 25th April of 1689 a warrant was issued continuing him in his post. He was to hold his Surveyorship during the King's pleasure; his retaining fee was still 2s. a day for himself and 6d. for his clerk, with 4s. allowed daily, for times when he was travelling on official business, for "diet, boat hire, and riding charges".[1] He was also reappointed in his surveyorship at Windsor Castle. By now, moreover, Wren was actively at work, apart from such details as the preparations for William and Mary's coronation, on important designing jobs of the type best suited to his position as Court Architect. He had also appeared, for the second time, as a Member of Parliament. The fact that his second parliamentary spell soon ended in a humiliating fiasco was no fault of his own. It arose, one assumes with the new king from the Netherlands unaware of the local complexities involved, from the local politics of an ancient borough which Wren knew well, and which would have made him a constituency more familiar and congenial than remote and 'rotten' Plympton.

The constituency now chosen for Wren was New Windsor. He knew it from his early days, and more recently he had often been there as Surveyor at the Castle. He could, with such a parliamentary seat, have expected to see something of his constituents. But as it suited William III as well as it had suited James II to have so important a public servant in Parliament it was again as a court nominee that Wren tried his fortunes at Windsor. What neither he nor the king may have known was that a dispute had long existed over which of two methods of choice should decide the royal borough's representation. The choice of Windsor's two Members of Parliament could be made either by the Mayor, the bailiffs, and a select number of burgesses or, rather more democratically, by a considerably wider range of the town's inhabitants.[2] At Windsor, as in some other boroughs, both methods were sometimes simultaneously tried, with double returns and with resulting petitions, appeals, and unseatings.

Windsor's election for the Convention Parliament of 1689 saw a double, and therefore contested return. The royal nominees were Wren and Henry Powle, a Berkshire man well known as a Whig lawyer. Their election was by the Mayor, the Corporation, and a reliably select number of burgesses, while Powle's position was soon strengthened by his choice as the Convention Parliament's Speaker. Sir Algernon May and one William Adderley were, on the other hand, chosen by the wider range of Windsor's inhabitants who paid scot and lot. May and Adderley petitioned against Powle and Wren, suggesting that the Committee of Privileges should take no action before a settlement of the thorny problem of Windsor's electoral methods.[3] But the committee took a decision, resolving that, as Windsor's right of election lay solely with the smaller body Powle had been rightly chosen; the House as a whole confirmed the ruling. For Sir Algernon pointed out that he had received twelve corporation votes without that of the Mayor, while Wren's dozen voices included the mayoral vote. The committee therefore ruled, with the House's support, that Wren's election was void, so that in May, 1689, a writ went out for the election of *one* new Member for Windsor;[4] Henry Powle the Speaker continued in Parliament.

Doubts about Wren's parliamentary position had not, however, stopped the Members from consulting him, as Surveyor General, on a problem bearing on their own convenience and comfort. Early in April of 1689 a committee of the House was set up to consider how

Members could most conveniently watch the Coronation of William and Mary.[5] It was to confer with Wren, and to take account of the arrangements made for going to and coming back from Westminster Abbey. Along with the Surveyor General they soon visited the relevant spots, and in a mere two days they reported. They found, with the ceremony soon due, that the galleries in the Abbey and in Westminster Hall were still unfinished. But Wren promised their swift completion, and in particular to check the strength of the supporting scaffolding.

Once his tenure of power in England was secure William of Orange lost no time in setting Wren to work on important projects for the improvement, and in one case for the ambitious glorification, of two royal residences. What Wren achieved, and the degree in which his work fell short of what was first proposed, stemmed from the new king's health and personal preferences, and from the punctuation of his short reign by major operations of war.

The new king was of slight build and short stature, and though he was often less frail than he seemed he suffered much from asthma and found it hard to live and work in mist and damp. He had, therefore, as Stadholder of the Netherlands, spent much money, in the dry, sandy, gently hilly heathland of the Veluwe country well away from the dikes, inundations, and polders of North and South Holland, on the large new palace which he built, by 1688, on his estate at Het Loo near Apeldoorn. He continued, when he was also King of England, to do much work both on the house and on its formal gardens, and he often resided there during the inevitably long spells which he spent on the Continent. Back in England he launched out on no equivalent venture in the somewhat similar heathland terrain of Camberley, Chobham, or Aldershot. But he did take drastic action, away from the architectural chaos of Whitehall and a good distance from the muddy and misty miasma of its stinking tidal riverside, on sites much closer to the political fulcrum of his British domains.

The new king's ventures in palace-building, both of them swiftly started and with as much haste on the queen's part as from her husband, were at Kensington and Hampton Court. Inevitably and properly within the terms of his Surveyor's post, they both caused much work, and many journeys of inspection, for Sir Christopher Wren.

Though William III, for reasons both of health and working convenience, disliked the palace at Whitehall he needed a home, particularly in winter, at a really convenient distance both from the scene of government and from Parliament at Westminster. Two miles from Whitehall, on the edge of what was still the mere village of Kensington, he found the comparatively modern house which he could use as the nucleus of a more ambitious place of residence. The mansion, mainly Jacobean and not much altered since the early years of the seventeenth century, had been owned, till he died in 1682, by Heneage Finch, one of Charles II's Lord Chancellors and in 1681 created Earl of Nottingham; from his final title he had called it Nottingham House. The Second Earl arranged to sell the house to the new sovereigns, and though the purchase was not complete for two years, effective royal occupation started by the middle of 1689.[6] For work was then commenced, in great haste, to fit Nottingham House as a royal residence, more healthy than Whitehall and, as the energetic and informal Queen Mary told a friend, at an easy walking distance from the older palace.[7]

Kensington Palace was another of Wren's commitments where the reality achieved, under Wren himself or other architects, fell far short of what might have been built; it was no surprise that Vanbrugh, almost certaintly before 1718 when Wren ceased to be Surveyor General, got out an ambitious project for the almost complete replacement of the rambling, haphazardly composed palace as it stood by about 1700. But campaigns in Ireland and on the Continent soon strained the national finances, work on Hampton Court diverted money and building talent, while at the end of 1694 Queen Mary's death, at Kensington itself, much lessened, without removing, the impetus behind the Kensington project. But while she was alive, and in particular during the first year of the joint reign, the Queen seems, on one occasion with sad results, to have been the main driving force behind the repairs and the new work which were taken in hand.

Whatever Wren and his royal patrons may have envisaged for a grandiose new palace at Kensington, what was actually built by the time of the King's death in 1702 amounted to some separate additions to the compact Jacobean block of Kensington House. Four corner buildings were added, in the manner of pavilions, to the earlier buildings. There were also, at differing dates, two long, narrow wings or galleries, and some entrance buildings, with an attractive cupola finished by April, 1690, leading in from the west. Attractive gardens, in the Dutch manner which was congenial to William and Mary's taste, were formally laid out, by George London the royal gardener, east and south of the palace.* To provide easy access from Whitehall and St James's a wide new road, forty feet broad and wide enough to allow three coach lanes, was to be laid out through Hyde Park.† Its surface was well gravelled, it had broad and amply deep drainage ditches, and it was also to be lined, at regular intervals, with posts bearing lanterns. Captain Michael Studholme, who held the post of

*In June, 1690, London claimed and Wren allowed, £1540 3s.8d. for work at Kensington (C.T.B.IX, p. 715).

†The line of this road can now be traced in Rotten Row.

Keeper and Guide of His Majesty's Roads, was the official responsible for this imposing highway; late in August of 1689 his estimate, for £4,277, was referred, for their comments, to Wren, and to William Talman who now held the post of Comptroller of the Royal Works.[8] Construction must, however, have started, for early next month, when Wren reckoned that what had already been done would be inadequate, the contract was called in. The work was, however, carried on, and in May, 1693, Studholme sent in two estimates; Wren agreed them, after Hawksmoor had measured the proposed work, at a sum very near Studholme's higher figure.[9] Later in the same year Studholme submitted, for the expert opinion of Wren and his colleagues, a scheme, which Wren passed, for the improvement of a road (now Gloucester Road) from Kensington Palace to Chelsea and its completed Hospital.[10]

Wren's main work at Kensington came in two phases. Firstly there was a new range of apartments for the special use of the Queen, complete by the end of 1691 and accompanied, in the same building operation, by a Grand Staircase, with a simple delicate balustrade of Baroque ironwork by the Huguenot smith Jean Tijou, to give ceremonial access to the King's apartments. A few years later work started, for the widower king, on the more ambitious King's Gallery. Whatever may first have been intended, what was done was, as at Chelsea and as in Winchester Palace for Charles II, an imposing work in the main of brick, but with dressings of stone. Such a mixture would not, for the monarch who had commissioned the new palace at Het Loo,[11] have seemed unfamiliar or beneath his sovereign dignity.

So anxious was the queen to occupy her new home that normal building procedure was riskily short-circuited. Early in July of 1689 contracts were signed, for the main work of this first phase, with Thomas Hues as bricklayer and with John Hayward as carpenter.[12] Both contracts stipulated that the workmen were to follow directions from the officers of the Royal Works; the "draught", or drawings, had been approved, not by both sovereigns but by Mary alone. The outer walls, for the corner additions to Nottingham House or for the considerably larger Queen's Gallery with its fine oak staircase, were soon run up in brick. Internal subdivisions were not, however, so durably started, and such heavy items as chimney stacks and marble chimney pieces were dangerously poised over nothing stronger than timber partitions. Wren could hardly have been happy with so precarious a contrivance. Any extra weight was likely to cause trouble. Early in November, when the roofing was leaded, trouble came with a vengeance. Some walling collapsed, some workmen were killed, and several were injured.[13] The Queen, whose impatience, and whose frequent visits to view the work and hasten the men, had in part caused the trouble, was duly and humbly penitent for what had happened.

The first part of what Wren and his assistants designed and built at
Kensington was finished in about two years. Though the new
buildings were mainly of brick Portland stone was used for dressings.
Its supply, in the late summer of 1690 when the sea battle off Beachy
Head for a time gave the French the command of the Channel, was
liable to hostile interception; the same factor could also have worried
Wren over building progress in the City. "King Billy", in the
meantime, was away on his successful Irish campaign. For the king's
comfort in the field Wren had, in March of 1690, been asked to
superintend the making of a marquee, or "itinerant house" to cover
the royal travelling tent; two waggons were to be set aside to carry the
contraption.[14]

The Queen's Gallery, a long, narrow block with its staircase at one
end and some private apartments to the south, was like a
sophisticated version of the Tudor or early Stuart long galleries. With
its simple bolection panelling, bolection mouldings round marble
fireplaces, and an unadorned ceiling, it was one of Wren's less
remarkable though far from unseemly works.[15] What later followed at
Kensington was of considerably more note. Meanwhile, and at the
same time as the first operations at Kensington, Wren worked, for
erection elsewhere, on some of his finest and most mature designs.

Wren's involvement with Hampton Court well proved how much
his career as a designer was swayed by events, in no way architectural
in character, which occurred amid England's swift political changes
at that time. The personal tastes of William and Mary, the king's
campaigns out of England and his frequent spells of residence on the
Continent, the Queen's early death, a short spell of peace which
included a disastrous fire at Whitehall, and William's death after a
reign of only thirteen years, all contributed to the frustration, the
interruption and the actual achievement of what Wren designed, in
person and with no debt of inspiration to his official colleagues, for his
most important commission, so far, as official Court architect. Yet
although, for more than a dozen years of his life, he found Hampton
Court a leading preoccupation his main designing work for the palace
was swiftly done in the year 1689.

Though any riverside site can be damp and trying for an asthmatic,
William and his wife much liked Hampton Court, finding it greatly
preferable to Whitehall on its muddy tidestream and, in a situation
which was still rural, more secluded than suburban Kensington.
Transformed, or perhaps wholly rebuilt, the palace up the river could
be something of an opposite number to what William's great rival
Louis XIV had by now created at Versailles; one has to recall, when
assessing the prospect as the new sovereigns saw it, that they could
reasonably expect a reign of twenty years or more. Though Hampton
Court, even in its portions by Wren, falls short of Versailles' vaunting
splendour, and though it has rather been seen as a parallel to the

Louvre whose enlargement Wren personally knew, a study of what Wren first proposed shows that Hampton Court might have been a palace more nearly an equivalent to the Sun King's residence out of town.

In brick, with stone dressings, the Perpendicular Gothic palace of Wolsey and Henry VIII was, by 1689, a sadly unfashionable house. No more than Audley End was it a building congenial to Wren's mature Renaissance taste, or one which he would have wished to retain. Though his first, more drastic project for Hampton Court would still have allowed the preservation and continued use of one important element of the late Gothic palace that building, in one and perhaps in both versions of Wren's proposals, would have been masked and marred by new features unsympathetic to its real design; this was not the first time when Wren somewhat arrogantly suggested the unsympathetic embellishment of an earlier master's work.

As William and Mary wished to use Hampton Court as soon as they could alterations to the old palace were started in April, 1689.[16] Some recently installed fitments could, moreover, be re-used; one notes, for instance, the ironic point that some fireplaces in the Wren buildings have iron firebacks, dated 1687, with the arms of the uncle-cum-father-in-law whom William had lately supplanted. But plans were soon afoot for more drastic changes than the repair and patching of early Tudor courtyards. With Wren's alternative schemes for what was called the "Grand Project" we come to what would, had it been finished at Hampton Court, have been one of his noblest works.

What Wren proposed early in 1689 was to pull down almost all of the Tudor Hampton Court, and to replace it, in the seventeenth-century Renaissance taste as this was understood in France, by a spacious new palace, like its predecessor with three main courts but with the first two, significantly for the visitor's approach to the building's most monumental front, united into a single space. Alone of the other buildings the Great Hall, built by Henry VIII and on any reckoning of great and stately splendour, was due to survive as the central feature, from the Bushey Park side, of one avenue of approach. Yet even here some refacing, and the building out of a small terrace or platform, with curved walls to form a kind of exedra, would have made an unsympathetic interference, on the northern side, with John Molton and James Needham's Great Hall of the 1530s.[17]

For the new work, one preliminary design apart, Wren got out two main versions of what he proposed. The new palace was to be aligned onto the Bushey Park Avenue with its circular basin, also onto Charles II's 'canal' with whose water supply Wren had, as Surveyor General, already been concerned. The visitors' entrance, from the road leading down to the river, was to be through the double space of the new entrance court. The Palace's southern and eastern sides were to look out, as they actually do, over more private gardens.

Though the first designs were for a palace smaller than the Louvre which Wren had seen, and far smaller than Versailles of whose layout he must, by now, have been well aware, they had about them a magnificent dignity akin to the stately residences of the French king; they were, so Wren and his employees hoped, to be a suitable setting for monarchs who could hope, in Anne and in her still living son the little Duke of Gloucester, to have successors of their own line.

The surviving drawings tell us nothing of what Wren proposed for the new buildings due to flank the western, or outermost section of his great entrance court, to arise on the site of the early Tudor Base Court whose buildings in fact survive. They were, perhaps, to have been a modest prelude to the more vaunting scale of the Grand Front of the block whose first floor was to be used less for private residence than for purposes of government. A Council Chamber was in the middle of the first floor. It was to be flanked by an ante-room and a withdrawing room, and even by a 'stool room' to the last named official apartment. More notable, and well fitting what could, with the King in residence, be the country's place of decision, was the elevation designed to confront approaching councillors.[18] Eight giant Corinthian half-columns were to adorn the rooms for the council, and, below them, the entrance to the Privy Court and to the park and Charles II's 'canal'. Above the central opening the royal arms and a somewhat cramped equestrian figure of William III were to lend dignity to the building, while in the central block, and in the wings which were to flank it, boldy edged windows were to add to the masonry's dramatic effect. Above the council block a finely detailed, balustraded attic storey was to have as its centrepiece a great crowned cartouche, with heroic human supporters, but with no indication, in the drawing of the block, of what device or design it was to have contained. The topmost feature, full of Baroque panache and with a particularly happy stroke of design, was to be a dome, bell-shaped and with a richly detailed finial, and with a concave drum whose surface was to be varied with formalised lambrequins. The whole composition, 150 feet across, would have been of truly royal magnificance and can rank among Wren's finest designs. Though without a dome, the block on the eastern side of the Privy Court was also to be of much splendour and would have answered, with its giant order, its three openings to the park, its attic storey, and in some of its fenestration, to the Council range.[19] Distinctive features of this residential range would have been some open arcading, some niches for urns or statues, and staircase towers nicely capped by gently concave *cupoletti*. As it faced the park this same block was to be the centrepiece of a long frontage whose flanking wings were to have their own attic storeys; only in the central block, above its giant order, a pediment was to correspond with the one actually erected in this ceremonial position; the pencilling of its drawing is too faint to give a certain clue to the subject of its sculpture; it could, like the actual pediment, have enshrined a Herculean theme.

Whatever hopes Wren may have had for a totally new Hampton Court his "Grand Project" soon fell victim to the political and financial problems which beset William and Mary in the first year of their reign. The royal finances were straitened even before the Irish campaign. By the end of 1689 work had started on the less ambitious replacement scheme whose result was the present palace – half Tudor-Gothic and half by Wren, whose stylistic contrasts one can still admire. Wren's replacement of some of Wolsey's work suffers from an obvious incompleteness; the Tudor buildings, superb in their own category, are in some ways more satisfying, and more in keeping with the spirit of their own time, than what Wren and his collaborators were able to achieve.

Intelligent and sympathetic as architectural patrons William and Mary were closely interested in what was done at Hampton Court; as at Kensington their haste caused practical problems. With the King often away the Queen was more in evidence than her husband; *Parentalia* records that she suggested improvements in the gardens, and tells how she often came to "inspect and observe" the work, frequently meeting Wren on site and having lively discussions with him on "architecture, mathematics, and other learning".[20] The two palaces on which he was now engaged naturally required large slices of Wren's time. His record of riding charges shows that in 1689–91 he was at Hampton on 308 days – nearly one in three from the time when William and Mary decided to build there.[21] The even greater frequency – 384 days in a shorter period, of his visits to Kensington may be explained by the more modest palace's greater nearness to Scotland Yard.[22]

What was decided, as the year 1689 progressed, was to leave the Tudor Base Court, the Great Hall, and much of Clock Court as they were. The old chapel, with a new altarpiece and other fittings by Wren, was also to survive; so too were some buildings to the north of it. But as one saw the palace from the south-east, the eastern and southern fronts were to convey the illusion of a wholly new set of buildings, of brick with important features and dressings of Portland stone and in a French Renaissance taste fully mature though less splendid than what was allowed for in Wren's first designs. Some features in the new work did, however, correspond, at least in the park front, to some set out in the "Grand Project". Behind those two long frontages, with their impression of a less grandiose Versailles, a courtyard, to Wren's design on all of its four sides replaced the Green Court of Wolsey's palace. Its alignment, with three openings leading to Charles II's 'canal' or Long Water and like similar openings in the

"Grand Project" piercing the middle of the eastern front, was to be a little south of the Tudor court which it replaced. Out in Clock Court another feature by Wren was to screen the entrance to the new state apartments. The main survivals of the Tudor palace were to lie north-west of Wren's suites of royal apartments. It was on this reduced, but still important scheme that work started, in the summer of 1689; then and later re-usable materials came from the unfinished palace of Winchester. I will deal later with features of Wren's design; for the moment one has historic and biographical points.

Quick building being required there was the risk and soon the reality of accidents on site. In June of 1689 a labourer names Harrison was killed when an old wall collapsed; £2 compensation was authorised for his widow.[22] Six months later a worse collapse involved new work. The cause may have been the structural expedient which had caused the disaster at Kensington. It seems, however, more likely that a new wall, apparently sound, collapsed. The situation caused, or perhaps served to reveal, an acrimonious situation between Wren and an architect associate.

Two men were killed in the accident and were buried on the spot, while eleven were hurt.[23] The King sought an early report, and on 18th December Wren had to attend at the Treasury about the fallen wall.[24] Then at the end of the year, as the King was impatient to see a statement on the whole condition of Hampton Court, Wren and William Talman, who was now his uneasy colleague as Comptroller of the Royal Works, again attended and were to prepare a written report.[25] As a Treasury minute put it, the matter was "a thing so nice" that an account was required without delay. It was arranged that Wren was to examine on oath a range of such "disinterested men" as bricklayers, carpenters, and other building craftsmen who "had left off their aprons" and were under no suspicion of being under his influence.[26] Talman, so one assumes, was to do something similar. Sharp disagreement soon arose, between the two architects, on the quality of the work done before the disaster; Talman seems to have hoped that the controversy, and any discredit falling on Wren, would help him to the full control of operations at Hampton Court.

In January 1690 Wren and Talman sent in their reports, contradictory but each backed by constructional experts.[27] Talman had got an opinion from the London mason Jasper Latham who must have backed the contention that the collapsed wall had been unsoundly built. Wren, on the other hand, protested that Latham, who had worked a little, but not prominently, on City churches, must have been a madman to pass such an opinion; he assured the officials that the new walling had withstood winds of a hurricane force. Talman countered with a statement that Latham was not mad, and that other buildings had shielded the new wall from the wind's supposed force.

His own witness was the carpenter Matthew Banks; he and Talman soon started a dispute on cracks in some piers and on the use, which Wren supported, and which the Surveyor General reckoned should not be "maliciously interpreted", of iron cramps. Arbitrators were appointed to inspect the work done; the quarrel, with its "general dispute" between Wren and Talman, highlighted, though it may not have started, a sequence of bad feeling between the two men. The episode did not, however, interrupt progress at Hampton Court.

Wren had still, in these first three years of the new reign, to tackle various minor tasks which arose from his Surveyor's post. St James's Park and its waterfowl continued to claim some attention from him and his colleagues; he must, of course, have known the birds well from his walks in the park. In September, 1689, the Treasury asked him to report on various bills for their upkeep.[28] A year later there was a similar query, looking back to the previous winter when men were hired to break the ice on the canal.[29] Nor were these waterfowl of purely ornamental interest, for in the summer of 1690 John Webb, the park's fowlkeeper and pondkeeper, put in bills not only for feeding the birds but for serving some of them to the royal table at Kensington and Hampton Court.[30] Ice, moreover, soon became relevant to Wren in another form. For James Frontin, the "yeoman" of their Majesties' icehouse, asked for a long lease of some of the royal icehouses. He proposed, with the profits, to build "commodious icehouses near St James's and at Hampton Court; later in the same year Wren had to value the sites for Frontin's new Erections in the London park.[31] At Windsor Wren and Talman were concerned, as Wren had been in earlier years, with the water engine which, like that at Marly near Versailles, raised Thames water to the castle. John Taylor asked, late in the summer of 1689, for the renewal of his post as its caretaker. Both Wren and Talman certified his competence and he was duly reappointed in 1690.[32] By then, moreover, Wren was again involved in Windsor's parliamentary representation.

The Convention Parliament was dissolved early in 1690 and the second, more Tory Parliament of William and Mary's reign met in March. The King and his advisors must still have thought it fitting to have the Surveyor General in the Commons, for Wren again appeared, by the same, restricted electoral procedure as that used in the previous year, as a Member for New Windsor: his colleague was Baptist May, once a court crony of Charles II who had, during that reign of revels, gained none too good a reputation.[33] He had later settled down as Clerk of the Works at Windsor Castle, with a residence in the park on which Alexander Fort, the Master Joiner of the Works, did some repairs on which Wren later had to report. The unsuccessful candidates were William Adderley again, and Sir Charles Porter, a Berkshire lawyer, a close adherent of William III, and later in the same year Lord Chancellor of a subdued Ireland. They claimed that most of the legal electors had returned them, and that the Mayor, notwithstanding had unduly declared May and Wren to be Windsor's representatives in Parliament. The Committee of Privileges, more mindful of royal policy than an increasingly restive parliamentary majority, considered the case and in two months resolved that Wren and Baptist May had been properly elected. But the Commons overruled the committee, deciding, albeit by a small majority, that Porter and Adderley were Windsor's properly elected Members. The formal papers of return had thus to be altered, and the names of Wren and Porter were stricken from the file.[35]

Apart from major commissions in what was probably the busiest phase of his career Wren also continued to deal with various issues coming naturally to the Works office. One petition, coming in 1690 from an old friend and technical associate, looked back at the politics of the Exclusion controversy and of James II. Alexander Fort complained of the loss of his post, as Master Joiner of the Works, because he had, from late in 1683 and after James II's accession, worked as designer and supervisor on the Duke of Monmouth's town mansion in Soho. Wren had looked into the complaint of Fort who had reckoned, on a predecessor's death, to get the official post. But James II, being offended with Monmouth's joiner (Wren said, somewhat innocently, that he did not know the king's reasons) gave positive orders, privately at his bedchamber levée and more publicly before the Treasury lords, that Fort should be kept from the succession. Wren had obeyed without question, and Fort had to await the new reign before he could secure his promised place.[36]

Fort was also concerned, early in William and Mary's reign, with another commission which may have involved Wren as a designer and which was certainly started by Wren's old friend, collaborator and, over Hungerford Market, business associate Sir Stephen Fox. At Farley, his native village near Salisbury Fox had already employed his fellow Wiltshireman Fort on the attractive almshouse with its central wardenry. Now, in 1689-90, he employed Fort as the main contractor for the new church across the road.[37] Wren could well have sent down the building's basic plan, with a chancel whose southern doorway is survivally Perpendicular, but most of whose windows, like others in the building are round-headed as in many of Wren's City churches. The body of the church, on a Greek cross plan, gives an "auditory" effect, while the tower, whose southern doorway has an open pediment, came close in its design to some of Wren's simpler towers in London.

Palaces and parks apart, the years 1690 and 1691 showed how many topics could come officially to Wren's attention. In April 1690, when England was at war with France, and when the capture of a French merchantman had yielded, among the booty, a consignment of marble, Wren reported on its quality. The less good blocks, he recommended, were to be sold, the proceeds helping to pay for the storage of the rest; the workmen on the job were to be protected from the attentions of the press gang.[38] Then in 1691 he and his staff had to face a problem with a nautical relevance. The townsmen of Margate, not yet a seaside resort but of some note as a coasting port and, as Defoe wrote later, a landing place much favoured by William III as he journeyed to and from the Netherlands, were in trouble when, in the autumn of 1690, a gale from the north-west much damaged one of their harbour works. In the following January, a nasty time of the year for a journey to so exposed a part of Kent, Wren travelled to inspect the havoc;[39] the trip could have recalled his consultation about the Tangier mole or, earlier still, his Wadham display on building in deep water or building piers and moles into the sea. His opinion, backed by sworn local statements, was that repairs would cost the sum, large for such a place, of £2,500. So in July a petition went up asking for royal help; one imagines that Sir Christopher, with his memories of a wintry inspection in Thanet, supported the plea. Next month he was slightly concerned with a site soon to witness his noblest secular achievement. Gunpowder removed from warships needed safe storage. So the Queen, with her husband away abroad, gave orders for its lodgement in the comparatively recent building in the palace at Greenwich. Wren, as the official custodian of such a building, was thus told to allow the Ordnance officers to make, in Queen Elizabeth's neglected birthplace, what arrangements they pleased.[40]

Early in September of 1691 Queen Mary also gave orders for some politically interesting work in the Tower of London. Wren thus had to see that three or four rooms, in the Beauchamp and Bloody Towers, were fitted out for the safe keeping of important prisoners.[41] Conditions were not, however, to be of dungeon grimness, for in another three years we hear, in addition to tighter security measures, of the wainscoting or panelling of these apartments. Not far from the Tower, the Mint was now well established; within it there stood a building, known as Moneyers' Hall, which the Corporation of Moneyers used as their headquarters. Late in November they petitioned over its condition, and Wren was asked to inspect the building and to "do as is desired if you find it convenient". The work was carried out, and nearly a year later the Warden of the Mint was ordered to procure, out of coinage money, enough silver to yield £1,362 to pay for the work done, not only for the Moneyers' Hall but also, according to an estimate sent in by Wren, for a new engravers' house in the Mint itself.[42]

Late in the same year, 1691, Wren was asked to do some work which arose from an important personal inspection which he, and the Master Carpenter of the Works, had made in the previous summer.[43]

It had been on the meeting place of the House of Commons, in other words the once splendid chapel of St Stephen in the Palace of Westminster, used since Tudor times for its political purpose and refitted for Parliamentary uses under Wren's own direction; the inspection had involved climbing and peering into roofing timbers. Gutters had been uncovered, the timber of the roof had been opened out for inspection, and much of the one-time chapel's roof had been covered with new lead. Wren had thought that "all was firm"; now in the winter trouble had arisen over the ceiling of the Commons chamber. It was eight years since this ceiling, as well as the roof, had been properly examined; Wren now found that the ceiling was of plaster of Paris, not of the mixture of lime and hair which was less liable to cracking. The roof timbers were, however, very old (presumably of the fourteenth century when the chapel had been finished) and their long continuance could not be presumed. The real solution, Wren felt, was more drastic. To him it seemed reasonable that "ere long a new Roome be thought of where the important affairs of the nation may be transacted without suspicion of this sort". It was, however, another century and a half before anything of this kind was done. In the meantime he could do no more than provide a new ceiling and authorise repairs; the exclusion of cold draughts blowing in on the legislators was later to cause him some trouble. Moreover, he had already tackled a practical problem arising from the interaction of gusty air and smoke. For when, on October 28th, 1691 the Royal Society (on whose Council Wren had again sat in 1689–90) had a general discussion on chimneys, the astronomer Edmund Halley told the members how Wren had devised a new way whereby smoke could escape from the gunner's room which lay close "under the eddy" of the Whitehall Banqueting House. What Wren had done was to construct a "double funnel", one inlet providing an air current for the gunner's fire, the other, by a forced draught which ensured that the outgoing smoke was not "prest down" by the eddies swiring round the larger building, providing for the smoke's convenient emission.[44]

The last weeks of 1691 also found Wren concerned with a project which also looked back to a long period of service to education. Since early in Charles II's reign Wren, along with Sir Robert Clayton and Sir Jonas Moore, had been a governor of Christ's Hospital School in its quarters off Newgate Street. But Hooke, with John Oliver who was Wren's deputy at St Paul's, seems for some years to have been more important for the school's post-fire building programme. So when in 1682–84 a new block for the mathematical school was put up along the southern side of the buildings Wren may only have exercised general supervision. The design of the frontage was certainly not of his normal quality. The pavilion ends, with open pediments and pairs of Ionic pilasters were, indeed, respectable compositions, but the central part, with a large curved pediment over four widely spaced Ionic pilasters, was crude and loosely composed, a typical work of artisan Baroque. More sophisticated, though not built as they were first achieved, were the plans which Wren presented, early in 1692, for a new Writing and Drawing School.

The new building's chief benefactor was Sir Jonas Moore, ten years earlier Lord Mayor of London and in 1691/92 the President of Christ's Hospital. By 18th December 1691, designs for the new block, to run north and south over the site of the old city wall and ditch, were in Wren's hands; he soon presented them and they were approved.[45] Their actual rendering came a little later in Wren's career. But as the designs, as one has them in the drawings at All Souls',[46] were made in 1691, and as they may not wholly have been Wren's work, they can now be considered.

The drawings show a simple block, with round-arched arcading opening, at groundfloor level, into a covered piazza. The building was to be of three storeys, and the great open school room was of six bays with a gallery. Each bay was to have four 'classes', or double desks. With two feet of elbow room allowed for each boy, 336 were to do their lessons on the main floor. The end elevations were to have pleasingly panelled chimney stacks. More ornamental, on some corner turrets, pert *cupoletti* of a Baroque flavour were to have concave drums surmounted by simple caps. From the handwriting of their notes, and from other indications, Hawksmoor, by now Wren's trusted assistant, may have made these drawings, and may also have conceived some points in their design; in such a case they foreshadow the time when Wren would no longer be his country's greatest living architect.

Two Cambridge colleges were still, in this last decade of the century, of professional interest to Wren; one of them also saw the revival of a family connection.

At Trinity the library staircase had already, in 1686–87, received the noble covering of John Grove's plaster ceiling, with rich wreathing and the winged heads of cherubs in its rectangular portion, and a profusion of foliage, along with suitable heraldry, in its gently curved cove. Now in the 1690s the great work was completed. The masonry was finished in 1690 and in the same year, now that fitting and furnishing were afoot, Cornelius Austin went twice to London to see Wren about the panelling and bookcases.[47] It was against the oaken background of the bookcase ends that Gibbons set his limewood carvings whose shields, amid profuse cherubs and foliage, commemorate many Trinity worthies. Gibbons also made the plaster busts which, as a weak substitute for the fullsized statues which Wren envisaged, surmount the bookcases, while over one of the doorways his limewood carving includes the arms of the joint sovereigns in whose reign the carving was done. Caius Gabriel Cibber carved the library's stone statues; unlike Wren in these last years of the job he went personally to Cambridge to keep an eye on the finishing and placing of his work.[48]

The other Cambridge college with which Wren was now involved, indirectly on important fittings and decorations and more directly as the father of one of its junior members, was Pembroke. Since the new chapel, which Wren had designed for his uncle the bishop, had been opened for worship, the old chapel, going back to the foundation period of the fourteenth century, had been little used. But in the summer of 1688, while James II was still on the throne, the Pembroke dons ordered that their old chapel should be turned into a library. Such a task, with the structural work and new fittings involved, needed more money than the college could normally find. A significant donor, who gave the useful sum of £100, was Dr William Holder, a Pembroke man, Wren's brother-in-law, and an associate in many of Sir Christopher's activities.[49] Though the bookcases, and other woodwork, could well have been made by such a Cambridge joiner as Cornelius Austin, the splendid plaster ceiling, with its floral and animal motifs, its books to denote learning, and its completion dating of 1690, was by no local craftsman but was wrought by Henry Doogood, the plasterer for Wren in several of the City churches; so too were the plaster arms of William and Mary in whose reign the work was finished. Wren may not have worked out the whole design for this splendid covering of the old chapel, but it seems most likely, with Holder so prominent a donor and with his own previous connection with Pembroke, that he gave the college his "interest and advice".[50] Then in 1691, the year after the new ceiling was finished, the Wren link with Pembroke was reinforced when the Surveyor General sent his son, aged sixteen when he came up as a Fellow Commoner (*ad secundam mensam**) under Dr Westfield as his tutor.[51] The younger Christopher was there when, in 1693, the books were carried into the newly equipped library.

In periods so full of official work it was as well for Wren that his church commissions were a comparatively light burden. In the City no more parish churches were commenced at this time, and those finished under William and Mary were, in the main though under Wren's general supervision, the concern of joiners, carvers, plasterers, and other craftsmen. Nor, before 1694, was it time to finish the steeples left incomplete above their towers. At St Paul's work went steadily both on the choir and transepts, on the main fabric of the nave, and on much of Gibbons's rich exterior carving, best seen in panels below the windows of the aisles. The most important frontages

*The Pembroke Fellow Commoners must have dined at a 'second table' ranking between those of the Fellows and the scholars.

were those of the two transepts. Wren seems to have decided, almost
simultaneously with his presentation of the 'Warrant' design, to make
important changes in this aspect of his cathedral. For the entrance
vestibules, demurely recessed behind columns *in antis*, he substituted a
pair of porches, boldly curving out as does that of Sta Maria della
Pace in Rome, a church of whose appearance Wren could have known
through illustrated books. His drawings show that one version of this
porch was semicircular;[52] what one has in practice, with six fine
Corinthian columns for each porch, is more gently segmental. Above
the top of each porch large windows were headed, to make a shape
much favoured by Wren, by a gently segmental curve, while drawings
show various designs for the great doorways into the cathedral's
transepts.[53] Several years before the transepts were built Wren also
kept his options open, between a triangle or a segmental curve,[54] for
the shape of his transepts' pediments, while the sculpture to go in the
lunettes of those pediments also admitted variations. A phoenix above
the auspicious word RESURGAM seems always to have been the choice
for Gibbons's carving in the southern pediment. But for the northern
side a drawing has various schemes for the arms of the City of
London;[55] those of William and Mary, with their significant
inescutcheon of Nassau, were what Gibbons actually rendered.

The drawings for the arrangement of the morning prayer chapel,
with no altar provided and with a mention of paving "arras ways", in
Swedish stone,[56] must date from about now. More important, as the
nave neared completion, were Wren's ideas for its western
termination. Inigo Jones's one-tiered portico had only lately been
pulled down. Wren still hoped as at the time of the 'Model' design, for
the impressive effect of a one-tiered western portico, whose vast
columns would powerfully impress those who approached the new
cathedral up Ludgate Hill. Some drawings survive to show alternative
schemes for such a facade. Two projects allow, as in the 'Model'
design, for a stupendous Corinthian giant order whose columns would
have been taller than those of Inigo Jones. Another, with a marked
Hawksmoorian touch where a semicircle is scopped out of the lower
edge of an open pediment, has an Ionic giant order of square piers and
rounded columns.[57] A similar design was rendered by Hawksmoor,
with a Doric order, in the east end of the new parish church at
Greenwich. But none of these imposing designs could be built; what
defeated Wren were geological problems in the Dorset quarries.

Wren was more concerned, in this first half of William and Mary's
short reign, with his Surveyor's jobs at Kensington and Hampton
Court; the commission at Hampton Court was the more testing, and
architecturally the more important of the two. For the moment, and in
fact lastingly, the notion of an almost wholly new palace had been
given up; what Wren achieved, by the end of 1691, were the essential
first stages of new buildings which were, on two sides in close

promixity to Tudor work, to enclose a single court and, at least form
the fine ornamental gardens laid out by Le Nôtre, and with Tijou's
brilliant Baroque ironwork, to give the illusion of a new building, not
all of stone but in an attractive blend of red brick and Wren's
favoured, silvery Portland stone; Reigate, Headington, and Beer stone
were also used.[58] Though the fitting and furnishing of the rooms lay
some distance in the future the external design of the palace blocks
had by now been settled.

Dr Kerry Downes has well pointed out the essentially French
nature of Wren's Hampton Court elevations, and the relationship of
the scheme with the enclosed courtyard of the Louvre[59] rather than
with Versailles whose central portion, even after its enlargement and
envelopment under Louis XIV, did not much exceed Hampton
Court's dimensions. Wren's elevations thus, in their out-of-town
setting, reflected the restrained, somewhat heavy classicism of the late
French Renaissance. More sculpturally Baroque effects were reserved
for the designs, nearly all unexecuted, which Wren and Gibbons got
out for various internal features. Though the new palace, as started in
1689 and somewhat spasmodically continued till after 1700, is
somewhat less in reality than what Wren and his associates had in
mind, what was actually built is among Wren's most important
works; in its inner courtyard it displays structural ingenuity sparked
off by the visual preferences of a royal patron.

Though the two outward elevations display four tiers of openings
their real composition is in three storeys; the round windows, whose
sequence is at some points interrupted by applied decoration or by the
monumental main features of the park and garden fronts, belong to
the *piano nobile* and are many of them blank because of high-rising
coved ceilings behind them. Above them, the attic storey has a long
series of square windows, closely paned and set below a stone
balustrade. The ground floor is almost wholly faced with Portland
stone which appears, more sparsely, in the window edgings and other
dressings of the upper storeys. Over some of the windows the
keystones are boldly carved with crowns above crossed sceptres and
the royal cipher with its initials W (not G) MRR (*Willelmus et Maria
Rex et Regina*). The orangery on the south side, and the openings from
the Fountain Court to the park, diminished the accommodation
provided at ground level; the essence of the palace, as a royal home or
as a place of dignified reception, was contained in its first floor.

The central feature of the eastern, or park, front best conveys the
notions of regal grandeur held by Wren's patrons and expressed in the
architect's designs. Four fluted Corinthian half-columns, and four
pilasters of the same order, have rich garlanding between their
capitals. Above the trabeation and a modillioned cornice a triangular
pediment awkwardly interrupts the attic storey and contains
Gibbons's fine relief of Hercules overcoming envy. The king, despite

his unherculean physique, liked to revive the notion, held earlier by the Dutch Republic in its struggle against Spain, of himself as Hercules defeating the overweaning power of the Sun King. Herculean iconography is thus somewhat profuse at Hampton Court.

The southern or garden front is better for its lack of a pediment; its central feature is narrower and more modest than its eastern counterpart. The sculptural decoration here is more sparse, but no less politically pointed, than on the other side. A fine trophy of arms rises above the central window, the arms of William and Mary rise above two others which have pediments, while the Royal Arms and Garter badges cap two windows at the level of the orangery. Rainwater heads dated 1690 prove the swift execution of this outward elevation of what Wren, Talman, and the Works craftsmen quickly achieved under the queen's constant supervision.

Equally interesting are the more secluded elevations of Fountain Court. The round windows, many of them false openings as in the park and garden fronts, were wreathed round, at the king's desire, with Hercules' lion's skin. The windows along the court's southern side, being masked by the ceiling of the cartoon gallery, were insipidly filled by Laguerre with grisaille paintings showing the twelve labours of Dutch William's tutelary demigod. The main windows are simply pedimented; below them the rounded arches of the cloister arcade mask one of the more interesting features, alike biographical and architectural, of all Wren's work.

Wren's first idea had been to repeat, in this arcaded enclosure of Hampton Court, what he had done at Cambridge in the library at Trinity. The floor level of the ceremonial rooms round the court, and of the long, narrow, dull Communication Gallery which recalled Tudor or Jacobean long galleries, was to lie not on a level with the tops of the arches but a few feet lower on a level with the simply moulded caps of the square piers; the device would, as at Trinity, have increased the height of rooms above the alleyways. But William III, concerned over the dignity of passages by which courtiers would approach the park, complained with some justice that Wren's design for the cloister walks would make them too low and dark.[60] So Wren ingeniously raised the ceilings not to the full height of the main arches but to the tops of low segmental arches inserted below them. The blank spaces so created were filled, less elaborately than in the arches at Trinity, by wisps of floral and foliage carving, while the alleyways, slightly heightened but with little effect on the dignity of the rooms above them, were improved by a shallow vault. The king, one assumes, was satisfied and work went on, in Wren's busy years of 1690 and 1691, on the palace which William saw as something of a counterpart to his French enemy's vaunting Versailles.

II   1692–1694

The year 1692, which included Wren's sixtieth birthday, found him involved, St Paul's and the City churches apart, in a few projects lying away from the cares of his Surveyorship. But despite the expense of Continental campaigning, and the king's frequent absence from England, this last phase of Queen Mary's life was in essence one in which Sir Christopher's main preoccupations were with Kensington House (not yet called a palace) and the more obviously palatial alterations at Hampton Court.

A few matters of consultation still, however, came Wren's way and he still had the minor cares of his official post. In 1692 he had to deal, without visiting the estate, with the schemes of the Earl of Devonshire, soon to be the first Duke, for the gradual rebuilding of Chatsworth; the episode reveals an attitude to Talman somewhat better, for the time being, than that which had prevailed when the wall collapsed at Hampton Court.[71] The Earl sent to Wren, for his comments and a report, the account of Jackson, the chief mason whom he had employed on the South front. Wren sent men to Derbyshire to "examine and bring into form and make a book containing every particular work" done by the previous May; Alexander Fort went, at the same time, to measure the carpenters' work. Wren reported early in August; he took account of the qualities of the local limestone, and of the point that Derbyshire wages, even for masons brought from London, were only half the London rates. He abated and corrected some of Jacksons' prices, and the entire account, as Wren revised it, came to £9025 16s.6¾d. Wren reckoned, when all was done, that the Earl would not be unwilling to reward the "skill, care, journeys, and attendance" of the architect. Commendation from so high a source may well have encouraged the Earl to continue, in 1693 when the contract was signed for the building of the eastern front, with his employment of Talman.

Other consultations in 1692 arose from Wren's old relationship with a former patron. At Oxford Ralph Bathurst, having refused the bishopric of Bristol but still Dean of Wells, continued in his long presidency of Trinity. He had long been keen on the replacement of his college's small mediaeval chapel. Back in 1683 he had told a correspondent that the chapel was "the chief thing that now calls for help."[62] The actual new chapel was not, however, started till 1691. It was longer and wider than its predecessor, and no use was made of the mediaeval foundations. Its plan, like that of the chapel which Wren seems, some ten years earlier, to have designed for Trinity was the conventional rectangle of Oxford's less ambitious college chapels. The only unusual feature, now as in the scheme of the 1680s, was the somewhat squat and stumpy tower which had to rise above the gateway, with rooms above it, which led into the original quad of the monastic Durham College. Wren was not the main designer of a building probably planned by Henry Aldrich, the amateur who had, for two years in 1691, been Dean of Christ Church. Where in 1692 Wren came in was as Bathurst's adviser over some points of detail.

Late in 1691 Bathurst told Wren that the college, with the assistance (in the plural) of "very able architects" had completed the main fabric of the chapel.[63] But in the coming February Bathurst sent Phips, his surveyor, to consult Wren with a scheme for further embellishments; he particularly asked the architect for his ideas on the pinnacles proposed for the tower; he himself would be happy to omit them.[64] Within a week Wren sent the president his opinion.[65] In general he approved the design of the building which was, in any case, too far advanced for any advice of his to make any difference. He did, however, send down some ideas which the mason would find useful when he came to mouldings and the cornice. To allow better support for the tower he suggested some changes in the walling and stairs of the gateway. He agreed with Bathurst that there was no need for the tower to have pinnacles, and neither he nor the president could have been much enamoured with the emblematic statues which actually arose above the tower's corners. Another suggestion by Wren, and one which was carried out, was for the main body of the chapel to have a parapet with runs of engaged balustrading, and with gadrooned and flaming urns above each of the pilasters which stand between the windows. Wren may also have advised about the rich interior woodwork, and Gibbons seems to have carved some of it in the altarpiece.

Another famous Oxford building, started early in 1692 and well in progress by the spring of 1694 when Trinity chapel was consecrated, seems not to have concerned Wren though it probably owes some inspiration to one of his masterpieces. The splendid library at Queen's was started in 1692, and Dean Aldrich may have designed it. But some ideas, for a library range which first stood above an arcaded piazza, could have come from what Wren had done, as the first of a small series of really stately college libraries, at Trinity in Cambridge.

Back in London some jobs still involved Wren as Surveyor General. Early in 1692 he and Talman were asked to estimate for repairs to the House of Commons.[66] The work went on into 1693, and a final point concerned the exclusion of cold air which could come in, where the east end of St Stephen's Chapel had originally stood, at that end of the debating chamber.[67] Wren reckoned that the chief cause of the annoying inrush was the opening of these windows, and he had ordered that in winter at all events they should be secured. But double sashing and double glazing were also reckoned to bring extra comfort to the legislators. So early in the autumn of 1693 Wren was ordered for the modest outlay of £42 14s.0d. to have the work done.

Another Westminster item, in the summer of 1692, concerned a whimsical little sidetrack in the jungle of officialdom. Stephen Chase, a functionary who held the post of Chafewax to the Great Seal, had been allowed a small building, hard by one end of Westminster Hall, for the melting and stirring of the wax needed to seal official documents.[68] Twelve years earlier the buildings had fallen down, so that Chase had needed, till the Surveyor General rebuilt and furnished his quarters, to hire what he called a wax house. He now, so it seems had to repair the building which he had rented, and for this he sought repayment. The little incident shows how, at a time when Wren and his colleagues were busy on two new royal residences their cares could range from the sublime to something near the ridiculous.

In 1692, and all through 1693, work continued at Kensington House and on the exteriors at Hampton Court. The sum of over £80,000 was spent, for the years 1691–94, at Hampton Court.[69] The record of riding charges for the Senior Works officials shows that Wren, Talman, John Oliver the master mason, and the "Surveyor's man" (presumably Hawksmoor) were most regular in their attendances at the more distant site.[70] It was as well for Wren that his multiple preoccupations in the City were now much less, that he was no longer on the Hudson's Bay committee, and that his membership of the Royal Society laid fewer burdens on him than in Charles II's reign. He was still, however, active as a Fellow. He was on the council, with fewer attendances than in earlier years, from 1692 to 1694,[71] while in November of 1693 his son Christopher, aged only eighteen and still an undergraduate at Cambridge, was chosen as a Fellow;[72] parental influence was, one assumes, at work behind this early selection. The young Wren was not, however, present at the relevant annual meeting, and five years were to pass before he actually took up his Fellowship.

The gardens and ornamental surroundings at Hampton Court now claimed attention. Jean Tijou was paid £360, between 1691 and 1694, for some of his superb Baroque ironwork in the gardens, while Hawksmoor, not Wren, got £10 for some garden plans which George London, in charge of the actual laying out of beds and lawns, was to render on the ground. For the ornamental waters William Bushnell and Arnold Thompson got £538 6s.7d. for bringing water from the Longford New River with which, in James II's reign, Wren had been concerned.[73] With the king often away, and personally present at such battles as those of Steenkerk and Landen, it was the queen who exercised royal supervision on the spot; she would have had many more chances, on such visits, for the architectural and other discussions which seem to have left so pleasing an impression on the mind of the elderly Surveyor General.

Another 'new river' came, in 1693, within Wren's official

cognisance. For several years a contract had run, between the Treasury and the New River Company whose artificial watercourse came into London from springs in Hertfordshire, for a supply of water to St James's Palace, the older arrangements being insufficient to meet the needs of larger kitchens and laundries. In March, 1693, the company petitioned over arrears of the rent, at £27 a year, which had been allowed to accumulate, and whose payment the Board of Green Cloth had stopped. So Wren had to report; it was a matter on which he could have put a subordinate to work. Late in April he told his superiors that he believed what the company alleged, adding that the rent should be paid as before.[74]

Not far from the source of the New River Company's water the buildings of Christ's Hospital Girls' School were now, between 1693 and 1696, going up at Hertford. John Oliver, Wren's deputy at St Paul's, was in charge of the work and Wren, without being principally responsible for the design may, in view of his simultaneous association with the same foundation's new buildings in London, have cast an amending eye over the drawings.

With Sir John Moore's writing school in Christ's Hospital's City buildings we are on firmer Wren ground. However much Hawksmoor may have had to do with the original designs the erection of the actual block, considerably different from that shown in the drawings at Oxford, was certainly a Wren responsibility. Moreover, a letter which Wren wrote while work was in progress most valuably reveals his views on some matters of great professional note.

Work started in 1694 and the new block was formally opened in the following spring. Late in 1694 Wren wrote, on general topics rather than business practicalities, to the Hospital Treasurer.[75] He was ill at the time, and illness, along with the pressure of work, had kept him from any recent interview with the Treasurer. He recalled how someone on the committee had observed that "English artists are dull enough at inventions", but that once they had a pattern from abroad they "imitate so well that commonly they exceed the original". Wren admitted the general truth of the unnamed committeeman's remark; to him it proved that what Englishmen lacked was not talent but "education in what is the foundation of all mechanic arts, a practice in designing or drawing, in which everyone in Italy, France, and the Low Countries pretends to more or less". After good writing nothing, he considered, could be more usefully taught in the school than drawing; on a practical note he reminded his correspondent that boys so trained would be useful not only to painters, sculptors, and engravers but also to "artificers".

The craftsmen who worked on this job at Christ's Hospital were paid in accordance with their quoted prices as allowed or altered by Wren. Henry Doogood was the plasterer and Jonathan Mayne did the carving round the niche which held Gibbons's statue (altered to make it a better likeness) of Sir John Moore. When all was done a dispute arose over the total cost which had shot well above the £4,000 which the irate benefactor was prepared to pay. "Long discourse" followed with Wren, who gave his architectural services free and who adjusted the bills downwards by at least £450.[76] The hospital itself, due to profit by rents from small houses and shops built in the covered piazza below the new Writing School, in the end paid a final balance. Nor did Wren's relationship with the testy Sir John Moore end with the building of the new Writing School. He had, in 1693, given him designs for a new school in his native village of Appleby Magna in western Leicestershire.[77] But these, a few years later, were so much altered by Sir William Wilson or some other Midland architect, that the finished school can hardly be claimed among Wren's more personal works.

Heavy adaptation seems also to have occurred to the designs, perhaps by Wren or by one of his works colleagues, for an educational establishment more distant than Appleby from Wren's office near Whitehall.

The idea that a college, of university standing, should be founded in the colony of Virginia was not new when William and Mary came to the throne. But nothing practical had been done before their reign. In 1690, however, James Blair, the Bishop of London's commissary in Virginia, actively renewed the proposal. Preliminary moves were made in Virginia and London. Early in 1693 the Charter of William and Mary College was granted; its precise site, and its location at Middle Plantation in Bruton parish, had yet to be decided. When Blair, as the new college's first president, went back to America he may have taken the ground plan, and some elevation drawings, of a quadrangular building to accommodate the new foundation. Such plans could have been prepared in the new office over which Wren presided; they could thus have given rise to Hugh James's later statement that the building "as first modeled" was by Wren. But he added the point that it was "adapted" to the nature of the country by local builders.[78] So the new building was started in 1695 and determined the location, in a few more years, of Virginia's new capital of Williamsburg. It was never completed according to its full quadrangular plan and it may, like Sir John Moore's school in Leicestershire, have been so changed as to bear little relationship to anything that may have come from the Works Office drawing boards. With a basement, a facade of three main storeys of locally made brick, dormer windows to light its attics, three balustraded balconies, and a cupola, the building was of more dignity than any so far put up in the colony; it lasted less than ten years till a fire gutted it in 1705.

Before 1693 was out Wren was involved, with a certainty better proved than his associations with Appleby or Williamsburg, on a project for a site which was to see the last of his really great commencements.

As befitted a sovereign who was so keen on the navy, and who had been immersed in naval administration, James II had hoped for a seaman's equivalent to Chelsea Hospital. But nothing was done in his reign, nor had action been taken by the early summer of 1692 when the victories of Barfleur and La Hogue alike improved the popular standing of the Navy and increased the throng of wounded and disabled seamen. Queen Mary, on the spot in England and an enthusiast for the succour of naval heroes, was the one of the two joint sovereigns who set in motion the scheme which led, some thirteen years later, to the admission to the Royal Naval Hospital at Greenwich of its first pensioners. The site of the palace, royal property and no longer needed as a residence, and occupied by a mixture of decayed mediaeval and Tudor buildings and by important works of the seventeenth century, was chosen to accommodate the new charity; the idea that the empty shell of the palace at Winchester should be fitted out for the same purpose was soon passed over. In March of 1693 the Treasury asked Wren (who had already been to Greenwich on the same business) to comment on a report, got out by one Tailer, "for making an Hospital of Their Majesties' house at Greenwich for Seamen."[79] Whatever Tailer's paper may have proposed Wren, who must have realised the fine opportunities of so good a riverside site, still almost rural and not too heavily cumbered by buildings worthy of preservation, was soon at work on ideas of his own which harked back to Webb's scheme for a complete new palace for Charles II. His project, and its alteration at Queen Mary's insistence, comes into the next year of his life and the last of that of the Queen. But from now onwards a major new preoccupation was added to Sir Christopher's cares.

The early summer of 1693 brought Wren some work, between the City and the Government quarter of Whitehall, which one can link with one of the finest of his ecclesiastical schemes. The Treasury asked him to go to Powys House in Lincoln's Inn Fields, and there to make an estimate for its conversion into a residence for the Lord Keeper of the Great Seal. Wren reckoned that the job would cost £910, and at the end of June he got authority, confirmed in a few days by the Queen's pleasure, to execute the repairs.[80] Lincoln's Inn Fields, being near the Inns of Court, was clearly a desirable living place for legal luminaries. Wren's work at Powys House can be associated, in approximate dating if not in style, with his scheme, probably evolved in William and Mary's reign but never started, for a splendid church, square in plan to correspond to the great space of Lincoln's Inn Fields in whose middle it was to stand.

Wren's church in Lincoln's Inn Fields could have been a most satisfying masterpiece of his Baroque eclecticism. Unlike his City churches, but in a more effective way like St James's in Jermyn Street, it would have been an important feature in a scheme of urbanism.[81] Its site was of the geometrical character that a Baroque architect liked to adorn with such a building, and while Archer's later church in the small central space of Smith Square showed that a public building, however fine in itself, could somewhat heavily dominate such a site, Wren's smaller project would, in the manner of a pavilion, have been more happily in scale with the far greater expanse which was to contain it. Above an arched and rusticated base each side would have had four Corinthian three-quarter columns, while above each corner there would have been a small dome, conventionally rounded or with concave drums. A main dome was to support a lantern and a tall spirelet, rising proudly above a church of whose proposed interior we know nothing but which could well have been among London's loveliest places of worship.

The parish churches in the City were no longer among Wren's major commitments. But a start was soon made on the completion of some steeples to arise above the main structure of their towers. The upper stages of St Vedast's were started in 1694 and may have been designed, probably by Wren himself though not without Hawksmoor's knowledge, in the previous year. Here, with a plastic effect coming from the gently concave sides of the two stages below the spirelet, one had a touch of Roman Baroque as Borromini and his contemporaries had practised it, an idiom out of date by the Roman standards of 1694 but a work of much grace and sculptural quality, foreshadowing another Roman borrowing soon, a short distance away, to grace the western end of St Paul's.

The year 1694 was to be significant for Wren; in the summer he had, as Surveyor General, to handle a politically interesting job which had first come his way in 1692. For in August of that earlier year he had sent in an estimate for the conversion of some buildings in the Savoy Palace, used under James II as a residence by some Benedictine monks, and as a college and chapel by a group of Jesuits. Their new use, during the war then in progress, was to be as a hospital for sick and wounded soldiers and seamen, and the Surveyor General was soon bidden to do the work at a modest cost. Then in July of 1694 the Commissioners for Sick and Wounded Seamen asked Wren to fit up buildings, within the same precincts and already used as barracks, as quarters for Irish prisoners of war. Wren personally looked at the buildings, which lay close to his official residence. He reckoned that the portion of the barracks proposed for this new use was most suitable for its purpose; he also considered that the £189 10s.0d. mentioned in his estimate was as little as one could pay for such a job.[82]

Hampton Court, whose new exteriors were rising fast, was clearly

among Wren's leading commitments in what proved to be the last
year of his royal patroness's life. Outbuildings as well as the main
fabric lay within the Surveyor General's scope, so that in September
he had to consider a petition from Samuel Shute, the Surveyor of the
Mews, who put in an estimate, for £925, for work due to be done there
under instructions from M. Auvergne (Ouwerkerk), the Master of the
King's Horse.[83] Wren took two months to report, but he then
reckoned that the work asked for by this official from abroad was
indeed required, and that if it were "well performed" it might fairly
cost the estimated sum; it was actually done for £7 less. Materials for
use at Hampton Court still came from Winchester. There was also the
question of the possible completion of the palace in Hampshire. Wren
went there, with William III, during 1694. His purpose was to survey
the unfinished buildings, but nothing was done.[84]

Crucial decisions for the buildings of Greenwich Hospital were
taken, by Queen Mary and Wren, during 1694. Decisive moves seem
to have started in September, though important discussions may well
have occurred by that time. On 21st September an announcement was
made of the Queen's pleasure that enough ground, adjoining the
"new unfinished house" (Webb's Charles II block) should be set out
"for the convenience of a Hospital for the relief of seamen".[85] Wren
was to inspect the site and to report on the amount of land which he
considered sufficient for the purpose in hand. By the first days of
October he had got out a plan of the site; he and a colleague reckoned
that the land included within the site's measurements might
reasonably granted for the new foundation.[86] Later in the same
month the site was granted to the commissioners who were to carry
out the Queen's intentions. Their eventual chairman was Prince
George of Denmark, the husband of the future Queen Anne. Evelyn
and Sir Robert Clayton the City magnate were among them. So too,
of course, was Wren who donated his architectural services to a
project which lay, strictly speaking, outside his responsibilities as
Surveyor General.

By the time that the Greenwich Hospital commissioners
commenced their task there had been some brisk infighting, over the
layout of the buildings, between the architect and the scheme's
leading patron.

On one vital point no difference seems to have existed between
Wren and the Queen. Both of them wanted the hospital to be on a
palatial scale; as Hawksmoor later put it Mary II had "a fix't
intention for Magnificence", while Wren, assessing the great
possibilities of so fine a riverside site, and probably recalling the work
he had seen in progress on the three-sided courtyard, looking down to
the Seihe, of the Collège des Quatre Nations in Paris, had it in mind to
complete the open courtyard whose dome and portico were to survey

the Thames. While Chelsea, for all its beauties, and its anticipation both of the dome structure of St Paul's and of such academic groupings as Queen's College, Oxford, was a glorified almshouse, the seamen's hospital at Greenwich was, like Blenheim in the next reign, in essence to be a palace. Where Wren and Mary were at odds was over the degree of survival to be allowed to other buildings on or just south of the site, and over the impact which the new buildings were to have on its landward aspect.

Despite the existence of the Charles II block it was not certain, in Wren's earlier schemes, that the new buildings would allow for the preservation and continued use of so important an earlier work. Webb himself had made plans for a three-sided court,[87] with a pedimented and domed main building, of which his existing block, on the side of the court towards London, would have been the western wing. But Wren, with his Baroque architect's preference for new schemes on empty sites, had it in mind to create a new layout, three-sided like that planned by Webb and facing the river but on a site, closer to Woolwich, to the east both of the remains of the old palace and of the pathway leading down from the Queen's House. The scheme was for a capacious hospital, with accommodation blocks of three storeys and large enough to hold 2,376 sick or wounded seamen.[88] Another project, of stately splendour and worth judging as one of Wren's most notable unexecuted schemes, would have kept and included Webb's block in its western wing. It was for a deep court, looking down to the river and with a principal block which would have masked the Queen's House even if that charming building by Inigo Jones had been allowed to survive.[89]

The court itself would have been in two sections, one wider than the other. Close by the river, the exterior of a block opposite the Charles II building would have reproduced that of its predecessor. But the two blocks forming the inner part of the court would have lain a little closer to each other; the lesser breadth of the inner section would have led the eye, via a pair of low colonnades curved on the plan of an exedra, to the main block whose hall and chapel wings would have risen high above the twin colonnades. A slightly bunched and cramped effect would have prevailed in this southern end of the enclosure, but the splendour of the ceremonial block would have been little impaired.

The principal block would have had a central element leading direct, on each side, to cruciform wings containing the hall and the chapel. A pedimented portico, with its Corinthian columns on the pattern of 2:1:1:2, would have led to a circular vestibule lying, like its equivalent at Chelsea, between the chapel on the east and the western hall. Above that vestibule the drum and cupola of a fine dome were to rise as the main outward feature of the hospital. With its two tiers of lucarnes this dome, unlike that which Wren soon designed for St Paul's, would have had a kinship with that of St Peter's in Rome, but the whole scheme, allowing for the greater distance of its main block from the river, would have owed more, portico, dome and exedra included, to Le Vau's Collège des Quatre Nations. Nor would its stately dome have been the hall and chapel block's only intrusion into the Greenwich skyline. Wren's drawings show alternative plans for cupolas on the hall and chapel roofs; in one version a corona of gracefully curved brackets would have upheld a cap and a pert little spirelet. We know nothing, however, on how the chapel and hall would have looked inside.

Wren's scheme for this great three-sided court would certainly have produced a splendid set of buildings. But the Queen, who knew Greenwich well, often visited the site, and took a deep interest in the planning of this nautical 'Invalides', firmly rejected the idea of the domed block which would have closed the vista from the river.[90] She was anxious, not unreasonably in view of its classical style and comparatively recent completion date, to keep the Queen's House. She also intended that there should still, from Inigo Jones's building, be an uninterrupted view, between new hospital buildings, which would include Webb's Charles II block, down to the tideway. Once she knew her mind the queen was firm with her architect, so much so that a belt of ground, leading straight from the Queen's House to the Thames was excluded from the site which the Hospital Commissioners were granted for their use.[91] Wren had to bow to the royal inevitable. His next designs had to allow, with separate hall and chapel blocks, for buildings on each side of the Queen's central avenue. For various reasons, one of them unexpected and tragic, the start of actual building work was delayed till after the beginning of the year 1695.

Among Wren's drawings for work to be done at Hampton Court there are some, for the ornate, colourful interior decoration of 'Queen Mary's Closet'.[92] Coloured panels and a painting of a romantic scene were to adorn the walls. Exterior features were also to complement the work. For some other drawings, dated in innocence of what was soon to happen, show a bridge and some portals close by the same apartments; some ironwork with attractive detail was also to be included.[93] But if this work was ever started it may never have been finished, and it seems certain that Wren's royal patroness never used and admired it. For on 28th December 1694, Queen Mary died of smallpox at Kensington. Friendly feelings apart, the event concerned Wren professionally. One of his drawings is a plan of Kensington Palace, with a dotted line to show the tortuous route by which the queen's body was borne out to its funeral procession.[94] The funeral itself, in Westminster Abbey, was among Wren's responsibilities, and in the coming spring he had to consider Alexander Fort's request for

£328 16s.0d. for the "coffins and work about them" of the late queen.[95]
Wren also, in 1695, designed the queen's monument, due for a place
in the Abbey but never in fact set up. His drawing shows a work of
vaunting splendour in the full Baroque taste.[96] Its paired Corinthian
columns were to be plainly unfluted or slightly twisted and wreathed;
while the architrave was to bear Garter and thistle badges. But Mary
II's real monument, like that of Wren himself, was to be a building, or
more precisely the noble group of hospital buildings soon started at
Greenwich.

12

William III

I   1695–1697

Despite some infidelities William III had sincerely loved his queen, and Mary's death, with the war against Louis XIV still in progress and unresolved, was a severe blow. He never married again. His immediate task was to pursue the war to what degree of success he and his allies could achieve. For the succession he looked to Anne, the sister-in-law to whom he now became reasonably reconciled and, beyond her, to William, Duke of Gloucester, the one among Anne's many children whose life had reached well into boyhood and who might yet live to reign as William IV and to perpetuate the Protestant Stuart line. But over one matter, specially dear to the late queen, William for the moment lost heart. Though the shell of the new buildings at Hampton Court was well advanced by the early months of 1695 their covering and furnishing was postponed. Royal residences remained, however, of much concern to Wren, while Greenwich Hospital could be the more keenly pursued both as a matter of wartime medical need and as a memorial to Queen Mary II.

The year 1695 also brought another royal residence to notice, not for continuance or completion but soon before an act of abandonment. Though its purchase had never been completed, the Jacobean mansion of Audley End was still occupied by the Crown. But the Earl of Suffolk, to whom the property reverted while William III still lived, drew the Government's attention to the state of the house. In December Wren explained[1] that the annual £500, with which a fair amount had for some years been done, had ended in the autumn of 1688. Since then the Office of Works, with considerable difficulty, had been able to spend £200 each year. Some £1,500 was still owing for what had been done, and over £1,300 was still needed for work which Wren held to be necessary to avoid still heavier expense. He added the point, on a house for whose style and construction he had little liking, that "much should be done to make this house a residence". But with Windsor considerably renovated, and with the royal commitments at Hampton Court and Kensington, Audley End never blossomed out as a palace fit for a Baroque Sovereign. Indeed, by the time that Wren explained the situation at the mansion in Essex, work had started on another phase of building operations at Kensington.

Though Hampton Court was for a time laid aside William III, still disliking Whitehall, had a real need for better ceremonial quarters within a short distance of Westminster. The King's Gallery at Kensington, started in 1695 and in progress for another two years, was built across the southern sides of two of Wren's square corner pavilions;[2] it disregarded the previously sunny outlook of their rooms, leaving a small and somewhat gloomy courtyard between the new block and the Jacobean southern wall of Nottingham House. As in the Queen's Gallery the main interior was simple in its decoration, with plain bolectioned panelling, a coved ceiling, and some pedimented doorways. More impressive, with its brickwork in two mellow hues of red, and with its three central elements slightly projecting and varied by severely plain pilaster strips, is its southern exterior, devoid of dormer windows but made more impressive by the simple panelling and surmounting urns of a central attic feature. John Evelyn, who visited the house when the gallery already had its pictures and a fine collection of porcelain, held that the building, as altered by that time, was "very noble, though not great".[3] Dr Whinney has suggested that Hawksmoor, who certainly worked on this attractive building, may actually have been allowed to design it.[4] The simple drama of the handling of its brick masses (without any dressings of Portland stone) is certainly akin to some of Hawksmoor's authentic work. Yet it seems unlikely that Wren, to whom royal residences fell as Surveyor General, and who was, in the close aftermath of Queen Mary's death, less busy than before on Hampton Court, would have failed to concern himself, at least as a supervisor if not as the main designer of apartments for his royal master's personal use. The road through Hyde Park also came in for attention at a time when it must often have been used. In September of 1695, Capt. Studholme sent in an estimate, for a little over £466, for the repairs to the royal highway, and in the coming year Wren had to certify what needed to be done; late in August payment was made to Studholme of the sum which Wren and his assistants had estimated.[5]

The Treasury records still show that Wren had a wide range of minor official business. The Savoy came up again when he was asked, in the middle of 1695, to find a suitable place, and then to get out an estimate for a house to be used by the Provost Marshal; a prison for military offenders was also to be a part of the job. Wren's figure came to £531; in the following year he was asked, as a matter of some urgency, to put the matter in hand.[6] More whimsical, in the hot June weather of 1695, had been the request from William Lowndes, the Secretary of the Treasury, that Wren should take a look at the cellars and stores below the clerks' room at the Treasury, the rooms in question being so noisome from the rising miasma of "ill scents" that the clerks could not carry out the business of the office.[7]

Of greater political and financial interest were some transactions made necessary by the reminting of the coinage carried out in 1696 and 1697. This was a major operation, so that provincial mints were temporarily set up in such cities as Exeter, Bristol and York. But the main work fell on the long established Mint within the Tower of London. The officers of the Mint needed extra space for the important work now due to be done. The Office of Works had a building in the Mint, and in May of 1696 Wren was consulted, not only about new construction but on the temporary loan of this building, for use as a melting house, till the clipped money, which had caused the review of the currency, could be melted down and recoined.[8] The Works storehouse was duly handed over, and in November Wren had to survey the new work, to report whether the bills seemed reasonable, and if so to settle them.[9]

From the spring of 1695, the designing and building of The Naval Hospital at Greenwich became one of Wren's leading tasks. The commissioners had as their chairman Prince George of Denmark, the husband of the future Queen Anne. Though inactive he was of some note as a figure head; his appointment marked better relations now prevailing between the widower king and the sister-in-law who was, within the Protestant line, his designate successor. An early point for determination was whether or not the layout of the hospital was to be that on which the late queen had insisted.

The commissioners, who included Wren, got quickly to work. They soon appointed a committee with Wren (who took no payment as their architect) an essential member, to inspect the available site. On 21st may of 1695 they met on the spot. John Evelyn, who was the new charity's treasurer, was also there; so too were Sir Robert Clayton and two others.[10]

The commissioners' immediate task was to consider how Webb's Charles II block might be fitted out to receive a first intake of pensioners. They quickly reported that the existing building could, with the addition of a new block on its western side, be adapated, for about £6,000, to house between 300 and 400 men. But if, as the committee hoped, the Commissioners' policy was to house a much larger number, something larger and more spacious would clearly be needed. Wren obviously hankered for his scheme which Queen Mary had vetoed. It must have been at his insistance that the committee urged the grant to the commissioners of the strip of land, "designed for an avenue or vista,' and running down from the Queen's House to the river, which had, by the late queen's wish, been excluded from the earlier grant. They also pressed, and here again we see the workings of

Wren's wide technical experience, that the springs and conduits which had served the old palace, and which had been diverted or even blocked by various private persons, should securely be made available to the new hospital.

The basic policy, both of immediate repairs to the Charles II block and of later, more ambitious buildings, was accepted without trouble. But over the site, and over the alignment of the ceremonial blocks, the king respected his late wife's wishes. Wren thus had to plan on the assumption that the riverward 'vista' was still to preclude his notion of a three-sided court. But in a few months another committee, with Wren among its members, proposed some adjustments and additions on the eastern and western sides of the site.[11] More ambitiously, and with the idea that benefactors should be encouraged for a scheme covering the widows and children of seamen as well as seaman pensioners, they suggested that the Queen's House, and over two hundred acres of the park, should also be added to the hospital area. Here again their ideas were rejected, and the Naval Hospital had to stay within the boundaries laid down when Queen Mary had still lived.

The next important move was on 16th December, when the commissioners held a general meeting; their gathering place, as for some of the committee, was in Guildhall.[12] They chose a large committee of sixty whose members inevitably included Wren, William Lowndes the Secretary of the Treasury, Sir Robert Clayton, and John Evelyn, also that doughty seaman, the future Admiral Benbow, soon to be Evelyn's tenant at Deptford and thus close enough to keep an eye on progress at Greenwich. For the hastening of their business they at once formed three sub-committees. The elderly Pepys, one of the commissioners and retaining his interest in maritime affairs, sat on that which considered the charity's constitution. Benbow, Lowndes, and Evelyn helped to deal with its finances, while Wren was obviously prominent on the Committee of Fabric whose powers were to "design and frame draughts and models" of the proposed hospital, to "prepare estimates and contracts" and to send for suitable contractors.[12] That body's proceedings are important for the hospital's building history. A little later the Grand Committee asked Wren for his estimates of what he proposed to do at Greenwich, also for some indication of any other schemes he had in mind.[13] But for the moment the work done on the riverward part of the site, was all to be on the Charles II block and on its nearby extension.

The Committee of Fabric met at Guildhall on 21st April 1696;[14] some of its later gatherings were in Wren's office at Scotland Yard. The members present perused Wren's drawings for the alteration of Webb's block, also for "some additional building" to go up so that the hospital could initially hold 350 seamen, along with some fifty people to care for them; his present estimate was about £15,250. The new block (pulled down in 1811–14) was to lie a little west of, and parallel to, the building by Webb. Wren's design was for a narrow block of two storeys, with a segmental pediment in its middle and with three-storeyed pavilion ends.[15] At the end of May, as Evelyn put it, they "settled divers officers" and authorised Wren to employ labourers on excavation work for new foundations.[16] John Scarborough, the Clerk of Works and an officer whose post was "settled" that day, was to get tenders from "able-workmen and artificers". In a week's time they made their first contract, for excavation and clearing brickwork surviving from the mediaeval palace, and for the supply of some new materials;[17] the occasion was one when the name of a man, later famous in a sphere far removed from builders' materials, came to Wren's notice. For on this day (which Evelyn gives as the 4th rather than the 5th June) when the Fabric Committee made agreements "with divers workmen and for materials", and when they arranged for the supply of stationery, ink, and "200 Dutch quills" they contracted, for bricks, with Daniel Foe whose flourishing brickyard at Tilbury was well sited for transport up river to Greenwich; Wren and his colleagues could not have known that in another twenty three years, and still within Wren's lifetime, their supplier (who may have been present) was to burst into literary immortality as the author of 'Robinson Crusoe'.

In a few more days they arranged, for masonry, with Thomas Hill and with Wren's trusted associate Edward Strong.[18] Wren was also asked, at this meeting, to fit out two rooms, in the pavilion of Webb's block which lay pleasantly next to the river, for the meetings of the hospital commissioners. Later still Henry Doogood, another of Wren's Works craftsmen, was to carry out the plasterwork.[19] By then, on 30th June 1696, Wren and a dozen of his Grand-Committee colleagues had met on site to lay the foundation, or corner stone of the new building. They dined together on what must have been a genial occasion and then, precisely at five in the afternoon, with Flamsteed the Astronomer Royal coming down from the Observatory, with his instruments, to observe what Evelyn called "the punctual time", the stone was well and truly laid; each committee man present gave tips to the workmen.[20]

Once work had started, and despite frequent interruptions in the supply of ready money, progress was good. On 11th September, the Committee of Fabric heard, perhaps to its members' surprise, that work was "in a greater state of forwardness than could be expected". Materials were more amply available than money, and in four more days the commissioners asked Wren and his committee to start the foundations of the block (the Queen Anne Building) which would be "answerable" to the King Charles II block and its additon.[21] There

St Paul's, interior; central space and choir

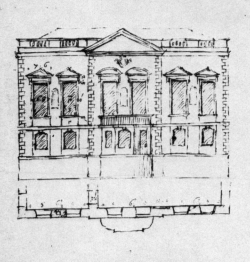
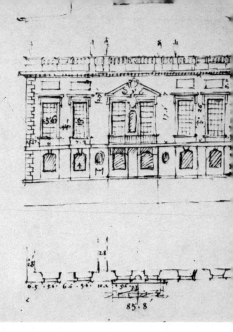

Whitehall Palace, Drawing
Room block scheme of 1687–
1688, both elevations

Lincoln's Inn Fields: scheme
for church, 1692

Chelsea: portico and lantern

ROYAL HOSPITALS

Greenwich: scheme for hall block and a dome

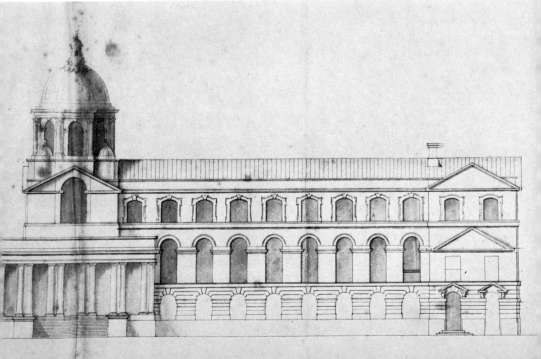

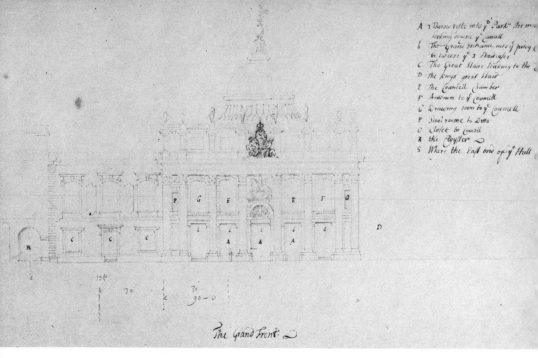

A 3 Therow visto into y Park the me
    looking down y Canall
b The Grane intrance into y passge
    between y 2 Stadrfes
C The Great Stairs leading to the
D the Kings great Stair
E The Councell Chamber
F Antiroom to y Councell
G Drawing room to y Councell
P Stool roome to Ditto
O Closet to Councell
R the Cloyster
S Where the East end of y Hall

The Grand Front

Project for the Grand Front, 1689

HAMPTON COURT

The actual palace, from the south-east

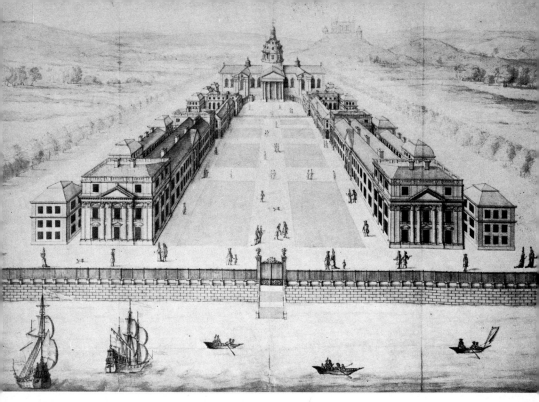

Wren's rejected project

GREENWICH HOSPITAL

The actual buildings, now Royal Naval College

St Paul's: south transept and dome

St Paul's: a western *campanile*

(*below*) Westminster School;
projected dormitory, 1711, altered
1719
(*bottom*) Burlington's drawing for the
actual dormitory, 1722

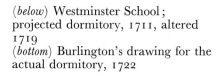

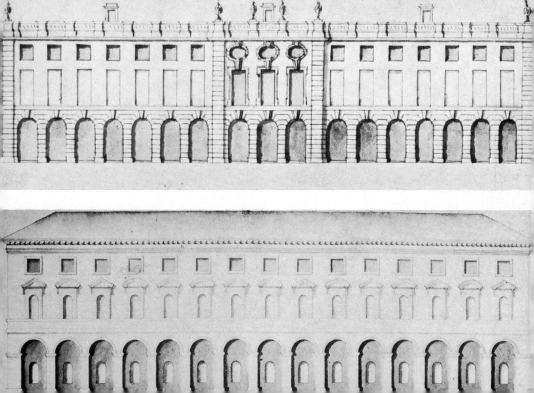

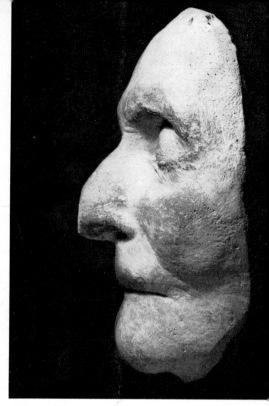

(*left*) St Paul's: memorial to Jane Wren, d. 1702 (*right*) Death mask of Sir Christopher Wren, 1723

FAMILY AND PERSONAL

(*left*) Hampton Court: doorway of Wren's house (*right*) Christopher Wren, 1675–1747

was, in fact, a delay for some months, but in May of 1697 the Committee heard that the foundations of the hospital's second block was soon to be laid.[22] But by now they had encountered some trouble with a subordinate member of their staff. Daniel Sheppard had, in 1696, been made assistant to the Treasurer, with other duties which meant that he was often on site. Late in the spring of 1697 a whole list of complaints was laid against Sheppard, among them that he, though a married man, 'courted' a woman at Greenwich and that he had shown an impudent bearing to the Archbishop of Canterbury. He was suspended from duty, though when in the summer Evelyn and another commissioner persuaded Dr Tenison to pardon Sheppard his suspension was lifted. He was, however, sharply reprimanded, and warned that if any of his offences were repeated he would be dismissed.[23] Had Pepys been chairman of that particular committee he might, perhaps, in view of the indiscretions of his own younger days, have smiled kindly on at least one of Sheppard's peccadilloes. But I cannot imagine that Wren, who was at most of the commissioners' meetings and attended these disciplinary hearings, showed over much sympathy to the Assistant Treasurer.

In August, in Wren's absence, some of the Fabric Committee's members saw the foundations by then put down. Next month the committee decided that the new building was to be wainscoted "as near the manner, as may be, at Chelsea College", while in October, Hawksmoor, as Surveyor General's clerk, got £20 for preparing all the drawings for the new buildings.[24] By now, in the autumn of 1697, the time drew near for detailed work on the more ceremonial buildings on the southern half of the hospital site. These, however, fall into the later section on William III's sole rule.

Wren's minor tasks as Surveyor General seem, at this time, to have been of no great structural note. Ancillary buildings at Kensington came to his notice, and in September of 1697, at a time when the ending of the war of the League of Augsburg suggested that William might spend more time in his English residences, Wren got out an estimate for the barracks planned, at Kensington, for the Guards.[25] Another scheme which must have occupied his mind, if not his draughtsman's pencil, links him to a notable scholar and brings us to one of the more fascinating 'might have beens' in Sir Christopher's career.

On Wren's sixty-fifth birthday the Treasury sent him a petition from a man who was already Wren's social friend and who had the care of some rooms, in St James's Palace, whose condition came automatically within the Surveyor General's scope. Richard Bentley, as Keeper of the Royal Libraries, asked for the speedy repair of the King's Library at St James's;[26] what he now sought was a reduced version of a more ambitious idea of which Wren, already the designer of new libraries at Lincoln and Cambridge, must have been well aware.

Wren had probably known Bentley for some years before 1697, for the future Master of Trinity had, as a young cleric in his early twenties, been a tutor and chaplain in the household of Dr Edward Stillingfleet, the learned theologian and the owner of a splendid private library, who had, for over ten years, been Dean of St Paul's and hence in frequent contact with Wren. The connection continued after William and Mary had made Stillingfleet Bishop of Worcester, and the Bishop's patronage, early in 1694, helped Bentley to his royal librarian's post. Bentley soon, in a phase of his career more charismatic than his later years at Cambridge, combined agreeable social activity with his official duties. He had, since the end of November in 1695, been a Fellow of the Royal Society,[27] with additional reasons for meeting Wren, and such other Fellows as Evelyn and Newton. Wren was again on the society's council in 1695–96.[28] Bentley formed a conversational club of his own, with its meetings in his rooms at St James's. Wren, Evelyn, Newton who was in London as Warden of the Mint, Locke the Philosopher, and others met regularly on these social occasions.[29] Nor was Bentley, always keen on the enlargement and redecoration of buildings under his care, content with the accommodation available in the palace for the royal collection of books. Queen Mary's death had already postponed a scheme for a wholly new library. But now, in 1696 and 1697, when Evelyn recorded his opinion that "the books want place", Bentley's ideas went well beyond the "speedy repair" for which he petitioned in October of 1697. What Bentley really wanted was a totally new building to provide worthy housing for the King's books. Such a building would certainly have been a commission for the elderly Surveyor General whom this rising scholar in his thirties, now immersed in his famous Phalaris controversy, could meet and entertain on even terms. We shall see how the project continued almost to the time when Bentley relinquished his post at Court. In the meantime, Wren had given some attention to a building problem in the Cambridge college of which both Stillingfleet and Bentley were members.

It was probably late in 1696 when Dr Humphrey Gower, the Master of St John's, first consulted Wren about his scheme for the replacement of the college's bridge,[30] a timber structure which led out across the river to a pathway at whose far end the dons of St John's had their bowling green. Wren gave the matter some thought. What he proposed, in a letter of 31st March 1697[31] in which he told Dr Gower that nothing was more acceptable to him than to promote "any public ornament", especially in the universities, went considerably further than the mere replacement of a timber bridge by one of stone. Landscaping, in the Backs which had yet to assume their present aspect, was also involved. What Wren suggested was that the authorities of St John's should divert the Cam, cutting a new channel, 700 feet long and fifty across, which would straighten the river's course on an alignment west of the college's recently completed third court. This would give St John's a parterre, or regular expanse of lawn, immediately beyond their new buildings; it would also, incidentally, give Trinity, on the riverward side of Wren's recently completed library, a more regular parterre than the triangular space which one then found in that part of the college. What would also be necessary, should the Cam behind St John's be diverted into a new channel, was the resiting of the college's boghouse which then, and for many more years, discharged its effluvia direct into the river. This practical point does not, however, seem to have given Wren much worry. What had more concerned him, without his visiting St John's in person, was the landscaping of the college's back side and the mathematically precise siting of any new bridge which the college might build.

What Wren wanted to do was not to build a new bridge on the site of the old one, but to align his new structure "directly in the middle vista" of the three succeeding courts of St John's; by such a device one could have seen straight through, for over five hundred feet, from the High Street to the new bridge. What Wren may not have realised, when he suggested a new bridge very nearly on the alignment of Hutchinson's "Bridge of Sighs", was that a bridge on the existing site would have been far more convenient, for access to the bowling green and other parts of St John's College's ornamental grounds, than the more geometrically sited structure of his own preference.[32] Where he did, however, make a shrewd point, with no expectation of the aesthetic sensitivities of those who now glide through the Backs in punts or canoes, was when he suggested that the elevations of any new bridge could be simple, and well within the capacity of local masons. For the college dons did not need to assume that their new bridge "should appear fine to the river and the bargemen". All that they need provide, for their own pleasurable transit, was a fine balustrade, perhaps with urns, pyramids, and statues on its piers. He added, at the end of his letter, that if Dr Gower and his colleagues approved of his ideas they should send him a map both of their own grounds and of the course of the Cam as far up as Trinity's existing bridge; he would then get out fuller designs and an estimate for what the whole job might cost.

Wren's ideas seem, however, to have been too ambitious for Dr Gower, particularly over his proposed, and admittedly costly, new channel for a stretch of the river. In the following year St John's was in touch· with Hawksmoor, not Wren, about a bridge, on Wren's 'mathemtatical' alignment but leading straight over the river from the western block of the third court. Even so, nothing was done for a few more years, and when in 1709–12 Robert Grumbold built the older of the college's two present bridges,[33] it was on the site of its timber predecessor, and with sculpture for the admiration both of 'bargemen' and latter-day tourists.

The same years of 1697 and 1698 still found Wren busy over the final fitting and furnishing of some City churches whose main fabrics he had designed, likewise with the completion of some steeples left unfinished when naves and sanctuaries were built. Among his more interesting achievements was the Gothic completion of the steeple of his early church of St Dunstan-in-the-East. Along with its four corner pinnacles the tower was also capped by a central pinnacle upheld from below, like the orb and cross of a crown, by four gracefully curved flying supports. St Mary le Bow, before 1666, had boasted a 'corona' of this type, but its flying supporters rose much less steeply than those now seen in a more riverside part of the City. Another, more distant source of inspiration may not be past possibility. St Dunstan's, near the river and the most easterly part of the City, lay in a district specially linked with the seaborne trade in coal and hence with Newcastle. Its parish must have been known to many Geordies away from home; they could, before the Fire and now well after it, have been glad, in this steeple whose silhouette much resembled that of St Nicholas's in Newcastle, to see a reminder of Tyneside close by the Thames.

At St Paul's work now entered a crucial phase; things were complicated by trouble in the Isle of Portland and by smouldering disagreement between Wren and some of his colleagues on the rebuilding Commission.

Much of the trouble at St Paul's was of long standing, arising, since 1676 at least, from a dispute between the cathedral authorities and their local agents and many of the island quarrymen who lifted stone not only from the king's quarries on the royal demesne but from many workings, on the commons, where they were entitled to a large share of the duty money levied on stone from this source.[34] A rough, isolated, inbred set of men, they were remote from the cathedral commissioners or from such sophisticated officials as Wren. Personalities intruded into a situation already fraught with an animosity whose causes Wren barely understood, and bedevilled by financial dispute. Thomas Gilbert, a local mason who had long been the commissioners' chief agent at Portland, gave considerable trouble, so that back in 1693 Wren had insisted on the appointment of John Toby, a quarryman who also worked as a wharfinger, as an additional agent.[35] In 1693 Gilbert died; his successor, as controller of the local stone trade, being his young son and namesake. Then on 3rd February 1696 a catastrophic landslip devastated Portland. Gilbert reported the "dismal destruction" of the roadways and cranes, and of the piers whence blocks of stone were taken in barges to the waiting coasters. The Royal Society, a few days later, heard an account of the disaster, whose cause was credibly linked to recent heavy rains.[36] There seem, at this time, to have been two piers, or roughly built jetties, for the loading of the stone once it had been laboriously brought down from the hillside workings. The more northerly pier, comparatively little damaged by the landslip, was probably close by Henry VIII's coastal fort of Portland Castle. The other one, known as the King's Pier, was more to the south; on the shoulder of the island, not far below the site of the present Anti-Submarine School. Wren was told to send more associates to inspect the devastation; next month, on 18th March, they told Gilbert, in accordance with Wren's instructions, to repair the damage.[37] More orders went out in the coming month; they included a point on which Wren, with his Tangier advice and Margate experience, would have had some expertise, that the North Pier should be lengthened, by some five or six yards, to take it into deeper water.[38] But the sea bottom was in any case too rough for the easy approach of hoys or coasters. The work never seems to have been done, and later loading work was long concentrated at the King's Pier. Meanwhile the work on the cathedral continued, and in July 1696, the commissioners decided that the morning-prayer chapel, off the nave's western vestibule, should go ahead so that its first use should coincide with that of the choir.[39]

The year 1697 was one of important decisions, of controversy, and of (literally) puerile vexation. The unfinished cathedral was a tempting playground as well as one of the City's sights, and the commissioners were worried by the mischievous behaviour, within the unfinished fabric, of great numbers of boys "who daily resort thither . . . and do many times harm to the building". They ordered the Clerk of the Cheque, who then had an easy time as few men, while stone from Portland was scarce, were working on the site, to keep the urchins out.[40]

Action against the boys of the City was agreed at the end of March in 1697. By that time, however, a far more serious issue had come to a head; a sharp blow at Wren himself was linked to less controversial measures on other matters.

In these early months of 1697 trouble seemed imminent over the financing of St Paul's. The supply of money from the coal tax was due to end in 1700. In the meantime, so a petition by the commissioners told the House of Commons,[41] the price of materials had so greatly increased that the cathedral could not be finished within the time set by earlier Acts. Much money was owing to the workmen, while the "dreadful accident" at Portland, making the quarries and harbours temporarily useless, had made matters worse; one had, in addition,

higher wartime freight charges caused by the danger of French
warships, or from privateers from such enemy ports as St Malo and
Dunkirk. The commissioners, with Wren among their number but at
the moment without a seat in Parliament, asked leave to bring in a bill
which would continue the help they had from the coal duties. Other
ecclesiastical bodies had, however, similar ideas and put in for their
shares in so copious and reliable a source of funds. Early in February
the Dean and Chapter of Westminster Abbey pointed out that they
alone, till now, had borne the burden of their great church's repair.[42]
Though they had, since a heavy outlay in 1660–62, spent nearly
£20,000 the structure was still "so very defective" that about £40,000
was needed, in the opinion of their technical advisers, "to support and
repair" the church. Many other churches in London put in claims,
but a church in Southwark was alone heeded. But the Westminster
Chapter was successful, and St Paul in the City of London was, by an
amendment to the original Bill, relieved of a sixth of his coal money to
help St Peter at Westminster. Repairs to "the Collegiate Church of
St Peter in Westminster" were specifically included in the title of the
Act eventually passed, at the end of March. Another amendment,
inserted as the Bill went through committee,[43] laid it down that
Wren's stipend, as Surveyor for the building of St Paul's, should half
of it be paid each year, but that the other half should be held over, to
be paid "in one intire sum" within six months of the eventual finishing
of the cathedral. Those who had pressed for the cut may not have
realised that nearly fifteen years were to pass before Wren got all that
was due to him.

By the end of 1696 thirty years had passed since the gutting of Old
St Paul's. It was twenty-three years since Wren had presented his
'Model' design, and twenty-one years since the approval of the
'Warrant' design had led to the laying of the foundation stone of a
cathedral which could, if the ideas inherent in the 'Warrant' design
were followed, have been more easily built "by Parts" than the more
geometrically integrated church of the model. Not only had the
'Warrant' elevations been much altered as work went along but the
cathedral had not, despite the operative warrant's wording, been built
"by parts" so that the choir could be finished and used before the rest
of the cathedral. (see page 154) Not only had Wren made important
visual changes from the design approved in 1675, but to the
"variations, rather ornamental then essential" which Charles II had
covertly allowed him he had added a sequence of building operations
which had meant the construction, in such quick sequence as to make
the work a virtually simultaneous process of the choir limb along with
the transept and the main fabric of the nave. The whole area of his
proposed cathedral was thus covered with new work before any of it,
above the great crypt which lay, in an unmediaeval manner, below

nave and choir alike, was ready for worship. The cathedral clergy could already, by 1696, have held services in the crypt. But a crypt was not what they had long hoped for. After so many years, and with the promise of 1675 in their minds, their impatience for a complete cathedral, or at all events for a choir, was easy to understand. Though their new choir was now almost ready, the commissioners were now confronted with ideas which, for some of them, seem to have put a severe strain on their patience.

On 23rd March 1697, at a time when he must have known that the halving of his salary was almost through Parliament, Wren brought to a commissioners' meeting a paper on the present state and condition of the new St Paul's; Archbishop Tenison of Canterbury and Bishop Compton of London were there to mark the importance of the occasion.[44] Wren's ideas set out in the paper, of which copies were to be circulated, must have been known already and may have contributed to the dispute which caused the temporary halving of Wren's cathedral stipend. The point over which argument was likely to arise was essentially the same – mathematics versus liturgy – which had caused the rejection of the 'Model' design. Wren's paper was read and considered at a commissioners' meeting on 30th March.[45] Isaac Newton was there, for the first time as a commissioner; one can imagine that the great mathematician supported Wren in the following argument.

Wren reported that the nave had now risen, in several places, to the level of its upper cornice, but that it must so remain along with the western portico for whose giant order he still hoped, till the restoration of the cranes and piers at Portland made it possible to ship blocks of stone of sufficient size. The circular wall which formed the lower part of the drum of his projected dome could, however, be built up, for another twenty feet, so that the roofs of the nave and transepts, and later that of the nave could join onto it and so protect the supports of the dome from the weather. For this part of the building, which would not lastingly be exposed to wind, rain and smoky grime, freestone (perhaps from Burford) would do as well as the temporarily unavailable Portland blocks and would work out cheaper. More crucial, and more open to dispute, were Wren's thoughts for the rest of the dome, and for the 'cupola' which would surmount his composition. It was clear that what he really wanted now was not the finishing and furnishing of the nave but the full completion of a great cathedral dome which would crown and dominate the City of London.

Wren based his plea for the dome's completion on the two arguments to some extent linked, of finance and architectural pride; considerations of the clergy's practical convenience also came in. He could not have been sure, when he prepared his memorandum, that the coal money would be available beyond 1700, for he reckoned that he could only count on it for three and a half years. If the dome were not started within that time it could not reasonably be considered "a fit enterprise for a smaller revenue". But were it built it would, in a city so far undistinguished, compared to others of less wealth and note, for its public buildings, be "so remarkable an ornament" that everyone in London would be satisfied, and that no one would "repine at the charge of completing the whole work". But if the nave and the 'great' portico alone were finished, a second boarded partition, additional to one which must have screened the choir, would be needed between the nave and the unroofed central space. The cathedral as a whole would thus give an odd impression, like two separate buildings parted by a circular open court, with the choir, inconveniently in times of rain or snow, separated by an open space from the vestries of the choir and clergy.

Coming to the consideration of money Wren gave it as his opinion that the completion of the nave and its western portico would cost as much as it would to build the cupola (as then envisaged with a modest lantern) to its very top. His estimate for the rest of the dome was £55,000 with a completion time, conveniently within the span of the coal money as originally allowed, of three to four years. If, as he obviously hoped, his darling project of a great dome was agreed all available workmen must now be concentrated on this aspect of the cathedral; the work, once started, "must be finished with all application".

But the commissioners, perhaps by a majority, disregarded most of the plea of the Surveyor with whom their relations, by now, were clearly soured. They agreed that the drum of the dome should be carried up as Sir Christopher had suggested. But for the rest they preferred that the nave, without prejudice to the precise nature of its portico, should be continued. Then in the middle of May they ordered Wren to go to Portland, with suitable people and at the expense of the cathedral, to report on the situation as it was over a year after the great landslide.[46] Late that month Wren, Hawksmoor, and Edward Strong, drove down to the Isle; their coach trip to the Dorset coast, in late spring, could have been a pleasant relief from strained conditions in London. Wren and his colleagues soon got to terms with what was still an unhappy situation. When they saw the pier hard by the castle, or coastal fort, which Henry VIII had built they considered that the rocky sea-bed was too much for the dredging technology of those times. An alternative way to this north pier was apt to be clogged by the heavy shingle of what Wren vividly called the "driving beach" of the Chesil Bank. They held that the way to the King's Pier could be restored by cutting across what they mentioned as the "broken common" below the quarries.[47] On these technical and practical matters the colleagues from St Paul's were better able, in a short visit, to propose solutions than they were to deal with local problems of quarrying rights and finance. In the upshot, the commissioners decided on yet another way to the more southerly pier, and a mason named John Wray, who was clerk of works at Portland, was ordered, under Wren's direction, to make new ways for the downward movement of the vital stone.[48] Soon, moreover, one problem which had long bedevilled the seaborne transport of the blocks was eased by the coming of peace with France. In the autumn of 1697 the Peace of Rijswijk, from the English, Dutch, and Spanish points of view a satisfactory bargain, ended the war of the League of Augsburg, and with it the danger from privateers. The occasion was soon marked by an auspicious event in the new St Paul's.

As the year 1697 progressed the choir became nearly ready for use. Grinling Gibbons' splendid stalls, rich with their floral panels and their cresting of palm branches enfolding winged cherubs' heads, were being set up. The richly carved organ case, originally on the screen which lay across the entrance to the choir, was being erected, with William III's arms to indicate its dating. In November the King made a splendid *joyeuse entrée* (but without the triumphal arches which Wren and his works colleagues might have been asked to erect) into the City of London. Then on 2nd December a solemn service of Thanksgiving was held in St Paul's. The King did not come as he had planned to do, but the occasion was one of solemnity and splendour, and if all the residentiary canons attended the elderly William Holder would have been gladdened that public worship now started in his brother-in-law's great building; ordinary Sunday services started in another three days.

As the year 1697 ended the political scene in England seemed favourable for new or continued architectural ventures. The King, aged forty-seven, could reasonably hope for at least another dozen years on the throne; hazards from the "Little Gentleman in Black Velvet' were obviously unforeseen. The worst sorrow of William's bereavement had eased; there seemed no reason, in finance or personal feeling, why such projects as Hampton Court should not now be resumed. The politically ominous deaths of the Electoral Prince of Bavaria, of Charles II of Spain, and of the young Duke of Gloucester had yet to occur, so that neither the Spanish nor the English succession gave undue prospects of international war or conflict at home. In a few more days a fiery disaster at Whitehall gave added importance to Kensington and Hampton Court and presented Wren with another great opportunity for stately designing.

II   1698-1702

The year 1698, which included Wren's sixty-sixth birthday, turned out to be one of the busiest in his professional life. It started, on a smaller scale and in a more limited area than the City of London, with a fiery reminiscence of 1666. For on 4th January the ancient, jumbled, chaotic palace of Whitehall was, between the river and the line of the present Whitehall, almost wholly burnt to the ground. As Evelyn put it, exaggerating over one specially important building, "nothing but walls and ruins" remained.[49] The devastation included the block, with its chapel but without the altarpiece which had already been dismantled and stored away, which Wren had designed for James II; it was the first of his buildings to be destroyed. But Inigo Jones's Banqueting Hall, significant as architecture and hallowed, in monarchist eyes, by its memories of royal martyrdom, was saved by strenuous efforts. Having survived, and with its associations with another sad January day, it was obviously due for preservation in any new palace complex which might arise by the tidal Thames.

Though William III disliked Whitehall he had to think of the future. A fine palace, here rather than at Kensington or Hampton Court, was important both for administration and for easy contact with the Parliamentary purlieus a little way upstream. Even if William himself was seldom to be at Whitehall he had to think of the governmental needs of his successors – of Anne and even more of the boy who hoped to become King William IV. A new palace, corresponding to the Louvre if not to out-of-town Versailles, was thus, when a newly concluded peace seemed to offer good chances of its being built, an item of immediate policy. So Wren, in these early months of 1698, quickly made the designs for what would, had it been finished, have been his most ambitious secular building. It could, in a great expanse which must have included offices as well as ceremonial apartments, have contained the new Royal Library to replace the rooms at St James's for whose repair Bentley had, a few months earlier, put in a petition.

The Surveyor General had got to work as soon as he could after 4th January. Narcissus Luttrell noted that Wren had, by 20th January, surveyed the ruins and measured the available site. Rebuilding was the immediate policy of the King whose ideas for "a noble palace" could, "by computation" be finished in the optimistically short time of four years. Luttrell also saw, in the first days of March, that about two hundred labourers were daily at work in Whitehall, clearing debris round the Banqueting Hall so that it could be fitted up as a chapel royal.[50] The work was hastened, and Wren promised, about

8th November, that the conversion would be done by the end of the month.[51] It was, indeed, as a chapel, and not for court functions, that Inigo Jones's Palladian masterpiece was used till as late as 1890.* Wren's alterations, with a simple reredos, an organ by 'Father' Smith in a dignified case, a pulpit, and appropriate pews, seem not to have been of major note; as it happened his conversion of the hall to religious uses was all that he ever carried out on the site whose devastation must, after the patchwork chaos which had previously prevailed, have seemed a golden opportunity. The King also directed Wren to build, at the southern end of the hall, a range which would contain a council chamber and five rooms for his own short-term lodging.[52] But nothing came of the idea. It seemed more important, for reasons more valid in 1698 than they were in another two or three years, to plan for a virtually new, ambitious palace, planned and furnished for a succession of monarchs whose courts were to be of a full Baroque splendour.

Wren presented two alternative schemes.[53] Both were to keep the Banqueting Hall. In one case it was to receive additions which would largely have spoilt it. In the other, it was, like the Charles II block at Greenwich, to be duplicated. Its retention, particularly in the first project, recalls what had been due to happen, in an otherwise new palace, over Henry VIII's great hall at Hampton Court. The preservation of so pronouncedly Renaissance a building would have been more pleasing to Wren than the keeping of a Tudor Gothic hall. One can, however, sense royal insistence, from the partially Stuart William III and still more from Princess Anne with her devotion to the memory of a martyred grandfather, on the continuance of a building with so poignant an association.

Wren's first, more imposing scheme was to make the Banqueting House the central feature of a new palace which was, with the sweeping away of the 'Holbein' gateway which had survived the fire, to stretch from the river, across the line of the present Whitehall, and well into the eastern end of St James's Park. The project also included some ambitious planning, in a manner foreshadowing what Hawksmoor (who knew the scheme in all its details) was later to suggest for Cambridge, for other parts of Whitehall and Westminster. A leading element in Wren's suggestion was to be a new Parliament House whose need he had already mentioned. Almost square, it was to lie north of Westminster Hall and of the buildings already used by the Lords and Commons. Being closer to the new palace than were the older Houses of Parliament it was linked, by a long corridor

---

*It had, once already, witnessed a religious ceremony, when under James II, in April 1688, Bonaventure Giffard was consecrated, as a titular bishop *in partibus*, for service as the Catholic Vicar Apostolic of the Midland District.

gallery of classical character, to the symmetrically disposed blocks of the palace which was to enshrine the Banqueting Hall.

Though Inigo Jones's hall was, under this project, to be preserved it was to be roughly handled to make it part of a Baroque composition whose two domes, with their low drums and pedimented lucarnes, were to display a skyline akin to that with which Wren had now to be content at Greenwich. On its river side it was, in part, to be masked by the four giant Corinthian columns of an imposing portico whose architrave was to conceal much of the hall's frieze and balustrade. At each end of the hall, a circular pavilion, likewise with a giant Corinthian order and with great trophies of arms and royal heraldry to adorn its lower spaces, was to support one of the two domes. Superb in themselves these buildings would not have so closely adjoined Jones's simpler Palladianism. On its western side, where it was to face a large enclosed court, the hall was to be unaltered bar the addition of a shallow staircase; in the court itself the elevations of the flanking buildings would have had paired Ionic columns, at intervals along a lengthy expanse and giving an unduly repetitive effect. Facing the park, the elevations were to be of great dignity, with a Corinthian giant order and smaller Ionic half columns, but without the sculptural effects which were to add to the splendour of the palace's eastern side. Facing the river the two flanking blocks were to have been of an overpowering dignity. More giant columns were to mask the two main storeys, while the sculptured pediments were to contain historic or allegorical scenes; between those columns, and below the great windows, a central cartouche was, in each block, to have the letter 'W', flanked by trophies, trumpets, garlands, and branches. Statues and large urns were to cap the balustrading of those buildings, with trophies of arms and statues along the parapet of the Banqueting Hall and its added portico. The northern elevation, towards Charing Cross, was planned, one supposes, to correspond to a southern equivalent. The second and third storeys were to be awkwardly elided, but a central window, below a plain pediment, was to be nicely flanked by palm branch brackets.

The other scheme, also allowing much accommodation for administration and ceremonies, was to leave the Banqueting Hall unaltered but was to duplicate it and provide, between the two Palladian buildings, a narrow linking block whose elements were to be a Baroque contrast to Inigo Jones's more restrained Classicism. On the river side a central pavilion, with giant Corinthian columns and *antae* was to have a richly carved relief of a battle scene, four symbolic statues, and an equestrian statue of William III – clearly a notion dear to the king's heart but only fulfilled, over thirty years after his death, in Bristol and at Hull. Archways, with small domes above them, were, in a somewhat cramped fashion, to link this vaunting building with the two Palladian halls; the genuine one could still, after 1698, have served as a chapel. The palace's other buildings, mostly along the sides of three rectangular courtyards, were to be comparatively modest. Here again the park front was to be less elaborate than that facing the river. Its central block would have had a giant Corinthian order, and urns and statues along its parapet. More linking buildings, with small domes, were to be wedged between the ends of the long central block and the narrow ends of the side buildings which were themselves to have a further display of giant Corinthian columns *in antis*. These outer blocks were to run back along the northern and southern sides of the great palace. The Westminster front, with a trophy of arms in a triangular pediment, would have had a central composition more elaborate, in the manner of the garden front at Hampton Court, than that in Wren's other design. What both versions of this imposing Whitehall Palace would have lacked was a high-rising focal point equivalent to the dome which the architect had originally proposed for Hampton Court. Either palace would however, have been a work of sweeping ambition, and however much Hawksmoor and other Works officials may have helped Wren over details the basic conceptions, for a building which would have crowned his official career and whose progress would have gone well into the eighteenth century, must mainly have been Wren's responsibility in a scheme which gave him the last of his really great secular opportunities.

In the meantime the early months of 1698 brought Wren a bereavement, a new commission, and the chance of personal service to an old and dear friend.

Early in the year he lost his brother in law, William Holder, the canon of St Paul's who had, as rector of Bletchington over forty years back, sheltered the Dean his father-in-law in the dark Commonwealth days, at the same time giving a stable home to the young mathematician who had yet to find his place in the world. Though Holder died at Hertford he was buried, as seemed fitting, in the crypt of the new cathedral in which he may, for a few months, have taken his turn to take services in the completed choir. For Wren the occasion could have been one for wistful reminiscence both of kinship and of long and varied points of association.

In the same month Wren was appointed Surveyor of Westminster Abbey. No equivalent post had existed before. Now with Thomas Sprat, his old college friend and close associate in the Royal Society, as Dean of Westminster and also (as was normal at that time) the Bishop of Rochester, Wren took up a post which he was, unlike his Crown surveyorship, to hold for the rest of his life. It was clear, from what had happened in Parliament the year before, that someone of Wren's calibre was needed to care for the great mediaeval building whose Gothic fabric dominated Westminster.

The Act of Parliament which allowed a sixth of the money from the

coal tax to be used on repairs to the abbey, and which also halved
Wren's salary at St Paul's, had been passed, as we have seen, in
March of 1697. Wren's appointment, a year later, was made to ensure
that the necessary work was actually and expertly carried out. Like
his other commitments, his Westminster surveyorship meant
attendance at many committee or council meetings; for a man in his
position work at the drawing board and on site took part only of his
heavily engaged time.

The first work to be done was on the restoration and repair of the
Abbey's existing stonework. Not much was done in 1698, but over
£2,000 was laid out in the next two years.[54] Buttresses, pinnacles, and
a flying buttress were repaired on the abbey's northern side.
Windows were mended and repairs to the lofty choir vault meant the
erection of special scaffolding. The eleven arches of the monastic
presbytery were repaired, while in 1701, as work proceeded with more
money being spent, four clerestory windows, in the same part of the
church, were repaired for £50 apiece.[55] But major designs, for the
virtual rebuilding of the abbey's transept fronts, and for alterations in
its silhouette, came a few years later in Wren's career.

In the late spring of 1698 Wren received an official commission
arising from the activities of a man very different from Canon Holder
or the clerics for whom he worked at Westminster.

Early in 1698 the Czar Peter the Great of Russia, aged twenty-five
and in the full, uncurbed vigour of his youth, came to England. He
had already met William III in the Netherlands; as the enthusiastic
founder of the Russian Navy he was anxious, in both countries, to
study shipbuilding, on whose carpentry he worked in person. He
could study his subject, and work on ships' timbers, in the Dockyard
at Deptford; for this purpose he needed to stay near at hand. Admiral
Benbow being away in the West Indies, John Evelyn's house at Sayes
Court seemed a suitable lodging for the Czar and his servants; the
subtenancy, of whose bestial disorders Benbow saw nothing, was
disastrous for the owner. Evelyn's servants were loud in their
complaints, and the trim garden suffered as greatly from Peter's
boorishness as the house itself. So when the Czar had gone home
Benbow, as the tenant liable for repairs, petitioned the Treasury over
the damage done to the house, to the garden, and his own
belongings,[56] while in June John Evelyn went to see "how miserably"
the Czar had left his much loved property. Wren, and George London
the King's head gardener, had to go to Sayes Court to view the
devastation and to estimate the necessary repairs. They reported that
£150 was needed, and this the Treasury duly paid.[57]

St Paul's was still, of course, among Wren's concerns, but with a
certain sourness now about the financial side of his commitment.
There were, however, from the cathedral and from other buildings he

had designed, some possibilities of compensation. By the summer of 1698 he had spent much time and money on the engraving on copper of several designs of St Paul's, as already rebuilt and still due to be finished; he had already made similar plates of some City churches, and of such royally commissioned buildings as Chelsea Hospital, the Palace at Winchester, Hampton Court and Greenwich Hospital. In July of 1698 he was officially given the exclusive right, for fifteen years, to publish and print his "delineations and descriptions"; the grant makes the point that the work, still due to include some more views of St Paul's, had been done "with great truth and exactness, according to the rules of art".[58] The venture may well have brought Sir Christopher, who was not really wealthy though comfortably placed, some useful sums of money at a time when his children must, in their varying ways, have been a source of fair expense.

Whatever might happen about a new palace at Whitehall, there were other royal residences, at Windsor and Hampton Court, on which work could, at this juncture of affairs, be contemplated or pursued, while the palatial, though now charitable buildings at Greenwich commanded much of Wren's attention alike in his office and at frequent committee sessions.

At Greenwich the hospital project was now, in the spring of 1698, in a phase which was, for the basic plan of the buildings, of decisive note. Wren's idea of a domed block running across the site had now to be given up; the architect had to content himself, with results which we can now admire, to two groups of buildings lying on each side of the vista from the Queen's House to the river. The hall was to be the first of the more ceremonial buildings, and on 1st February the Committee of Fabric asked Wren, "in pursuance of the general design" to present plans and an estimate.[59] By early April Wren, as always a quick worker, had done what they asked. His design for the hall, with one of the hospital's two domes above its entrance, was approved, and Hawksmoor, as Wren's clerk, was to mark out the ground. By 3rd May, when a meeting was held without Wren's presence, Hawksmoor reported that he had done what the committee asked; Wren was to be told to let them know what materials would be needed.[60]

For the rest of 1698, and in 1699, the Greenwich scheme gave Wren a good amount of work. Window details, for sashes or for casements in transomed designs, had to be considered both for the Charles II block and the new building behind it,[61] while at a meeting, held at Wren's office on 22nd July 1698, Hawksmoor was formally appointed Clerk of Works in succession to a predecessor who had died.[62] He was to "reside upon the place" and his salary, £50 a year as Clerk to the Surveyor, was to go up by nearly half. Four days later the committee members decided that they would like to see statues of William and Mary set up somewhere in the front (i.e. on the river side) of the buildings, and Wren was to consider a good site, for these adornments which were never in fact erected. He was also to estimate for a facing of Portland stone on the northern side of the hall.[63]

Other practical details, among them the poor quality of the bricks delivered in the previous year, came up at what was obviously a full session; a final order was for two hogsheads of "good strong beer" for the workmen on the site. Then in September, Wren had the unusual pleasure of reporting that materials were now cheaper than when the earlier contracts had been made;[64] the coming of peace with France would certainly have lowered the cost of freighting Portland stone up the English Channel. The point was to be considered when new contracts were made, while Hawksmoor, later in the year, visited quarries in Kent and made a wide range of enquiries, under Wren's instructions, into the current prices of bricks, timber, and wood for panelling.[65] The hall apart, one ward was, in the winter of 1698–99, to be fitted out for the reception of pensioners, so that Wren got out plans for the completion of the old sailors' cabins not with panelling in front of the beds, but, as at Chelsea, with curtains.[66] By the end of 1698, Hawksmoor was making drawings, under Wren's direction, so that an engraving could be published on the whole hospital as it was due to be completed. Such an engraving would, by a device common in the building projects of those times, be circulated to prospective and actual subscribers.[67] The domes above the chapel and hall are more fanciful than what one actually sees at Greenwich, with niches and open arches alternating round the drums, and with urns above the windows. Fine trophies of arms, rather than the statues once proposed, flank the steps to the upper piazza. For the upper courtyard itself Wren got out alternative schemes, both of them different from what was actually built. In one scheme each side of the piazza was to have six pavilion wards, in conception like those of the French country palace at Marly le Roi, which were to be linked by continuous colonnades running all the way to the Queen's House. In another scheme, appearing in the engraving of 1699, a single ward block was to run back, on each side of the piazza, at right angles to the colonnade and half way between the hall or the chapel and the block, as now actually existing, on the southern side of the site.

Though Whitehall and Hampton Court might both be administrative centres as well as residences the residential character of Windsor, of which William III was personally fond, was more exclusively pronounced. A scheme of 1698 for important changes at the castle, sparing the work done under Hugh May but much altering its character and its landscape effect, were got out in the Works office; it seems likely that Hawksmoor, under Wren's overriding authority, had a considerable hand in the scheme.[68]

A grouping of buildings so mediaevally irregular as those at

Windsor Castle could never be forced into the mathematical precision of Renaissance or Baroque planning. But these proposals would have done much, in one area of the castle most unhappily, to change the ancient layout of the castle. West of St George's Chapel the Horseshoe Cloister was to disappear, and a vista, recalling that which was to have linked the palace and the cathedral's west front at Winchester, was to have been opened up from the royal chapel to the nearest part of the town. Within the castle a colonnaded portico was to connect the Upper and Middle Wards, while the keep, still squat and Norman, was to have been approached by an imposing grand stairway. North of the castle, and down towards the Thames, a magnificent formal garden, on a south-north alignment, was to contain geometrical beds, a canal with ponds, and fountains; more formal gardens were to run, west to east, at right angles to this composition.[69] Though the rest of Wren's landscaping schemes for Windsor Castle remained unfulfilled something was done, under Queen Anne, to formalise this area downhill from the castle. On the southern side of the Upper Ward an imposing new block of state apartments would have looked out over the avenue of Long Walk. Wren planned that it should, in the middle of its main facade, have a large segmental pediment, with a seated figure (perhaps of Victory) amid trophies of arms as its sculptural adornment; statues of kings and queens were to fill niches in its rusticated base. Another version of the project has a rusticated lowermost story of a strongly Hawksmoorian character, so much so that Hawksmoor, in a year when Wren his official superior was unusually busy, may have had a large share in the designing work.[70]

After the Whitehall fire, and despite such political difficulties as William's trouble with Parliament over a peacetime standing army, the completion of the work at Hampton Court was obviously a matter of urgency. But the renewal of work belongs rather to 1699 than to the previous year. In the meantime one can look within 1698, at lesser building commissions and to Wren's more personal life.

The minor and routine commitments of the Works Office, as noted in the Treasury records, seem not to have caused Wren much trouble or controversy. He was still, of course, a fellow of the Royal Society, and at the end of November he again joined the society's council. Isaac Newton, on the same occasion, became one of his colleagues, and on the same day the younger Christopher Wren took up the Fellowship to which he had, five years earlier, been elected.[71] In another five yers he was to join his father as a valued colleague on the council. In the meantime, in the first months of 1699, we have a glimpse of the continued education, after his Cambridge days, of a young man whose career was in large measure to lie within Sir Christopher's sphere.

What the younger Christopher Wren, aged twenty four in February of 1699, did was to make the Grand Tour, already of increasing importance for the 'finishing' of any young man who aspired, particularly in architecture and the visual arts, to culture and sophistication. Christopher Wren himself tells us that his journey included the Netherlands as well as France and Italy; his companion was the son of Wren's much trusted master mason Edward Strong. It is from the time that he was in France, and still to extend his journey to Italy to see the "fine buildings" of which both the young men, understandably from their backgrounds, were keen to gain personal experience, that Sir Christopher's letter of 7th March 1699 is a valuable document for the great architect's personal attitudes and anxieties.[72]

Wren was sixty-six when he wrote this letter to his son. He may have been ill, and he seems to have reckoned that his death might not be long delayed; he was not to know that he still had nearly a quarter of a century to live. He was obviously anxious for his son's speedy return to his father and to Jane his sister, and his letter suggests, at a time when the Whitehall commission still hung fire and when he lacked half his salary as Surveyor for St Paul's, that his finances were somewhat strained. There is also the feeling that he was none too satisfied with the promise and progress of a young man who, though he proved competent in various fields, was no genius like his father and may, in his twenties, have seemed something of a dilettante when compared to the more purposeful application of his travelling companion. One also gets a suspicion that Sir Christopher, whose foreign travels had never taken him beyond northern France, was a little envious of the more ambitious journey which his son had now proposed.

What Wren had in mind for his son was a career in the Office of Works. Significantly, during what turned out to be a short spell of peace between England and France, it was to the France of Louis XIV, with Versailles, the Louvre, and other buildings virtually complete, that Wren sent his son so that he could "make observations and find acquaintance who might hereafter be useful to you in the future concerns of your life". Baroque and Papal Italy was, though agreeable, of less relevance for this purpose. One had also to think of other problems and dangers, and of awkwardly increased expense. Poor food, the journey across the Alps, and "abominable lodgings" had all to be risked. So too, with the war not long over, were the "dangers of disbanded armies"; brigandage on land and piracy at sea were always, in those days, worse in times of peace than during wars when men enlisted as soldiers and seamen had other things to do. Sir Christopher doubted, bearing in mind that "a hundred others" could claim that they had seen Rome, Naples, and other sightseers' towns, that his son's journey so far south would justify the hazard and expense. He would, however, let his son go on to Italy as he clearly wished to do; he added the point that anything the younger Christopher spent would in any case soon be his. Sir Christopher's presentiment of death, in fact amply falsified, was clearly strong in these last few years of the century in which most of his career had been cast. He hoped, however, that the younger Christopher, would "look about you . . . and penetrate into what occurs", that his experiences in Italy would not be those of a dreamer or what we now call a playboy, and that he would soon return, not only to "comfort and assist" his father but also to understand family affairs which might otherwise find him in "perplexity and loss". A postscript is the most pathetic touch in a revealing letter. In a brief reference to William, Christopher's younger half brother who was now nineteen and hopelessly afflicted with what seems to have been mental deficiency, his father says that "poor Billy" continued in his illness and was, he feared, "lost to me and to the world to my great discomfort and your future trouble". The younger Christopher was, however, to be forty-eight before he had the sole burden of his unhappy brother's care.

Wren had, in the meantime, the routine work of his Whitehall and Windsor surveyorships. Whitehall was clearly in abeyance till the king made a firm decision about replacing the burnt palace, though we find, in May of 1699, that he had to fit up a shed, near the Banqueting Hall which was now a chapel, for 'Father' Smith while he was installing an organ in the newly converted place of worship.[73] He had also been ordered, both at Kensington and Windsor, to repair damage caused by a severe gale, less spectacular than the great hurricane to come in 1703, but none the less, by Evelyn's reckoning, the worst for many years and the cause of several deaths. The work at Windsor was also, by the King's personal order, to include seven 'shash' windows.[74]

St James's also, in these early months of 1699, had another chance of an important building which Wren would have gleefully designed. The recent death of the learned Bishop Stillingfleet, Bentley's old patron and Bishop of Worcester, had put the bishop's important library for disposal. Evelyn and Bentley were most anxious that the king should buy so outstanding a collection, and Evelyn, at the end of April, had a working dinner with Archbishop Tenison, urging him to get the king to make the purchase and also, as the existing library at St James's was too small, to build a new block, for an augmented royal library, in the nearby park.[75] The Royal Society had its own ideas for Bishop Stillingfleet's books. Dr Sloane, its energetic secretary, hoped that William III, having bought the library intact, would give it to the Society. Early in May the society, having fully discussed the matter, formed a committee, with Wren, Evelyn and Bentley among its members, to wait on Lord Chancellor Somers urging that legal luminary to tell the King "how worthy it will be his royal care to preserve such a learned library entire".[76] But whatever entreaties Wren and his colleague may have made nothing came of these ideas, and Bentley soon left London, to the discontent of his new colleagues, from the potentiality to the newly finished actuality of a library designed by Wren.

As the year 1699 proceded Wren became more deeply involved in the finishing of the new work already started at Hampton Court. Some of the designing, by him and others, may already have been done, but now was the time for the palace again to become important in the Surveyor General's life and activity. William Talman, as Controller of the Works at Hampton Court, was also much involved and he may, during 1699, and in 1700 till his dismissal later that year, have been at Hampton Court more often than Wren himself. The gardens were also important at this time. Much had already been done on their layout and achievement, but more was still carried out, so that in 1700 Wren and his colleagues were asked by the Treasury to give their opinion on a large estimate, for nearly £1,300, sent in by the gardener Henry Wise for what he was to do in the park and gardens; they "abated" his price by £47, while later in the same year they took note of work done on the bowling green.[77] Wren, Talman, and Banks did not, however, consider themselves expert in the more horticultural details of such undertakings, for earlier in 1700, when asked to comment on a wide range of work, costing £10,864, done in the palace gardens, they reduced the amount by the tidy sum of £1,930 9s.0d. but did not venture to comment on the prices given for trees and plantations.[78] On another subject, which came up at about the same time, Wren also confessed himself inexpert. For when he received memoranda from William Lowndes at the Treasury, and from Horatio Moore, the keeper of His Majesty's Tennis Courts, he quoted a figure of £200 for mending the brick paving of the real tennis court which already existed at Hampton Court. But Wren, "being unacquainted with tennis play", consulted Moore who sent in an estimate for a stone floor, a boarded ceiling, a penthouse frame for nets, and the repair of the lodges provided for the King and the players. The total would have run well above £500, but the king ordered that the repairs should none the less be done, for £200, more modestly in brick.[79] Some of the work involved the pulling down of an existing building by Wren himself. For in July of 1700 the King, at Het Loo where he soon heard of the young Duke of Gloucester's death, sent orders for the demolition of the Water Gallery, built early in his reign and a special favourite of Queen Mary. But as its materials were valuable they were to be carefully preserved, and their re-use elsewhere was to be considered by Wren and his colleagues; at the end of the month Wren and Talman had to ask for a storehouse for the safe keeping of the gallery's costly fittings.[80] The Banqueting House, of modest size and with a segmental and broken pediment above its doorway, replaced the gallery at the very edge of the river. The king had approved Wren's design at the time when he ordered the destruction of the Water Gallery, and it seems fair to assume that its construction, perhaps with the re-use of some of the carefully stored materials, went on in the second half of the year. Another aquatic feature must have been relevant at about the same time. For in the previous autumn Talman had reported the completion of the avenue coming in from the north through Bushey Park, and of the "bason", four hundred feet across, which was to stand in a circle of trees. The two drawings for a Britannia Fountain to go in this bason, in each case for a splendid Baroque composition and preserved amid Wren's drawings at Oxford, may date from about this time.[81]

More strictly within Wren's sphere were the schemes for the internal completion of a large part of the actual palace, in particular the suite of rooms, for the king's ceremonial use, along the southern wing of Wren's new work. On 28th April Wren sent in his estimate for the completion of this part of Hampton Court.[82] As the cost of furnishing was "more or less according to the intention of the owner" a perfect estimate was somewhat a matter of guess work. What he proposed was on the assumption that William III would furnish "as decently as the greatness of the rooms seems to require", and he had worked out a total cost of £6,800. The grand stairs, like the King's Stairway at Kensington, were to be of Irish stone, but they were to be longer and easier to climb. The iron rails were to be of "good work"; the promise was well and delicately achieved by Tijou. When he came to consider the actual rooms Wren pointed out that all the interiors had been "long since designed" and that the king would soon see his designs. Work must have started quickly, for in September Talman reported to the king that five rooms were almost complete.[83] These, in addition to the King's Grand Staircase and the Guard Room, are the rooms en suite along the first floor, or *piano nobile*, of the southern wing, now seen in something of the condition in which Wren and his decorative team left them. There are some points of difference from what Wren mentioned in his estimate of April 1699. The grand stairway, for instance, lacks the wainscoting up to twenty feet for which Wren allowed, and the fine doorcase, with its broken pediment, bust, and splendid rolled brackets, makes four less than what Wren proposed. The stairway's architectural effects are, in fact, mainly found in the miniature composite capitals in Tijou's ironwork, and in the *trompe d'oeil* splendour of the fluted Corinthian columns of Verrio's elaborately Baroque mural painting. The Guard Chamber, with its walls lined, as at Windsor and other royal residences, with carefully arranged weapons of war, is unremarkable as a piece of architectural design; its main architectural effect comes from the likeness to fluted pilasters of its groups of pikes.

The following rooms, from the first Presence Chamber through the Audience Chamber to the King's Drawing Room to his sleeping and dressing quarters, are undramatic as architecture, with their bolection fireplaces in marbles of various colours and some of the doorways simply pedimented, owe more to their decorative features – splendid carving by Gibbons or Verrio's Baroque painted ceiling above a towering state bed in the King's bedroom – than to anything that Wren designed. More impressive, with its paired Corinthian pilasters along the inner wall and single pilasters between the windows, is the architectural effect of the long gallery which was fitted up to display the cartoons of tapestries. Despite the excellence of Gibbons's woodcarving these rooms at Hampton Court would be more impressive if they contained some fireplaces and chimneypieces rendered from the designs, many of them by Gibbons and considered, by the Wren Society, to be earlier than Queen Mary's death at the end of 1694, which survive in the Soane Museum.[84] Their architectural invention is often more interesting than what one actually sees in the palace, while their figure carving includes heroic and mythological scenes, Garter badges, monograms of William and Mary, and a bust of Charles I which would fittingly have been installed by a grandson of the Martyr King who emphasised Stuart rather than Dutch connections. But in two of them the faintly indicated Royal arms suggest a date in Charles II's reign or that of his brother.[85]

By the end of 1700 King William must have decided, no doubt to Wren's disappointment, not to build a new palace at Whitehall. There were, however, good political and financial reasons for the decision. The Duke of Gloucester's death had made it likely that the English succession would in time by hotly disputed. Even if the Act of Succession secured the House of Hanover on the throne William III may have felt, from what he personally knew of the future George I, that the first Hanoverian king of England would take less interest in a new palace in London than in his electoral *residenz* in Germany. Then at the end of 1700 the death of Charles II made it virtually certain, as the young Bavarian prince's death in 1698 had made it likely, that the Spanish succession, and the World balance of power, would have to be settled by another, and expensive Continental war. Nor was William, though he died earlier than he might have expected, in a state of health that seemed to guarantee long continuance as the sole sovereign of England. Hampton Court, Windsor, and Kensington had therefore to suffice as his English places of residence and administration. Early in 1701 we come to an incident, concerning Wren as Surveyor General and his colleagues in the Works office, which points to the piecemeal redevelopment of the ruined expanse at Whitehall. On the last day of February Wren made representations on a warrant from the Lord Chamberlain whereby John Vanbrugh, already, after a chequered military and dramatic career, a rising star in the architectural firmament, was licensed to build himself lodgings in Whitehall; it was later insisted that his new house should not be over sixty-four feet square, and that the somewhat parvenu architect should use brick and stone salvaged from the débris of the gutted palace.[86]

Some of the drawings in the All Souls' collection[87] cause regret that Wren could never blossom out as a designer of country mansions. But his duties as Surveyor General, and the pressure on his time of his various commitments, made it impossible for him to embark on this kind of work. But once at least, at the very end of the seventeenth century he did act, perhaps with some technical advice and certainly as a financial scrutineer, on a country mansion of moderate note. William Lowndes, since 1695 the Secretary of the Treasury and thus Wren's colleague, and frequent consultant, in the higher operations of government, came of a family which had, for some decades, been settled at Winslow in central Buckinghamshire. About 1697 he bought the manor house in the village, soon replacing it by Winslow Hall which he dated 1700, and whose construction spanned some two or three years.[88] The house, in the main of brick but with some stone dressings and segmentally pedimented main doorways, is of a type that many contemporary masons or brick-layer craftsmen could readily have designed. The designer could, in view of the craftsmen involved, have been one of Wren's distinguished team in the Office of Works. For Matthew Banks the headcarpenter of the Works, Charles Hopson the King's joiner, and Robert Greenway the royal locksmith were all involved on the job. So too, in the gardens, were George London and Henry Wise. Their employment by so high a government official was natural enough, and Wren must, during his frequent dealings both with Lowndes and his craftsmen in the Works Office, have known of the project. The use, moreover, of his much favoured Ketton stone for some of the paving and steps could have been by his advice, while some corner fireplaces, not a very common feature, could have derived from those in the domestic quarters of the Royal Observatory, or in the vestry at St Lawrence, Jewry. Where Wren certainly came in perhaps in 1701, was over the checking and "abatement" of many of the contractors' accounts; he here did his friend Lowndes a service like that which he had performed for others. He knocked £100 off Hopson's account, and £10 from another bill for £263. He "corrected" Greenway's account for locks, bolts, and keys, and in all he must have saved Lowndes a reasonable amount of his total expense of over £6,000.[89] Where he could not help was over the high cost of transporting such heavy materials as timber, bricks, and stone to a place far from any navigable waterway.

At St Paul's, in these last four years of William III, work in hand

was on the finishing of the nave; it included the Morning Prayer
Chapel which had not, after all, been ready for worship
simultaneously with the choir, and was opened early in 1700. The
dome, despite Wren's plea of 1697, remained in the initial stages of its
drum, and its final design had yet to be worked out. The nave's upper
stages, the main structure of the two western towers, and the
decorative carving, below windows and elsewhere, in this part of the
cathedral, belong to these few years each side of 1700. The western
portico was also started, but not, as Wren had hoped, with its
columns in a giant order. The Portland quarries could not, in the
aftermath of the disaster of 1696, yield blocks large enough for so
impressive a composition. So Wren opted, with considerable success,
for two tiers of fluted Corinthian pillars. Unlike those of Inigo Jones's
portico they were not evenly spaced, but were grouped in pairs. A
reason for this, so one finds in *Parentalia*, was that the broader spaces
so obtained better allowed, in front of the new cathedral's main
doorway, for processional and ceremonial entrance.[90] Wren may have
seen, when he so arranged his columns, that their equal spacing, in a
traditional classical portico of the type originally placed across the
doorways of temples not meant for congregational worship, had a
defect when applied to the main way into a great Christian church.
Above his upper colonnade Wren made his pediment a simple triangle;
it would be more interesting, and more in tune with Baroque invention,
were it broken or segmental. Its triangular tympanum was, at first, left
empty; by the time that it was filled Wren had employed its sculptor on
a commission of a more poignantly personal interest.

Wren's supervision of St Paul's was still complicated by trouble at
Portland. Though a contract was made, on 26th January 1699, with
Thomas Gilbert for the supply of as much stone as he was directed to
send,[91] and though he was to make an adequate carriage way, wide
enough for two mule carts to pass without danger, from the King's
Quarry to the south pier, things did not go as smoothly as Wren
hoped. Gilbert at once complained that some other quarrymen,
among them a comtumacious islander named Mitchell, had
obstructed his work, lured away his best men, and illegally extracted
stone from the royal quarries. Wren took steps, about the time of the
new contract, to get Mitchell sued for riot.[92] Next month a case came
up between Gilbert and his partner, a Weymouth stone merchant
named Ezekiel Russell who was also a shopkeeper, and some of the
quarrymen.[93] Judgment, predictably with such influences behind
Wren, Gilbert, and Russell went in the official favour, but it did not
end the trouble. Lawrence Spencer, the Clerk of Works at St Paul's,
had soon to go down to Portland with Wren's instructions for ending
the local quarrels. The problems at Portland were also worrying Wren
and his fellow commissioners for building Greenwich Hospital, and

they planned, at the same time, to send Hawksmoor, as Clerk of the Works at Greenwich, along with Spencer "to rectify the disorders of the quarrymen" and, to "concert for the interest of the Hospital".[94] He does not, however, seem to have accompanied Spencer on this mission. But the cathedral's Clerk of Works did repair to Dorset, reporting, in May of 1699, that he had heard the quarrymen, but that those tough individualists (who had some right on their side) "could not be brought to any reasonable terms." Gilbert was therefore told, with the labour situation as it was in Portland, to recruit more quarry workers from within the Isle itself, from Dorset's other stone-working district of Purbeck, or from any other place.[95] Then by the end of the year there was an incident, from within Wren's own domain of the Royal Works, which must have much annoyed the Surveyor General. For Sir Christopher heard from Gilbert that William Talman, as Controller of the Works at Hampton Court, had authorised Gilbert's rival Mitchell to lift five hundred tons of Portland stone for use in the gardens. This was, of course, against the rules prevalent in the royal quarries. As the stone was for the king's service Wren let Talman's action stand.[97] The episode could, however, have contributed to the tension in which, next year, Talman lost his position in favour of Vanbrugh.

Things at St Paul's improved, from Wren's point of view, in what turned out to be the last two years of William III's reign. Early in 1700 the Surveyor was asked, when indicating his proposals for the coming year's work, to present his designs for "the whole fabric". On 1st February he handed them in; one assumes that they included his latest thoughts for the dome.[98] The commissioners were well pleased with what they saw. On 8th March, Wren was allowed to continue with the dome as far up as he could conveniently do so. The continuance of the north-western tower, whose great bell was now ordered, was also allowed.[99]

Wren's dealings with Portland, and his renewed contacts with men of some prominence in southern Dorset, may have had some bearing on Sir Christopher's choice of the last place for which he ever sat in Parliament.

As Surveyor General Wren had, in 1700 and 1701, renewed his concern for the physical comfort of the House of Commons. In April of 1700 he had, on the roof of the one-time St Stephen's Chapel, made four "funnels", or ventilators, to let out hot air, reckoned in the physical rather than the oratorical sense, should Parliament sit in summer.[100] Then in March of the following year, collaborating with a committee of the House which included Lowndes, Wren had to survey the building so as to see, "for the conveniency of Members", how cool air could be let in.[101] By the end of the year he was back again as a Member.

The occasion for Wren's return to Parliament was the election of a new House which first met at the very end of 1701. Wren's constituency was Melcombe Regis, across the narrow harbour from Weymouth. Melcombe Regis, considerably larger than Weymouth which has now, for many practical purposes, given its name to the combined town, still awaited its fame, under royal patronage, as a seaside resort; its activity, in 1701, was all that of a seaport town. The town's records throw no extra light, in terms of local personalities and intrigues, on Wren's election,[102] but Melcombe Regis could have been a useful parliamentary foothold in a district where Wren had, and still needed, good contacts and in which he was yet to face considerable problems. He could, at the end of 1701, have expected a reasonable tenure of his seat. But in the coming March the death of William III, unforeseen so soon and arising from an accident, put a stop to Wren's career in Parliament. He was not among the Members of the first House of Commons elected in the new reign of Queen Anne.

In the meantime, the hospital at Greenwich had been among Wren's main concerns in these last three years of William III. We find, from the minutes of the Committee of Fabric, that he was on site, to give "various directions", in April of 1699,[103] but for most of the time he could rely, for on-the-spot supervision, on Hawksmoor as Clerk of Works. He was, however, most regular, up in London, in his committee attendances; there were occasions, in 1700 and 1701, when he and one other were the only members who put in an appearance. Important matters were the promulgation of the hospital's design, work on the first of the two domes, and the supply of stone.

In June of 1699 the committee arranged for the printing of five hundred copies of the engraving which gave a general view of the hospital as its buildings were then proposed; two dozen of these, perhaps for commissioners or important donors, were to be mounted and put into black frames. Three months later a hundred copies of the ground plan were to be run off, again with the framing of twenty-four;[104] a few days later the "prospect and plan" of the hospital were put to the Grand Committee.[105] In the following spring Wren, Evelyn and another commissioner had an audience at Kensington with the king and gave him copies of the Greenwich prints. William "graciously received" them, and pressed for the "diligent carrying on" of the building work.[106] The hall block was now, by April 1700, well advanced, Wren having told the masons, in the previous month, to work quickly on the roofing and finishing of this particular building.[107] The entrance columns, and the fine composite pilasters, could thus take shape. But the leaded dome, its Baroque design now determined with its irregular sequence of Corinthian colonnettes and its four buttresses, effectively projecting and with similar Corinthian embellishment, could not yet be finished. Its completion, and the building "by bays", of the portico along that side of the upper court, had to be taken in hand in 1701.[108]

Stone, both in its quality and in the way in which its supply was enmeshed in the peculiar problems of the Isle of Portland, was a continued worry. Back in the spring of 1699, some of that which came up from Dorset proved defective, so that Wren told the quarrymen that he would "take none but what shall be from the king's quarry and sound".[109] Hawksmoor, a man from northern Nottinghamshire who probably knew the country just over the Yorkshire border, mentioned the existence of good stone at Roche Abbey, so in the two following years he was asked to get 1,500 tons from Roche, and a similar amount of Ketton stone which Wren knew well from his Cambridge commissions, to supplement the Dorset supplies.[110] Then, at the beginning of 1702, while Wren was a Member of Parliament for nearby Melcombe Regis, he reported on a demand, by George Stillingfleet (almost certainly a relative of the late bishop), who farmed the royal demesne land on the Isle, for a tonnage duty on stone used by the hospital. But Wren and his colleagues assumed that, as the hospital at Greenwich was a royal foundation, the building operations were "king's work", and so not liable; they ordered an enquiry into the relevant papers.[111]

The year 1702 included the opening of a new reign and, a few weeks after Anne's accession, the declaration of a major war whose financing was bound to have a severe effect on some of Wren's leading building projects. Later in the year Sir Christopher entered his seventies, while in its last few days he faced poignant personal tragedy.

13

Septuagenarian

One

The years of Queen Anne's reign almost coincided with those of Wren as a septuagenarian. Despite his being well past what we now regard as the retiring age of a public servant Wren continued in office as Surveyor General; the preparations for the Queen's coronation, on St George's day in 1702, were naturally among the tasks of him and his colleagues in the Works Office. Soon after that ceremonial event England's formal entry into the war of the Spanish Succession made it unlikely that much royal money would be available for ambitious building schemes. The fate of one modest project gave an indication of what was likely, in Court residences at all events, to occur in the new reign.

In July of 1702 Wren and Vanbrugh, working as colleagues in the Works Office, got out estimates, by the queen's direction, for some alterations and extensions at St James's Palace which was now, with the abandonment of the ambitious scheme for a new Whitehall Palace, to be more important than before as a central scene of Court activity.[1] The proposed works were largely a matter of enlarging such existing buildings as the Council Chamber, the Drawing Room, and the Chapel, though a portico, leading in from the main gate with twelve pairs of Portland stone pillars, would have been a new structure recalling Wren's idiom at Chelsea and Hampton Court. The total estimate was for £3775 16s.6d, though Wren, with his preference for completely new buildings, pointed out that, as most of the proposed work was to be "but peecing old and new," there might be unforeseen contingencies.[2] But when, in a few days, the estimates were read to the Queen she at once stopped the proposal.[3] Some smaller projects may, however, have been taken in hand later in 1702, and some alterations, which cost £249, were certainly made in 1704. Work left over from the previous reign, was, moreover, continued both at Kensington and Hampton Court, particularly over the layout and perfection of formal gardens. But ambitious schemes of palace building were out of the question while England was again immersed, in several areas simultaneously and all the time at sea, in a long, expensive war. Under Anne, Wren never had the great chances of new work which came to him from William and Mary, and though he remained her trusty servant, his personal relations with the new queen were never of the closeness that he had enjoyed with the previous sovereigns.

The two greatest of Wren's projects still in hand, now and at the time when the architect kept his seventieth birthday, were Greenwich and St Paul's. Renewed war made it likely that more sick and wounded seamen would need the refuge of the naval hospital. So it was no surprise when, at the beginning of April, orders went to Hawksmoor, as Clerk of the Works, that building operations were still to be carried on "with care and vigour".[4] Finance, however, was still a problem, and in July a petition, on the whole state of progress, went up to the Queen. Wren and his colleagues pointed out that over £19,000 was still owing for work done, but that four years' worth of the late king's annual allowance of £2,000 was in arrears; the Committee of Fabric urgently pressed that the royal £8,000 should be paid.[5] Supplies of stone from Portland still caused Wren anxiety, and Thomas Gilbert was blamed, by letter and in an interview when he came to London, for sending blocks corrupted with saltpetre.[6] At St Paul's work proceeded on what were evidently the final phases of the body of the cathedral, and on the beginning of its dome. It was in 1702 that the engravings of the supposedly finished cathedral were run off to be sent round to final benefactors of the great project. They still showed the two western towers on a comparatively simple *tempietto* design, and although the drum of the dome, bar a cresting of flaming urns along its balustrade, was shown very much as it was built, the dome itself was still, with its emphasised ribs, its two tiers of lucarnes, and its small lanterns, far closer to that of St Peter's in Rome than to what Wren actually perfected.

On 29th December 1702, Jane Wren, Sir Christopher's much loved daughter by his second wife, and his favourite among his three surviving children, died at the age of twenty-six. She had been her elderly father's best companion and consolation; her musical gifts added to the domestic pleasures of his home. Jane's musical leanings were enshrined in her monument in St Paul's. For down in the crypt a fine plaque, with the usual Baroque embellishments of foliage and cherubs' heads, shows her as St Cecilia at her organ. Wren's choice of sculptor, and of the man who became his favourite stone-carver, is of interest. For Francis Bird, a Londoner who had trained in Flanders and Italy and who later worked under Gibbons and Cibber, was a Catholic recusant; if Wren was aware of this his patronage was typical of an open-minded, tolerant approach to the problems of his time.[7]

An incident of the year 1703 reminds us that Wren's great achievement with the City churches had still to see its final stages. For the tallest, and on any count one of the noblest of his steeples, that of St Bride's off Fleet Street, was finished in that year. One of the Oxford drawings shows an attractive, but much less ambitious alternative version not unlike a mediaeval tent or pavilion,* while another drawing may possibly be for the steeple of the same church.[8] But the actual steeple, with its spirelet rising gracefully above a diminishing series of octagonal stages, is of a vaunting grace with no real rival in any of Wren's parish churches. In the following year the steeple of Christ Church, Newgate Street, with the angular emphasis of its square, diminishing stages, came as the final feature of another large, important church.

Wren and his subordinates in the Works Office still had their range of routine tasks; the staff now included the younger Christopher Wren as "Clerk Engrosser". Wren had to see to the measurement of Verrio's painting on the walls of the Great Staircase at Windsor; the Italian artist was duly paid £300 in accordance with a report by Wren, and by an assistant named John Ball who may well have done much of the measuring.[9] The housing of State papers was still, in default of a purpose-built repository, an increasing problem, and in July the Treasury asked Wren to make an estimate for the erection, in the Chapter House at Westminster Abbey which had not, since the Reformation, been under clerical control, of a gallery for the housing of public records.[10] There were also the first indications of a scheme which bore on the problem, already faced in the 1690s by Wren, Evelyn, and Bentley, of proper housing for a national or royal library.

In 1700 Sir John Cotton, the third baronet and the descendant of Sir Robert Cotton who had built up the famous Cottonian Library, bequeathed his ancestor's collection to the nation.[11] He had, in Cotton House which lay, amid the buildings of the Palace of Westminster, between the House of Commons and the Lords, built a special room to house his literary treasures.[12] As the library was now a national possession, its future housing, and the immediate problem of any improvements that might be needed, became a responsibility of the Surveyor General. So Wren, in the summer of 1703, was asked to report on any changes and enlargements which might be needed; a few months later the Library's Trustees specifically asked that the rooms which contained the manuscripts and books should be made larger and more convenient for readers.[13] Wren produced estimates both for wholly new quarters and (more expensively) for alterations in Cotton House. But for the moment changes were confined to refurnishing, and by July of the following year John Heisenbuttel, the joiner with whose work Wren was fully familiar, had made twenty-seven new presses to hold items in the Cotton collection; along with their locks

*This design has been rendered as a font cover in the restored church.

by Kay, their price, on whose fairness Wren was asked to comment, came to £137 10s.0d[14], and the Cottonian Library was again to concern Wren in the next few years. One finds, in the meantime, that the elderly Surveyor General still played his part, under Newton's long presidency, in the affairs of the Royal Society.

Wren was again on the council of the Royal Society in 1703, and since the previous year his son Christopher had been one of his council colleagues;[15] he was in later years, to be a useful *alter ego* for his father whose attendances, as he neared and passed his eightieth birthday, were inevitably fewer than they had been in his more vigorous days. But in 1703, and again at a later time in Queen Anne's reign, Sir Christopher Wren was able to give his personal help to the society in an architectural connection. The affairs of Gresham College were, at that time, in some confusion, and complaints were soon made that the professors were not giving their discourses in accordance with the founder's scheme. There seems also to have been a project to build a wholly new college. So early in 1703 the council of the Royal Society asked Wren both to inspect the designs for a new Gresham College and also to consider what alternative accommodation the society might need should the hospitality of Gresham College no longer be available; he was thanked both for his trouble in coming to the meeting and for accepting the task.[16] In another two months the council decided that the society should have its own "place of abode", and a committee, somewhat strangely not including Wren, was to consider the buying of some existing building or a site for something new.[17] It was, however, a few years before things came to a head.

While work continued at Greenwich and St Paul's the supply of stone from Portland continued to bother Wren and his colleagues. Thomas Gilbert, who seems to have been ailing and was dead by the spring of 1704, had in 1702 been dismissed as the Cathedral Commissioners' Agent in the Isle.[18] Despite his plea for reinstatement, referred to Wren at the end of the year, Sir Christopher had his own ideas, and in March of 1703 gave his fellow commissioners his proposals for the running of the quarries; he included the point that all matters relating to the supply of his favourite stone should wholly be left to his discretion.[19] The Cathedral Commissioners agreed that an official named Henry Wood was to go to Portland to take over the running of the quarries and to send "useful stones" as he was, from time to time, instructed by Wren. The islanders themselves put up some proposals, and these were agreed. Wood was to employ these particular quarrymen; he was also in consultation with the disfavoured Gilbert, to compensate the one-time agent.[20] But the main control was to lie with Wren. He was already dissatisfied with the system whereby all the local quarrymen had their chance to supply the stone, and in the early autumn of 1703 he suggested to the Queen, who was then at Bath, that short supply and high prices were likely result of such arrangements. He got official authority forbidding *all* the Portland quarrymen from cutting stone without his licence.[21] But this, not unnaturally, in view of the local situation, was reckoned to be against the customs of the manor, and although stone was still supplied, Sir Christopher's vexations on this score were by no means over.

The year 1704 was more notable for Blenheim and the capture of Gibraltar than for any new architectural venture by Wren. Sir Christopher had, however, his routine tasks as well as the continuance of the two major schemes which remained under his care. One of them flowed from a great natural catastrophe of the year before. The great storm of November 1703 must have worred men like Wren whose concern lay with such things as growing timber, scaffolding, and buildings under construction. Some outright damage was done, at Windsor, to the indoor tennis court, so in the following May Wren went there to arrange for repairs "to make it wind tyde (tight) and water tyde".[22] A week earlier he had been asked to inspect 'Caesar's' tower in the Tower of London, not for its furnishing as a prison but to report on the cleaning, tidying, and new cataloguing of various records which were housed there. A fair amount had been done. For, structural repairs apart, £150 had to be laid out on new presses and drawers.[23] Elsewhere in the City the time of final decision was now approaching on the most famous of all Sir Christopher's works of architecture.

For aesthetic reasons a double dome for St Paul's, with an inner ceiling for the crossing and an outer, more lofty covering may have been decided by Wren before the late months of 1704. What was crucial for his final design, and for his constructional methods, was the enlargement, beyond previous schemes, of the cathedral's topmost lantern. Wren's final design was for a structure of stone and with colonnettes, and with decorative urns above its cornice. It was to be of considerable height before one reached the small dome which itself upholds the bronze ball and summit cross. The height and weight of such a structure, larger than many of the steeples of his City churches, made it too heavy to rest on the timber framing of the dome below it. Some support, quite separate from the outer skin or the inner framework of the dome, was a structural necessity. Wren turned to a device which he had already used, at Chelsea Hospital, to support a lantern or cupola too massive for the roof beneath it. A brick-built cone, concealed both from outside observers and from those in the cathedral's central space, was to arise, from within the attic stage of the dome's drum, to uphold the lantern and to relieve the timbers of the dome itself. As often with his most important schemes Wren sketched variants of his design before he evolved its final version. His drawings in the cathedral show several versions of the device whereby he so cleverly solved his problem. To save weight and brick, the cone is pierced by tiers of oval openings in a way corresponding to the lucarnes which Wren's outer dome does not possess. The outer dome, less exciting in its decoration than some earlier sketches, and with its ribs only slightly emphasised, is of a noble simplicity akin to that of Les Invalides in Paris, which Wren never saw but of whose details he could have known from engravings. Some of the commissioners wanted copper for its covering, but Wren preferred lead, and Joseph Roberts, who had worked already on the cathedral's roofs, was in 1707 ordered to use lead from Derbyshire, twelve pounds of it to a square foot, for the sheathing of a dome whose supporting structure must by then have been well advanced; he was, in the carrying out of his task, to submit to Wren's judgment.[24]

As the west front was complete the sculptured filling of its pediment, and the statues which serve as that pediment's acroteria, were taken in hand about 1705. The main subject, appropriately for its setting and giving fine dramatic opportunities, was the conversion of St Paul. Its carver, as also for the statues of apostles, was Wren's favourite sculptor Francis Bird. Though sculpture in the Baroque manner was somewhat sparsely used inside the cathedral one had it here in full profusion, stylistically a fitting accompaniment to the two western towers whose final design, now at last perfected after early versions in the manner of Bramante's *tempietto*, made them the most Baroque, and among the most effective elements of the new cathedral's exterior.

The two western towers of St Paul's are as much of a masterpiece as anything about the cathedral, while inside the south-western tower, below that particular campanile, the circular stairway, to Wren's design and with its splendidly simple masonry by William Kempster, is among its architect's most boldy effective works. The bell towers rest perfectly on their well proportioned bases, and have as their top stages varied compositions of masonry arches, urns, curved supports, and at last of bell cupolas, in shape Baroque and ending, above scrolled brackets, in pineapple finials. More interesting in its stylistic derivation, and rich with its sequence of recessed and projecting pairs of short Corinthian columns, is the intermediate stage of each one of these towers. Wren's immediate inspiration, from a pair of buildings in progress at the time, may well have been the somewhat larger main drum of each one of his two domes at Greenwich. But another parallel, alike for Greenwich and for this stage of the St Paul's towers between its base and the variegated motifs of its topmost section, lay in the middle stages of Borromini's twin *campanili* which rise dramatically above each side of the facade of the Roman church of S. Agnese in Piazza Navona. Wren could have known of these towers from engravings in books, improving on their proportions in his lower stages and in the graceful upward diminution of his cupolas. But now at last, in the first years of the eighteenth century and at a time when Borrominian Baroque was out of date in Rome itself, he achieved brilliant work which owed little to the mainly French idiom of most of St Paul's.

Wren's impact on the City of London's skyline was not confined, about this time, to what he was doing at St Paul's. A few parish churches now received their steeples as the ornamental terminations of their existing, comparatively simple towers. Wren had made alternative designs, perhaps in earlier years, for a steeple on the tower of St Magnus's close by London Bridge. What he now finished in 1705 was unique among his London steeples. The topmost cupola and spirelet was upheld by a slender, octagonal lantern, which arched openings and Corinthian pilasters at the corners. Dr Whinney, who points out that Wren had, much earlier, sketched out a similar design for St Mary le Bow, suggests an Antwerp derivation for what is, on any count, one of Wren's most characterful steeples; the basic design is, indeed, reasonably common in the Low Countries.[25] In another three years a trumpet-shaped spire, leaded and at first with a good profusion of flaming urns, capped the considerably older tower of St Edmund's; agreeably Baroque in its silhouette it recalled, in its upper section, what Wren had already done at St Nicholas's, Cole Abbey.

Wren's personal and family life, in these first years of Queen Anne, remains obscure but must, after his daughter's death, have been quiet and lonely. Many of his old friends and patrons were dead by now. Hooke died in 1703, and Evelyn's death, three years later at the end of February of 1706, must have been, for Sir Christopher, a keenly felt loss. With Jane no longer alive Wren's household was, one presumes, run by servants; I do not know whether "poor Billy" was, at this time, cared for by his father or by his brother. One of Wren's few family letters dates from October of 1705.[26] It was written to the younger Christopher, away from London at the time and perhaps in the Netherlands. For his father refers to the receipt of letters from Holland; he was also pleased that his son had "laid aside" a proposal for entering the army. He made the point, over Lord Peterborough's dashing capture of Barcelona which was then known in London, that "we have not yet rejoiced for Barcelona, though you have"; he goes to say that he had been asked (with what result we do not know) to journey out of London for a family christening.

Though Wren never went again to Portland the islanders, and problems connected with the supply of stone, continued to worry him; at one sharp moment they gave rise to one of the testiest letters which he ever wrote. There had been renewed trouble when the royal authorities had tried to prevent the export of any stone from the island except by the permission of Wren whose authority for this purpose, whether or not the blocks sent up Channel were for royal residences, was that of Surveyor General of the Works. In 1704 the order was withdrawn. But the disputes, in large measure arising from Wren's misunderstanding of the local position, continued in the late spring of the following year.

What seems to have happened was that Henry Wood, the Dean and Chapter's agent at Portland, paid over to the local quarrymen some tonnage money to which Wren, who reckoned that stone raised for St Paul's was "for the king's service", did not consider them entitled. So on 12th May Wren wrote at length[27] to John Elliott and sixty other Portlanders; some at least of them must, one imagines, have been men who raised stone on the commons, away from the royal workings. It was in a postscript that the Surveyor General told Elliott and his confederates that he was sorry that Wood had let them have the money, and that if he did not hear better things of their conduct he would try to get the sums refunded. As he sharply put it, "'tis all one to me" whether or not the islanders' grand jury brought in a presentation against Wood; he added the warning that if the quarrymen ventured to pay duty on stone for St Paul's, or for any other purpose which lay within his Surveyor General's scope, they would not have a farthing allowed for their payment. But the postscript was soothing compared to what Wren had said to the Portlanders in the main part of his letter. He had, so he told them, read their letter to himself and to Bateman, the Assistant Surveyor at St Paul's; he reckoned that they would never "make a right use of any kindness, for which reason you may expect less of mine for the future". While he assured the quarrymen that they would always be paid what was right, he reckoned (despite the resumption of war and therefore of privateering) that the stone they had sent to Greenwich had been at no special risk which might justify a higher payment. Nothing that their jury could do would alter his own action, except for his extra endeavours to ensure that the tonnage money which "by a pretended grant from the Crown" they now claimed was better disposed than by the Portlanders themselves. Wren insisted that they had "no manner of right" to duty money on royal consignments; he added the threat that he could easily prove his point, and that he would make the Queen aware of the way in which the islanders were contesting her rights and despising her authority. He ended, tartly and in dudgeon, with what now follows.

For though 'tis in your power to be as ungrateful as you will, yet you must not think that your insolence will be always borne with, and though you will not be sensible of the advantage you receive by the present working of the quarries, yet, if they were taken from you I believe you find the want of them in a very little time; and you may be sure that care will be taken both to maintain the Queen's right, and that such only be employed in the quarries as will work regularly and quietly, and submit to proper and reasonable directions, which I leave you to consider of.

But some tonnage money was still paid to the islanders, and in another couple of years Wren was still to be troubled over the promiscuous, or "squatting" way in which some of the islanders still opened up new workings.

Work still went steadily at Greenwich and in 1705, rather later than seemed likely in the last years of William III, the first pensioners actually entered their new quarters. In July of the same year Wren made a journey, without further involvement, which had its bearing on the future housing, in buildings as palatial as those of Greenwich, of a warrior of far higher rank than these unlettered seamen. The historic royal manor of Woodstock having been granted, as a reward for his military successes, to the Duke of Marlborough the project for what came to be known as Blenheim Palace was started in that year. Vanbrugh and Hawksmoor were the designers concerned, and though Wren must have been well aware of the scheme he was no more the new mansion's architect than he was the designer of the "greenhouse" at Kensington (better known as the Orangery) with which Vanbrugh and Hawksmoor had also been involved. But Lowndes at the Treasury heard, in July of 1705, that Wren intended "speedily to go to Woodstock". So he asked him to look at the building contracts, to inspect the recently started building operations, and to make an estimate for the whole scheme.[28] Wren must, as he got older and perhaps less even tempered, have been glad, when he knew how others working at Blenheim fared with the termagant Duchess, that his concern with the nation's gift to Marlborough was no greater than it was.

The Cotton Library, and the idea that the Royal Library should be accommodated in Cotton House, came again to Wren's notice in 1705 and the following year; the possibility that Gresham College might move also bore on the problem.

In the spring of 1705 a committee, which included Wren and one Travers whose title was that of Supervisor General, viewed Cotton House both to report on its condition and to consider its purchase by the Crown. They considered that the room which housed the valuable Cottonian collection to be "damp and improper" and "partly ruinous"; £100, without prejudice to any eventual buying of the house, was soon authorised for emergency repairs, and more money, as certified by Wren, was spent on the building later in the year.[29] There followed, with Wren much involved, the negotiations for the purchase by the Crown of the house whose destiny, so it seemed, was to contain books belonging to the nation. Sir John Cotton, the fourth baronet, and members of his family had other ideas for the development of the site, and when active discussions started for the buying of the property they stuck out for £5,000. This was more than Wren and Travers thought right, but Wren wryly declared that he could hardly object if the Queen was prepared to give more than he and his colleague considered reasonable.[30] But haggling continued, on and off, for another six months; the final stage came in the last month of 1706. On 4th December Lowndes asked Wren to negotiate again on the purchase price, also to report on the space available not only for the combined Cottonian and Royal Libraries but also the library of Gresham College (which also contained what Wren mentioned as "rarities and instruments") should this also be moved from its quarters in the City.[31] In the middle of the month Wren reported on a series of meetings with Sir John Cotton.[32] The baronet had agreed to lop £200 off his asking price; he agreed that such a sum was anyhow needed to make the mansion properly fit for an expanded library. But Wren also sent in a plan of the Royal Library in St James's Palace, "shelved as full as it can be" and yet with many of its books in heaps on the floor. There was no chance, for the moment and indeed for many more years, for a spacious, purpose-built library such as he himself had designed for Trinity at Cambridge. He foresaw that the combined Royal and Cottonian Libraries would be congested in their present setting; he went on to make a pithy observation which must ring sadly true to most librarians. For he reckoned that both of the libraries due to share the space in Cotton House should be "purged of much useless trash", but that this purgation had to be "the drudgery of librarians". In the end, in 1708, the Surveyor General arranged for suitable repairs and shelving at Cotton House so that the old Royal Library could be moved in.[33] The joint collection's later moves, the fire of 1731, and the indignities and renovations which followed do not concern a biographer of Wren. One notes, however, as a demonstration of the haphazard way in which the English authorities dealt with such matters, that Smirke's commencement, in the British Museum of a really worthy Grecian home for these and other collections did not come till exactly a hundred years after Sir Christopher's death.

With Blenheim left to Vanbrugh and Hawksmoor, Wren turned, in 1706, to a residential problem of his own. Unlike his friend and official colleague William Lowndes, he had never had a country estate, though in a few more years he provided such a residence for his son. He had his official residence in Scotland Yard, but he must have felt the need for some out of town retreat, semi-rural yet not too far from the buildings for which, as Surveyor General, he and his works colleagues were still responsible. The eighteenth century was, as Pope, Garrick, and others were later to show, a time when riverside residences became popular among men who were prominent in London life and society. Wren had, in his particular position, no need to buy a property. For a riverside house, conveniently placed and already belonging to the Crown, lay to hand on the southern side of the Green at Hampton Court. Modern traffic apart, the scene was still more rural, and less suburban, than it is to-day, while upstream, in Hampton village, there were, and are, some houses earlier than Wren's time along with the mediaeval forerunner of the present church. In the nearby palace the Surveyor General could, albeit in a state much less ambitious than what he had first proposed, have seen one of his most important buildings, while if he did not wish to go as far as his parish church he could worship in the royal chapel whose reredos, with its paired Corinthian columns and curved open pediment, was to his designs. For Quellinus's marble altarpiece from James II's Whitehall Chapel, had never, though stored for some years at Hampton Court and probably intended for use there, been actually set up. In 1706, the year when Wren went to divide his time between Scotland Yard and his new home, he was asked (perhaps at his own prompting as Surveyor of Westminster Abbey) to dispatch the Baroque marble composition to the Dean and Chapter; as the royal warrant put it, the reredos "might be very ornamental to our said College Church".[34]

Once he had moved to the house at Hampton Court Green Wren soon found that it was in poor repair, and that much money would be needed to put it right. So in August he petitioned the Treasury, describing the bad state of his new home, and pointing out that over £340 was still due to him for work done in the previous reign.[35] Wren rightly said that he had faithfully served the Crown for over forty years; this was, he added, "without any consideration for extraordinary services". He therefore asked, as a recompense for those services and in lieu of the money due to him, for a fifty-year lease of the house hard by Hampton Court. No great haste was displayed over the consideration of Sir Christopher's request. His use of the house may have been unimpeded from 1706, but it was not till the middle of 1708 that Wren's petition was effectively considered.[36] The officials pointed out that the Crown must still reserve a yearly rent of £10, and that as Wren considered the house to be old and decayed he must repair it at his own cost; they noted the Surveyor General's offer to waive the £341 3s.4d. due to him if the repairs were done. Queen Anne, when she saw the papers, pointed out that a lease for fifty years to a man of seventy-five would mean that Wren's executors, and no holder of his Surveyor General's office, would have the house once Wren had died. But as Wren "had been an old servant of the Crown" she was ready to overlook the point. So in the following month the Treasury asked for full details of the house, and on 20th August 1708 formal authority went out for the grant of the lease for which Wren had asked.[37] The repairs, reckoned to be an expensive job, must then have been carried out, presumably under the supervision of the illustrious occupant. Since Wren's time there have been some additions to the house, but the bold modillioned cornice, and the main doorway with its segmental broken pediment and fluted Corinthian pilasters, seems likely to be part of the repairs and refurbishings done for Sir Christopher.

Two

During 1707 St Paul's, continued well on its way to structural completion, but the same year saw a change in its deanery which augured ill for Wren's relations, already under strain, with the cathedral Chapter. For Henry Godolphin, long a prebend of St Paul's, now became its Dean, holding his deanery in plurality with the Provostship of Eton. He was a younger brother of the powerful Sidney Godolphin, recently made an Earl and for the third time Lord Treasurer who seems, in that high capacity, to have worked well enough with the Surveyor General. But the new dean who may, as a prebend, have pressed for the suspension of half of Wren's salary, was Sir Christopher's strong opponent. It was another three years before he had his main quarrel with the great architect, but Wren could hardly have welcomed Henry Godolphin's appointment.

In the meantime Wren was consulted, as Surveyor General and as a man of science, on such varied problems as the comfort of Parliamentarians from Scotland and on liquid fire. The Act of Union had increased the number of Members of Parliament, and in May of 1707 Lowndes asked Wren to report on the additional space which could be provided to hold them in the House of Commons; he was to say how soon the work could be done and how much it would cost.[38] Then in August a somewhat bizarre petition, by John Orlebar and William Powell, was referred to Wren. What Orlebar and Powell asked was for an advance of £200 to help them in the construction of a "large engine" which would squirt out, for offensive or defensive purposes and both at sea or on land, what they described as "a liquid composition of very inflammable nature". They claimed that the concoction could, if used at sea, save the expense of fireships. Wren, who had, with several noblemen, seen a demonstration of a small model of the device, considered that the "engine" could be of use, and the £200 was paid, with what results I do not know, before the end of the month.[39]

Trouble over stone from Portland came up again before 1707 was out. Late in September the Directors of Greenwich Hospital sought the removal of the duty paid, on each ton of stone, to the islanders and to the Dean and Chapter of St Paul's.[40] Wren was asked to comment, and in November he did so at some length.[41] He repeated his point that the quarries belonged to the Crown, and that they yielded finer and better blocks than any others in England. Care must, Wren said, be taken to preserve the stone from wasteful use and to prevent "irregular and promiscuous working". He went on to claim that he, as Surveyor General, had long exercised his official right to direct the raising of Portland stone. Wren went, for his legal opinion, to the Attorney General who must have reckoned that the architect had a case. So in the following April the Lord Treasurer wrote to Samuel Stillingfleet, the successor to his relative as steward of the royal manor, referring to what Wren had said in his paper. Godolphin added that some quarrymen contested the royal right, opening new, or "squatter" quarries without leave and despising all prohibitions. The royal agent was to enquire into the offences but the problem, being linked to rooted local customs and insular obstinacies, was unlikely to disappear. Wren must have been glad that St Paul's and the City churches would, at all events, need little more of what the Portland quarries had to send.

The year 1709 was of modest architectural concern to Wren. Some minor points cropped up over lodgings in Whitehall, and Wren's office was twice concerned over the raw material of sculpture. Early in the year he was asked to make available, as a gift from the Queen, a large block of white marble to the Earl of Pembroke who was now Lord High Admiral. It had been taken in prize during William III's reign and it had lain, for a dozen years at least, in storage at Scotland Yard. Four months later a similar request concerned a larger quantity of stored marble. This time it was to go, for use at Blenheim, to the Surveyor of Works at Woodstock; three other blocks were also to be used, outside St Paul's, for a statue of Queen Anne and its supporting pedestal.[42]

The year 1709 seems also to have been one of friendly conversations between Wren and a young architect from Scotland who was, by the time that Wren died and in later years, to be one of his important followers on the English building scene.

James Gibbs, at the beginning of 1709 in his mid-twenties, was then in London after five and a half years in Rome, most of them spent learning architecture under Carlo Fontana, *Capo Architetto* to the Pope and thus, in Papal Rome, the opposite number to Sir Christopher.[43] Gibbs had good contacts in London and an introduction to Wren, in Scotland Yard or down at Hampton, would have been easy to arrange. It is clear, from what Gibbs said of his own activities, that he saw much of the great designer who was, despite the growing eminence of Hawksmoor and Vanbrugh, the doyen of English architects. What was not true, despite what some writers have suggested, was that James Gibbs, about to commence his important career in England, was Wren's 'pupil'. For Gibbs's time with Fontana had given him an architectural training more thorough than Wren had ever had, while his drawings, with which Wren was clearly impressed and which continued to be of a splendid quality, are better, on the whole, than those of Wren himself. What did occur, as Gibbs recorded, was that Sir Christopher "was much his friend", and that he was pleased, as well he might be, with Gibbs's drawings.[44] Wren had little to teach Gibbs, but so eminent a man could, like Gibbs's aristocratic fellow countryman the Earl of Mar, put the aspiring young architect in the way of patrons and work. An important chance, with which Wren as well as Mar may have been concerned, came to Gibbs in another four years. We can also see, in a matter less architectural than akin to Wren's old discipline of astronomy, that Wren may, a little later, have recommended Gibbs as a decorative designer. For when, in 1712, John Flamsteed the Astronomer Royal brought out his *Historia Caelestis* its boldly Baroque dedication page,* with space for lettering enclosed in a grouping of wreathed and twisted composite columns, and a Roman Baroque pediment, was laid out by Gibbs.

A job which came Wren's way in the spring of 1709 lay within his responsibility but may not have caused him much detailed work. The Duke and Duchess of Marlborough, and more particularly Sarah the Duchess, were anxious, in addition to Blenheim whose palatial character the Duchess disliked, to have a town residence of reasonable pretension. It was the Duchess, with her husband abroad in this year of Malplaquet, who pressed on with the project for the original Marlborough House, handsome in its blend of brick and stone, at first with two main storeys and simple in the modest display of its architectural features.[45] Though Sir Christopher may, overall, have been responsible for the design, his son, with his post in the Works Office, may, to his elderly father's content, have got out the main features of the design, while a Hawksmoorian touch comes in the horizontally rusticated quoins. Vanbrugh, so one reckons from his unhappy relationship with Sarah Churchill, would have left the project severely alone. Unlike Wren's other buildings, Marlborough House has a visible, and inscribed foundation stone. It was the Duchess's idea, and she laid it herself, recording both the old style date of 24th May 1709 and the new style, or Continental, equivalent

*Despite its publication date, the dedication was still, with Queen Anne still alive, to Prince George of Denmark who had been four years dead.

day of 4th June.[46] Progress was well maintained, but the health of Wren, whom the Duchess in her termagant impatience mentioned as a "poor old man", impaired the intensity of his supervision; he was probably pleased when the Duchess relieved him of contact with herself and of the needful supervision of those who worked on the job which was none the less finished in 1711, by which time 'Mrs Freeman' had fallen out with 'Mrs Morley', with a later effect on one aspect of the career of the younger Christopher Wren.

The year 1710 was not without interest and variety in the life of the ageing Surveyor General. Early in the year he had to see to the speedy erection, in Westminster Hall, of enough staging for 200 peers, and 558 Commons men, to watch Dr Sacheverell's trial.[47] He was consulted over such matters as due payment for gardening work in Windsor Great Park and, also at Windsor, for gravelling one of Studholme's new roads.[48] Then in the autumn he was able to be of service to his old friends in the Royal Society.

Though Gresham College remained in its old buildings, the Fellows of the Royal Society felt that their position there was precarious and that they should have buildings of their own. In September 1710, they heard that Dr Brown's house, in Crane Court off Fleet Street, was up for sale; they noted that it was "in the middle of the town out of noise", and that it might be a "proper place" for the Royal Society. A committee, including Newton who was still president, Wren, and Dr Sloane was set up. They soon inspected the house, found it "very convenient", and agreed to buy it for £1,450.[49] Some Fellows opposed the move, pointing out that the house in Crane Court was "less commodious" than the Society's quarters in Gresham College. But the purchase went through, and at the end of the year Sir Christopher, his son who was now frequent in his council attendances, and another Fellow were to visit the house and decide which of the previous occupant's leavings would be useful to the society.[50] Some alterations had to be made at Crane Court before the society could move in. Wren's hand was probably behind the employment, for these purposes, of William Dickinson and of some craftsmen from the Works Office, and then in July of 1711 he was consulted, as over other building jobs, on "abatements" that could be made in relevant bills.[51] He had, in the meantime, been concerned in another of the society's activities. For in December of 1710 he was on a committee, along with Newton, Halley, Dr Sloane, the physician Dr Mead, and others which was to go down to Greenwich, and there to report on the condition of the Observatory and its instruments. For such a delegation Sir Christopher, once an astronomer and the Observatory's architect, was, one imagines to his great satisfaction, an obvious choice.[52]

Apart from the Works Office and the Royal Society, Sir Christopher and his son also came, in 1710, to a historic episode in the history of St Paul's. Work on the dome, now rising high above the cathedral's completed walls, had gone steadily forward. Sir Christopher still supervised the task as best as he could, but as his age and health told now on his agility he could no longer climb the stairways and ladders which led to the topmost heights. So when, in 1710, the time came for the laying of the last of the stonework, in the lantern which supported the topmost cupola and the cross above it, the topping out was done, not by the architect himself, but by the younger Christopher; he had been born in the year of the great church's commencement and was, at his age of thirty-five, more nimble in such matters than his father. The younger Edward Strong, who had been with Christopher Wren on his travels abroad, was with him, along with other masons, on the festive occasion. One might reasonably say that the main structure of St Paul's, as distinct from its embellishment, was now complete. But what should have been a pleasing episode was not, to Wren's sorrow in the coming years, by any means the end of the story. A sharp controversy over the payment of the suspended moiety of Wren's cathedral salary, and over certain other matters, had actually started before the little ceremony high up on the lantern. The situation was made worse by Wren's bad personal relations with Dean Godolphin and the more assiduously attending members of the Cathedral Commission. Its partial resolution was linked to a major church building project with which Wren was involved, and which gave him his best chance of expressing views which he had formed while planning the rebuilding of parish churches in the City of London.

Wren reckoned, in 1710, that St Paul's was so nearly complete that he should be paid the half of his salary which the Act of 1697 had suspended and which had now accumulated to a considerable sum. Two remaining points at issue were not on matters of basic structure. One, over which Wren complained of active obstruction by most of his colleagues, was the commissioners' wish, now a firm decision, to have cast iron railings round the building, and not the wrought iron embellishment which he himself preferred. The railings, along with the internal painting of the dome for which Wren preferred mosaics, had in fact been discussed as far back as the spring of 1709. The choice at that time was between the Wealden ironfounder Richard Jones and another founder named Robinson.[53] Early in 1710 the commissioners, at a meeting which Wren attended and at which he was outvoted, firmly decided on a fence of cast and turned iron; they appointed Jones to do the work, with his design to be subject to alterations by Wren.[54] For the dome paintings their choice was now between Thornhill and a Venetian named Pellegrini, and in February they arranged for the making of model domes on whose inner sides the artists could paint "specimens" of the scenes, to be drawn from the

Acts of the Apostles, which they proposed.[55] For the rails the commissioners' preference was not, in fact, unreasonable, for the actual railings placed round the new cathedral were fine work from the historic forges of eastern Sussex. Another point at issue with Wren was the commissioners' wish to dismiss and prosecute Jennings, the Master Carpenter of St Paul's whom they accused of corrupt dealing in timber belonging to the Dean and Chapter. There seem, in fact, to have been some good reasons for suspecting Jennings and he was dismissed, though without prosecution, in 1711.[56] But neither the trouble with Jennings, nor the railings over which Wren continued to fight a rearguard action, need have blocked the payment of Wren's money had there been reasonable goodwill on both sides.

But goodwill was lacking, so on 10th February 1710, Wren petitioned the Queen, not asking in so many words for the money but seeking her permission to finish the cathedral to designs approved by her or suitable delegates.[57] Anne returned the petition to the commissioners who considered it late in April. They denied obstruction, accused Wren of the same offence, and resented his reference to their "arbitrary proceedings". So Wren, having failed in his first petition, and at a time when he had ceased to attend the commissioners' meetings, wrote in January 1711 to his old friends Archbishop Tenison of Canterbury and Bishop Compton of London; he made the point that nothing but the iron railings, and the idea that the inner side of the dome should be painted, prevented his completion of the cathedral. The prelates passed Wren's letter to the Attorney General who agreed that the architect's case was "very hard", but who correctly ruled that as Parliament had suspended Wren's salary only Parliament, by a new Act or by deciding that its stipulations of 1697 had been fulfilled, could pay Wren his arrears.[58] As it happened, an excellent opportunity for suitable parliamentary action now lay to hand.

Late in 1710 the roof of the old parish church at Greenwich collapsed. The damage was such that a wholly new building was needed. As the parishioners were poor they turned for help to that well tried device of church-building finance, the tax on coal coming up the Thames. Several other parishes in or near the fringes of London came in with similar requests. There were others, however, who reckoned, in this winter of 1710–11, that help could now be obtained for a much wider scheme. The Parliament of 1710 was strongly Tory and High Anglican. Its members were worried, when they noted the continued outward growth of London and Westminster into what had once been a lightly peopled countryside. The new suburbs, with some chapels of ease but few fully constituted parishes, were an area where Nonconformity could and did flourish, and where "anarchy and schism" could grow with little restraint. Spine-chilling statistics were given, for the parishes concerned, of the meeting houses, seventy-five in all, put up by the Presbyterians, Anabaptists, Independants and Quakers.[59] A committee of the House of Commons, set up to consider the petitions of Greenwich and various other parishes in and near London, enlarged its vision and urged that no less than fifty new churches should be built, and that suitable chapels of ease should get full parochial status. The new buildings were to be of stone, and unlike the Dissenters' hated meeting houses they could advertise their presence, as did Wren's churches in the City, by uprising towers and steeples. Allowing, as had to be done under the law as it stood, for reluctantly tolerated non-Anglicans (but not of course, for Catholics) each church was to provide for 4,750 souls.[60] Queen Anne, always anxious for the advancement of her beloved Church of England, enthusiastically backed the scheme. By now, moreover, the matter of St Paul's had come into the parliamentary discussion.

The Commons were told[61] that the sum of £756,837 4s.0½d. had by now been laid out on the cathedral, and that £29,187 was still needed; this included money for the "cast iron fence", for painting the inside of the dome, and for a new Chapter House. Wren proposed, optimistically as things happened, to have all this work done by Christmas of 1711, but only provided that the work was left "to his management and direction". The sum of £1,325 had also to be allowed for "the Surveyor's suspended salary", and £10,500 for the joint item of statues on the three pediments and what turned out, in a few more years, to be the contentious item of "pinnacles and other ornaments round the top of the church". The Dean and Chapter characteristically doubled Wren's estimates, but Sir Christopher countered with an offer, conditional on his having "the management thereof" to undertake the work for the sums mentioned.

Wren waited till the New Churches Bill was going through its committee stage. He then took the Attorney General's hint, putting in a petition which largely repeated his previous arguments; his plea was backed by the argument that he could, if given a free hand, get the work done by Christmas.[62] The committee's recommendation, by now, was that a sum not over £350,000 should be granted for the new churches, and for the completion of the repairs to Westminster Abbey in which Wren, as the Abbey's Surveyor, was also interested.[63] Late in May the Bill, with various amendments over what had originally been proposed, went through all its stages, and got the Royal Assent. The coal tax money was to be used, for eight years from May 1716 to the early autumn of 1724, for the new parochial places of worship. Westminster Abbey was to get £4,000 a year, and £6,000 was to go to the completion of Greenwich Hospital, including the chapel, across the central space from the hall, for which a specific petition had been made. The only parish church mentioned was the new one at

Greenwich; the locations and precise sites of the rest were to be decided by commissioners. Clause IX, covering the last of the "other purposes" mentioned in the Act's title, declared that St Paul's was finished according to the terms of the Act of 1697. It gave authority, on or before Christmas Day, to pay Wren's "suspended salary". Just as that salary had, in 1697, been halved by an Act whose main purpose was to apply coal tax money to the building and repair of churches, so now, in 1711, an Act with a similar purpose did belated financial justice to Sir Christopher. It was by no means the end of his troubles over St Paul's, but it was a move in the right direction.

An important task was the choice of commissioners to work those parts of the Act which applied to new churches in and near London. Archbishop Tenison was one of them, so too, at Queen Anne's insistence, was Wren who knew more than anyone, from his personal thinking and experience, on the planning and building of Anglican parish churches. His son Christopher was also on the Commission. So too were Vanbrugh who was not a church architect, and Thomas Archer whose fine new church of St Philip, on the edge of the growing town of Birmingham, had lately been started.

The commissioners got quickly to work, and we hear, from the autumn of 1711, of "frequent meetings and consultations" over the siting of the new churches and their graveyards, and over other aspects of what would, had it been fully carried out, have been a major building achievement.[64] The commissioners' minutes show that Wren and his son were both in regular attendance at the meetings which occurred, not far from Wren's house in Scotland Yard, in the Whitehall Banqueting House. Sir Christopher, who must still have spent much of his time in town, was at ten of the twelve meetings held between October of 1711 and the end of that year. He and the younger Christopher also served, along with Vanbrugh and Archer, on committees set up to get out instructions for the surveyors and to view nearly forty sites suggested for new churches and agreed, by Hawksmoor and Dickinson, as being suitable for their purpose.[65] A committeeman can, also, help by written memoranda as well as by his personal appearances. Wren took the opportunity, for his colleagues' benefit and guidance, to get out his "Thoughts on Churches" which expressed his "sentiments after long experience", and which were a major statement of his thinking on a problem which had long occupied his mind.[66]

Parentalia shows that some of Wren's ideas of 1711 went back, with little change, to 1666 when his plans for a rebuilt City of London included churches as well as houses and secular public buildings. For his earlier insistence that the new churches in a newly planned city should be "conspicuous and regular" was now repeated in his plea that new suburban places of worship should not be "in obscure lanes" but in "the larger and more open streets". His advocacy, in 1666, of "useful porticoes, and lofty ornamental towers" found its echo in his argument, to Queen Anne's commissioners, for the adornment of the new churches' most conspicuous sides with porticos and with "handsome spires or lanterns". On both occasions Wren urged cemeteries, away from town centres, rather than cramped churchyards round the churches themselves; he made the point that they should, unlike some of the City churchyards, be accessible to coaches and hearses. Other arguments were more specific to the out-of-town provisions required in 1711. He hoped, for example, that churchyard monuments would be "regulated" by the architects of the buildings, and not left to the "fancy of every mason". The cemeteries themselves would, to his town planner's eye, restrain urban growth "with a graceful border". More important were his suggestions for the churches themselves. They must, if each one was to cater for 4,750 people, be large buildings but not, with the vernacular Anglican liturgy in mind, so large as to hold more congregations of more than 2,000. The pulpit being the main liturgical focal point the hearers of a preacher with a "moderate voice" would sit, in front of the clergyman, as much as fifty feet away in an auditory church which would be a broad rectangle rather than a circle or a polygon allowing for a more "fan-shaped" disposition of the worshippers; one can liken Wren's proviso to the arrangement, in such a modern episcopal and parish church as the new Clifton Cathedral, whereby a "radial" plan means that no one sits more than fifty feet from the High Altar. Wren hoped that the new churches should not be so cluttered with rented pews that the poor, to whom equally the Gospel was preached, had no room to sit or stand in the aisles. He would also have preferred open benches to the proprietorial system of lockable pews, but he wryly commented that there was "no stemming the tide of profit and the advantage of pew keepers". On another aspect of ecclesiastical sociology Wren was, however, less progressive. For the new churches must not be built, in outer suburbs where growth was still likely to occur, on empty and comparatively inexpensive sites, but "among the thicker inhabitants for the convenience of the *better* sort". The "better" (or richer) inhabitants would then raise the most money for maintenance and repairs.

Wren and his fellow commissioners of 1711 could not, of course, know that a mere dozen churches, not forty-nine plus Greenwich, would ever be built under the new Act, and that of those which did get built not all would be the wholly new foundations which the Tory Parliament of 1710 had in the main envisaged. Had the whole scheme been carried out it could, with such architects as Hawksmoor and Archer at work, have been a more significant contribution to English church planning and architecture than what Wren achieved in the

City. Archer's new church at Birmingham, of which Wren must have been aware, well fulfilled the idea, of a new church on the outskirts of a growing town, which Wren had in mind when he wrote out his orderly document of his whole thinking on the matter. Had he himself had the designing of many new churches built under the Act they might, as Mr Howard Colvin has suggested, have tended to repeat Wren's favoured, and none too exciting, "galleried basilica" of St James's off Jermyn Street.[67] But some by Hawksmoor, who knew Wren's thoughts and built them in new areas where they certainly fulfilled Wren's provisos, were more original masterpieces by an architect who could now be said to have outstrippd his old master. The new Act had, moreover, given Wren his chance, a he neared the age of eighty, to codify the thinking of a lifetime in which, in such matters, theory had been tempered by some hard experiences.

With no new palaces in prospect, Wren's commitments as head of the Works Office continued to be on a minor scale. He and his colleagues had to see to the repair of Guard Houses at Kensington, Whitehall and Hampton Court, while there was still the increasingly vexatious problem of finding space for the records of such Courts as those of Wards and Requests and the Queen's Bench.[68] The repairing of the road in Hyde Park by Captain Studholme, by now a veteran in his post, had also to be checked, the sum in question in November of 1711 being the considerable one of £1,085 11s. 1d.[69]

So at the beginning of 1712 (New Style) one came to the year in which Sir Christopher would achieve what was, by the standard of those times, the great age of eighy. The year started with an event which, by a happy piece of parliamentary irony, mainly concerned the architect's namesake son.

The rise of Harley and his colleagues had meant the replacement, in the favour of Queen Anne, of the Duchess of Marlborough by her distant and disliked kinswoman Mrs Masham, *née* Abigail Hill. Though he was a political and personal lightweight, Abigail's husband was found a seat in Parliament, his constituency being New Windsor, the borough which had, in 1689 and 1690, brought an ignominious rebuff to Sir Christopher Wren. But when on 1st January 1712, Samuel Masham got a peerage, with Mrs Masham becoming Baroness Masham, the resulting vacancy[70] was filled, this time apparently without trouble or controversy, by the younger Christopher Wren. He sat for Windsor again in the Parliament which met early in 1714, but Queen Anne's death, and the Whig complexion of the first Hanoverian Parliament, meant that the parliamentary career of the great architect's son was comparatively short. He had, in the meantime, and as we shall notice, seen great changes in the domestic and personal circumstances of his life.

At the end of 1712 the younger Christopher Wren become a

widower. His wife, whom he married in 1706, seems to have died in childbed or very soon after the birth of the fifth Christopher Wren, who himself died, aged sixty, in 1773; the episode, though all too common at that time, must have been a poignant experience both for the bereaved husband and his aging father. The first Mrs Wren was Mary, the daughter of Philip Mussard, by descent a Huguenot and since 1677 a naturalised Englishman. *Parentalia* (perhaps mistakenly) makes the point that he was Court jeweller to Queen Anne, and he certainly supplied jewels to Charles II and his queen. As he and his forbears were connected with the gold and jewellery trades, Wren's interest in coins and medals, and his collection of classical coins on which, in 1708, had he published a descriptive catalogue,[71] could have made the two men kindred spirits. Then in 1713 Sir Christopher set events in train which duly led to another marriage for his son, and to the further continuance of the family line.

On 20th October 1712 Sir Christopher reached the age of eighty. His career as an architect was now near its end. But the last decade of his life was not to be lacking in incidents, and is full of interest for his biography.

14

Declining Years

The year 1713, the last complete twelvemonth of Queen Anne's invalid life, included the Treaty of Utrecht and, for England, the end of a ten-years' war. It did not, however, see any resumption of palace building. Sir Christopher Wren, for whom the year was soon full of unexpected and varied activity, still had his routine commitments at the Works Office. He also worked on a project which, had it ever been started, would have produced a building on a major scale.

Wren's Works enquiries of this year concerned the accommodation of soldiers, the checking, at Windsor, of another of Studholme's new roads,[1] and a matter of ecclesiastical concern. He had also, in the middle of the year, to see the erection, in St Paul's, of special fittings so that the Queen could attend the service of thanksgiving for the peace which the Tories had arranged at Utrecht.[2]

An early project of 1713 was the fitting out, in the Savoy, of barracks for 500 infantry. The Queen approved the project, but Robert Harley her Lord Treasurer felt that the work could be done for less than the £1,600 of Wren's estimate. So the Surveyor General was asked to reconsider his figures. By the end of November the scheme had changed into one for an infirmary. Wren, whose supervision of the office may, by now, have begun to slacken, was asked to speed his report.[3] By now he was busied over a far more ambitious project of military housing.

Hampton Court and Windsor apart, Queen Anne's residence was now divided between St James's and Kensington. Troops for guard duty were needed in both places; their barracks could thus conveniently be placed between the two. So late in the spring of 1713 Wren was told that the Queen intended, for the housing of some of her Guards, to have barracks built, in Hyde Park, on a site well placed for the soldiers to do duty at both royal residences. Wren, who would obviously be in charge of such a job, was to hear about the numbers to be housed* and to work out an estimate.[4] From what he was told Wren made the plans, two-dimensional and without elevations, for what would have been an ambitious grouping. The parade ground

---

Parentalia, on page 334, mentions 1,000 Horse Guards and 2,000 private soldiers.

was to have measured 175 feet by 240, an infirmary and a wide-aisled chapel were to be provided, and the "necessary places" were to be little cabins round circular courts.[5] But Anne's death, within little more than a year, prevented the commencement of one of Wren's last imposing or monumental schemes.

Another idea, with which Anne as a devout churchwoman interested herself, was for better worshipping facilities while she resided at St James's. The queen had the idea that Inigo Jones's chapel, originally put up for the Catholic devotions of the Spanish Infanta who never in fact came to marry Charles I, and which was actually used by Henrietta Maria and later by Catherine of Braganza, could be turned over to the Anglican services which she devoutly followed. By 1713 the chapel, in sharp contrast to its original use, become the home of French and Dutch Calvinist congregations. Wren was now to inspect it, see if it was larger than the chapel within St James's Palace in which Anne already worshipped, and if so to work out the cost of its conversion to the Queen's use.[6] Here again no actual change was made while Queen Anne still lived, and the Hanoverians did not pursue the matter. An episode of more personal importance concerned the officers working for the New Churches Commission.

The commission's original surveyors had been Hawksmoor and the younger William Dickinson whose father had served the Works Office and who had helped Wren over St Paul's, on some of the later work on the City churches, and at Westminster Abbey. Now in 1713 Dickinson, who had designed none of the new churches, resigned his surveyorship for an important post in the Office of Works; as its holder he could relieve Wren of his work in the Palace of St James, Whitehall, and Westminster. His successor, as things turned out for only two years, was James Gibbs. Though the Earl of Mar's influence, and Mar's letters to Harley, now the Earl of Oxford and strategically placed as Lord High Treasurer, may have been important for Gibbs's success the good opinion of Wren, whose professional knowledge and expertise in such matters was unrivalled, seems certain to have been vital. Sir Christopher seldom, in this ninth decade of his life, attended the meetings of the New Churches Commissioners. But on 18th November, when the business in hand included the choice of a Surveyor to take over from Dickinson, he seems to have made a special effort to come. His son was also there, and the commissioners' choice was to be made by ballot. Gibbs was the winner, and it seems that Wren's recommendation, as well as the votes of him and his son, helped his colleagues towards their decision. At a time when Gibbs was, for professional reasons, concealing his Catholicism Wren may not have known of his young friend's religious beliefs. But Gibbs's Jacobite loyalties, which were, after the designing of his one 'New Church' of St Mary le Strand, to cost him his surveyorship, were less effectively hidden.

In this same busy year Wren came into professional contact with another prominent Stuart supporter, whose loudly advertised opinions were in the end to lead him to Jacobite exile. In 1713 Wren's old friend Sprat died as the holder both of the see of Rochester and the deanery of Westminster. His successor, by an act of high Tory patronage very typical of that particular year, was Francis Atterbury; as was normal at that time he held both appointments, the poor bishopric and the rich deanery, in plurality. As Bishop of Rochester he was of no interest to Wren. But he was much concerned with Sir Christopher as the Surveyor of the Abbey. He noted the advanced age of his eighty-year old archiect. It seemed prudent to ask him for a memorandum setting out what he had already, since 1698, achieved as Surveyor, and giving his thoughts on future repairs. Wren answered with the last of his important documents on any great mediaeval church;[7] he used some nice phrases about the style which he really disliked.

Wren was critical of the "flutter of archbuttresses," or rather flying buttresses, which supported the vaults both of the choir and the nave; as a man deeply interested in structure he also wrote disapprovingly of the "indiscreet form" of the high-pitched roof whose acute slope, unlike that of St George's at Windsor, caused the sheets of lead to slip, but which could not be altered; the roof timbers he found to be a mixture of oak and Normandy chestnut. He said that he had found traces of the "Saxon" (i.e. of the Norman) church, and he pointed out, in a reference to the west end of the nave, that the great church had never been finished. Henry VII's chapel he found to be a "nice embroidered work" in serious decay; his son was later to speak vividly of the "cut work and crinkle crancle" of the same late Perpendicular masterpiece. He begged for "some compassion" for that part of the Abbey, hoping that as the chapel was a "regal sepulture", holding as it did such recent royal corpses as those of Charles II, William and Mary, and Prince George of Denmark its repair might get royal assistance in addition to the money from the London coal tax.

Wren went on to speak of work he had done on the Abbey, replacing the severely worn Reigate stone with Burford stone sent down, past Oxford, by river. On the church's southern side he had carried out considerable repairs, but on the north the close proximity of houses and gardens, with such apanages as wash houses, cellars, and privies, had stopped him from doing much. The most dangerous part of the choir vault would, he said, be made good in a few months, but the main repairs needed on the northern side had yet to be put in hand. He assumed, mistakenly perhaps in view of the French Gothic character of the new church which Henry III had started, that a central steeple perhaps like that which he knew well at Salisbury, had originally been intended; to remedy the omission he had proposed the heightening of the tower, with the addition of a spire. Anything classical, in the manner of his City steeples would, he felt, be a "disagreeable mixture", so he sympathetically put in a somewhat stiff and insipid Gothic design. For the north transept he later got out designs and sketches which may be those, dated in 1719 when they were used as guide to actual building work, which bear Wren's signature.[8]* One is of a character more Romanesque than the geometrical Gothic of the other. But both are in sympathy with the Abbey as Wren knew it. So too, "without any modern mixtures to show my own inventions", were Wren's notions for the two western towers, actually built by Hawksmoor and with unmediaevally Baroque details mixed in with their basically Gothic idiom.

Another ecclesiastical work which was finished in 1713 gave the final touch to one of Wren's City churches; two others, in the next few years, were similarly involved. By no means all of the City steeples had been finished in the main building processes of their churches. One such was at St Michael Paternoster Royal, where an upper stage was now added to a comparatively simple tower. Like other steeples built late in Wren's lifetime the composition, delightfully Baroque with its octagonal plan and with Ionic pillarets jutting out, at intervals, from the polygonal core, does not wholly integrate with the tower below it. Plainly an afterthought, it is none the less a splendid, characterful addition to the church; aesthetically it is akin to the drums of the domes at Greenwich and to the fine Borrominian *campanili* of St Paul's.

Other events of 1713 concerned Wren's arrangements for the future of his family.

On 14th April 1713 Sir Christopher Wren made his final will;[9] as was not unnatural for a man of eighty he signed it with a somewhat shaky hand. He left all his property to the younger Christopher whom he also made his sole executor. He desired him to take "particular care" that "poor Billy" should be comfortably maintained and cared for as long as he lived. Other clauses looked back to arrangements made, but never completed, while Christopher Wren was married to Mary Mussard. Sir Christopher had clearly intended, during that time, to set up his son as a man of independent property. For that purpose he had arranged, with two trustees, to lay out £10,000, plus Mary's marriage portion, for the buying of suitable land. He now desired his son and the trustees to make the necessary arrangements "with as much convenient speed as may be". Though Wren's wishes

---

*The Thomas Sprat who also signed them was one of the canons, not the Dean who died in 1713.

were expressed in a will which was not proved till 1723 immediate action was taken to set up the younger Christopher as a country squire.

The property bought, for £19,000, was at Wroxall in rural Warwickshire; there may already, in 1713 when the deal was made, have been some idea that the new owner's relationship with the vendors might one day be more than commercial. The site, and the half of the church which has been destroyed, was once that of a small priory of Benedictine nuns. Not long after the dissolution Thomas Burgoyne, a commissioner for monastic surrenders and thus well placed to acquire such property, obtained Wroxall Priory, as also an estate at Sutton in Bedfordshire. The family kept both estates, but Sutton seems to have been their main home.[10] At Wroxall they built an Elizabethan mansion on the western side of the nunnery site, while under Charles I a baronetcy came their way. Sir Roger, the fifth baronet, married Constance, a daughter of a City magnate, Sir Thomas Middleton. Sir Roger soon died, in 1713, and in August of that year Dame Constance sold the Wroxall estate, for his son's use, to Sir Christopher Wren. The Wrens thus came to be the owners of the Wroxall property, semantically elevated, for the estate purposes of the eighteenth century, into an 'Abbey'. More remarkable, though perhaps foreseen in 1713, was that in another two years, by which time he was no longer in Parliament, the younger Christopher Wren became the second husband of the Bedfordshire widow from whom Wroxall had been bought. He settled, one hopes to his father's pleasure, as a squire on his Midland estate. Though he does not seem, at all events on the outside, to have altered his gabled Elizabethan house some gate posts and garden walls were apparently of his time and design.

Queen Anne's last seven months found Wren on a variety of Surveyor's minor tasks at Windsor and in London. The running of his office seems to have aroused criticism, for late in February he had to prepare, for the Lord Treasurer, his proposals for cutting what were thought to be its "exorbitant charges".[11] The military quarters in the Savoy still concerned him, with a report requested early in June and orders, a few days later, to fit out houses for military use – some for officers, one as an infirmary, a large house for the Provost Marshall and prisoners, and other buildings for coal stores and other purposes – all for the none too large sum of £600.[12] At Windsor Wren, still surveyor for the castle, faced such mundane problems as the emptying of the boghouses and, at the Queen's personal insistance not long before she died, the whole problem of laying running water into the castle and the gathering into a single head of several inlets.[13]

The smooth and peaceful Hanoverian succession made little immediate difference to Wren who was soon reappointed both as

Surveyor General and as Controller of the Works at Windsor. As it happened, the Windsor post was abolished early in 1716, the work being merged with that of the Works Office.[14] To ease Wren's burden as head of that office a commission, including the newly knighted Vanbrugh, was set up to exercise the Surveyor General's office; the younger Christopher, despite his new interests, remained its employee as Clerk Engrosser.[15] The Board of Works, as the new body was called, took over the work which had nominally been the Surveyor General's sole responsibility. Wren attended its meeting as often as his age and physical weakness allowed. For the moment, in the conciliatory opening year of George I's reign, all seemed well. What was to make things more difficult, at once for such known Jacobites as Gibbs, and in due course for others who had long and devotedly served the Stuarts, was Mar's rising of 1715, intended to burst out elsewhere than in Scotland and the North of England and a serious threat, before he had settled into his new kingdom, to George I and his Whig supporters.

When the '15 started Sir Christopher Wren was nearly eighty-three. Under modern conditions such a public servant would, by that time, have long retired on pension. But no pensioned retirement had then been organised; the holders of such posts as Wren's would, if not dismissed, ease off their activity, as Wren was for a few years allowed to do, while more of their work was done by trusted deputies or less senior members of their staff. Though Wren remained mentally alert the more physically exacting work of a post which was now burdened with few major tasks could be left to the other members of the Board of Works, and to the technical team built up at the Works Office. The holder of Wren's official post need not, under the new dynasty, have expected the brusque harshness of outright dismissal. Yet there remained, for consideration not only by so veteran a designer as Wren but by others among his colleagues, the position, in the English architectural climate early in the eighteenth century, of architects whose instinct and preferences were Baroque.

Colen Campbell's *Vitruvius Brittanicus*, with its homage to Inigo Jones and his more or less Palladian followers, started to come out in 1715. The English edition of Palladio's *Quattro Libri dell' Architettura*, under the sponsorship of the Earl of Burlington and with its Italian text translated by Giacomo Leoni, also came out that year. Their publication heralded the English Palladian revival of the eighteenth century. Palladianism, for great country mansions and for other buildings, alike urban and rural, became the architectural idiom most favoured among the newly dominant Whig aristocrats. The Roman classicism of Palladio was not a style which Wren disliked, but it was not, despite Inigo Jones's achievements a little before his time, the style in which he had worked. In the new Palladian age a Surveyor

General who was not a Palladian might well seem an out-of-date anachronism. Architects like Wren, Hawksmoor, Archer, and Vanbrugh who had, in their varying ways, given England its demonstrations of Baroque, were out of sympathy with the new fashion. James Gibbs, a younger man and, despite his admiration of Palladio as "the Great Restorer of architecture", a non-Palladian architect by training and instinct, could to some extent adapt himself to the new trend. But for Wren, as for others among his associates, it was now too late. What remained, in a few more years, was the actual manner of Wren's departure from the post which he had held for nearly half a century, and whose detailed working he had controlled for nearly all of that time. In the meantime some incidents affected Wren's position at St Paul's and Greenwich. A new commission for St Paul's was appointed in 1715, while John James, a carpenter by training who had, in 1711, succeeded Jennings as the cathedral's master carpenter, now became its Assistant Surveyor. Wren was on the new commission. But only twice, on 28th June and 2nd July, did he attend its meetings.[16] On the first of those occasions James Thornhill was, to Wren's displeasure, formally asked to paint the inner surfaces of the dome. He was already at work, with no apparent protest by Wren, on the first of his wall decorations in the hall at Greenwich. His achievement there was to be a triumph of richly coloured allegorical Baroque wall decoration; it was a pity that a similar technique, linking the dome paintings in St Paul's with the work of such Italian exponents as Pozzo and da Cortona, was not used in the cathedral. It would certainly have been more effective than the insipid grisaille, less happy in actuality than sketches suggested, which adorns the dome. It would also have been better than the mosaic decoration which Wren had favoured. But from July of that politically fateful year, with his opponent Godolphin still Dean and to be in that office till after his death, Wren ceased to sit on the St Paul's Commission. John James took over the work of the surveyorship, and Wren's later visits were affairs of contemplation and no longer of official business.

His age and increasing bodily infirmity caused Wren to give up his Greenwich surveyorship in 1716. Vanbrugh, already at work on buildings within the Hospital, succeeded Wren, but Hawksmoor the Assistant Surveyor was at least as much involved in the fulfilment of Wren's plan.

In the following May Wren, along with others, went to Windsor to inspect the "water engine" which raised water from the river to the castle. The visit may, at so late a time in Wren's life, have been the last he ever paid to a place he had known since childhood; his commitment there would, by now, have been part of his activity on the new Board of Works. He and his colleagues found "great ruination" in the approaches to the pumping device. The engine itself, so they reckoned, would have to be renewed, while the building which housed it, the sluices, and the great water wheel would all have to be rebuilt. New bridges, to give passage over the sluices to the horses which towed the river barges, would also be needed. They estimated that the whole job would cost about £1,600. The work was put in hand by one John Rowley whose bill, in the middle of 1718, was referred to the Board of Works.[17]

Wren was also concerned, at this time, with the last of his City steeples and with final embellishments on St Paul's. The steeple of St James's Garlickhythe, like that of St Michael Royal resting on a tower completed some years earlier, was finished, after a building process of about three years, in 1717. Of a rich Baroque invention in its octagonal mainstage it is akin, though with its pillarets and their capping urns paired and not evenly spaced, to that of St Michael's. But the octagonal or circular emphasis of that slightly older steeple fades in its equally delightful upper stages. At St Stephen's Walbrook the lantern, of the same years and with pairs of Ionic pillarets grouped at its corners, is more rigidly squared in a reminiscence of Christ Church, Newgate Street.

The year 1717 also saw the outbreak, between Wren and the cathedral authorities, of a last flurry of disagreement over St Paul's. Most of the cathedral commissioners wanted to erect a balustrade, instead of the plain parapet of Wren's intention, above the topmost cornice and round the walls of the new building; one recalls the reference, when the New Churches Bill was going through Parliament, to the idea, with its details unspecified, of "pinnacles and other ornaments round the top of the church".[18] Sir Christopher, when the scheme was mentioned to him, criticised it for the plausible reason that such a feature would be too much of a target for the destructive power of high winds; he could also, had he known what would happen to Bird's prominent statues, have realised that even Portland stone would suffer, if put up in thin enough units, from rain and mordant London grime. His aesthetic condemnation of the notion was, one feels less soundly based. He had not, in his own various drawings, allowed for a balustrade round the choir, transepts, and nave of his new St Paul's. Yet he had, at Hampton Court, for example, designed buildings which did have balustrades, while he knew of other buildings, such as the Banqueting House in Whitehall, to which balusters were an accepted embellishment. His remark, that "ladies think nothing well without an edging", seems less than charitable. Despite Wren's disapproval the commissioners went ahead, under James's supervision, with the project which their norminal Chief Surveyor had disliked. By now, however, at the end of 1717, there were the first indications of the sharp blow which his enemies were soon to direct against Wren as royal Surveyor General.

Whatever intrigues may have started before the end of 1717, Wren's position was finally challenged in the following spring; political jobbery, aided perhaps by suspicion of a man whose background and long years of service to the Stuarts might be held to incline him unduly to anti-Hanoverian sympathies, was certainly behind what now occurred. On 21st April a Royal Warrant went out for the grant to William Benson of the office of Surveyor within the Tower of London and in other residences, especially castles and palaces, as a rule reserved for royal "repair and abode".[19] Benson was to enjoy all the profits and emoluments of the Surveyorship, as fully as Inigo Jones or Denham, or Wren on the day when the warrant went out, had earlier enjoyed them. Wren's tenure of the office was specifically revoked. By his deprivation he lost the use of his official residence, the brick-built[29] house in Scotland Yard which had for years been his main home. He was lucky that he still had the lease of the house on Hampton Green, and that he owned or rented a house, more convenient for London visits and London concerns, in St James's Street.

William Benson, who now succeeded Wren as Surveyor General, was a "gentleman architect" of a type common in the early Georgian age. His designs, made a few years earlier, for his country mansion at Wilbury in eastern Wiltshire suggest that he was less of an architectural ignoramus than some of Wren's defenders have supposed.[21] By now, moreover, the Surveyor General's post was one, in the main, for an administrator; as such Benson was so inept that he was dismissed in the following year. But before that event his precautionary attack on the efficiency of the Board of Works which had, with reasonable efficiency and with Wren attending it when his health allowed, functioned for some four years, produced a last little protest from the old architect in his riverside retreat.[22] He referred to his own attendance at the Board of Works and came to the defence of "former managements", meaning the recent Board of Works and his own conduct for more than forty years before George I's arrival. He ended with the assertion that there were no just grounds for censuring those who had run the Royal Works before Benson was put over them. His last words were these "And as I am dismiss'd, having worn out (by God's mercy) a long life in the Royal Service, and having made some figure in the World, I hope it will be allowed me to Die in Peace". Benson's dismissal must have made it easier for Sir Christopher, aged eighty-six when he wrote the letter, to have his wish.

Wren kept his surveyorship of Westminster Abbey till his death, but apart from Westminster his architectural activity was, by the year 1719, almost at an end. So when in that year the parishioners of St Clement Danes decided to add a steeple to the tower which Wren had started it was Gibbs, not Wren, who made the design, sympathetic to Wren's later manner yet distinctively of the eighteenth century. When, at about the same time, the tower of St Michael's Cornhill was to be finished Wren's old associate Hawksmoor, designing in his somewhat graceless and eccentric Gothic, was the chosen architect. By now, moreover, an important ecclesiastical scheme, in the end producing a masterpiece by Gibbs but possibly involving some private consultations with Wren, was under way elsewhere in London.

Back in 1708 a visitor to St Martin-in-the-Fields had noted that the old church, despite its fairly recent "beautification", was "low and ordinary" and much in need of rebuilding on a larger scale.[23] Only the steeple was in good condition. The parishioners, till the spring of 1718 including Wren, were soon of the same opinion. An Act of Parliament, authorising a wholly new church to replace a "decayed and ruinous" building, was passed in 1720. Commissioners were appointed to carry out the work. Had Sir Christopher still been a parishioner he could well have been one of them. He could also, at Hampton or in St James's Street, have easily been consulted by the commissioners, some of whom must have known him in person. The commissioners first met in June of 1720 when four architects, one of whom soon withdrew, sent in their schemes.[24] One of them was Gibbs who could, like the commissioners, have had personal discussions with Wren – by now his friend for some eleven years. Gibbs clearly wanted to impress the commissioners with Wren's merits as an inspiration for what he himself might do in the designing of the new St Martin's. So on 17th August he took the Building Committee to see some of Wren's churches;[25] in view of his alternative designs for a circular or basilican nave he may have taken them both to centrally planned buildings and to some which were more conventionally rectangular. The final choice, towards the end of the year, lay between Gibbs and John James. If Wren had any influence with the commissioners he could well have disposed them to his friend Gibbs rather than to James for whom, as Jennings's successor at St Paul's and as the builder of the uncongenial balustrade, Wren's feelings may not, at that particular time, have been very agreeable. He must have known what was happening when, in the autumn of 1721, demolition work, involving the destruction of the graves of his two wives and of Gilbert his infant son, was started on the old St Martin's in which he had often worshipped.

On 20th May 1719 Wren wrote, in the scrawling hand of a very old man, that he approved the more Gothic of the two available designs for a new facade for the north transept of Westminster Abbey.[26] He may have made it himself, or Dickinson may have drawn it out in collaboration with the older architect. Now, however, it was under Dickinson's close supervision that it was carried out, being replaced, in Queen Victoria's reign, from the designs of Scott and Pearson. The work was finished, with Wren still the Abbey's Surveyor, in 1722. What was never achieved, in Wren's life or at any other time, was the risky operation of building a central tower and steeple. Such an adornment was, however, intended. One may suppose that Wren, despite a knowledge of structure which should have made him realise the heavy strain it would impose on the crossing piers of a French Gothic church never meant to have a central tower and spire, countenanced, if he did not authorise in detail, what was now proposed in the last year of his life. A print of the Abbey, published by John James, shows it with an insignificant tower, and with an ornate spire "as designed by Wren".[27] Sir Christopher may not, however, have made any such design. More important, though never carried out, are some schemes of 1722, bearing Dickinson's initials and of more interest than beauty. One is for a spire, while two others show an unhappy combination of a Gothicised dome and a more truly Gothic spirelet.[28] More interesting, for Wren's old school in the shadow of the Abbey, were schemes for a scholars' dormitory. Like many of Wren's projects they got enmeshed, in a last demonstration of the importance of factors outside architectural aesthetics, in political turmoil.

The idea went back to 1708, when the school got a legacy of £1,000 for the building of a new dormitory; the donor asked that those eminent Old Westminsters Dean Aldrich at Oxford, and Wren whose Abbey surveyorship reinforced his interest as an old boy of the school, were to be consulted. Aldrich soon died, and Wren held that the bequest was too small for a new dormitory but that improvements could be made in the existing room which had once been the monks' granary. Yet he made two designs, in March of 1711, for a fine new dormitory block, to be built along one side of the college garden;[29] such a scheme fitted his basic preference for new sites and new buildings rather than the patching of ancient and stylistically uncongenial structures. One of Wren's two schemes, with its sleeping accommodation to be supported on a rusticated arcade, was to form the basis of what he and his colleagues later proposed. When Atterbury came to Westminster as Dean he pressed, no doubt with Wren's approval and despite the obvious inadequacy of the legacy for so ambitious a work, for a wholly new building, and early in 1714 an altered version (perhaps changed by Hawksmoor) of Wren's arcaded design was engraved for the information and encouragement of extra benefactors.[30] But Queen Anne's death, and the troubles of 1715 and 1716, supervened so that nothing was done for some years, while drawings of 1717 suggest that work may, in the meantime, have been considered on the scholars' hall fitted out in what had been the abbot's dining hall.[31]

The idea of a wholly new dormitory was what in the end held the field. Later in 1718 donations came from the Treasury, from George I, and from the future George II,[32] and at the same time work went ahead with the final presentation of designs. There was, however, a split in the Chapter, to some extent on Tory and Whig lines, over whether or not a new dormitory should be put up in the garden. In the meantime there was a return, not to the scheme published in 1714 but the essence, particularly in its central section, of one of Wren's eight-year-old designs. The elevation drawing, "examined" on 14th January of 1719,[33] shows the rusticated arcade of the earlier design, and a fine central feature where the main windows have about them, in a likeness to what one sees in the Fountain Court at Hampton Court, oval windows wreathed not with the Nemean lion skins of those made to please William III but with floral carving of a more ordinary Baroque type. Niches in the two pavilion blocks were to have similarly adorned windows above them, while a row of flaming urns was to cap the unbalustraded parapet of the proposed building. Even if Dickinson assisted Wren over some details the veteran architect would, as an old boy of the school where he had been Busby's favoured pupil, have taken a close interest in what was now proposed. Other designs, some of them perhaps by Dickinson, were made at about the same time, while on 24th May, when the canons were still disputing over the renovation of the old dormitory or the building of a new one, Wren wrote to say that the new site in the garden or orchard was "much more proper and convenient in all respects" than the converted granary.[34] But the dispute, with the Chapter, at this time including Bishop Bradford of Carlisle the eventual (and Whig) successor to Atterbury, almost equally divided, could now be solved only by a somewhat lengthy process at law. By the time that the legal issue was decided high politics had given their twist to the architectural character of any dormitory which might get built for the Westminster scholars.

On the last day of 1720 the birth of the boy later known as Bonnie Prince Charlie gave encouragement to the more fervent Jacobites such as Francis Atterbury; it was also the signal for new plots and endeavours on behalf of the 'King over the Water'. A few months later, at the beginning of April, the accession of Walpole as Chancellor of the Exchequer and First Lord of the Treasury gave power to the most effective of the Jacobites' opponents. With Walpole in charge increasing suspicion was bound to fall on men like Atterbury who made no concealment of their Stuart sympathies.

On 16th May of 1721 the House of Lords, to which the dispute over the Westminster dormitory had gone, ruled in favour of its erection on the garden site.[35] The basic policy which had triumphed was that of Atterbury and Wren; other influences prevailed in its detailed execution. Lord Burlington, an amateur architect as well as a Whig, was an important figure in the Lords, while the high Tory bishop cum dean, and those who had backed him, were increasingly under a cloud. Though some of Wren's architectural friends seem still to have persisted with designs in the Baroque tradition it was now more likely that one of the 'Burlington School' of Palladians should have the commission. In the end it was Burlington himself, both as patron and as designer of the actual new dormitory, who on 21st April of 1722 laid its foundation stone.[36] The new dormitory, of whose details Wren must have known, and of which he need not have violently disapproved, was laid out, with no variation in the middle of its frontage, as a dignified Paladian range,[37] a good work in the newly fashionable taste but of less character than what Wren, in 1719 but reviving his more Baroque ideas of Queen Anne's time, had proposed for the site. At Westminster as in other places Whiggery and Palladianism were now triumphant. During the month in which Burlington started the Westminster dormitory Walpole got reliable news of yet another serious Jacobite plot. Atterbury was strongly suspected, and in another four months he was in the Tower. His sojourn, unlike that, under Henry VIII, of John Fisher, his illustrious predecessor in the Rochester diocese, was not to cost him his life. But his trial, a *cause celèbre* of the coming year, was to end in his deprivation and to his banishment to the Pretender's Court. By that time his illustrious Abbey surveyor had met his peaceful end.

Since he had ceased to be Surveyor General Sir Christopher Wren had lived more and more in retirement, for the most part in the riverside quiet of his house on Hampton Green. His son and his grandson tell us, in *Parentalia* which Stephen Wren brought out after his own father's death,[38] that Wren betook himself, in his home in what was still rural Middlesex, "to a country retirement", and that there, "free from Worldly Affairs", he passed much of the time, in his last five years, in contemplation and study, particularly of the Scriptures. He was, we hear, cheerful despite the lack of close relatives which his age, and family circumstances, had imposed on him; he was, the narrative tells us, "as well pleased to die in the shade as in the light". Though his limbs were now feeble his mind remained vigorous, to a degree unusual in a man of his age, almost to the end.

Though Wren now spent most of his time at Hampton he sometimes came up to London. Apart from matters to do with the abbey and the school at Westminster he could not, at this late stage, have had much business to conduct. But he could, and did, pay reflective visits to buildings, most notably in the City, which had arisen to his designs. Chief among them, and complete by now in all things but some details, was the new cathedral. He must have wished, as the designer of such a building would do today, that all the details not only of the main structure but of the furnishings and decoration had been carried out under his will and direction. The story that he would sit, in recollection and reverie, immediately below the dome may not, perhaps, be precisely accurate, for the great space beneath the dome would not, at the time when Thornhill's paintings were in progress, have been the most peaceful or emotionally happy setting for the architect of St Paul's to dwell on his chief ecclesiastical achievement. But somewhere in the cathedral Sir Christopher could still have found good places wherein he might sit and indulge in the reminiscences of a designer whose connection with St Paul's, old and new had, by the last year of his life, continued through sixty years.

By the early weeks of 1723 (New Style) Sir Christopher Wren had well passed his ninetieth birthday. He could look back on a full life which had stretched from the time of Laud and Cromwell to that of Walpole and Atterbury. He had seen, and could recall, the halcyon days, from the Wrens' point of view, of the Laudian ascendancy, the harder times of the Civil War and the Commonwealth, and the Restoration which had opened the way to his own active career. Politics apart, the accident of fire had given him one of his greatest chances, while other potentialities had been blighted by the political ups and downs of Charles II's reign. He had passed through the short reign of James II to a fruitful yet precarious spell of favour and creative maturity while Mary II and her Dutch husband were on the throne. His old age, with Anne as queen and the long war of the Spanish succession a dominant factor, had been fuller and more busy than a man in his seventies could normally have hoped. In the end he had lived, firstly without controversy but in the end with official dismissal and the outright supersession of one of his designs, to see the coming of George I and over eight years of Hanoverian power. His closest friends were all dead by now, he had long been a widower, his favourite child had predeceased him, and his namesake son had set up on his own and must often, as a squire in the Midlands, have been away from London. Testy and sarcastic at times Sir Christopher had none the less, more than most of his contemporaries, lived well and cleanly, and without the taint of political scandal or financial corruption. "Benevolence and complacency", so his son and grandson put it, were the marks of his last, declining years.

Sir Christopher Wren died, on 25th February of 1723, and like Wellington, asleep in an armchair. His servant found that his master had failed to wake from an early evening nap. The event was not at Hampton, but during one of Wren's London visits, in the house in St James's Street. He was buried, not in the parish church which he had liked better than most of his parochial churches, but in the great cathedral of his own designing where the coolness of Dean Godolphin could hardly deny him his last resting place. His grave, in the extreme south-eastern corner of the crypt, has above it no more than a plain slab. In this respect it is less impressive than William Holder's double cartouche, or Bird's fine plaque to Jane Wren, or the Baroque cartouche, with its skull and weeping *putti*, which commemorates Mary Wren and also, with their respective death dates of 1713 and 1729, her Mussard parents Philip and Constantia. For Wren's real visible memorial one must look, as his son explained in one of the most famous of all epitaphs, elsewhere than his actual grave.

There were, in fact two versions of Wren's funerary insciption. One, described as an "After-Thought for the Inscription in St Paul's", makes points unmentioned on the actual stone.[39] The record of Wren's years is not the plain *annos ultra nonaginta* of the better known inscription but, in a reference to the venerable Homeric hero whose exact attaintment of ninety years was quoted, in antiquity, by those who wished their friends long life, the words given are annos ultra Nestoreos.* Wren's devotion, not to his own interests but to the public good, is mentioned in both texts. There are, however, two versions of the epitaph's most famous phrase. The "After-Thought", with greater physical accuracy, says *si* TUMULUM *requiris despice*, but adds the point *si* MONUMENTUM *circumspice*. The actual engraving has *Lector, si monumentum requiris circumspice*. The looking round is better done upstairs than here in the least impressive part of the cathedral's crypt, but so far as it goes, with no mention made of Sir Christopher's other buildings, the sentiment is true.

Yet for a fuller appreciation of the range of Wren's genius and inventive power one needs to see more than the actual buildings of an architect who evolved several versions of what he actually saw built and whose career, over decades in which politics and a State finance inevitably bore heavily on his activity, included the making of many important designs for buildings never started. For a fuller memorial of Wren the architect one must also turn to the greater collections of his drawings. In the Soane Museum there is vital material on Hampton Court and other buildings. The library of the Royal Institute of British Architects, with material once in the Bute Collection, illuminates City churches and St Paul's. In the library of St Paul's, though not only there, drawings show what Wren did, or what he contemplated, for his best known building. Above all comes the great insight into Wren's mind provided in the five volumes of drawings lovingly cared for in the Oxford college of which he was a Fellow. They are in a building designed by his pupil and fellow worker Nicholas Hawksmoor though provided, later on, with its Palladian fittings, the stately library at All Souls'.

*Steele made the same classical point in an obituary article.

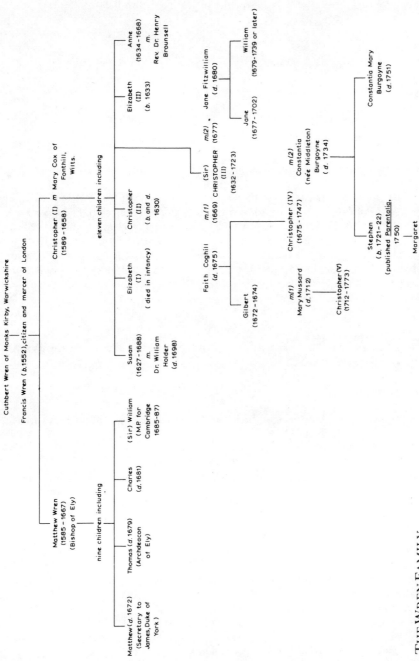

Cuthbert Wren of Monks Kirby, Warwickshire

Francis Wren (b.1552), citizen and mercer of London

Christopher (I) m Mary Cox of
(1589-1658)   Fonthill,
                     Wilts.

nine children including

Matthew Wren
(1585-1667)
(Bishop of Ely)

Matthew (d.1672)   Thomas (d.1679)   Charles   (Sir) William
(Secretary to   (Archdeacon   (d.1681)   (M.P. for
James, Duke of   of Ely)   Cambridge
York)   1685-87)

eleven children including

Susan   Elizabeth   Christopher   Elizabeth   Anne
(1627-1688)   (I)   (II)   (II)   (1634-1668)
m.   (died in infancy) (b. and d.   (b. 1633)   m.
Dr. William   1630)   Rev. Dr. Henry
Holder   Brounsell
(d. 1698)

                    Faith Coghill m(1)   (Sir)   m(2) Jane Fitzwilliam
                    (d. 1675)   (1669) CHRISTOPHER   (1677) (d. 1680)
                                          (III)
                                          (1632-1723)

Gilbert   Christopher (IV)   m(2)   Jane   William
(1672-1674)   (1675-1747)   Constantia   (1677-1702)   (1679-1739 or later)
                                         (née Middleton)
                    m(1)   (d. 1734)
                    Mary Mussard
                    (d. 1712)

Christopher (V)   Stephen   Constantia Mary
(1712-1773)   (b. 1721-22)   Burgoyne
                                         (published Parentalia,   (d. 1751)
                                         1750)

                                         Margaret
                                         (owned "Heirloom" copy
                                         of Parentalia)

THE WREN FAMILY

Notes

Abbreviations

The following abbreviations are used to denote various sources of information:

CSP(D): Calendar of State Papers (Domestic), CSP(A and WI): Calendar of State Papers (America and West Indies), DNB: Dictionary of National Biography, VCH: Victoria County History, WS: Transaction volumes of the Wren Society, AS: Drawings in the Wren Collection, All Souls' College, Oxford, R.C.H.M.: Volumes published by the Royal Commission on Historic Monuments, HBRS: Volumes issued by the Hudson's Bay Record Society, CTB: Calendar of Treasury Books, CJ: House of Commons Journals, RS: Records of the Royal Society, PRO: Public Record Office.

Chapter 1

1. Christopher Wren, *Parentalia, or Memoirs of the Family of the Wrens,* Introduction, p. viii.
2. *Parentalia,* p.1.
3. *Parentalia,* p.2.
4. *Parentalia,* p.135 *et seq.*
5. Information kindly supplied by Mr Maurice Rathbone, Archivist, Wiltshire Record Office, Trowbridge.
6. *The Builder,* 11th May 1872.
7. Wiltshire Record Office, East Knoyle Registers.
8. Information kindly supplied by Mr Maurice Bond, O.B.E., F.S.A., Hon. Custodian of Monuments, St George's, Windsor.
9. CSP(D), 1634–5, p.455.
10. *Parentalia,* p.135.
11. *Parentalia,* p.142.
12. N. Pevsner, *Wiltshire,* 1963, p.206.
13. *Parentalia,* p.138.
14. For Busby, *see* entry in DNB.
15. *Parentalia,* Interleaved "Heirloom" copy, Library of the R.I.B.A., inserted opposite p.181.
16. *Parentalia,* p.182.
17. See DNB.
18. John Aubrey, *Brief Lives,* ed. O.L. Dick, 1949, p.161.
19. See DNB.

Chapter 2

1. H.B. Wells in VCH Oxfordshire, II, pp.279-87
2. For Wilkins, see Barbara Shapiro, *John Wilkins, 1614-1672; An Intellectual Biography*, Univ. of California, 1969.
3. Shapiro, *op. cit.*, p.22.
4. Wadham College, Oxford; Muniments 110/2, Caution Book.
5. Shapiro, *op. cit.*, p.111.
6. For Byrd, *see* Mrs J.C. Cole in *Oxoniensia*, XIV, p.63.
7. Shapiro, *op. cit.*, Ch. V. *passim*.
8. John Evelyn, *Diary*, ed. E.S. de Beer, III, p.106.
9. Evelyn, *op. cit.*, III, p.111.
10. *Parentalia*, p.200.
11. For Claypole, *see* DNB.
12. *Parentalia*, pp.33-4.
13. *Parentalia*, pp. p. 198.
14. Aubrey, *op. cit.*, p.191.

Chapter 3

1. Samuel Pepys, *Diary*, ed. Wheatley, I, p.313.
2. Evelyn, *op. cit.*, III, p.259.
3. Evelyn, *op. cit.*, III, p.271.
4. *Parentalia*, p.53.
5. Aubrey, *op. cit.*, p.161.
6. Pepys, *op. cit.*, I. p.263.
7. Evelyn, *op. cit.*, III, pp.384-5.
8. Viktor Fürst, *The Architecture of Sir Christopher Wren*, 1956, p.1.
9. Evelyn, *op. cit.*, III, p.297.
10. For this gift to Charles II, *see* John Lindsey, *Wren: His Work and Times*, 1951, pp. 67-8.
11. *Parentalia*, p.260.
12. For Denham, *see* DNB.
13. *Parentalia*, p.260.
14. Bodleian, Rawlinson MSS, A 341, f. 99 *et seq*.
15. Bodleian, Rawlinson A 341, ff. 125-7.
16. For Willis, *see* DNB and *Cerebri Anatome*, 1664, also *The Anatomy of the Brain and Nerves*, Tercentenary edn., ed. William Feindel, 2 vols., 1965.
17. *Parentalia*, p.260; the date is wrongly given.

Chapter 4

1. John Summerson, *The Sheldonian in its Time*, 1964, p.5.
2. Evelyn, *op. cit.* III, p.385.
3. For this building, *see* Louis Hautecoeur, *Histoire de l'Architecture Classique en France; Le Regne de Louis XIV*, I, 1948, pp.234-7.
4. David Loggan, *Oxonia Illustrata*, 1675, plate IX.
5. Summerson, *op. cit.*, p.8; Margaret Whinney, *Wren*, 1971, pp.19-22; Kerry Downes, *Christopher Wren*, 1971, pp.51-5. *See also* WS IX and XIX.
6. *Parentalia*, p.33.
7. Robert Willis and J. Willis Clark, *The Architectural History of the University of Cambridge*, 1886, I, p.147.

8. Pembroke College, Cambridge, Archives F I.
9. For the interior, and other points, *see* E.H. Minns in *Pembroke College Annual Gazette*, Dec. 1946.
10. T. Warton, *Life of Ralph Bathurst*, 1761, p.87.
11. H.E.D. Blakiston, *History of Trinity College, Oxford*, and the same author in VCH Oxfordshire, III, pp.238–51.
12. Trinity College, Oxford, Miscellaneous Letter Book, Wren to Bathurst, 22nd June 1665. The same letter book contains a loose drawing which may be a plan by Wren for a staircase arrangement. Opposite, a manuscript note refer to "Dr Wren's dessign for building in the little garden towards Balliol", with an estimate for £735.
13. Downes, *op. cit.,* p.56; *see also* AS IV, 73.
14. Pepys, *op. cit.* IV, p.203.

Chapter 5

1. Briggs, *op. cit.,* p.38.
2. *Parentalia*, p.261.
3. *Parentalia*, p.261.
4. *See* Chapter 4, note 12.
5. Quoted in full by M.S. Briggs, *Wren the Incomparable*, 1953, pp.42-3.
6. For Compton *see* DNB, *also* Edward Carpenter, *The Protestant Bishop*, 1956.
7. *Parentalia*, pp.261-2.
8. *Parentalia*, p.262.
9. Reginald Blomfield, *A History of French Architecture, Eighth century – 1661*, II (1911), pp.127-8; Hautecoeur, *op. cit., L'Architecture sous Henri IV et Louis XIII*, p.551.
10. Evelyn, *op. cit.*, III, p.133.
11. Whinney, *op. cit.*, p.32.
12. Hautecoeur, *op. cit.* Louis XIV, I, pp.70-1; Anthony Blunt, *Art and Architecture in France*, 1500-1700, 2nd edn., 1970, p.133.
13. *Parentalia*, pp.261, 262.
14. Hautecoeur, Louis XIV, I, p.429.
15. Briggs, *op. cit.,* p.42.
16. *Parentalia*, pp.261-2 for Wren on various chateaux.
17. *Parentalia*, p.261.
18. For Maisons, *see* Blunt, *op. cit.,* pp.131-2 and plates 97-100; for Vaux le Vicomte *see* Hautecoeur, Louis XIV, I, pp.101-9.
19. Hautecoeur, Louis XIV, I. *passim*
20. Hautecoeur, Louis XIV, I, pp.260-6.
21. For Wren and Bernini, *see Parentalia*, p.262.
22. *Parentalia*, p.261.
23. For Gobert, *see* Hautecoeur, Louis XIV, I, pp.161-3, 164, 180, 286.
24. Whinney, *op. cit.*, p.19.
25. Willis and Clark, *op. cit.* II, p.702.
26. Bodleian, Tanner MSS 145, nos. 110-12.
27. Evelyn, *op. cit.* II, pp.448-9.
28. For this scheme, *see* AS II 4-7.

Chapter 6

1. Briggs, *op. cit.*, p.47 (quoting Evelyn).
2. CSP(D) 1666-67, p.121.
3. Evelyn, *op. cit.*, III, p.463.
4. *Parentalia*, p.267.
5. *Parentalia*, p.269.
6. AS I, 8.
7. AS I, 7.
8. Whinney, *op. cit.*, pp.82-3 and plates 74-5.
9. 19 Charles II, c. III, preamble.
10. London Rebuilding Act, clause V.
11. London Rebuilding Act, clause XV.
12. London Rebuilding Act, clause XVI.
13. London Rebuilding Act, clause XXXVI.
14. Millicent Barton Rex, *University Representation in England, 1609-90*, 1954, pp.243-4.
15. Willis and Clark, *op. cit.* II, p.702.
16. Willis and Clark, *op. cit.* II, p. 704.
17. Bodleian, Tanner MSS 155, f. 44.
18. Willis and Clark, *op. cit.* II, p.704.
19. Bodleian, Tanner MSS 155, f. 60 (Breton to Sancroft, 27th March 1667).
20. Bodleian, Tanner MSS 155, f. 35 (Breton to Sancroft, 6th July 1667).
21. Bodleian, Tanner MSS 155, ff. 37 and 105 (Breton to Sancroft 28th Jan. and 5th Feb. 1668.
22. Bodleian, Tanner MSS 155, f. 17 (Breton to Sancroft).
23. Emmanuel College, Cambridge, Chapel Account, entry for Oct. 1669.
24. AS I, 100.
25. Emmanual College, Chapel Account Book.
26. WS XIII, p.21 (quoting Wren's report of 26th Feb. 1667 in Bodleian, Tanner MSS 145, f.129).
27. Downes, *op. cit.*, p.139.
28. WS XIII, p.22.
29. *Parentalia*, pp.278-9.
30. *See* note 29 above.
31. *See* note 29 above.
32. WS V, plate 27 and C.R. Weld *A History of the Royal Society*, 1848, I, pp.212-13.
32. Weld, *op. cit.* I, pp.212-13 and Thomas Birch, *The History of the Royal Society from its First Rise*, 4 vols., 1756-7, II, p.194.
34. Birch, *op. cit.* II, report of Council, 28th June 1670.
35. Birch, *op. cit.*, Council, 10th April 1672.
36. Salisbury Cathedral, Chapter Act Book (in Diocesan Archive Office); letter to non-residentiary canons, 5th Oct. 1669.
37. Pepys, *op. cit.* VIII, p.40.
38. WS XI, pp.21-6 (quoting Wren's report of 31st August 1668, in the Cathedral Library).
39. *See* note 36 above.
40. Salisbury Cathedral, Chapter Archives, fabric bills, 1671.

41. His report is among the Chapter Archives.
42. CSP(D), 1668-9, pp.224, 227.
43. CSP(D), 1668-9, p.132.
44. CSP(D), 1668-9, p.615.
45. CSP(D), 1668-9, p.309.
46. Evelyn, *op. cit.* III, p. 531.
47. For the Coghills of Bletchington see VCH Oxfordshire VI, pp.56-71.
48. *Parentalia*, Heirloom copy, and facsimile reprint of 1965.

Chapter 7

1. AS III, 106.
2. CSP(D), 1671, p.206.
3. Evelyn, *op. cit.* III, p.554.
4. CSP(D), 1671-72, p.98.
5. CSP(D), 1671-72, pp.128-9.
6. *The Diary of Robert Hooke*, ed. Robinson and Adams, 1935, 6th March 1675.
7. William Addison, *Audley End*, 1953, p.41.
8. Evelyn, *op. cit.* III, p.556.
9. WS XVIII, pp.122-3.
10. WS XVIII, pp.174-7 *passim*.
11. CSP(D) 1673-75, p.26.
12. CSP(D) 1673-75, p.26.
13. CSP(D) 1673-75, p.230.
14. WS XVIII, p.35.
15. CSP(D) 1673-75, p.153; WS XVIII, p.36.
16. WS XVIII, p.40.
17. WS XVIII, p.41.
18. WS XVIII, p.13.
19. WS XVIII, p.34.
20. WS XVII, p.32.
21. WS XVIII, p.34.
22. CSP(D), 1673, p.31.
23. WS XVIII, p.34.
24. WS XVIII, pp.36-7.
25. WS XVIII, p.45.
26. CSP(D) 1671-2, p.4; VCH Oxfordshire III, p.138.
27. CSP(D) 1671-2, p.31.
28. VCH Oxfordshire III, p.122.
29. In *Oxonia Illustrata*, 1675.
30. *Parentalia*, p.283 *et seq.*
31. Whinney, *op. cit.*, p.84; *see also* the Great Model in the Model Room (over the Morning Prayer Chapel) of the present St Paul's.
32. WS IX (quoting *Parentalia*)
33. RCHM London IV, 1939, p.16.
34. Whinney, *op. cit.*, p.63; important ideas, especially for steeples, could have come from illustrations in Cornelis Danckert, *Architectura Moderna*, 1631.
35. For the auditory qualities of this church, *see Parentalia*, p.310.

36. James Gibbs, *Book of Architecture*, 1728, p.viii and plate 28.
37. AS II, 49.
38. Hooke, *Diary*, 11th July 1674.
39. Downes, *op. cit.*, p.99.
40. AS II, 71.
41. Hooke, *Diary*, 3rd August and 5th April 1675.
42. Eduard Sekler, *Wren and his Place in European Architecture*, 1956, p.62.
43. Chapter Act Book, *Decretum de Ornando Choro*, 5th Oct. 1671.
44. Chapter Act Book, Articles of Agreement, Nov., 1671.
45. Cathedral Archives, Memo. of Agreement, 4th Jan. 1672.
46. Chapter Act Book, Memo of 6th May 1673 and comment by Wren, 1st June.
47. Chapter Act Book, Agreement of 1673.
48. Salisbury Diocesan Archives, Agreement of 8th March 1683.
49. *Parentalia*, p.286.
50. *Parentalia*, p.287.
51. *Parentalia*, p.282.
52. AS II, 21.
53. In the Model Room at St Paul's.
54. *See* note 51 above.
55. Whinney, *op. cit.*, p.86.
56. *Parentalia*, p.282.
57. *Parentalia*, p.282.
58. Hooke, *Diary*, 14th Nov. 1673; Anthony Wood, *Life and Times*, ed. Clark, Oxford Historical Society, XXI, 1892. p.274. For the younger Wren's letter on the bust, which he gave to Oxford University in 1737, *see* Mrs R.L. Poole in Walpole Society, vol XI (1922-23) p.40.
59. Barton Rex, *op. cit.*
60. Information kindly sent by Mr T.H. Aston, University Archivist.
61. Anthony Wood, *op. cit.*, p.279.
62. WS XVII, pp.76-7.
63. *The Builder*, 2nd April 1892, pp.259-63 (information kindly sent by Rev. Canon Peter Binnall, M.A., F.S.A., The Subdeanery, Lincoln).
64. Survey of London, XXXV, 1970, especially p.9; also Richard Leacroft in the *Architectural Review*, 1951, pp.43-6 and *Theatre Notebook* XVIII, 1964 and XXI, 1967.
65. AS II, 51.
66. Hooke, *Diary*, 20th June 1674.
67. Hooke, *Diary*, 31st March 1675.
68. Hooke, *Diary*, 1st June 1675.
69. Hooke, *Diary*, 12th June 1675.
70. Hooke, *Diary*, 12th Oct. 1672.
71. Hooke, *Diary*, 24th August 1674.
72. Hooke, *Diary*, 26th July 1675.
73. Westminster Public Library, Archives Dept., Registers of St Martin-in-the-Fields, Christenings 1672-81, 26th Oct. 1672.
74. Hooke, *Diary*, 15th Sept. 1673.
75. Hooke, *Diary*, 23rd March 1674; St Martin's Registers, Burials, 23rd March 1675.

76. Hooke, *Diary*, 28th Aug. 1675.
77. St Martin's Registers, Burials, 4th Sept. 1675.
78. Hooke, *Diary*, 11th Sept. 1675.
79. Information kindly sent by Mr Howard Colvin, St John's College, Oxford.
80. AS II, 65.

Chapter 8

1. WS XIX, pp. 113-15, quoting Royal Warrant of 22nd June 1675; see also Hooke, *Diary*, 22nd June 1675 and CSP(D) 1675-76, p.173.
2. C.R. Weld, *A History of the Royal Society*, 2 vols. 1848, I, p.251.
3. Weld, *op. cit.* I, p.254.
4. Royal Warrant, 22nd June 1675.
5. Hautecoeur, *op. cit.* Louis XIV, I, pp.453-5.
6. CSP(D) 1675-6, p.173.
7. WS V, p.21, Wren to Fell, 3rd Dec. 1681.
8. AS II, 8-14.
9. *Burlington Magazine*, March, 1961, pp.83-9.
10. AS II, 7.
11. AS II, 32, 34, 36-7; *see also* note 9 above.
12. AS II, 32.
13. AS II, 29; WS I, plate 19.
14. Whinney, *op. cit.*, p.97.
15. Whinney, *op. cit.*, p.102.
16. WS XVI, p.9.
17. *Parentalia*, p.292.
18. WS XIII, p.56.
19. WS XIII, p.69.
20. Hooke, *Diary*, 9th Sept. and 21st Oct. 1676.
21. Hooke, *Diary*, 20th Oct. 1676.
22. Hooke, *Diary*, 17th Nov. 1676.
23. Hooke, *Diary*, 13th and 17th Jan. 1680.
24. Hooke, *Diary*, 18th March 1676.
25. Hooke, *Diary*, 24th Feb. 1677.
26. For the Fitzwilliams, *see* DNB.
27. Hooke, *Diary*, 20th Dec. 1678.
28. Hooke, *Diary*, 24th Aug. 1676.
29. Hooke, *Diary*, 1st Sept. 1679.
30. Hooke, *Diary*, 1st Dec. 1676.
31. Hooke, *Diary*, 31st Oct. 1677.
32. Hooke, *Diary*, 7th, 11th, and 16th Jan. 1679.
33. Hooke, *Diary*, 26th March 1676.
34. Hooke, *Diary*, 8th Aug. 1676.
35. Hooke, *Diary*, 5th Oct. 1676.
36. Shapiro, *op. cit.*, p.143.
37. Willis and Clark, *op. cit.*, II, p.532; *see* also Philip Gaskell and Robert Robson *The Library of Trinity College, Cambridge*, 1971, p.14.
38. For these, *see* AS I 52-5.

39. Willis and Clark, *op. cit.* II, p.532; Gaskell and Robson, *op. cit.*, pp.15-16. 14-15.
40. Gaskell and Robson, *op. cit.*, pp. 15-16.
41. AS I 39.
42. Gaskell and Robson, *op. cit.*, p.16.
43. Details, in Trinity College Library, in a report and photographs by Mr Donald Insall, F.R.I.B.A. Further details kindly sent by Mr Peter Locke, A.R.I.B.A., of Donald W. Insall and Associates, London SWI.
44. Willis and Clark, *op. cit.* II, p.546.
45. Willis and Clark, *op. cit.* II, p.535 (from Wren's draft letter with the drawings at All Souls').
46. Wren's draft at All Souls'.
47. Bodleian Tanner MSS 155. ff. 43-4.
48. Willis and Clark, *op. cit.* II, p.537.
49. Trinity College, Account Book of Robert Grumbold, item under 12th May 1677.
50. Willis and Clark, *op. cit.* II, p.540.
51. St Martin-in-theFields Registers, Christenings 1672-81.
52. St Martin-in-the-Fields Registers, Christenings 1672-81; Evelyn, *op. cit.* IV, pp.169-70.
53. Bodleian Tanner MSS 40, f.123.
54. Hooke, *Diary*, 31st Dec. 1677.
55. *Parentalia*, p.331.
56. Hooke, *Diary*, 2nd Feb. 1678.
57. *Parentalia*, p.332; WS V, p.52.
58. For drawings, *see* AS II, 89-95.
59. *See* page 52.
60. AS II, 89.
61. Hooke, *Diary,* 11th Sept. 1676.
62. Hooke, *Diary,* 2nd July 1679.
63. E.E. Rich, "History of the Hudson's Bay Company, 1670-80", HBRS I, 1958, p.88.
64. HBRS VIII (Minutes of the Company 1679-84), Part I (to 1682), 1945, p. xxv.
65. *See* note 64 above.
66. HBRS VIII, minutes for 31st Dec. 1679 and 18th Feb. 1680.
67. HBRS VIII, minutes for 26th Jan. 1680, 2nd Feb. 1680, etc.
68. HBRS VIII, minutes for 25th May 1675.
69. HBRS I, p.171.
70. Hooke, *Diary*, 20th Dec. 1675.
71. Hooke, *Diary*, 31st Dec. 1676, 1st Jan. 1677.
72. Hooke, *Diary*, 5th Feb. 1676.
73. Hooke, *Diary*, 10th, 11th, 25th, and 31st Oct. 1677.
74. Hooke, *Diary*, 14th Nov. 1677.
75. Hooke, *Diary*, 17th Nov. 1677.
76. Birch, *op. cit.* III, p.352.
77. e.g. on 4th May 1678 (Birch).
78. Birch, *op. cit.* III, Council meeting 27th Nov. 1679.

79. Birch, *op. cit.* III, meeting, 17th Jan. 1678.
80. Birch, *op. cit.* III. pp.347, 350.
81. Birch, *op. cit.* IV, meeting 27th May 1680.
82. Birch, *op. cit.* IV, meeting 3rd June 1680; *see also* Bryan Little, *The Monmouth Episode*, 1956, p. 79.
83. Birch, *op. cit.* IV, meeting 12th Jan. 1681.
84. Birch, *op. cit.* III, p.362.
85. Birch, *op. cit.* III, Council 5th May 1678.
86. Hooke, *Diary*, 10th, 13th, 14th May 1678.
87. Birch, *op. cit.* III, Council 30th May 1678.
88. Hooke, *Diary*, 23rd Oct. 1679.
89. For Moses Pitt *see* D.N.B.
90. Birch, *op. cit.* III, meeting 28th March 1678.
91. CSP(D), 1678, p.167.
92. Hooke, *Diary*, 14th Nov. 1678.
93. Hooke, *Diary*, 14th Jan. 1679.
94. Birch, *op. cit.* IV, Council 21st Jan. 1680.
95. *The English Atlas*, 4 vols, Oxford, 1680-82, Vol. I.
96. Birch, *op. cit.* IV, meeting 30th Nov. 1680.
97. Evelyn, *op. cit.* IV. p.225; *see also* Hooke, *Diary*, 1st Dec. 1680.
98. Hooke, *Diary*, 18th Sept. 1680.
99. Hooke, *Diary*, 16th Oct. 1680; St Martin-in-the-Fields Registers, Burials.

Chapter 9

1. Hooke, *Diary*, 25th March 1676.
2. Hooke, *Diary*, 29th April 1676.
3. Hooke, *Diary*, 2nd May 1676.
4. *Parentalia*, p.309.
5. Hooke, *Diary*, 16th Dec. 1676.
6. Hooke, *Diary*, 15th April 1680.
7. Bodleian, Rawlinson MSS 387 B, f. 204 r.
8. Bodleian, Rawlinson MSS 387B, ff. 2r, 175 r, and B 389, f. 113v.
9. Bodleian, Rawlinson MSS 389, f. 99 v.
10. Bodleian, Rawlinson MSS B 389, f. 112 v.
11. See, for example, Bodleian Rawlinson MSS B 389 ff. 112 v, 115 r, and 116 r.
12. Bodleian Rawlinson MSS B 389, f. 116 v.
13. Bodleian Rawlinson MSS B 389, f. 123 v.
14. Bodleian Rawlinson MSS B 389, f. 126 r.
15. Bodleian Rawlinson MSS B 389, ff. 129 r and 130 r.
16. Bodleian Rawlinson MSS B 389, f. 131r.
17. Bodleian Rawlinson MSS B 389, ff. 113 r and 114 r.
18. Bodleian Rawlinson MSS B 389, f. 124 r.
19. Bodleian Rawlinson MSS B 389, f. 112 r.
20. Bodleian Rawlinson MSS B 389, f. 122 v.
21. Bodleian Rawlinson MSS B 389, f. 131 r.
22. *Parentalia* p.320.
23. Evelyn, *op. cit.* IV, p.397.

24. See.WS X, pp.58-60.
25. The particulars in the rest of this section are abstracted from the tables in WS X, pp.46-53.
26. Evelyn, *op. cit.* IV, p.293.
27. Birch, *op. cit.* IV, Council 4th May 1681.
29. Birch, *op. cit.* IV, Meeting, 27th April 1681.
30. Birch, *op. cit.* IV, Meeting, 29th June 1681.
31. Birch, *op. cit.* IV, Council 16th Nov. 1681.
32. Birch, *op. cit.* IV, Council 18th Jan. 1682.
33. Birch, *op. cit.* IV, Council 8th March 1682.
34. Birch, *op. cit.* IX, Council 10th May 1682.
35. Birch, *op. cit.* IX, Council 9th Aug. 1682.
36. HBRS VIII, p.xxv.
37. HBRS VIII, p.132.
38. HBRS VIII, Committee, 8th Nov. 1681.
39. HBRS VIII, Committees 25th Jan, 10th and 13th Feb. 1682.
40. HBRS VIII, Committee 29th Sept. 1682.
41. HBRS XI (Letters Outward), 1679-84, pp.34-7.
42. HBRS VIII, Committee 12th July 1682.
43. Birch, *op. cit.* IV, Council 27th April 1681.
44. Birch, *op. cit.* IV, Council 5th Oct. 1681.
45. C.G.T. Dean, *The Royal Hospital, Chelsea*, 1950, p.25.
46. Evelyn, *op. cit.* IV, p.257.
47. *See* note 44 above.
48. Birch, *op. cit.* IV, Council 11th Jan. 1682.
49. Birch, *op. cit.* IV, Council 8th Feb. 1682.
50. Evelyn, *op. cit.* IV, p.281.
51. Dean, *op. cit.* p. 38.
52. Evelyn, *op. cit.* IV p. 281.
53. Dean, *op. cit.*, p.39.
54. Dean, *op. cit.*, pp.122-3.
55. Dean, *op. cit.*, p.47.
56. W.H.St. John Hope, *Windsor Castle, An Architectural History*, II, 1953, p.386 (Chapter Acts, 23rd Jan 1682).
57. Hope, *op. cit.*, Chapter Acts, 1st May 1682.
58. Hope, *op. cit.*, pp.386-88.
59. WS IV, pp.17-23 and W.D. Caroë, "Tom Tower", 1923.
60. WS IV, p.17.
61. *See* note 60 above.
62. WS V, p.18.
63. WS V, p.20 (Wren to Fell, 30th June 1681).
64. WS V, p.21.
65. WS V, p.21.
66. WS V, p.21.
67. *See* note 66 above.
68. Christ Church Archives, Disbursement Book, New Building.
69. Whinney, *op. cit.*, p.104.
70. *Parentalia*, p.292.
71. WS V, p.42 (Trinity College archives)

72. WS V, p.43 (Trinity College archives)
73. CSP(D) 1680-81, p.209.
74. WS V, p.19.
75. HBRS VIII, Part 2, minutes for 3rd Jan. 1683.
76. HBRS VIII, Part 2, minutes for 27th June 1683.
77. HBRS VIII, Part 2, minutes for 7th Aug. 1683; CSP (A & WI) 1681-85, p.471.
78. HBRS VIII, Part 2, Committee 20th Nov. 1683.
79. CSP(D) 1683 (Jan-June), pp. 173-4.
80. CSP(D) 1683 (Jan-June), p.295.
81. CTB VII (1681-5), p.850.
82. CTB VII, p.861.
83. CSP(D) 1682, p.356.
84. CSP(D) 1683 (Jan-June), p.22.
85. WS VII, p.12.
86. *Parentalia*, p.325.
87. CTB VII, p.985.
88. CTB VII, p.727; WS VIII, pp.22-4.
89. CTB VII, p.705 (8th Feb. 1683).
90. CTB VII, pp.972-74.
91. Bodleian Rawlinson MSS B 389, f. 126 r.
92. WS VII, p.63.
93. WS VII, pp.23, 28-9.
94. WS VII, pp.22-4 and 42-3.
95. Evelyn, *op. cit.* IV, p.341; Daniel Defoe, *A Tour Through England and Wales*, Everyman Library, I, p.185.
96. CSP(D) 1683 (July-Sept), p.344 etc.
97. CTB VII, p.707.
98. Evelyn, *op. cit.* IV, p.471.
99. CTB VII, pp.1303, 1315.
100. WS VII, p.929.
101. CTB VII, p.929.
102. CTB VII, p.581.
103. CTB VII, p.1074.
104. CTB VII, p.1166.
105. CTB VII, p.1313.
106. CTB VII, p.1165.
107. CSP(D) 1684-5, pp.82, 115.
108. CTB VII, pp.1317 and 1521.
109. St Martin-in-the-Fields, Vestry Minutes, 1666-83 (F 2004), meeting 7th Dec. 1681.
110. St Martin-in-the-Fields, Vestry Minutes, 1666-83, meeting 26th Jan. 1682.
111. Evelyn, *op. cit.* IV, p.767.
112. John McMaster *A Short History of . . . St Martin-in-the-Fields*, 1914, pp. 263 and 276 (illustration opposite).
113. St Martin-in-the-Fields, Vestry Minutes, 1683-1716 (F 2005), meetings 14th July and 23rd Sept. 1685.
114. Evelyn, *op. cit.* IV, p.455.

Chapter 10

1. CTB VIII, p.137.
2. *See* note 1 above.
3. CTB VIII, p.138.
4. CTB VIII, p.89.
5. CTB VIII, pp.58, 115, etc.
6. For Treby *see* DNB.
7. CSP (D), James II, vol I, p.363
8. For the above episodes, *see* CJ, 1667-87, pp.718, 719, 720, 726.
9. CJ 1667-87, pp.727, 730, 733, 744, 752.
10. CJ 1667-87, pp.727, 742.
11. CJ 1667-87, pp.730, 735.
12. CJ 1667-87, p.736.
13. CJ 1667-87, p.740.
14. CJ 1667-87, pp.744, 748.
15. CJ 1667-87, p.752.
16. CJ 1667-87, p.755.
17. CJ 1667-87, p.761 etc.
18. Survey of London, XVIII, p.44.
19. *Gentleman's Magazine*, 1832, p.113.
20. CTB VIII, p.17.
21. Evelyn, *op. cit.*, IV, p.472.
22. CTB VIII, pp.168, 215.
23. CTB VIII, pp.210, 280.
24. CTB VIII, pp.353. 394.
25. CTB VIII, pp.408, 694-5.
26. CTB VIII, pp.457, 807.
27. CTB VIII, p.502.
28. CTB VIII, pp.587, 589.
29. CTB VIII, pp.1102, 1417.
30. CTB VIII, p.915.
31. CTB VIII, p.1033.
32. CTB VIII, p.1011.
33. AS II, 100.
34. WS XVIII, p.56.
35. *see* note 34 above.
36. WS XVIII, p.57.
37. WS XVIII, pp.61-3.
38. *see* note 37 above.
39. CTB VIII, pp.1149, 1153.
40. CTB VIII, p.1299.
41. CTB VIII, p.1463.
42. CTB VII, p.1437.
43. AS I, 85, IV, 142.
44. AS IV, 142; *see also* WS VII, pp.73-7.
45. AS I, 85.
46. WS XVIII, p.63.
47. *See* note 46 above.
48. AS IV, 97.

49. Evelyn, *op. cit.* IV, p.534.
50. Bodleian, Rawlinson MSS C 987, ff.12, 14.
51. CTB VIII, p.738.
52. Whinney, *op. cit.*, p.105.
53. Bodleian, Tanner MSS 40, f. 27.
54. Bodleian, Rawlinson MSS D 862, f. 12.
55. Dean, *op. cit.*, p.77.
56. CTB VIII, p.1446.
57. CTB VIII, pp.1847-8.
58. Willis and Clark, *op. cit.* II, p.540.
59. CTB VIII, p.1533.
60. CTB VIII, p.1652.
61. CTB VIII, pp.1521, 1637.
62. WS XVIII, p.68.
63. Briggs, *op. cit.*, p.257.
64. CTB VIII, p.2121.
65. CTB VIII, pp.2126, 2129.

Chapter 11

1. CSP(D) 1689-90, p.67.
2. *See* John Stoughton, *Windsor*, 1862, p.180 *et seq.*
3. CJ 1688-93, p.118.
4. CJ 1688-93, p.82.
5. CJ 1688-93, p.82.
6. For the Palace *see* WS VII, pp.135-96 and 240-3, RCHM West London, 1925, pp.67-78, and G.H. Chettle and P. Faulkner in the *Journal of the British Archaeological Association*, 1951.
7. WS VII, p.136.
8. CTB IX, p.232.
9. CTB IX, p.200; WS XVIII, pp.96-101.
10. WS XVIII, p.103.
11. Information on the original construction of Het Loo kindly sent by the Assistant Representative, British Council, Amsterdam.
12. WS VII, pp.143-5.
13. WS VII, p.135.
14. CSP(D) 1689-90, pp.526-7, also Narcissus Luttrell, *A Brief Historical Relation of State Affairs . . . 1678-1714*, 6 vols., 1857, II, p. 12.
15. For this, and other interiors at Kensington, *see* the plates in RCHM West London, pp.67-78.
16. WS IV, p.38.
17. WS IV, plate 4.
18. Soane Museum, London; volume of Wren's drawings for Hampton Court, dated 1694 and acquired by Soane in 1817, no 7; *see also* WS IV, plates 11 and 12.
19. Soane volume, no. 8.
20. *Parentalia*, p.326.
21. WS IV, p.22.
22. WS VII, p.182.
23. WS IV, p.43.

24. CTB IX, p.74.
25. CTB IX, pp. 77-8.
26. WS IX, pp.72-4.
27. *See* note 26 above, *also* CTB IX, p.355.
28. CTB IX, p.244.
29. WS XVII, p.72.
30. CTB IX, p.749.
31. CTB IX, pp.1048, 1402.
32. CTB IX, p.255.
33. For Baptist May, *see* DNB.
34. CJ 1688-93, p.350.
35. CJ 1688-93, pp.418, 420.
36. WS XVIII, p.66.
37. For Farley, *see* WS XIX, pp.87-90.
38. CTB IX, p.563.
39. CSP(D) 1690-91, p.434.
40. CTB IX, p.1279.
41. CTB IX, p.1292; CSP(D) 1690-91, p.509.
42. CTB IX, pp.1385, 1867.
43. WS XVIII, p.84.
44. RS, Journal Book VIII (1690-96), p.79.
45. WS XI, p.72.
46. AS IV, 28-34.
47. Willis and Clark, *op. cit.* II, p.537.
48. Willis and Clark, *op. cit.* II. p.542.
49. Pembroke College, Register of College Orders, 14th Aug. and 8th Dec. 1688.
50. E.H. Minns in Pembroke College Society Annual Gazette, 1945, pp.7-12.
51. Pembroke College, Admission Book, 6th Oct. 1691.
52. St Paul's Cathedral Library, Wren Drawings II, 136 a and b.
53. e.g. St Paul's Drawings I, 43, 48a, II, 137.
54. St Paul's Drawings I, 27.
55. *See* note 54 above.
56. St Paul's Drawings I, 77.
57. St Paul's Drawings I, 50 and II, 140, 141.
58. WS IV, p.38.
59. Downes, *op. cit.*, pp. 82, 87.
60. *Parentalia*, pp.326-7.
61. For this episode *see* WS XVII, pp.22-37.
62. Letters among correspondence at Trinity College.
63. Draft letter among correspondence at Trinity College.
64. Warton, *op. cit.*, p.68.
65. Warton, *op. cit.*, p.69.
66. CTB IX, p.1477.
67. CTB X, 333, 341; WS XVIII, p.101.
68. CTB IX, p.1718.
69. WS IV, p.26.
70. WS IV, p.25.

71. RS Journal Book VIII, meeting 30th Nov. 1692, and p.208.
72. RS Journal Book VIII, p.208.
73. For these outdoor items *see* WS IV, pp. 25, 32, 34.
74. CTB X, p.76; WS XVIII, p.95.
75. WS XI, p.74, letter of 24th Nov. 1694.
76. WS XI, p.75.
77. For the school at Appleby Magna, *see* WS XI.
78. Marcus Whiffen, *The Public Buildings of Williamsburg*, 1958, pp.28-32.
79. Luttrell, *op. cit.* II, p.21; CTB X, p.90.
80. CTB X, pp.220, 264.
81. WS IX, plate 31.
82. WS XVIII, pp.89, 108-9.
83. WS XVIII, pp.112-15.
84. Luttrell, *op. cit.* III, p.280.
85. CTB X, p.770.
86. WS XVIII, p.111.
87. Downes, *op. cit.* p.112.
88. AS V, 28.
89. AS V, 21-4.
90. *Parentalia*, p.328.
91. Greenwich Hospital, Commissioners' Minutes (PRO Adm 67/1), Minutes of the Grand Committee, report of 21st May 1685.
92. Soane volume, nos.63-4.
93. Soane volume, no.19.
94. AS I, 12.
95. CTB X, p.1098.
96. AS I, 5.

Chapter 12

1. WS XVIII, pp.122-3.
2. Chettle and Faulkner, *op cit.*
3. Evelyn, *op. cit.* V, p.237.
4. Whinney, *op. cit.*, p.162.
5. CTB X, pp.1195, 1401.
6. CTB X, pp.1106, 1353.
7. CTB X, p.1126.
8. CTB XI, pp.11-12.
9. CTB XI, p.312.
10. PRO Adm 67/1; Evelyn, *op. cit.* V, p.211.
11. PRO Adm 67/1, Grand Committee, 25th Sept. 1695.
12. PRO Adm 67/1; Adm 67/2 (Committee of Fabric), p.1.
13. PRO Adm 67/1, Grand Committee, 9th Jan 1696.
14. WS VI, pp.33-4.
15. WS VIII, plate 23.
16. Evelyn, *op. cit.* V, p.243; WS VI, p.34.
17. PRO Adm 67/2, 5th June, 1696; Evelyn, *op. cit.* V, p.244.
18. WS VI, p.34.
19. WS VI, p.34.

20. PRO Adm 67/1, 30th June 1696; Evelyn, *op. cit.* V, p.249.
21. WS VI, p.35.
22. WS VI, p.36.
23. PRO Adm 67/2, Aug, 7th, 1696, 11th and 25th June, 9th July 1697.
24. WS VI, p.36.
25. CTB XII, p.342.
26. CTB XIII, p.131.
27. RS Journal Book VIII, p.320.
28. *See* note 27 above.
29. R.J. White, *Dr Bentley*, 1965, p.86.
30. M.H.A.M. Newman in *The Eagle*, Vol. XLVII (1932), pp.63-70.
31. In the Muniment Room, St John's College; reproduced by R.F. Scott in the Proceedings of the Cambridge Antiquarian Society, vol VII (1890-91), pp.256-7.
32. David Loggan, *Cantabrigia Illustrata*, 1688, plate 26.
33. Willis and Clark, *op. cit.* II, p.276.
34. For the whole question of the supply of stone from Portland *see* J.H. Bettey in *Archaeological Journal*, Vol. CXXVIII (1971), pp.176-85.
35. Bettey, *op. cit.*, p.180.
36. WS XVI, p.79; RS Journal Book VIII, p.332.
37. WS XVI, p.80.
38. *see* note 37 above.
39. WS XVI, p.81.
40. WS XVI, pp.82-4, 84-6.
41. CJ 1693-7, p.665.
42. CJ 1693-7, p.686.
43. See 8 and 9 William III, cap. XIV.
44. WS XVI, pp.84-6.
45. WS XVI, pp.84-6.
46. WS XVI, p.86.
47. WS XVI, p.88.
48. WS XVI, p.89.
49. Evelyn, *op. cit.* V, p.283.
50. Luttrell, *op. cit.* IV, pages 334, 351.
51. Luttrell, *op. cit.* IV, p.448.
52. Luttrell, *op. cit.* IV, p.351.
53. For his drawings *see* AS V, 1-14 and WS VIII.
54. WS XI, p.13.
55. WS XI, p.27.
56. CTB XIII, p.325.
57. Evelyn, *op. cit.* V. p.290.
58. CSP(D) 1698, p.343.
59. WS VI, p.37: PRO Adm 67/2, p.80
60. WS VI, p.37.
61. WS VI, p.37.
62. WS VI, p.37.
63 WS VI, p.38.
64. WS VI, p.38; for the bricks *see* PRO Adm 67/2, 2nd and 9th Sept. 1698.
65. WS VI, p.38.

66. WS VI, p.38.
67. WS VI, p.39.
68. AS V, 15.
69. AS V, 16.
70. AS V, 17. 20.
71. RS Council Minutes, Vol II, 30th Nov. 1968; Journal Book IX, p.115.
72. In *Parentalia*, Heirloom Copy, RIBA Library.
73. CTB XIV, p.357.
74. CTB XIV, p.283; Evelyn, *op. cit.* V, 315.
75. Evelyn, *op. cit.* V, p.323.
76. RS Journal Book IX, pp.148-9.
77. WS IV, pp.67-8.
78. WS IV, p.69.
80. WS IV, p.66.
81. WS IV, p.59; AS I, 79-80.
82. WS IV, p.58.
83. WS IV, p.59.
84. In a volume given to Soane by the younger George Dance, 1817.
85. Soane volume, ff. 45, 49.
86. CTB XVI, pp.48, 224.
87. E.g. AS I, 17, 18, 19, 24, 25; II, 83-8.
88. For the building process see G. Eland in "Records of Buckinghamshire", *Journal of the Bucks Architectural and Archaeological Society* Vol. XI, 7 (1926), pp. 406-29.
89. Eland, *op. cit.*, pp.421-2.
90. *Parentalia*, p.288.
91. WS XVI, p.26.
92. WS XVI, p.93.
93. WS XVI, p.94.
94. WS XVI, p.96; PRO Adm 67/2, 2nd May 1699.
95. WS XVI, p.97.
96. WS XVI, p.97.
97. *See* note 96 above.
98. WS XVI, pp.97-8.
99. WS XVI, p.98.
100. Luttrell, *op. cit.* V, p.36.
101. CJ 1699-1702, p.413.
102. Information kindly supplied by Mr J.A.C West, A.L.A., now of The Local History Museum, Weymouth and Melcombe Regis.
103. PRO Adm 67/2, 18th April 1699.
104. PRO Adm 67/2, 20th June and 12th Sept. 1699.
105. PRO Adm 67/2, 19th Sept. 1699.
106. PRO Adm 67/2, 9th April 1700; Evelyn, *op. cit.* V, p.399.
107. PRO Adm 67/2, p.179 (12th Feb. 1701).
108. PRO Adm 67/2, p.179 (12th Feb. 1701).
109. PRO Adm 67/2, 25th April 1699.
110. PRO Adm 67/2, 9th April 1700, and 5th Feb. 1701.
111. PRO Adm 67/2, p.194 (28th Jan. 1702).

Chapter 13

1. WS VII, pp.210-12.
2. WS VII, p.212; AS I, 30-2.
3. *See* note 2 above.
4. PRO Adm 67/2, 21st April 1702.
5. PRO Adm 67/2, 15th July 1702.
6. PRO Adm 67/2, 12th June 1702.
7. For Bird see Rupert Gunnis, *A Dictionary of English Sculptors*; Walpole Society, Vol XXII (Vol III of Vertue's notebooks), 1934, pp.18-9; Rosemary Rendel in *Recusant History*, 1972, pp.206-9.
8. AS II 46, IV, 85.
9. CTB XVIII, pp.30, 82.
10. CTB XVIII, p.336.
11. For the Cottonian Library, *see* Edward Miller, *That Noble Cabinet*, 1973, pp.28-36; *see also* WS XI, pp.48-59.
12. For the ground plan *see* AS III, 13.
13. CTB XVIII, p.437.
14. CTB XIX, p.300.
15. RS, Council Minutes, 1st April 1702.
16. RS, Council Minutes, 16th Feb. 1703.
17. RS, Council Minutes, 21st April 1703.
18. Bettey, *op. cit.*, p.183.
19. WS XVI, p.101.
20. WS XVI, pp.101-2.
21. CSP(D) 1703-4, p.455.
22. CTB XIX, p.236.
23. CTB XIX, pp.228, 349.
24. WS XVI, p.30.
25. Whinney, *op. cit.*, pp.77-8.
26. *Parentalia*, Heirloom Copy, Library of RIBA.
27. VCH Dorset, Vol II, pp.341-2.
28. CTB XX, p.356.
29. WS XI, pp.54-5; CTB XX, p.646.
30. WS XI, pp.57-8.
31. CTB XXI, p.118; Miller, *op. cit.*, p.58.
32. WS XI, p.58.
33. CTB XXII, p.131.
34. CTB XX, p.583.
35. CTB XX, p.749.
36. CTB XXII, p.26.
37. CTB XXII, pp.308, 370.
38. CTB XXI, pp.289, 296.
39. CTB XXI, pp.402, 423.
40. CTB XXI, p.445.
41. CTB XXII, p.223.
42. CTB XXIII, pp.41, 138.
43. For Gibbs' Roman training see Bryan Little, *The Life and Work of James Gibbs*, 1955, Chapter II.

44. Little, *op. cit.*, p.29; Soane Museum, MS Life of Gibbs.
45. For Marlborough House, *see* John Charlton, *Marlborough House* (HMSO, 1962), *also* plates 209-25 in RCHM West London, 1925.
46. Figured in Charlton, *op. cit.*, p.8.
47. Luttrell, *op. cit.* VI, p.544.
48. CTB XXIV, pp.307, 309.
49. RS Council Minutes, 8th and 20th Sept. 1710.
50. RS Council Minutes, 2nd Nov. 1710.
51. RS Council Minutes, 12th July 1711.
52. RS Council Minutes, 14th Dec. 1710.
53. WS XVI, p.107.
54. WS XVI, pp.108-9.
55. WS XVI, pp. 108, 109.
56. WS XVI, p.113.
57. Briggs, *op. cit.*, p.94, 95.
58. For Wren's letter and the Attorney General's opinion *see* WS XVI, pp.154-5.
59. CJ 1708-11, p.582.
60. CJ 1708-11, pp.583, 623; *see also* the text of 9 Anne, cap. XXII.
61. CJ 1708-11, pp.581-2.
62. CJ 1708-11, p.678.
63. CJ 1708-11, p.623.
64. CJ 1711-14, p.34.
65. Lambeth Palace Library, MS 2690.
66. *Parentalia*, pp.318-21.
67. *See* Howard Colvin on the New Churches Act, and the churches built under its provisions, in *Architectural Review*, Vol. CVII (1950), pp.189-96.
68. CTB XXV, pp.59, 98, 442-4 and XXVI, p.72.
69. CTB XXV, p.538.
70. CJ 1711-14, p.25.
71. *Numismatum Antiqurum Sylloge* etc (dedicated to the Royal Society) 1708.

Chapter 14

1. CTB XXVII, p.480.
2. CTB XXVII, p.264.
3. CTB XXVII, pp.102, 423.
4. CTB XXVII, pp.28, 201.
5. AS II, 99, 101.
6. CTB XXVII, pp.28, 264.
7. *Parentalia*, p.295 *et seq.*
8. WS XI, plates II-VI, *see also* p.20.
9. PRO, PROB II/590, f.65.
10. For Wroxall, *see* VCH Warwickshire Vol. II, pp.70-3 and Vol. III, pp.215-20; for Sutton *see* VCH Bedfordshire, Vol. II, pp.246-51.
11. CTB XXVIII, p.19.
12. CTB XXVIII, p.302.
13. CTB XXVIII, pp.54, 311.
14. CTB XXX, p.63.
15. *See* Geoffrey Webb, *Wren*, 1937, pp.131-2.

16. WS XVI, pp.116-17.
17. CTB XXXI, p.362; XXXII, p.64.
18. CJ 1708-11, p.582.
19. CTB XXXII, p.322.
20. CTB XXXI, p.269.
21. See N. Pevsner, *Wiltshire*, 1963, pp.510-11.
22. For his letter of 21st April 1719, *see* Webb, *op. cit.*, p.135, *also* WS XVIII, p.9.
23. Mrs K.A. Esdaile, *St Martin-in-theFields*, 1944, p.84.
24. McMaster, *op. cit.*, p.69 *et seq.*
25. *See* note 24 above.
26. WS XI, plate II (from the Abbey Library).
27. WS XI, plate VI.
28. WS XI, plate V.
29. WS XI, plate XV.
30. WS XI, plate XVII b.
31. AS II, 38-9.
32. WS XI, p.39.
33. AS III, 28.
34. WS XI, p.39.
35. WS XI, p.41.
36. WS XI, p.41.
37. WS XI, plates XXV-XXVII (drawings in the Bodleian, Gough Collection).
38. *Parentalia*, p.344.
39. *Parentalia*, p.347.

Bibliography

Leading primary sources for Sir Christopher Wren's life are the volume known as *Parentalia*, drawings surviving in Wren's own hand or from his office, the small number of Wren's letters, and various original documents relating to his work.

Parentalia, or *Memoirs of the Family of Wren*, was compiled by Wren's grandson Stephen Wren and brought out in 1750. The interleaved "Heirloom" copy, originally the property of Stephen Wren's daughter Margaret, and now in the library of the Royal Institute of British Architects, has valuable extra material, including a few of Sir Christopher's manuscript letters; it was published, in facsimile, by the Gregg Press in 1965.

The main collections of Wren's drawings are at All Souls' College, Oxford, in the library of St Paul's Cathedral, in the Soane Museum, London, and in the drawings collection of the R.I.B.A. (now housed at 22 Portman Square, London W.I). Memoranda on various subjects are printed in *Parentalia*. Wren's report on Salisbury Cathedral is in the cathedral archives, and has been printed by the Wren Society (Vol. VIII) as well as in *Parentalia*, while a copy of his recommendations for the new library at Trinity College, Cambridge is in Vol. I of the drawings at All Souls'. Important material is also in various college libraries and archive rooms at Oxford and Cambridge, in the Bodleian in the Tanner MSS and (particularly for the City churches) in the Rawlinson MSS, in the records of the Royal Society (partly printed by Thomas Birch in his four-volume history of the society which came out in 1756), in those of the Hudson's Bay Record Society), and in the minutes of such bodies as the Commissioners for rebuilding St Paul's, the Greenwich Hospital Commissioners, and the New Churches Commission of 1711. *The Diary of Robert Hooke*, as edited in 1935 by H.W. Robinson and W. Adams, is, for the period 1672–83, an authority of primary quality.

The most important corpus of material on Wren's work, reproducing hundreds of drawings and printing many documents, e.g. from the Treasury papers, comes in the twenty volumes, issued between 1924 and 1943, of the Wren Society; no equivalent treatment has so far been given to the drawings which, in 1951, came to light at the time of their sale from the Bute Collection. Sir John Summerson has, however, dealt with those on the City churches in *Architectural History*, Vol. XIII (1970).

Books specifically on Wren start with J. Elmes, *Memoirs of the Life and Works of Sir Christopher Wren*, 1823. Not much was written on Wren in the predominantly Gothic decades of the nineteenth century, but since 1900 there have been numerous books. These include: Lena Milman (the daughter of a Dean of St Paul's) *Sir Christopher Wren*, 1908; Lawrence Weaver, *Sir Christopher Wren*, 1923; *Sir Christopher Wren, His Life and Work* (Bicentenary Memorial Volume, R.I.B.A.), 1923; C. Whitaker Wilson, *Sir Christopher Wren, His Life and Times*, 1932; Geoffrey Webb, *Wren*, 1937; Martin Briggs, *Christopher Wren*, 1951; John Lindsey, *Wren, His Work and Times*, 1951; John Summerson, *Sir Christopher Wren*, 1953; Martin Briggs, *Wren the Incomparable*, 1953; Eduard Sekler, *Wren and his Place in European Architecture*, 1956; Viktor Fürst, *The Architecture of Sir Christopher Wren*, 1956; J. Lang, *Rebuilding St Paul's*, 1956; Kerry Downes, *Christopher Wren*, 1971; Margaret Whinney, *Wren*, 1971; Heywood Gould, *Sir Christopher Wren*, 1972.

Some other books, not exclusively on Wren, have important passages about him. They include Sir Reginald Blomfield, *A Short History of Renaissance Architecture in England*, 1900 etc; Ralph Dutton, *The Age of Wren*, 1951; John Summerson, *Architecture in Britain, 1950 to 1830*, 1953; Margaret Whinney and Oliver Millar, *English Art, 1625 to 1714*, 1957, and Kerry Downes, *English Baroque Architecture*, 1966.

Index